28 DAY BOOK

The Rise of the
Modern German Novel

The Rise of the
Modern German Novel

CRISIS AND CHARISMA

Russell A. Berman

Harvard University Press
Cambridge, Massachusetts, and
London, England
1986

833. 09

B

Publication of this book has been aided by a grant
from the Andrew W. Mellon Foundation.

This book is printed on acid-free paper, and its binding materials
have been chosen for strength and durability.

Library of Congress Cataloging-in-Publication Data

Berman, Russell A., 1950-
    The rise of the modern German novel.

    Bibliography: p.
    Includes index.
    1. German fiction—20th century—History and
criticism. 2. German fiction—19th century—History
and criticism. 3. Literature and society—Germany.
4. Modernism (Literature)—Germany. I. Title.
PT772.B38 1986   833'.009   85-24770
ISBN 0-674-77165-6 (alk. paper)

Preface

Early twentieth-century German culture is characterized by the concurrence of radical aesthetic innovation and profound social transformation. Modernism and modernization—the avant-garde revolt and the political upheavals culminating in fascism—mark a decisive turn in the possibilities and character of modern culture. In this study I explain the rise of the modern German novel in terms of social processes and political tensions that still operate in the contemporary world.

Although I do not exclude the kind of contextual material that the New Critics used to label "extrinsic," neither do I treat novels as mere illustrations of historical phenomena, as if they were polished mirrors reflecting their respective environments. Instead, I construct a literary sociology capable of demonstrating how the modern novel, as a paradigm for modern literature in general, attempted to intervene in the social crisis. At issue is not so much what the specific literary work or its author meant as how the innovative text operated vis-à-vis its recipient.

The insistence that literary sociology shift attention to the character of the social relationship between text and reader derives from reader response theory as well as from the subjectivist orientation of Max Weber's sociology. Weber's three categories of political legitimacy—traditional, legal, and charismatic—and his notion of bureaucratization clarify the Wilhelmine cultural crisis, which served as the background for the modernist revolt. The character of that crisis is also illuminated by key motifs from the critical theory of the Frankfurt school. Its sociological, contextual account of the shift from an ultimately unsuccessful liberal culture of the eighteenth and nineteenth centuries to the authoritarian stuctures of the twentieth century underscores the transformation of capitalist exchange mechanisms, a perspective which lends itself well to an investigation of the literary exchange of meaning between the novellistic text and the implied reader.

Although the Frankfurt school devotes much attention to the aesthetic substance of modern art, it never resolves the critical question of the cultural rupture around 1900. Paradoxically, Theodor Adorno, the most rigorous proponent of a modernist canon, derives modernism from a universal teleology of rationalization of aesthetic form and must consequently downplay the particular, qualitative leap that would seem to separate modern art from its nineteenth-century ancestors. His linear description of an inescapable history of domination is one of the least tenable features of classical critical theory. Peter Bürger addresses the modernist leap directly, but, like Adorno, he does so by describing the unfolding of an immanent logic within the aesthetic institution, as if modernism and the avant-garde had little to do with the transformation of the larger social order. Other participants in the Western marxist tradition, such as Walter Benjamin, Leo Lowenthal, and Georg Lukács, focus more closely, though in radically different ways, on the social contexts of literary production, but in the end the question of a modernist rupture remains unanswered. An answer is provided here by treating the rhetorical structures of the texts as aspects of a communicative strategy designed to produce a relationship with the recipient, a relationship that is always social and therefore responsive to the social crisis.

The study follows a circuitous path. It first relates the cultural crisis beneath the ideological facade of national unity in Wilhelmine Germany to Weber's treatment of charisma. Charisma implies not only the authoritarian leader but also the charismatic community, the new collective which the competing strategies of modern writing invoked. Weber's personal development, as shown in his wife's biographical narrative, provides one example of the experience of crisis, while shedding light on the intellectual historical genesis of the sociological categories underlying the literary transformations.

The study then traces the history of German realism, its reification, the imprisonment of the implied reader in the Weberian iron cage, and the development of the culture industry in the mid-nineteenth century. Gustav Freytag's *Soll und Haben*, Adalbert Stifter's *Der Nachsommer*, Theodor Fontane's *Irrungen, Wirrungen*, and Georg Hermann's *Jettchen Geberts Geschichte* illustrate the use of detail as the basic unit of exchange in the realist reception process, the institutionalization of literature through the text, and the overt thematization of exchange models.

The study next confronts the problem of modernism directly. In the criticism of German literature, the designation "modern" has never had the reverberations typical of Anglo-American debates. At best it has been associated with literary groupings that appropriated it explicitly for themselves, such as the naturalists of the 1880s. The reluctance to elaborate a broader usage probably reflects a conservative aesthetic taste, linked to the conservative politics of traditional literary scholarship. By refusing to underscore the specificity of the twentieth century, literary scholars could avoid recognizing the end of the monarchy and its cultural consequences. Yet the self-understandings and aesthetic practices of significant German authors after 1900 are at least as radically modern as those of Joyce and Eliot, Proust and Céline. They insist on the same rupture with nineteenth-century culture, as well as the same avant-gardist connection between aesthetic and social change. Responding to the endogenous weaknesses of hegemonic literary life, modern writing is forced to reflect on its own institutional status and undertake a relegitimation of its activity. Weber's account of legitimate political authority helps to explain this modernist literary effort to find new voices, both for the transformed notion of authorship and the reconstructed communities of recipients.

Finally, the study examines the charismatic project of modernist literature in texts by Robert Musil, Hermann Hesse, Elias Canetti, Gustav Frenssen, Ernst Jünger, Hans Grimm, Artur Dinter, Alfred Döblin, Oskar Maria Graf, and Thomas Mann. Instead of cataloging modern German novels, it treats three competing versions of modernist prose writing: fascist modernism, leftist modernism, and a modernism of social individuality. All are ideal types in terms of their characteristic tropes, understood as forms of address designed to generate the new communities of readers. The rise of the modern German novel and the associated aesthetic innovation are inseparable from the various programs for social and political transformation inscribed in the texts.

This book could not have been completed without a grant from the Andrew W. Mellon Foundation that allowed me to spend a year as a Faculty Fellow in the Humanities at Harvard University. I am indebted to many friends and colleagues for their help and support at various stages of the project, and want to express my special gratitude to Theodore Andersson, Peter Bürger, John Foster, William Harris, Jochen Schulte-Sasse, and Lindsay Waters. I owe special thanks to Virginia LaPlante for her generous editorial assistance.

I dedicate this book to the memory of Anna M. Alintuck, who in her inimitable fashion taught me about some of the issues I have tried to address: reading as exchange, public acts, and the vicissitudes of tradition.

Contents

*The Rise of the
Modern German Novel*

1

The Geography of Wilhelmine Culture

*L*iterature has its geography. New ways of writing the world and describing spatial structures establish new ways of literary writing. The priority of cartography over belles lettres explains the persistent organization of the history of literature along national lines: the place precedes the word and produces it. For literature itself the intimate relationship between the face of the map and the shape of the text becomes most evident when the question is reduced to a matter of size. Kafka, partaking of the ambivalent national loyalties of eastern European Jewry and identifying with a hostile German culture itself beleaguered by the Czech environment, proposes a "literature of small nations," a literature of small texts and fragments, paradox and noncompletion.[1] The proximity of borders makes for fragile forms. In contrast, the superpowers of the twentieth century, spanning continents with unified administrations, establish their greatness with a search for epic grandeur commensurate with their universe of power. The Soviet attacks on the Russian avant-garde, associated with an innovative prose style of radical brevity, called for a reappropriation of traditional forms in order to create the monumental novel of the Soviet experience, the breadth of which rivals the prototypically American narrative, the epic film with a cast of thousands. Be it the hidden borders of the polyglot city or the homogeneous topography of the self-enclosed empire, the contours of the world anticipate the forms of art; one writing (geography) sets up a second writing (literature).

This is not merely a matter of quantity, of texts big and small. The internal substance of literature also has a close relationship to the making and remaking of maps, as nineteenth-century German realism demonstrates. Its links to the process of national unification are manifold. Both movements take their characteristic turns in the wake of the defeat of the 1848 revolution, and the leaders of the new realism are outspoken advocates of a unified state. Yet the crucial relationship is not a matter of the explicit, extra-aesthetic politics of realist authors, but rather the politics implicit in the formal composition of realist works and articulated in the programmatic statements of the movement. On this intraliterary level the politics of national unification are repeated as aesthetic innovation. The Bismarckian vision of a new map, in which the traditional borders of particularism are surpassed by a single nation, generates a new literature in which the complicated variegations of earlier modes of writing—romanticism, Biedermeier restoration, the young German radicalism—are supplanted by the purported transparency, uniform perspective, and unified narration of the realist text.[2]

Since literature has its geography, the sociology of modern writing in Germany must try to reconstruct its map. The realist literary mode, which had been established as the corollary to the foundation of the German Empire, gradually lost its credibility as an aesthetic program and its viability as a form of cultural communication by the end of the nineteenth century. The subsequent paradigmatic shift in literary writing, which set in around the turn of the century and introduced specifically modern strategies, responded both to the literary crisis of the established mode and to an extraliterary crisis involving the culture's fundamental self-understanding as a specific organization of meaning. The crises to which modernity reacted gained expression in emphatically geographical terms. Realism had been the literary counterpart to Bismarck's Reich, a national construction that defined itself through the ideological exclusion of alleged outsiders: Catholics, Jews, Socialists.[3] The literary tendencies that struggled to replace realism identified themselves expressly with foreign influences: French, Russian, Scandinavian. These identifications were indicative less of an objective geography of literary innovation, typified by the contention that the force of Scandinavian drama had engendered German naturalism, than of a subjective revolt implicit in the ostentatious embrace of alien models. In a nation whose map had been so radically rewritten, thinkers were compelled to establish their own geographical identity, and literary history was forced to determine its own space. Thus the remarkable centralization of literary life in the large urban centers was not merely a mechanical reflection of the concentration of the publishing industry (had that been the case, Leipzig alone would have been the intellectual capital) but also a consequence of the desire to demonstrate geographical identity with the politics of Berlin, the bohemianism of Munich, or, in opposition to the metropolis, the anarchism of the rural retreats between Friedrichshagen, where the naturalists returned to nature on the outskirts of the Prussian capital, and Ascona, the alpine haven for reformers of all sorts.

Ultimately the competing versions of modern writing presented themselves as universal, or at least as not parochially regional in scope. They made their mark on the literary map not by restricting themselves to one particular place but by envisioning a new sort of space altogether, in which new kinds of social relations, denied by the older literature, might flourish. Modernism's writing envisioned a utopian place where emancipation, understood in various and often mutually exclusive manners, might occur, and where the restrictive social ties of the old world might be overcome: it offered so many maps to the buried treasure of a new freedom. The geography on which culture rests is always a social geography, and places act as ciphers for alternative versions of social existence: Jerusalem or Rome, Heidelberg or Schwabing. When the young writers of 1900 set out as mapmakers, pen in hand, to trace a social world opposed to the Wilhelmine environment—and such a revolutionary impulse lies at the root of all German modernism—they occupied the terrain on which the cultural opponents of established imperial society began to assemble.

Geographical designations, even the apparently most objective, are never neutral. Names, distances, and directions not only locate points but also establish conceptualizations of power relations. The nomenclature of space functions as a political medium. Recall the terms applied to the former European colonies in the mid-twentieth century and generated by the shifting geopolitical strategies of players in the international order: "the third world," the superior alternative to the first and second worlds, where freedom and justice would unite; "the nonaligned nations," the objects of perpetual economic desire coyly flirting with both suitors; "neocolonialism" and "imperialism," which cast the booty as a passive body, the object of external historical actors.

By now these terms of the fifties, sixties, and seventies have been overshadowed by the terminology of "north" and "south." Such directions seem at first value-free, serving only to locate without labeling. They act as mathematical vectors setting up a neutral space in which all relationships may occur and no particular politics is structured in advance. Of course, the Cartesian transparency of the fictional space is precisely what betrays its ideological nature, since the purported objectivity of the terminology banishes competing political categories from a discussion of fully political matters. The contemporary retreat from public political debate can be measured in the substance of language: what was once the third world, the victim of imperialism, or the "underdeveloped" is now just the south. Such a camouflage of power relations serves the interests of the privileged, especially when it has been internalized by the victims; the north-south conceptualization remains a northern strategy.

Yet the north-south dichotomy has a content beyond the *prima facie* ideological exclusion of politics. It presumes that the fundamental world problem is an unequal distribution of industrialization; starvation and poverty in the south are to be solved by increased acceptance of responsibility in the north. The geographical terms imply a specific discourse of quantity: the massive quantity of capitalist commodities in the north versus the astronomical numbers of people in the south. The north-south discourse counterposes a world of productive machines to a world of reproductive life and places the second at the mercy of the first, since the goal is always to spread industrial society and its cultural forms. Nevertheless, the fundamental dichotomy between a mechanical and an organic world also characterizes an antithetical tendency in contemporary culture: the neoromantic idealization of agrarian primitivism as an allegedly healthy escape from the corruption of the denatured city.[4] This neoromanticism and its purported opponent, the ideology of industrialization and development, divide the world in much the same way: city versus country, industry versus nature, object versus subject, north versus south.

The persistence of this trope of twentieth-century geopolitics indicates how the structuring of space, the geography of writing, draws on inherited motifs and figures which are appropriated and projected onto the uncomprehended immediacy of experience, endowing it with meaning. The occidental tradition is not an unbroken one, constantly projecting its structures outward, creating and recreating its south and its orient in order to render them victims. The tradition exists rather as a perpetually redefined goal or, above all, as literary rubble, with disjointed terms and broken images, which are constantly revivified and just as constantly exhausted.[5] Similarly the spatial organization that begins to emerge in opposition to the map of the new German Empire draws on a traditional term, the southern utopia, which is imbued with a new sense related specifically to the social crisis to which modern writing attempted to respond.

The archaeology of the south in central European culture uncovers many layers: the kingdom of the ultimate ally, the glorious Prester John, the classical source of science and art, the home of sensuality and rejuvenation—Goethe's "land where lemon trees blossom."[6] No matter how different the initial referents of these various designations—Ethiopia, Greece, and Italy—they converged in a geographical discourse which produced the south as a cipher associated with values that could at any time be mobilized and projected onto any specific place. In the culture of the German Empire the longitudinal distribution of meaning took on particular importance, since the process of national unification, at least in the post-1848 period, was perceived largely as a north-south conflict. The long-standing rivalry between Prussia and Austria, Berlin and Vienna, lent itself to a north-south reading; thus Austria's exclusion from German affairs during the 1860s is linked to the establishment of a confederation labeled specifically "North German." Certainly Prussian growth since the eighteenth century just as easily suggested a westward expansion by an eastern power. That sort of reading, however, rarely competed successfully with the vertical interpretation, which, given the associative significance of north and south, ascribed surplus strength to the northern power simply by force of rhetoric. In the war of 1870-1871 the German states, led by the northern forces of Prussia, opposed an enemy, France, perceived as southern, while in the process the southern German powers relinquished most of their autonomy; that is, the north conquered the south externally and internally. United by its northern part, Germany became "Prussianized."

Opposition to the empire and its society was soon expressed in spatial terms, as those writers dissatisfied with the character of

Wilhelmine culture attempted to draw an alternative map. Although this new geography borrowed traditional motifs, such as the aesthetic privilege of the south, it also began to open up the space in which a qualitatively innovative writing and opposition could operate. A theater review by Theodor Fontane is compelling evidence of cultural territorialization because the author, despite his dissatisfaction with the imperial world, was hardly an extremist opponent, eager to construct a radical alternative. Fontane's expression of discontent in his review is confirmed by similar geographical alternatives to Prussia in his novels.[7]

Fontane was regularly responsible for covering performances at Berlin's Royal Theater for the liberal newspaper *Die Vossische Zeitung*, and his impressionistic style permitted him to work into discussion of the theater his personal opinions and prejudices regarding contemporary developments. In a review of Goethe's *Egmont* on March 8, 1872, for example, he effusively praised the actress Marie Lehnbach for her treatment of the figure Clärchen, while seizing the opportunity to introduce the north-south code, thanks to the otherwise insignificant fact that the actress spoke with a southern German accent. This accent provided Fontane with the welcome excuse to slip away from the object at hand and introduce a short exposition on the character of imperial culture barely a year after the founding of the Reich:

> The voice. How this Rheinish-southern German wrapped itself pleasingly again around our heart! It makes us feel with a bit of pain that we, on our sandbar of the March, may be Germans in a *political* sense, but certainly not in a national one. We are something different, something peculiarly modern, perhaps (for those who care to hear it) something of greater intellectual potency, but we do *not* have the real German tone, at least not in our throats, and for the near future, Havelland and Zauche will not be the birthplaces of the Clärchens and Gretchens. The Main line still holds for *them*, and when they arrive here, we perceive with a sort of desire and humiliation how "She was not born in the valley." Each one of them is—a maid from afar, a relative of that family, doomed to extinction, which once under the name of "poesy" had its place in German hearts. She has now made room for the "founders." A horse, a horse! Seven Clärchens for one construction site.[8]

Stylistically the passage is typical of Fontane's feuilletonism: the delicate elision between literary and nonliterary matters; the willingness to present subjective judgments as his own; the amused, slightly disrespectful tone; the light cadence; and the active use of literary and other cultural allusions.[9] Its content, however, is a striking description of the internal cultural disintegration of the recently achieved political unity. Fontane's primary concern is the reality of diversity and contradiction beneath the superficial homogeneity of the nation. Both Clärchen and Gretchen, Goethe's victimized female lovers of the male heros Egmont and Faust, lose out—the former as a victim of political progress, the latter as a victim of the cultural advance from religion to science. Their sort of existence, with its Rheinish-southern German tone, cannot flourish in sandy Prussia. The Main River, the traditional border between the north and south, which lost its official significance with the foundation of the empire, in fact continues to divide the state into two realms, and the cultural antinomies therefore generate the crisis of Wilhelmine society. Opposed to the specifically "modern" character of the north, a traditional and therefore authentic German character prevails in the south. Thus, the geographic polarity is augmented by a temporal dimension, and the south's privileged link with the past makes it simultaneously the home of art, which Fontane treats as an anachronism in the modern world, in danger of extinction.

Fontane specifies two women as "maids from afar," a reference to a Schiller poem understood as an allegory of art. A sexual dimension is thereby introduced, underscored by the term chosen to express the higher northern intellectuality, "potency."[10] The southern world of art, traditionalism, and the female principle are opposed to the masculine and cerebral modernity of the north. Such projections of an aesthetic priority onto the south prepared the way for the establishment of an aesthetic counterculture in Munich, the southern capital, where it was already rhetorically inscribed. Fontane characterizes the northern opponent of the aesthetic principle even more precisely: the "founders" were the speculators and entrepreneurs who rode the crest of the economic upswing of the early years of the empire, the so-called founding years, transforming the face of Berlin with extensive construction projects, which were often criticized for a tasteless ostentation. Consequently, Fontane's critique of the the ideology of national unity and official

7

Wilhelmine culture is fundamentally a critique of capitalism, or at least of a specific phase of capitalist expansion, centered in Prussia and opposed to southern traditionalism and the possibility of beauty.

The opposition is reciprocal. Not only does capitalism deny art, but art now emerges as the mortal enemy of capitalism. Fontane may link art to the past because of his own romantic heritage from the 1840s, yet this link was responsible for the rise of an opposition to hegemonic imperial culture nearly simultaneously with the foundation of the empire. The opposition that Fontane constructs as the tendential southern secession created a space in which a secessionist art could thrive two decades later, as an early phase of German modernism. More generally, the text is symptomatic of a countercultural tendency within the Wilhelmine world which projected onto the south the possibility of an aesthetic individuality as one credible strategy of opposition. In fact, the reconstitution of the individual in society through aesthetic innovation eventually became one of the primary strategies of literary modernism.

In addition to the overriding antinomy of a prosaic north and a poetic south, Fontane finds a second cleavage under the veneer of national unification. In the phrase "we, on our sandbar of the March," Fontane speaks as a Prussian, from the standpoint of the conquering heroes who had led armies to victory over the French and who appeared to maintain their traditional identity in the empire, while the southern Germans of Bavaria, Baden, and Württemberg had been forced to relinquish theirs. The specific form of German national unification under Bismarck's leadership depended on the establishment of a cultural hegemony of one regional power, Prussia, over the smaller kingdoms of the south. The Prussians might therefore have been expected to be the privileged carriers of national identity in the empire. Indeed, such a privilege existed on an official level: the Prussian king was the German emperor, and the Prussian chancellor spoke as the chancellor of Germany.

Despite the culmination of the long process of national unification which had provided German culture with its driving force since the beginning of the nineteenth century, regional differences continued to operate, and the contention of homogeneity was as much an ideological illusion as was the purported civil equality proclaimed by the liberal legislation which ushered in the empire during the early seventies. The facade of social and national homogeneity obscured the continuity of real hierarchy, inequality, and power difference. The particular status of the hegemonic Prussian culture, based on its priority in both the unification and the constitution of the empire, did not at all lead to a congruence of Prussian and national identity. On the contrary, according to Fontane, the actual cleavage behind the illusion of unity implies a disjunction between political and national dimensions. Because the Prussians control the state, they remain necessarily distinct from the nation. This dynamic itself testifies to the nonidentity of the political administration and its objects, of the government and the people. "We, on the sandbar of our March," are political but not national Germans, because the Prussians hold the state in their hands but stand opposed to the nation with all the arrogance of a conquering power: it is a case of the state against society, the north against the south.

The assertions of both a unified national territory and a domestic civil equality are highly problematic. Regional differences remain strong, and social stratification has not diminished. Prussia may claim for itself the role of ruler and law-giver; it is the place of formal equality and abstract liberalism, since the "founders" were the advocates of laissez-faire doctrine. Yet Prussian speech, distorted and crippled, can never achieve either the political or the social unity that it promises. Because of its privilege, Prussia cannot be the *vox populi*: "we do *not* have the real German tone, at least not in our throats." Actress Lehnbach can speak as a German in a way that a Prussian cannot. Fontane turns the matter of her accent into a discourse on the politics of speech and the distribution of power, whereby the geography of the north-south struggle is transformed into a metaphor for hierarchy and the dialectic of domination.

Northern political privilege desiccates Prussian speech, which loses its national character at the moment of national unity, whereas the subordination of the south renders its spokeswomen, Clärchen and Gretchen, oracles of the nation. The diminutive form of their names indicates both the absence of power and the surplus of cultural meaning. While the north degenerates into a place of mere politics, the disenfranchised south becomes the home of a national collectivity and therefore the cipher for a potentially emancipatory politics opposed to the empty administrative character of Prussian ideology. Fontane's antinomy of politics and nation signifies alternative modes of social organization and therefore envisages a new dimension of possible opposition within Wilhelmine culture. The south is the locus of an epic form where the people speak as a totality in tones foreign to the administrative language of Prussia. Elsewhere Fontane explicitly criticises Prussian speech, but here the critique is implicit in the designation of the full national speech ascribed to the south.[11] By now geography has beome fully metaphorical, no longer tied to the empirical topography of Germany. The literary separation of north and south created the image, and therefore the cultural possibility, of a space in which the nation might reclaim for itself a full political voice against the distorted discourse of hierarchy and administration. Fontane's complaint that the Prussian accent lacks any national or popular substance suggests the desirability of finding a language fit for democratic speakers. By locating a place of collectivity, the critique of hegemonic rhetoric eventually engendered a new literary writing, for the construction of an epic, national-collective speech became a further characteristic version of modern literature in Germany.

Yet another issue indicative of the cultural crisis of the empire and relevant to the possibilities of literary innovation after 1918 is temporality. This problem arises as part of the aesthetic discussion because Fontane's own postromantic prejudices lead him to insist on a special relationship between art and the past. Conversely he implies that "modern" Prussia and, by extension, the whole process of modernization threaten beauty with extinction in the future. Aside from any particular assumptions regarding historic limitations on the possibility of art, Fontane diagnoses a dual chronology, or to use Ernst Bloch's term, an "asynchronicity," in which the present collapses into a simultaneous experience of the hegemonically modern and the still-present past.[12] Again Fontane debunks ideology by locating the contradictions within the superficial homogeneity of time. Ostensibly this temporal duality is projected onto the alternative geographic regions, suggesting an economistic interpretation of the cleavage between capitalist progress in the north and underdeveloped traditionalism in the south. This paradigm is a legitimate explanation, although the geographic distribution of modernization and time could fit just as easily into an east-west distinction. Yet for Fontane, the competing chronologies do not coincide fully with the north-south fault. Art is not threatened solely in Prussia; it is in danger of losing its place in "German hearts" in general because capitalist modernity is fully capable of penetrating the no-longer pristine world of the south.

Meanwhile, just as the present imposes itself in the place of the past, the past lingers on, albeit as a weak memory, in the place of the present. Fontane concludes with a rhetorically distorted quotation from *Richard III*, transformed into the battle-cry of a venal materialism. The "founders," who would sacrifice all the beauty of "seven Clärchens" for the profits of their enterprises, recall the language of a dramatist who, for Fontane, was the prototype of a romantic-popular force. Even the exponents of the most amnesiac present rely on the Shakespearean language of the past, while at the same time eroding its stability, both rhetorically and economically. The strategic memory of the passage is recovered in the implicit dynamic of exchange and displacement. On the surface, Fontane parodies and therefore criticizes the greed of the founders, who were willing to give up beauty in order to engage in capitalism. Meanwhile, the parodied speech of the entrepreneurs, based on the complex relationship to Shakespeare, carries out a specific exchange in the manner of the distortion of the original verse. Programmatically, construction sites will replace Clärchen; but rhetorically, the new speech of the empire has already displaced the one element of the original Shakespearean speech that is missing in Fontane's rendition: the kingdom to be exchanged for a horse. The solution to the linguistic equation touches on Fontane's highly ambivalent relationship to the empire, seen less as the institutionalization of Prussian hegemony within Germany than as the subordination of the kingdom, traditional Prussia, to the crassness of the empire, which is no longer Prussia.

Throughout his oeuvre Fontane echoes the resentment of the conservative gentry, the Junkers, who feared the erosion of their traditional status within the modern state, and even while treating their resistance to change with irony, Fontane himself gives expression to nostalgia as another mode of expressing dissatisfaction within Wilhelmine culture. Asynchronicity therefore characterizes both the north-south distinction and the north itself, in which the memory of a former social existence in a Prussia of the past coincided with the contemporary experience of the empire. Particularly after the German defeat in the First World War, this temporal ambivalence underwent a politicization that engendered a reactionary literary-cultural strategy, another version of modernism, oriented toward a repetition of the past and a regeneration of purportedly original social forms.

In the early 1870s, Wilhelmine culture was still sure of itself, and the signs of crisis were barely evident. The unified nation was young, and enthusiasm for the Reich was rarely questioned. Even Fontane's moderate doubts met resistance and incomprehension. Nevertheless Fontane touches on the important fissures in the national identity that gradually opened up space for a counterculture of opposition to emerge by the turn of the century, in anticipation of the various specifically modern styles of writing that developed and thrived until the end of the Weimar Republic. Fontane opposes the Reich on three grounds: it is materialistic and therefore hostile to art, political and administrative and therefore hostile to authentic collectivity, and ahistorically modern and therefore separated from the superior sociability of the past. These dimensions of opposition represent rudimentary formulations of three desiderata of the new writing strategies that subsequently took shape: aesthetic individuality, epic collectivity, and backward-looking regeneration. This fundamental structure of dissatisfaction with Wilhelmine society generated the categories for formulating the crisis of bourgeois culture in the early twentieth century. It sketched out the map of resistance, and resistance, in its various modes, functioned as the constitutive principle of the new literature.

In addition to the dichotomy between the prose of northern capitalism and the poesy of the backward south, the self-identity of German culture polarized along a latitudinal axis, setting up an east-west geography of further divergences beneath the ideological facade of national unity. Undoubtedly the economic conflict between, on the one hand, the large landowners east of the Elbe River and, on the other, the industrialists of the Ruhr, which increasingly dominated the political coalition-building of the Reich, formed the material basis for the superstructural interpretation of contemporary power struggles. Yet the discourse within which alternative images and motifs collide and interact has a literary dynamic all its own and consequently becomes more than a merely derivative disguise of economic forces. Though it would be senseless to deny this economic element within the east-west tension in Wilhelmine culture, it would be equally short-sighted to overlook the rhetoric of the tension as a constant restructuring of the verbal formulation of national identity. Designations of a cultural project can be appropriated by partisan interests and may therefore reflect the motivations of particular speakers, but the lexemic units within a culture's self-articulation also precede the speech of any particular interlocutor. They have their own internal etymology, just as they participate in historically structured literary configurations, and these parameters limit and shape the enunciations of the speakers, whose very self-identities, including their perceptions of material self-interest, are generated by the rules of verbal discourse. The material base can never fully account for ideology, but cultural discourse can account for the behavior of economic actors who are always caught in the rhetorical web of a social speech.

The Prussian Junkers, Ruhr industrialists, and the many others who perceived and described Germany in terms of its eastern and western extremities operated within a literary code as multifaceted as the north-south terminology. Politics, especially geopolitics, recapitulates a literary geography central to an occidental tradition which divides itself into opposing realms derived initially from the dramatic imagery of a solar myth, as the German terms for "east" and "west" designate: *Morgenland* and *Abendland*, the lands of "morning" and "evening." The terms themselves suggest a melancholy perception of the decline of the west, where the sun must set, condemned to a constant fear of the rising east.

Although these categories of myth and primitive religion continue to thrive long after the specialized intelligentsia of civilization have declared them anachronistic in order to establish their own privileged claim to knowledge, the historical experience of the post-mythic period reformulates and enriches the inherited latitudinal poles: the western Roman state opposes the religion of Judea or the mysticism of Byzantium; the rationalism of the European individual finds itself insufficient to understand the inscrutable empires of Asia. Both east and west can appear as places of poverty and suffering, but in different manners: the existential loneliness of the Christian sinner never satisfied in this western world because of a perennial dearth of signs of grace differs fundamentally from the abject misery of the silent masses in murky eastern realms. Each image corresponds to an alternative form of wealth: the senseless acquisition of material goods in the west, at best for mere pleasure, at worst for pure occidental greed, as opposed to the fabulous and magic luxuries of the Orient, the object of imperialist desire.

These variations indicate the sort of reverberations that the east-west terminology could carry as it was grafted onto the objective crisis of German national identity in the late nineteenth century, namely the dissatisfaction with Wilhelmine culture and the political tensions within the empire. The antinomic forces of the culture appropriated the discourse of geography in order to make space for competing modes of existence and alternative programs of social order. For the East Elbians were almost eastern, and the Ruhr was almost western, and the new capital, Berlin, could understand itself as a new Moscow or a new Paris. The ceremony in which the Reich was founded took place in 1871 in the Hall of Mirrors at Versailles, where the new state symbolically sought its own reflection in the image of the western metropolis. Yet later the annexationist projects in the two world wars were based largely on the desire for the east, the *Drang nach Osten,* presented as an instinctual drive, a longing for unlimited wealth and unheard-of destruction.

The formulation of the German crisis, as a matter of both cultural values and economic production of wealth constitutes a leading concern for the early Max Weber. As one of the towering intellectual figures in turn-of-the-century Germany, he offers insights into the contemporary social problematic. His life and work provide a seismographic record of the tensions and competing cultural possibilities in Wilhelmine society and thus serve to explain the cultural transformations. In many ways, Weber's crisis, his nervous breakdown of the late 1890s, paralleled the collective crisis, and the antinomic character of his experience sets up a map of the fragmentation of collective identity.

This map became an explicit description of the east and the west in the early 1890s when Weber undertook to investigate the transformation of agrarian society in the eastern provinces, especially the results of the capitalist modernization of the large land-holdings. But the east-west duality, with which he endeavored to interpret social change and its relevance to the national identity, was grounded on an earlier distinction, deemed equally urgent, in which the specifically geographical interpretation was still absent. The east-west projection rested on archaeological layers of ideology, which can be reconstructed from a letter of May 8, 1887, fifteen years after Fontane's review of *Egmont,* from the twenty-three-year-old Weber to his cousin and first fiancée, Emmy Baumgarten. In it Weber deals with the pair of signs, Goethe and Schiller, who would continue to provide German intellectuals with an opportunity to position themselves and declare fundamental allegiances:

I was very pleased to hear that you so enjoyed the certainly excellent performance of the *Maid of Orleans* by the Meininger troupe. I emphasize this because nowadays Schiller is not to everyone's liking. The exaggerated and exclusive idolization of Goethe ruins the taste for Schiller, especially for those people who are particularly literary and who become so unfair toward everything beside Goethe; this has often angered me in Alfred and his peers. For what good does it do me when people tell me now how universal Goethe's poetic concept is and how the whole substance of human life from A to Z can be found within it, if I find the *one* aspect, the most important, hardly touched at all? For people do not generally understand their lives as if it only mattered to have a good time and to find a perspective through which everything might be enjoyed; nor are they confronted *only* with the question as to how they might find happiness and personal satisfaction. Yet this question is the most profound one in Goethe's works, including for example *Faust,* if the matter is treated with sobriety and precision. Everything, even the most difficult ethical problems, is examined from this perspective. Look, it is rather curious that Goethe could recognize baseness only when it converged with the ugly and insignificant; he had no sense for it when it approached him in the form of certain beautiful feelings—cf. *Elective Affinities*—or in giant grandeur—cf. his meeting with Napoleon. For him everything was a matter of form, including his poetry, i.e. by "form" I do not mean solely the beauty of his verses but rather the form of his thoughts. And that is why he was a great artist, for he had a mastery of form like few others, and it is with form that the artist makes of his object what he wills. But as a poet and writer, I think, he is equaled by others.[13]

Emmy's attendance at a performance of Schiller's *Maid of Orleans* permits Weber to describe an antinomic relationship between the two canonic figures of German classicism and to develop a critique of the Goethean position. Regardless of the correctness of Weber's understanding, this letter reveals the character of the opposing values projected onto the two authors. Weber describes their relative popularity and complains that the admirers of Goethe have occupied a dominant position within contemporary taste—"the exaggerated and exclusive idealization of Goethe"—leading to the denigration of all other alternatives, especially Schiller, who was traditionally the only plausible literary rival. Thus, the attack that Weber launches on the cipher Goethe, at first glance gratuitously, as a rejoinder to Emmy's positive reactions to Schiller, implies a diagnosis of what Weber regarded as the characteristic ideology of the empire in the late 1880s. In fact, Goethe's historical reputation had reached its nadir by mid-century, and the nearly overlooked centennial of his birth in 1849 contrasted sharply with the next decade's widespread celebrations of Schiller, who was regarded as the prophet of national liberation. After the founding of the empire, the relationship began to reverse itself. In an era that adulated the heroic individual, literary scholarship rewrote the past as a sequence of great poets, and Goethe above all benefited from this revisionism, becoming the figurehead of a unified German literature, a literature of a unified Germany. During the conservative 1880s, the ideological understanding of "Germanness" was regularly reduced to the telling formula of "Goethe and Bismarck."[14]

Weber's attack thematizes this Goethean hegemony in the complaint that all other authors are tendentially excluded from consideration. He suggests the desirability of a plurality of literary modes, denied by the monological structure of contemporary culture. Yet literature as such does not constitute Weber's basic concern. Beneath the quantitative problem of relative popularity, Weber speaks to the qualitative content of the Goethe cult as a symbolic expression of the predominant mode of existence in the empire. Weber's Goethe exemplifies the reduction of the diversity of life to a one-dimensionality in which the sole dictate is an aesthetic one. Goethe's cult is not a cult of beauty but rather a cult of form, willing to embrace even the most reprehensible phenomena, subsumed in the word "baseness," as long as they appear in the appropriate form. Weber's two examples are telling. He alludes first to Goethe's novel *Elective Affinities* (1809), which nineteenth-century criticism often regarded as an immoral presentation of adultery. Weber adheres to this traditional reading when he addresses his young bride-to-be in an indisputably pedagogic tone so as to teach her the importance of an ethical commitment to the social institution of marriage. Weber, the perpetual patriot, next cites Napoleon, the epitome of the military threat to the institution of the German nation, as an exemplar of the sort of valuelessness that Goethe was unwilling or unable to condemn. Thus the failure of the Goethean position, like the failure of Wilhelmine culture in general, was its incapacity to articulate a substantive ethics, since "even the most difficult ethical problems" are subsumed under the aesthetic standpoint.

The mere formality of contemporary life, which culminates in the Goethean hegemony, leads to an aesthetic-hedonistic bias whereby the individual endeavors only "to have a good time and to find a perspective through which everything might be enjoyed." Imperial society turns out to be vacuous not only in its formality but also in its external materialism. Fontane's earlier antinomy of northern materialism and southern aestheticism has undergone a profound transformation. Now materialism and art coincide as complementary aspects of a decadent formalism oblivious to the "one aspect" which Weber deems "the most important." Although Weber does not elaborate on the Schillerian alternative, its character, as implied by the rest of the text, consists in the ability to recognize precisely those valueless and reprehensible phenomena that the Goethean perspective is willing to condone and, furthermore, the readiness to condemn them, even at the cost of limiting the sort of material pleasure and beauty that contemporary culture treats as the sole goal of social activity. Weber constructs a dimension of ethical discrimination—the example of Napoleon indicates that ethics is also politics—and counterposes to it a narcissistic formalism. Ethical behavior is not only a necessary addition to social life in the empire but also, implicitly, a preferred and superior mode of being. Desire is no longer directed toward Goethe's Clärchen and Gretchen, who, as figures of art, promised a pleasure unavailable in the desiccation of the sandy north, but rather toward the virginal Joan of Arc, the leader of ascetic ethics and national ideals.

This experience of an antinomic relationship between ethics and aesthetics, not yet interpreted within a geographic code, continued to occupy the cultural imagination in the following decades and was therefore a further symptomatic expression of the social crisis. Sixty years later, the opposition of the two existential possibilities structured the dual tragedies of the Rodde sisters in Thomas Mann's *Doctor Faustus* (1947). The bourgeois solidity of the older generation gives way to the divergence between the perfunctory marriage of Ines and the bohemian escapades of Clarissa, until the former's path leads dialectically to delinquency, and the latter's path to a fruitless attempt at social integration. After the historical catastrophes of the world wars and the holocaust, Mann could recognize the failure of both possibilities, but in 1887 Weber's goal was merely to articulate and defend the ethical alternative. His position at that time was hardly idiosyncratic. After the economic crisis of 1873, dissatisfaction with the venal character of the empire repeatedly thematized the cult of material accumulation as the cause of both social misery and moral decline. This diffuse anticapitalism accused the laissez-faire regime of an antisocial acquisitiveness and a subjective individualism, deaf to collective and national needs. Antiliberal rhetoric was appropriated by diverse political and cultural tendencies critical of imperial society, and these critiques gradually generated a geographical discourse. According to them, the empire, founded in a victory over France, rapidly became an imitation of France in its materialism and its frenetic search for pleasure. At times a sort of economic contamination was even suggested: the French reparation payments led to an economic upturn which in turn generated an empty, hedonistic culture, as if the victors had been physically infected by contact with the gold of the defeated carriers of Parisian immorality.

This sort of argument, which amounted to a defense of the allegedly German province of values and substance against the superficial formality of France, characterized the ideology of the naturalist movement as it gradually took shape in the course of the eighties. The features of naturalist literature included an extreme insistence on descriptive precision, a thematic interest in urban poverty, and a deterministic understanding of social conditions. Although these aspects indicate the vaguely leftist leanings of the members of the movement, they frequently gave voice to a surprisingly shrill nationalism. As early as 1882, the literary critical pathbreakers of naturalism, Julius and Heinrich Hart, complained that the decisive military victory of the Germans at Sedan in 1870 had been followed by no "Sedan of the spirit," no corresponding cultural liberation from a putative French hegemony. German literature, so they claimed, still lay prostrate beneath the weight of foreign models, which crippled authentic native creativity. At times the naturalists specifically attacked Grecophile tendencies; at other times French culture became their source of all evil; but at all times they denounced the alien paradigm as merely aesthetic and senselessly hedonistic. Its concerns appeared to them to be solely formal, and its status in Germany a veneer, temporarily grafted onto the essence of the national character. The Harts' formulation of the national project, their construction of German identity, depended on a reactivation of the antiformal, antiaesthetic ethics, which was constantly present, no matter how momentarily obscured, in the "spirit of the nation, hidden beneath the surface, resting in the depths, untouched by all changes, always the same."[15] Consequently they inscribed a new geography onto the map of Europe, wherein Germany became the privileged homeland of ethical substance, the potential bulwark against the external forces of moral and aesthetic decadence, which had penetrated the empire during the liberal heyday of the seventies but which the naturalists expected to overcome in the eighties with an idealist rearmament, an emphatic assertion of national identity and allegedly German values:

> The nation is pulling itself together, and the calls for a "national spirit" will cease to be an empty phrase. We consider ourselves Germans, representatives of Germanness against haughty Romanism and expansive Slavism. The blood flows more quickly in our veins, and after the dull digestive hours of the past decade, after the mere intoxication of pleasure, which dominated the arts as well as all other aspects of life, we again face the need for great ideals, which will elevate us and lead us beyond all everyday activity.[16]

Early naturalism's vision of a national rejuvenation soon engendered the explosive development of a naturalist theater, particularly in the plays of Gerhart Hauptmann, such as *Before Dawn* (1889) and *The Weavers* (1892). The specifically nationalist content of the initial vision was subsumed and modified in an aesthetic approach that favored the popular dialect language of everday life over the artificially formal German of the established stage, while simultaneously turning to contemporary themes and social questions. The rejection of the hegemonic literature of the seventies anticipated the modernists' self-understanding as a radical alternative to the bourgeois culture of the nineteenth century.

This cultural shift rested on the reformulated geography. No matter how much the naturalists claimed to borrow from foreign authors, especially Ibsen and Zola, the movement relied on the opposition of an authentic native experience to the false, formalistic liberal-capitalistic legacy regarded as a consequence of imitating the Parisian models—Dumas, Sardou, and Augier. An east-west polarity emerged, essentially identical to Weber's simultaneous antinomy of ethical and aesthetic modes. In 1887, when Weber wrote to Emmy

Baumgarten, the naturalist theater made its first important headway on the German stage with highly controversial performances of Ibsen's *Ghosts*. Thus Weber's categories were homologous with the basic self-conception of the naturalism of the day. His attack on Goethean aestheticism essentially coincided with the naturalists' cultural geography, especially the critique of an occidental, Francophile pole in his east-west reading of the agrarian question in Prussia.

Weber belonged to the Verein für Sozialpolitik (Association for Social Policy), an organization of academics, especially economists, and government officials, founded in 1873, the year of the first major economic crisis in the rapid process of German industrialization. Its members were troubled by the growing social costs of capitalist expansion. Although reaffirming their loyalty to the state and their own distance from the Socialists, these "academic Socialists," as their opponents labeled them derisively, attempted to develop strategies for state regulation of certain economic relations, such as protective labor laws, in order to blunt the edges of the increasingly sharp class conflict. This reformist stance was linked to a cultural geography, insofar as it treated the fully developed industrial capitalism as a foreign and western model. The constellation of expanding factories, a population explosion in the cities, and the emergence of new social problems was labeled "Manchesterism," referring to the center of the English industrial revolution, as if capitalist modernization were a peculiarity of British culture and not an international economic process. The asynchronicity generated by Germany's relative underdevelopment in the last decades of the century explained the paradox of German imperialism representing itself ideologically as the carrier of an anticapitalist culture, as Theodor W. Adorno has demonstrated.[17]

In the early nineties, however, when the Verein für Sozialpolitik turned its attention to the agrarian question, the "economic nationalist" Weber spoke to the east-west tension in terms not of a conflict with the western powers but of a conflict between economic forms within the empire, leading to social erosion (MW230). In Weber's view, the eastward penetration of the purportedly western capitalism and its corollary, subjective individualism, set off a chain reaction which transformed the patriarchal estates of Prussia into capitalist enterprises and consequently broke up the traditionalist cultural complex that had tied the rural population to the soil. The new economic rationality induced the landowners to relinquish their customary responsibilities to the peasantry, who in turn, inspired by ideals of economic independence and upward mobility, grew discontent with their own traditional status. As mass migration to the industrial west or abroad to North America set in, Polish and Russian laborers came to the estates, first as migrant workers, eventually as permanent settlers; indeed, the Slavic penetration of Prussia was both a cause and a result of the German exodus. Weber therefore blames the westernization, or capitalization, of the German east for both the immanent collapse of Prussian society and the dilution of the German character of the region, under the shadow of an ominous Pan-Slavism.

Regardless of the legitimacy of Weber's analysis, the structure of his geography and the character of the associations projected onto the two poles are crucial, for in Weber's mature thought, the industrial west and the agricultural east turn into two key categories, legal and traditional authority. His report for the Verein für Sozialpolitik on "The Conditions of Agricultural Workers in Germany East of the Elbe" (1892) demonstrates the complicated geographic dynamic:

It is the tragic fate of the German east that with its powerful achievements for the nation it has dug the grave of its own social organization. The establishment of the political greatness of the nation was above all *its* merit. "Bright from the north broke the light of freedom," sang the poet eighty years ago; the German east with its tight political and military organization was also the half-unwilling tool with which the nation reached its desired unity. It was not parochialism but uncertainty about what must follow that led excellent men in Prussia in the highest positions to resist dissolution into the greater unit of the Reich. The military and economic costs of Prussian hegemony have always been carried primarily by the naturally poor eastern regions of the state. With the unification of the empire, metropolitan and industrial developments made a great leap. The south and the west with their overpowering capital force the east to accept their manufactured products but turn down the bread that eastern agriculture squeezes, with difficulty and expense, from the native soil. Just as the east was the prime provider of the human material for the military foundation of the nation's political strength, it now provides the industry of the west with the labor force to establish the economic power status of

Germany; through the glorious development of German industry and urban centers, it has its life-blood, the future generations of laborers, sucked from its veins.[18]

Weber describes the Prussian role in the process of national unification as "tragic" because only the Junkers proved capable of carrying out the historic task at which the western liberals failed repeatedly, but the culmination of that process necessarily led to the erosion of the social basis of the same Prussian leadership. The traditionalist east, in Weber's view, provided the effective politicans as well as the best soldiers for the national birth; it was culturally prolific but economically poor. Even nature seems to have been parsimonious in its endowments to Weber's Prussia. Yet the relationship between cultural wealth and material poverty may have been in part a causal one, particularly in light of the Goethe-Schiller, materialist aesthetics versus national ethics antinomies. Eastern traditionalism, where ethics and austerity coexist, contrasts with the capitalist west, blessed with material affluence but unable to generate capable leaders: in the midst of surplus wealth, the west experiences a perpetual cultural deficit.

The crisis Weber describes was a complex combination of different processes. For example, the Junkers became the agents of the nation in the historical unification, but despite their privileged political role, the system of latifundia began to decay. Prussian traditionalism was additionally weakened by western capitalism, which sucked off its vitality like a vampire clinging to a healthy organism. The already sandy east was further desiccated by the westward flow of wealth. This tendential collapse of the East Elbian society set the stage for other developments that threatened the substance of the nation as a whole. German capitalism could not survive without a traditionalist hinterland as a cultural resource, because historically the Junkers alone had provided German national identity with its values and leadership. Since the beginning of the age of imperialism, capitalism had been unable to exist without the presence of a precapitalist other from which to extract its strength and wealth.

Above all, according to Weber, the Prussian crisis threatened national identity externally, for capitalist development opened the borders to foreign laborers and thereby endangered the German character of the region within the still young state: "Under the sign of capitalism, Germany will be denied the victory over Slavic propaganda."[19] The western model of wealth eroded the stability of Prussian traditionalism and subsequently the German identity of the region, drawing in a foreign and potentially subversive population. Like the historian Heinrich von Treitschke a decade earlier, Weber does not direct his antagonism toward the presence of a heterogeneous group because of an expicit xenophobia or cultural parochialism, though he often does display traits of chauvinism. The fundamental motivation for these two representatives of Wilhelmine academic politicians is rather a nearly frantic insistence on cultural stability and homogeneous national identity. To the extent that ethnic minorities appear as outsiders, their presence is quickly interpreted as a threat to the self-understanding of the empire, since the new geography underscores the importance of distinctions between insiders and outsiders, natives and foreigners. This dichotomous structure of national identity in turn explains why the crisis of Wilhelmine culture and the emergence of opposition can be traced in the reformulations of the geographic code.

When Weber resigned in 1899 from the Alldeutscher Verband (Pan-German League), a lobby for imperialist expansionism, he did so in protest not against the group's characteristic adventurism but against its opportunism, its unwillingness to cross the interests of Prussian agribusiness which profited from the pool of cheap migrant labor from the east at the expense of German national cohesion. Elsewhere the Alldeutscher Verband defended Germanism and damned foreigners with unbroken regularity; on this question alone it tolerated open borders, whereas for Weber on this question alone rests the whole weight of national identity. The traditional patriarchal latifundia, which had supported a German rural population, had also produced, in Weber's view, the personality types that filled the ranks of the military, the backbone of the nation. In his report "The Condition of Agricultural Workers," he comments:

> The stable closure of the official agrarian constitution was both a reflection and foundation of the tight state organization; it was above all the basis for the psychological prerequisites of military discipline. Military obedience was something normal for the peasant son or farm laborer from the east, used to patriarchal direction. It was part of his atmosphere, even outside the barracks, and particularly the attached laborer knew from his everyday experience on an estate that when the master commands, he does so in the common interest of all, including those who obey. This explains the role of the landed aristocracy in the officer corps. It is a common psychological error to believe that fully internalized subor-

dination excludes the possibility of a sense of personal honor and duty. Other aspects are decisive. Everyone who has seen a regiment recruited from different regions knows that the sons of the north-east, Prussia, Pomerania, Saxony and the March are still in the front ranks as far as typical soldierly honor goes. The relatively high level of nutrition combined with the readiness to do one's "damned duty" without reflection, as an inescapable legacy, created the capital with which Prussia fought her battles.[20]

Because precapitalist traditionalism had produced the cultural "capital" of Prussian strength, the capitalization of Prussia generated a cultural crisis. Weber's argument relies on a suggestive metaphoric logic. "Stable closure" corresponds to "discipline," "obedience," and doing one's duty "without reflection." Prussia, the east, is for Weber a place of stability and order, where, left to itself, change would not have occurred and traditional values would have remained intact if outside influences, the legacy of national unification, had not intervened from the west. The world Weber idealizes in Prussia could not resist the temptations of subjective idealism and material wealth associated with the fleshpots of western capitalism. And if Prussia was threatened, the empire could not last. The spread of western values and economic forms imperiled the reproduction of political leadership, the legitimacy of the borders and the substance of the military.[21]

In his report for the Verein für Sozialpolitik Weber describes the crisis as a destabilization of cultural identity and, in particular, as a conflict between eastern and western principles, between traditionalist and capitalist social forms. The geography of crisis is as antinomic for Weber in the early nineties as it was for Fontane in the early seventies: east and west or north and south. At the beginninng of the next decade, however, which was the beginning of the next century, a third term begins to emerge in Weber's work, in addition to traditionalism and capitalism, and a tripartite model of social forms evolves as a key feature of his oeuvre. Within the logic of the Weberian problematic, the third term, charisma, represents a response to the crisis of imperial identity, which his work of the early nineties had phrased within the geographic code of east and west. The introduction of the third term transcends the limits of the binary code, and Weber undertakes a global expansion of his project.

2

The Category
of Charisma:
Max Weber

*B*eyond the antinomy of traditionalism and capitalist rationality, the category of charisma constitutes Weber's response to the crisis of Wilhelmine society and is simultaneously a cipher of a cultural possibility beyond the organization of the bourgeois world. It is therefore the term from which a Weberian reading of modernism derives. The category itself was not simply the product of logical, intellectual labor; indeed, the specific nature of charisma implies a qualitative leap out of the inherited social logic and its formal constraints. The escape from the conceptual matrix of established culture and the answer to the antinomies of bourgeois life became a problem in Weber's own life before he articulated the solution in his professional writings. The social crisis described in the first half of the nineties within the geographical code corresponded to his psychological incapacitation after his father's death in 1897, and his discovery of charisma after the turn of the century was based on the climaxing of that personal crisis. Because charisma appeared first as a sword cutting through the Gordian knot of a single bourgeois identity, the biographical substrate to the intellectual progress clarifies the term.

Biography, however, like geography, is caught up in a medium of power. Just as geography transforms a material surface into an object of desire and conquest, fantasy and destruction, biography too is a discourse structured by vested interests. Writing a world and writing a life each has its political motor. Personal experiences, affinities, antipathies, and the choices between them are set out by writers with ulterior motives, for there is no transparent language of objectivity, certainly not for the emotions, and least of all for the biographer intimately tied to the object of study.

In the case of the key source on Weber's life, *Ein Lebensbild* (1926), a biography written shortly after his death in 1920 by his wife, Marianne, these motives are overwhelming. In the biography she not only heroizes her deceased husband as an Olympian figure but also positions herself as the sole legitimate heiress of his legacy. This is a key gesture, because, as Weber lay dying, he was watched over by two women: Marianne, who, by writing about him, established her own property rights against the competitor, and Elsa von Richthofen, Weber's student in his early Heidelberg days and, much later in Munich, his lover. With the biography, Marianne could claim the corpse and the title to the Weberian tradition, which she would guard and preserve in her Heidelberg salon for decades to come. To do so, however, she had to fashion the biography appropriately. References to Weber's infidelity had be to be avoided, even though the manner in which she skirts the issue makes it clear that she must have been aware of the liaison. Where a discussion of the affair would have been chronologically in order, Marianne portrays Weber as unquestionably loyal. The omission of adultery shows up as repression, just as any discussion of the sterility of the Weber marriage turns out to be denial, since Marianne simultaneously idealizes the values of family life, especially with reference to the Weber clan.

Marianne thereby avoids another painful topic, the character of her own background, which from the standpoint of the conservative German bourgeoisie, with its perennial insistence on behavior rigorously *comme il faut,* must have seemed dangerously questionable, replete with family insanity, unequal matches, and the loss of social prestige. Her mother, Anna Weber, was a first cousin of Max Weber and the daughter of a patrician textile merchant. Anna's husband, Eduard Schnitger, was a young doctor of few means, and Marianne suggests his incongruity in the wealthy family of his father-in-law. After Anna's early death, Eduard developed a severe psychological disorder, probably a persecution complex; two of his brothers succumbed to the same illness. Having been raised by her paternal grandmother in a family marked by tragedy and endowed with only modest financial resources, Marianne, the biographer, transforms Max and the other Webers into paragons of ethical rectitude and bourgeois solidity—everything her own father lacked—while presenting Max's mother, Helene, as a mythical matriarch, a constant source of life and nourishment. Marianne herself remained childless. This alliance with Helene, the real heroine of the biography, provides the basic structure of the narrative. Marianne presents Max's development as a righteous struggle to loose himself from his father's liberal freedom and to submit himself to his mother, whereby each parent takes on a metaphorical character. The father, the local politician in Berlin, is the principle of the north, while the mother, Helene Fallenstein, the daughter of a cultured Heidelberg patrician, is the south. Marianne is elated when she and Max, residing in Heidelberg, can move into Helene's childhood house; Max considers the move unimportant. Typically, this geographic code is linked to alternative existential modes: cold, patriarchal rationalism versus a traditionalist, female, ethical religiosity.

Although the hidden power struggle in Marianne's biographic project prevents acceptance of the presentation at face value, the account remains an important source on Weber's life, and not just because of the facts that filter out from the interpretation or because of the many interpolated letters within the text. Despite the unreliability of the narrator, who tells Max's story in the same way that the narrator in Thomas Mann's *Doctor Faustus*, Serenus Zeitblom, recounts the history of his friend, Adrian Leverkühn, the narrative gives evidence of the interpretive world within which Weber himself lived. Though it does not explain Weber's intellectual genesis with unclouded transparency (no text could achieve that goal), it provides partial explanations, as distorted as any other.

Whereas Marianne places her husband's origins in a genealogical context modeled on the form of the German novel of development, Weber himself understands the historical character of his intellectual straits as a matter of generation, of youth and the regeneration of its tasks. In his inaugural address as Professor of Economics at the University of Freiburg, titled "The Nation-State and Economic Policy" (1895), he places in context his own identity and the identity of his generation of German intellectuals:

> Even vis-à-vis the terrible needs of the masses of the nation which weigh heavily on the heightened social conscience of the new generation, we must frankly confess: the consciousness of our responsibility to history weighs more. It is not

27

granted to our generation to see whether the struggle that we are carrying out will bear fruit and whether posterity will look back on us as its ancestors. We will not succeed in banishing the curse upon us to be the epigones of a great political era, unless we can understand how to be the forerunners of a greater one. (MW 231)

Weber defines himself as an epigone, born after the heroic period of national unification and barred by history from participating in it directly. Although he expresses admiration for the ideals of the older political generation, including the National Liberalism of his own father in Berlin, the capital city and the center of national identity, he also distances himself from them, since he does not accept his epigonic status as a mandate for trivial imitation of the patriarchs. Born after the unification, he would carry it on and ensure the stability of national identity, not, however, by mimicking the liberal politics of the older generation. Instead, he would find his own identity and intellectual purpose by confronting the contemporary social conflicts and cultural crisis which had followed in the wake of the foundation of the empire and were now bequeathed as destiny to the generation of the 1890s. The fusion of east and west had generated the Reich, but it had also initiated a process that threatened the national cohesion, as the East Elbian investigations showed. Just as history denied Weber direct access to the project of the founders, it also prohibited him from falling behind the achievement of 1871 and taking the side of the east against the west—or in terms of the biographic code, his mother or his father. The epigone Weber operates simultaneously on the level of national identity and personal identity, politics and biography, and the impending catastrophe in his private life, the nervous breakdown, will eventually lead him to a resolution of the social crisis.

Because Marianne structures her account of the biographic genesis of Weber's personal crisis according to the rules of the Bildungsroman, she commences with a detailed account of his ancestors. Consequently, as a family history, the text offers considerable insights into German mores in the nineteenth century. But as a statement from the 1920s, it chiefly provides evidence of the cultural memory, of how Marianne and Max envisioned the various components of the cultural milieu. Thus, when she describes Helene's Heidelberg youth, the characterizations and values are testimony less to objective facts in mid-century Germany than to the manner in which the author and her husband understood the maternal component in his personality. The features ascribed to Helene are written into the biography so that Marianne can claim that Weber returned to the maternal legacy of Heidelberg.

Three elements dominate the character sketch of Helene. First, she is presented as a cipher of a practical immediacy, unwilling to stand on form or to respect the restrictive rules of conduct that tightly regulated behavior in the households of the nineteenth-century bourgeoisie. Marianne juxtaposes two anecdotes in a telling manner to convey this character. When a rat wandered into the living room, the young Helene neither froze in horror, as social mores dictated, nor called for a servant, but grabbed "the disgusting animal" bare-handed and drowned it in a well; and when a peasant woman, peddling apples, collapsed in the house and her death appeared inevitable, Helene insisted that the woman die there in peace rather than being transported laboriously to a hospital (MW 19). Each incident demonstrates Helene's ability to act immediately, as the situation demanded, without concern for the forms of social regulation or the rules of social conduct. Yet while the stories present Helene as the code-breaker, they also show Marianne to be caught up in a code of her own, for catastrophe is twice presented as the sudden and unmotivated penetration of external forces—the rat and the peasant, dirt and death—into the tranquil idyll of bourgeois domesticity. As Marianne tells it, Helene responded to the threat directly in order to preserve the interior, just as Max later responded to the social question in order to protect the national identity and to outflank the radical socialist alternatives.

This immediacy of action, particularly in terms of social issues, is linked to Helene's second feature, her roots in the liberal religiosity of the south. The lived religion of Heidelberg is contrasted with the dogmatism of the northern church, a polarity which echoes that between the notion of immediacy, the desire to engage in practical activity, and restrictive social regulations. It is not formal religion that concerned the young Helene, but a Christian life of the sort that ultimately led Max to cooperate with the Christian Socialist politician Friedrich Naumann. Yet the belief that Marianne ascribes to Helene, which contrasts with dogma, is not an apotheosis of irrationality, of tenets upheld despite their absurdity. That sort of belief would have returned Helene to the fold of the dogmatics. Neither is it an ecclesiastical or a mystical formalism. It is rather a religion of practical ethical commitment grounded in Christian ideals. This antinomy of form versus ethics, in which ethics holds priority over form, would return in Weber's letter to Emmy. Helene is the model of social concern opposed to any cult of form, be it a matter of etiquette or religion.

Marianne projects onto Helene's antiformalism an antiaesthetic component as well, which figures as her third character trait. Just as Max warned Emmy of the dangerous temptations of art, form, and pleasure with reference to Goethe, Marianne touches on the same issue by recounting Helene's reading Homer at the side of the literary historian Georg Gervinus, a close friend of the Fallenstein family. Although the literary experience seemed at first both enriching and idyllic, it turned out to threaten Helene's religiosity: "Her soul was too deep not to be shaken by the tension between Christian and pagan feelings, and she considered the attraction of her respected teacher to that world of earthly beauty as a 'temptation' to betray herself. The security of her childhood faith crumbled" (MW 21). Gervinus's Homer becomes a cipher of earthly beauty and sensuous pleasure opposed to Helene's native Christianity. This tension is heightened by another anecdote, in which Marianne shows how the lasciviousness of both Father Homer and his latter-day admirers can endanger even the most prudent virgin:

> She was sixteen years old, a chaste blossom still closed, when it happened one day that her respected teacher, beloved like a father, whom she had trusted for years, lost control. The aging man suddenly drenched the unsuspecting girl with the burning flow of an irresistible passion. Horror, disgust, pity and the old, thankful respect for the fatherly friend and teacher tore her in different directions and—because of her delicate nerves—to the edge of an abyss. Helene never forgot it. From then on, sensual passion seemed to her incriminated, guilty and subhuman. Even in her old age, the memory brought horror to her face. (MW 22)

Gervinus and Homer signify earthly pleasure, and Helene, falling back from them in disgusted horror, represents a sort of ethical asceticism, repelled by the things of this world and living solely for her faith and her ideals. Her rejection of Gervinus' world prefigures, within the biography, Weber's critique of Goethe and his praise of Schiller's ethical idealism just as Marianne's characterization of her mother-in-law as practical, religious, and ascetic anticipates elements that she would project onto her husband Max.

Helene's husband, Max senior, is not presented in any corresponding detail; instead, Marianne touches only on the steps of his career in liberal city politics from the Prussian constitutional conflict of the mid-sixties to the founding of the Reich in the seventies. This limited concern with the external trappings of his professional life indicates Marianne's judgment that his interior life was insignificant, as well as her own constant preference for Helene. The Weber family's religious practices appear rigid and formal when compared with the ethical, undogmatic faith of the southern Fallensteins, and Helene, who immersed herself in the works of theologians like Theodore Parker and William Channing, complained that her husband, attracted only to mundane affairs, "always has so much to do, reading newspapers and the like" (MW 31). The husband and father becomes the symbol of bourgeois liberalism during the foundation of the empire, the grand facade without intellectual substance or personal warmth, since the domestic sphere is fully subordinated to the exigencies of career and politics:

> Helene finds it increasingly difficult to explain her own intellectual and religious interests to her husband—because basically he has no such needs and is occupied instead with a worldly life, his office, politics and sociability. He has meetings all day, goes on campaign trips, travels considerably by himself on his vacations or later with the children and expects from his domestic situation—the center of which he naturally considers himself—the joy of love and comfort and service. Helene has much to do everyday. (MW 35).

Thus, the foundation is laid for the son's psychological and intellectual struggles between the north and the south, between Berlin and Heidelberg, between the patriarchal principle of political rationality, career, and progress and the matriarchal principle of religious ethics, interiority, and traditionalist social concerns. Marianne concludes that her husband's youth made a choice inevitable, since the latent crisis permitted no compromise: "In those years it was still unclear how 'the big one' [Weber] would choose between the model of his father and his mother. He already vaguely sensed that he would sometime have to make such a decision—as soon as he had control of himself and could purposefully begin to construct his own personality" (MW36).

Weber's early development was marked by the internalization of male ideals, a mimesis of the father within an overall patriarchal culture.[1] As a student in Heidelberg, he was less concerned with his maternal roots than with enjoying the good times of university life and becoming "a robust, powerful fellow" (MW 69). The initial escapades of the young student eventually gave way to a growing seriousness, but the ascetic turn had surprisingly little to do with the maternal influence, representing instead a subordination of the personal sphere to the demands of professional life in his father's careerist pattern. Weber studied law "like his father," and in a letter to his mother he explains that he prefers to devote himself to his intellectual work and vocational preparation without the senseless interruptions of social life. In correspondence with his mother he rejects her again by rejecting her theologian Channing, whose pacifism, in Weber's eyes, threatened the higher good of the national identity, the achievement of the father's National Liberal politics.

Finally, Weber chose his father over his mother in the symbolism of his marriage, but in a way that Marianne herself could never recognize. Weber initially courted his cousin Emmy, the daughter of Helene's sister Ida, who was married to the historian Hermann Baumgarten and lived in Strassburg. The Baumgarten world reproduced all the values associated by Marianne with Helene, but in even greater intensity, for it was Ida who was regarded as the fervently religious sister. Yet eventually Weber chose Marianne, not Emmy. Weber inscribed his marital choice within the limits of the family tree, for Marianne was also a relative, but her grandfather was the brother of Max senior. Thus, within the semiotics of family alliances, Weber tied himself to his father's side of the family, not his mother's; both possibilities were open, and he decided to identify with the patriarchal lineage. The issue, however, is deeper than the specific pattern of endogamy. Not only was Emmy a maternal relation, but she also shared the maternal principle, especially the religious background. Not only was Marianne a paternal relation but she shared the bourgeois traits of the lineage, its concern with social status, career, and intellectual labor as profession rather than religion. In the course of the biography, Marianne leaves no doubt that she considers religiosity superior to male rationality, but when Weber chose her over Emmy he was expressing an antithetical reading of the cultural alternatives: the modern world of rational activity and national-patriarchal identity was preferable to the powerless philistinism of provincial interiority.

The establishment of Weber's identity through the internalization of the patriarchal northern principle provided only a superficial stability for the young scholar and young husband. The patriarchal mimesis implied a constant repression of the maternal legacy, and on the personal level it caused a dialectical erosion that mirrored the cultural transformation of the period. The victory of German liberalism in the national unification was simultaneously more significant as a history of defeat. Since the Napoleonic Wars, the project of German national unification had been associated with liberal and democratic ideals. The envisioned national parliament promised to undermine the local power of the various aristocratic lineages and initiate an egalitarian transformation of traditionally hierarchical social structures. Yet when the empire was ultimately established, conservative forces led by Bismarck were able to appropriate the formerly progressive goal for their own purposes. The new state managed to unify the nation without any commitment to the earlier reformist hopes. Liberals who rallied to the banner of the empire were compelled to surrender their social values in the name of patriotism. Liberalism consequently lost its internal substance, and its vacuity provoked the anger of the younger generation of 1890, especially among Weber's naturalist contemporaries.

Although Weber himself mimetically appropriated elements of his father's liberal political rationality, such as the priority of politics over domesticity and the desire for national identity, he heightened precisely those aspects that necessitated a break with the same liberal ethos. In Germany at the end of the Bismarckian period, the liberal culture of the founders was remembered as little more than a cult of individuality and ornament, in which the content of laissez-faire behavior necessarily collided with the demands of collective identity. Weber insisted on the priority of the collectivity against eudaemonistic claims for individual happiness, for unlike the older liberals, including his father, Weber spoke with the pessimism of a new generation, unable to share the older faith in the inexorable confluence of individual and national progress. A return to the traditionalist world and its ethics, the matriarchal principle, was impossible, in terms of both national history and Weber's personal identity, but insight into the social question—to which the patriarchal laissez-faire liberalism was blind—grew increasingly necessary in order to guarantee the stability of national identity, just as it gradually occupied the central place in Weber's intellectual identity.

The path of cultural transformation led through a labyrinth of mirrors. Weber, whose patriarchal mimesis established the image of an identity constantly called into question by the denied maternal principle, had to overcome the paternal liberalism without regressing on either the individual or collective level. That liberalism, which Weber had denounced as the western capitalist model in the East Elbian study, had emerged as a reflection of France in the Hall of Mirrors in Versailles and had been denounced by its opponents as an imitation of English Manchesterism. Within the terms of this geographic code, Weber's journey through England, Scotland, and Ireland in the summer of 1895 took on particular significance. According to his letters included in the biography, the depopulation of the English countryside is a warning to him as to the future of Prussia if a similar process of enclosure and capitalist urbanization is left unchecked.

The trip also constituted a voyage into loneliness, into the destruction of all social bonds implicit in the logic of capitalist individualism. For Weber, liberalism turns out to threaten personal identity as much as national identity, and interiority as much as exteriority:

> This absolute absence of humans wherever one goes except for a few shepherd huts, and the splendid seriousness of this nature combine in a gripping manner, even though the landscape appears in such simple colors and shapes. . .The absence of forests and—with the exception of some parts of Loch Lomond and Trossachs—all significant trees contributes to this impression. It seems to me that this loneliness in the countryside which stretches to the gates of the cities is felt differently here than in England where one sees not a single peasant village on the whole trip from London to Edinburgh: instead only here and there a castle in a park separated from a few tenant dwellings and a single barn, and occasionally a church from the thirteenth or fourteenth century among a dozen workers' huts rather than, as in the past, fifty to sixty peasant homes—too big for its congregation, like a suit on a consumptive. And in England people think that a hundred thousand peasants could live here—although Scotland is made only for cattle or, better, sheep grazing. . .

By the way, even in Great Britain the world is just a village; can you believe that we met acquaintances from Berlin here? On the steamer to Loch Katrine I suddenly saw, among the faces of those pushing to board with their sharp English mouths, Gierke's Germanic face of a bard. We traveled together to Loch Lomond where our ways parted. Meeting compatriots is odd: we are otherwise so acclimatized that we have adopted the general whispering tone, pretend not to see the people sitting to our right and left and, only when asked, do we give short and very polite answers. We always eat a little less than we would like, open our mouths as little as possible, and even when the stomach is audibly growling, we just splash around with our spoon in the soup, as if we were not at all interested in the slop. But as soon as Germans were nearby, such a laughter arose among us when we were just waiting for the coach that all the English hurried over to see the barbarians, and I heard someone on the coach say "merry Germany." And before our departure we had a lunch that the waiters won't soon forget. G. started a meal like in the Teutoburger Forest, and I kept up. The confused waiters brought, as everything kept disappearing, ultimately superhuman quantities of roast beef, salmon, etc., probably fearing that we would otherwise start eating the guests. Three of them stood around our table, staring horrified at the destruction of their wares, and they were visibly relieved when the steamer tooted and put an end to the meal. (MW 219-221)

The peasants are gone now from England, and only the ruins of churches remain. The thriving world of medieval traditionalism, simple pleasure, and social cohesion has disappeared, replaced by an unnaturally barren nature: depopulation and deforestation are the same. England shocks the German nationalist with its picture of the future, the image of culture as a hollow shell, emptied of living substance. The same fate seems to await the East Elbian latifundia, and such a fate would be even more devastating for Prussia, since a hostile foreign population waits eagerly beyond the borders to enter the vacuum and call German national identity into question.

The process threatens individual identity as well, according to Weber, who augments the social analysis in his letter with a contrast of conflicting personality types. The English have "sharp" mouths, an adjective implying a cold, calculating rationality, which contrasts with the German's "face of a bard," implying poetry, joy, and pleasure. In Weber's eyes, the English of the capitalist age are trapped in their rules of discreet politeness. They eat too little, speak too quietly, and refuse to take notice of each other. The Germans, on the contrary, laugh and feast in a communal celebration of natural enjoyment. The reaction Weber imputes to the English indicates the terms of his own social thought: the German sees the English seeing the Germans as barbarians. The spirit of capitalism, Manchesterist culture, destroys the sensuousness that underdeveloped Germany still preserves. The laissez-faire liberalism of the father, which Weber imitated to establish his own identity, is now recognized as a danger to identity as Weber knows it. Merry old England has disappeared forever, and merry Germany is caught up in the same process that could put an end to the empire and to Weber as well. In his letters from England, Weber comes as close as he ever would to the cultural criticism of his intellectual Doppelgänger D. H. Lawrence, with his nostalgic idealization of a lost, natural world and his denunciation of the consequences of capitalist modernization.

As an encoded account of the crisis of bourgeois society, Weber's letters from England indicate his own impending breakdown. The mimetic dialectic takes its toll on two levels. Germany's imitation of western capitalism established the unified nation-state and unleashed a process of social erosion. Similarly Weber's appropriation of the patriarchal legacy allowed him to construct an identity that was threatened by the concomitant repression of Helene's values, which grew increasingly relevant in the face of the contemporary social question. At the moment when the repressed threatened to return, Weber returned to the origin of the repressed by accepting in 1896 a professorship of economics in Heidelberg, Helene's home, the southern source of the matriarchal principle. The stage was set for an explosive conflict in which the sharp tensions in Wilhelmine culture would overlap with the competing values in the Weber family.

The successful academic whose self-understanding had been made in the image of his father now witnessed the admission of the first women into the university. Marianne reports of these students that, "Each is moved by the consciousness of being a pioneer of a new world-order; each feels herself responsible for overcoming resistance. The new type [of woman] is severely attacked with arrows of derision and heavier ethical weapons and only gradually achieves acceptance and recognition" (MW 242). Among these students was

Elsa von Richthofen. Her sister, Frieda, was the lover of D. H. Lawrence, whose thoughts regarding the history of sensuous pleasure in industrial capitalism shared so much with Weber's cultural pessimism.

Weber's intellectual life, still caught in the antinomy of traditionalism and capitalist rationality, was subject to a subterranean tension which was brought to the surface through a family trauma. Helene desired to visit Max and Marianne in her native Heidelberg by herself, but her patriarchal husband objected. Against the background of the changing role of women at the university, the power struggle between mother and father was transformed into a matter of conflicting principles, touching the foundation of Max's identity. Unwilling to permit his wife to visit the young couple, the senior Weber failed "to break through the cage of his own being" (MW 245). The son took the side of his mother, and a bitter argument ensued between father and son in July of 1897. Communication between the two men broke down, and any hopes for reconciliation were shattered when the father died on August 10.

This transformation of the family constellation initiated a process through which Weber eventually overcame the early antinomies. Although the object of imitation was gone and Weber's personal critique of patriarchal liberalism was now irrevocably complete, he still had a painful road ahead of him. Soon after his father's death "an evil something stretched out its claws and reached for him out of the unconscious depths" (MW 246). Sleeplessness, nervousness, and irritation set in. In the course of the breakdown Weber was for long periods unable to pursue serious intellectual work. Interestingly, neither Marianne nor Max made any significant effort to interpret the collapse as an atonement for the father's death. Both regarded it as a consequence of Weber's own existential mode. But there the similarity between their responses ends, for the two perceptions of his psyche and, ultimately, the two prescriptions differed fundamentally.

According to Marianne, the matter amounted to a case of extreme exhaustion and overwork. Weber's career-oriented devotion had forced him to avoid participation in other dimensions of life; his professional rationality was antithetical to domesticity and friendship. This interpretation pervades Marianne's account of his condition: "When, during the week of Whitsuntide, he takes a hike in the Odenwald in order to escape the visit of a friend to which he was otherwise looking forward, the splendor of May is covered with a dark veil. He is exhausted, his rigid structure begins to loosen, tears pour out. Weber feels himself at a turning point. Nature, violated for so long, begins to take her revenge" (MW 248). Friendship, springtime, nature, even religion as indicated in the temporal setting of Whitsuntide, left him untouched as long as he imprisoned himself in the "rigid structure" of rational labor. His psychic breakdown was the breakdown of a mechanized rationality and thus a breakdown of the patriarchal coldness and severity. Elsewhere Marianne speaks of him explicitly as a machine. Her solution amounts to a return to the world of home life and social contact that has been repressed, the Helene-principle, and a deemphasis of career.

At times even Weber himself shared this vision of the desirability of a return to the female-matriarchal dimension. Marianne quotes from a letter of 1898: "The need to submit to the burden of work is gone. Above all, I want to live humanly with my little child and to see her as happy as I am allowed to make her" (MW 249). Yet even though he repeatedly insisted that his breakdown signified a profound dissatisfaction with the form in which he had organized his life in general and his professional work in particular, he did not reduce the problem to the alleged necessity of a return to nature, home, and family. The denial of a female, nurturing being was not what concerned him, but rather the specific form of the social existence he had experienced. Thus, he made repeated efforts to escape official professional obligations by giving up his civil service status as an employee of the state university. Not until 1903 did he succeed in shedding these contractual obligations. The delay was due to resistance both within the bureaucracy, which was hardly anxious to lose the promising scholar, and within his family. Weber believed, probably correctly, that the admiration and pride which Marianne and Helene felt for him depended largely on his successful career. Weber considered that these two advocates of the escape from male rationality in fact laid great stress on his professional achievements. Regardless of whether his estimation was correct, it made him distrust their call for a return to the female world as merely a sham effort to console the ailing patient.

His alternative to this regression took the shape of a perpetual effort to escape the demands of both the civil service and the weight of the Heidelberg legacy, of both father and mother. Although Marianne's heart and identity were tied to the Heidelberg of academics and to the Fallensteins, Weber, in another letter cited by Marianne, insists on his desire to leave:

> I have spoken at length with the doctor about my chances for the future, but apparently nothing definite can be said. It is almost out of the question to think that I might in the near future have a regular work schedule without running the risk of a quick return of the hellish state of the spring. Therefore we must not set our hearts on the Heidelberg position—I regard it as a gift from heaven that I am not ambitious and really don't care, and for the "world" no one is easier to replace than a teacher. Perhaps, if conditions had permitted, it would have been psychologically better to give up the position entirely from the start; then I could sail my ship out to sea as soon as the wind picks up instead of being anchored with my Heidelberg hopes. (MW 258)

Weber did indeed weigh anchor. He traveled extensively, sometimes with Marianne but more often without her, to Italy, Holland, and the United States, as if searching for a way out of the psychological and cultural conflicts. In 1903 he considered leaving Germany, the conflict-ridden empire, forever. If he remained too much of a nationalist to do so, he nevertheless transferred this sense of fundamental estrangement into his analyses of society and culture.

Through the imitation of his father, Weber had established his own identity and set up fundamental biographic and political commitments, but no matter how painful and ultimately intolerable his imprisonment in the patriarchal identity had become, Weber did not opt to renounce his career and return to the female world of Helene and Marianne, characterized by domesticity and interiority. Typically, as he gradually recovered, he carried on his intellectual labor but primarily outside of the bureaucratic mechanism of the university. This aspect of his solution testifies to the fact that he did not regard labor as such but rather the specific form ascribed to labor by society as the cause of his malaise. According to Marianne's biography, Weber escaped his crisis only by moving beyond the categories of the male principle of career and political rationality, not by returning to the female dimension of care and comfort, for he increasingly regarded his suffering as the inevitable consequence of rational labor and the promises for comfort as regressive and even illusory. The progress that had constructed individual and collective identities could not be reversed, although it might be transcended, and the siren song of amnesiac pleasure remained devoid of credibility.

Weber clarifies this view in a comment on Rembrandt's "Saul and David," which he saw in the Hague on one of his frantic trips in 1903:

> The gallery in The Hague has the advantage of being small, and one easily finds what one likes. The most beautiful of what I have seen so far is Rembrandt's *Saul and David* (playing on the harp). That one can paint two real Jews—and what's more, the king in a tasteless sultan costume and David as a real cutesy from a delicatessen—that one only sees the human beings and the gripping power of the music is nearly incomprehensible—but the piety of the musician is directly reminiscent of the expression in Giorgione's *Concert* and the one eye of the king that can be seen—he covers the other crying—indicates frighteningly how he is trying to forget that he is declining, how he sought forgetfulness in the music and does not find it. Photographs cannot convey the painting. Beside this picture, all the others with the "canalized" light seem to be nothing at all, and even the splended *Anatomy* shows that he was more a virtuoso in portraiture and technique than—as this picture shows—a soulful artist...I could not resist buying a print of the Rembrandt painting, although it is really only good for someone who has seen the original. The king's eye seems more powerful in the original. R. painted it when, after losing his Saskia, his wealth and his pictures, he declared bankruptcy and, although at the height of his powers, he wandered with his son and his loyal Hendrikkia through Amsterdam, feeling old age approach. (MW 283-284)

Identification with the figure of Saul explains Weber's fascination with the picture and imbues his description with passion. In the aging king he finds a symbol of a former greatness condemned to decline, the paragon of political rationality entrapped within the logic of an ineluctable failure. Neither David's songs nor Hendrikkia's loyalties nor even Marianne's entreaties compensate for the suffering of reason. The patriarchal world in its most excruciating misery still cannot regress to art, family, and comfort because the bridge that leads backward was long ago burned down by progress. Weber recognizes that the images of such regression hold out only illusory promises that could never resolve the fundamental conflicts of psyche and culture.

For Weber, reason might overcome its own melancholy not by capitulating to regressive temptations but by entering a third dimension: since David could not comfort Saul, the king would have to turn to Samuel the prophet. Ossified reason might undergo a sudden cultural rebirth effected by the representatives of an other-worldly grace and the promise of salvation. These are the "new prophets" of whom Weber speaks at the conclusion of *The Protestant Ethic and the Spirit of Capitalism* (1903-1904), written as he emerged from the depths of his own crisis.[2] Weber argues that, when left to itself, reason tends to prohibit sensuousness and pleasure. The rational organization of labor leads necessarily to the repression of traditionalism and the denial of individual satisfaction. Civilization's progress may accomplish grand feats, but it prohibits personal contentment and erodes the power of cultural structures to provide orientation in everyday life. Against the background of the increasingly meaningless culture of Wilhelmine Germany, Weber suggests that only a thorough transformation of values might guarantee social coherence. Such an act belongs properly to the province of the charismatic leader.

Weber's account of the contemporary cultural crisis consequently underwent a profound change. In place of the antinomic pairs—Schiller and Goethe, east and west, traditionalism and capitalism—he suggested a historical sequence from the innovative religious tenets of the Reformation to the reshaping of secular practice in an increasingly rational and self-disciplinary capitalism. This thesis, which is central to *The Protestant Ethic and the Spirit of Capitalism*, is a response to the vulgar versions of historical materialism that insisted on the constant and absolute priority of the economic base over the cultural superstructure. Even Friedrich Engels complained about such excessively deterministic tendencies in contemporary Marxism.[3] Yet to regard Weber's thesis as an essentially anti-Marxist statement because of its putative idealism obscures its protest against capitalism, articulated in the metaphor of the iron cage: the fully rationalized world imprisons the individual within the confinement of solely instrumental labor, leaving no room for either sensuous pleasure or authentic creativity. In addition, the focus on Weber's argument as an alternative to Marxism occludes its real political reverberations in terms of both the German Empire's ideological self-image as an expressly Protestant power and Weber's own earlier analyses. During the 1890s Weber counterposed the eastern ethics of Prussia and Germany to the acquisitive materialism of western capitalism; now it is a matter no longer of the choice between Schiller and Goethe or ethics and greed, but of a necessary and ineluctable relationship between the Protestant ethic and the superficially different but ultimately derivative spirit of capitalism.

Weber's turn to the sociology of religion at the beginning of this second phase of his intellectual development introduces two different themes. The more obvious, representing the substance of the essay's argument, is that religious beliefs establish and guide worldly practice and therefore generate new social formations, which are the ultimate object of Weber's investigations. This secularization rests on the other assumption regarding the innovative character of religious prophecy. Weber's account of the motion from Protestantism to capitalism is framed by prophetic activities with revolutionary consequences for social formations which, left to themselves, appear incapable of change. Thus, on the one hand, pre-Reformation Europe is a traditionalist culture, caught within the perpetual cycles of established economic practices, while on the other hand, capitalism—despite its explosively innovative character—leads directly to the rigidity of rationalized labor. The fact that the former period is described as halcyon and pleasurable and the latter as specifically unsensuous in its secular asceticism cannot hide the basic symmetry between the two static social forms. For the pessimist Weber, both the qualitative richness of traditionalism and the quantitative wealth of capitalism culminate in the empty repetition of eternal return. At this point, charismatic power takes on its full significance as a Nietzschean revaluation of values, since Luther was the one who initiated the revolution that overcame medieval stagnation, just as new prophets may be the only ones able to loosen the strictures of capitalist rationality.

This concern with the function of religion in social transformations led Weber during the following decades to both his seminal studies on the world religions and to his investigations into the character of charismatic legitimacy, or the reliance of particular forms of political authority on the credibility of prophetic promises of grace. Weber does not exactly discover religion in the midst of his own personal crisis. Although the biographic chronology suggests as much, the matter is more complex than such a simple formulation implies. For Weber, religion remains an object of study without becoming a source of substantive belief. He is fascinated by its capacity to ground new cultures and to destroy old ones, that is, as the mechanism for reordering social codes of meaning. In his early work the crisis of meaning in contemporary capitalist culture took on nefarious forms, such as the Goethe-cult of form and pleasure, the isolation of the individual in English society, the decay of political leadership in the empire, and, in the background, the vacuity of his own patriarchal role model. His turn to religion and charisma represents an effort to solve the cultural crisis through the examination of other processes of social and cultural valuation. In particular, Weber's turn to charisma is based on another discursive coding, a debate within Protestant church history on the notion of charisma in terms of the origin of Catholicism, a debate that itself displayed all the ruptures of Wilhelmine culture and anticipated the formulation of a specifically modernist theology. Weber appropriated the key term of that debate, with all of its hidden connotations, and transformed it into a central element in his own account of the crisis.

Under the influence of Friedrich Schleiermacher and Hegel, theology underwent a radical historicization in the early part of the nineteenth century. In place of the Enlightenment's theoretical concerns with the relationship between reason and faith and the concomitant designation of history as an abstract universal teleology, attention was redirected toward questions of the historical development of religion. Thus David Friedrich Strauss's *Life of Jesus* (1835-1836) attempted no philosophical formulation of the Gospel but rather a distinction between the historically accurate and the merely mythical in the accounts of Jesus, a distinction itself indebted to the Enlightenment's critique of myth. More characteristic of theological history in the period was the work of the Tübingen school under the leadership of Ferdinand Christian Baur, which displayed a strong Hegelian influence. Its approach to early church history emphasized a conflict between antithetical principles leading ultimately to a dialectical synthesis: the apostolic period was characterized by a contradiction between the Pauline version of the Gospel and the Judeo-Christianity of John, which found its synthetic resolution in the Catholicism of the second century. On the basis of this idealistic scheme, the theoretical contents of the various texts in the New Testament were deemed inauthentic if, when subjected to scrutiny and critique, they diverged from their ascribed role within the dialectic. Though the Tübingen school thereby set the stage for the many text-critical studies of the period, its Hegelian version of historical progress and its overwhelmingly philosophical concern were soon dismissed.

The break with Tübingen and the establishment of new theological and methodological paradigms, which would generally remain in force until 1918, came in the work of one of Baur's students, Albrecht Ritschl. Baur's concept of historical criticism as the central goal of theology had tended to deny any privileged position to the person of Jesus, while its scientific precepts excluded irrational phenomena, such as miracles or the personal experience of God. In the second edition of his *Origin of the Old Catholic Church* (1857) Ritschl reversed his teacher's orientation by focusing on the uniqueness of Jesus and the revelation, whereas Baur had seen only the struggle of competing ideas. Similarly, Ritschl replaced the Tübingen school's emphasis on Christianity's universal philosophical tenets with an emphasis on its personal religious encounters. This conservative theology of the era following the 1848 revolution supplanted grandiose Hegelian schemes by an apolitical and private individuality coupled with a hostility to theoretical claims. Thus, Baur's categories were rejected as empty metaphysics.[4] During the decade in which Marx made the transition from explicit philosophy to concrete economic analysis and in which the German literati, rejecting the earlier radical literature as excessively abstract and romantic, elaborated the program of realism, theology too underwent the shift characteristic of a conservative era from philosophy to revelation and from universality to the individual.

Ritschl's conclusions about the character of Christianity and the origin of Catholicism influenced the discourse of his followers, the Ritschlianers, who set the religious tone of the Wilhelmine era, especially in the journal *Christliche Welt*. In terms of methodology, Baur's philosophically inspired criticism gave way to a historical hermeneutics aimed at establishing the textual authenticity and philosophical legitimacy of documents in the New Testament. Not only did this gesture produce a new sort of scholarship parallel to developments in literary philology, but it also lent itself to a new sort of historical account of the early church. Where Baur had contended that Catholicism represented the dialectical supersession of earlier contradictions, Ritschl, anxious to separate authentic from inauthentic texts, treated the Catholic church of the second century as the result of a contamination of the initial Gospel by the culture of the Mediterranean milieu. The emergence of the episcopacy was henceforth viewed as the legacy of an impure, heathen Christianity. The specific methodological tools of textual philology were confronted with a problem that they were well-suited to solve, the elimination of textual contaminations essentially alien to genuine revelation. In addition, Ritschl's realist theology implied a specific characterization of the church beyond the formal insistence on its heterogeneous origin. Ritschl described Catholic piety as fundamentally mystical, and therefore heathen, be it in terms of the ascetic otherworldliness of the monks, the exaggerated emotionality of the masses, or the obsession of the clerics with elaborate speculation. To these allegedly Catholic elements he counterposed the purportedly Lutheran goal of an evangelical theology based solely on everyday faith and hence inimical to all mysticism.[5] Mysticism was thus linked to a contaminated church, while faith was a function of a free personality. After the establishment of the empire this ideological demarcation lent itself to extreme politicization during the cultural struggle or *Kulturkampf,* when a conflict arose between the new German state under Bismarck and the Catholic Church over the control of religious education, ecclesiastical administration, and, especially, the political allegiances of German Catholics, caught between the papacy and the Protestant rulers of Prussia. The terms of the theological discourse allowed Catholicism to be portrayed as foreign not only to Germany, because of its ties to Rome, but also to the authentic Gospel. Meanwhile the Lutheran faith, the religion of the new state, could claim a relationship to the increasingly privatized liberalism of the 1870s as the form of belief most appropriate to the free individual.

The elaboration of an alliance between Protestantism and the liberal culture of the Wilhelmine bourgeoisie, which was unquestionably loyal to contemporary social institutions, was the work of the foremost Ritschlianer, Adolf von Harnack. Named Professor of Theology in 1876 at the age of twenty-five, Harnack moved through the universities of Giessen and Marburg until his appointment to Berlin in 1888, despite opposition from orthodox conservatives uncomfortable with his willingness to question established liturgical practices from the standpoint of evangelical authenticity. In the capital he had access to the imperial court and actively engaged in university politics. Between 1903 and 1911 he headed the Evangelical-Social Congress, founded in 1890 to direct Protestant attention to social issues; from 1905 to 1921 he was general director of the Prussian State Library; in 1911 he helped initiate the Kaiser Wilhelm Society to promote scientific research; and in 1914 he received the aristocratic *von*. Thus the life of this theologian consciously participating in contemporary cultural institutions mirrored his theological project, to reconcile worldly culture and Christian faith, to make Lutheranism fully compatible with the culture of the founders of the empire. Practical, earthly activity was his ethos, not otherworldliness. Conversely, he claimed that true faith alone provided a basis for culture, since it secured the freedom of the personality against the external world.[6]

Given his cultural loyalties and overall Ritschlian orientation, Harnack developed an account of early Christianity and the rise of Catholicism that involved him in a dispute with Rudolph Sohm, a historian of canonic law from whom Weber would later borrow the concept of charisma. The ostensible subject of the controversy was the elaboration of a Protestant explanation of the transition from the early Christian communities of the first century to the established Catholic Church of the next. Because of the specific setting of the debate among Protestant scholars, this transition was understood as a decline from the pure faith of the initial apostolic period to the negative Catholic formations that Luther would later denounce.

Despite the seriousness of their conflict, the two men shared a fundamental paradigm, a pejorative view of the shift from an idealized first-century Christianity to Catholicism. Furthermore, both Harnack and Sohm identified the displacement of charismatic elements by hierarchical forms as the crux of the transition. Nevertheless the explanations for the change were subtly different. Harnack typically cast the early Christian communities as paragons of religious freedom and tolerance, characterized "by the lack of a set teaching in reference to the conceptual presentation of faith and hence by the multiplicity and freedom of Christian belief." The institutional corollary was "the absence of a clearly defined external authority in the congregations and therefore the independence and freedom of individual Christians."[7] Harnack thereby projected an idealized version of late nineteenth-century liberalism onto first-century Christianity, in order to contrast it with the purportedly intolerant organization of faith in the Catholic Church.

Harnack explained this change in terms of a contamination by contemporary secular "tendencies which attempted to accelerate the initial process of mixing the Gospel with the intellectual and religious interests of the period, i.e. with Hellenism, and by efforts to separate the Gospel from its sources by ascribing to it fully foreign assumptions. Among these belonged the (Hellenic) notion that knowledge is not a (charismatic) addition to faith or one possible extension of it but rather is identical with the essence of faith itself." Indeed, for Harnack, Christianity was mortally threatened by Greek philosophy and especially by Gnosticism, and he applauded the victory of the church over Gnosticism. Nevertheless Catholicism eventually succumbed to the Levantine setting and took on its characteristic form as "the Old Testament-Christian revelation, integrated and immersed in Hellenic thought, i.e. in contemporary syncretism and idealistic philosophy." The result was a loss of precisely that freedom Harnack cherished in the apostolic period and hence "a pedantic tutelage over the belief of the individual Christian," as well as severe limitations on "the immediacy of religious sentiment and thought." The many Christians who during the second century still insisted on "immediacy and freedom" lost out in the ecclesiastical struggles of the period.[8]

Harnack's account corresponded to important aspects of Wilhelmine ideology. Not only did he present Catholicism as an impure version of Christianity hampered by foreign elements, but he also described it as antithetical to freedom, which must have appeared plausible to liberal Protestants in the wake of the declaration of papal infallibility. Harnack's attack on the Catholic establishment, however, never implied a radical anti-institutional rejection of all legal and social orders. He complained not that elements of Greek or Jewish cult forms were carried on into Christianity, but that Catholicism declared these forms themselves to be divine— "the deification of the tradition"— and set them on an equal footing with the original Christian teachings.[9] Thus he was able to denounce Catholic hierarchy as illegitimate without falling into the anarchism that perpetually tempts laissez-faire liberalism.

This is precisely where the controversy with Sohm commenced, for Sohm insisted on the absolute incompatibility of hierarchy or legal forms with the essence of Christianity: "The essence of church law stands in opposition to the essence of the church." Whereas Harnack condemned the declaration of the divinity of the Mediterranean legacy, be it a matter of the pagan household cults or the inheritance of Greece or Israel, he recognized the need for the church to institute itself as a social organization; unfortunately, Catholicism had canonized that organization. In contrast, Sohm contended that the church, as a community of the divine order and the body of Christ, could in no way tolerate a secular or natural order: "Natural man is a born Catholic. Natural birth makes us the servants of God. Only rebirth makes us His children."[10] Where Harnack saw Catholicism succumbing to a heterogeneous heathen order, Sohm condemned the reconciliation with nature. Where Harnack described the contamination of faith with the loss of freedom, Sohm saw a fall from faith, the loss of the initial charismatic community, and the disappearance of "pneumatic anarchy" in the earthly maze of a legalized, institutionalized cult. Harnack attacked Catholic intolerance, but Sohm attacked Catholic bureaucratization as the antithesis of charisma, for the ossification of the ecclesiastical bureaucracy necessarily meant the demise of the community in which the spirit of grace could dwell.

In line with a romantic critique of enlightenment claims regarding natural law, Sohm rejected liberal notions of a natural order for the church as a secular institution compatible with the state. Therefore, while Harnack attacked Catholicism's deification of the ecclesiastical hierarchy but not its functional legitimacy, Sohm denounced legalization of the church as inimical to the spirit of religion. This contention of the incompatibility of law and faith derived from a variety of assumptions. For Sohm, law necessarily implied a fully developed "conceptual jurisprudence," deducible from a central legal principle and hence antithetical to Christianity, at the center of which was not a law but Christ. Second, Sohm insisted on the nation as the source of law; hence law did not derive from Christ and was, by definition, antithetical to Christianity. In addition to these characterizations of law as conceptual, national, and therefore secular, Sohm understood law—most importantly— as a system of formal violence fundamentally opposed to the essence of the Gospel. The denunciation of formal legality revealed Sohm's romantic heritage in which the wholesome unity of faith was counterposed to the negative totality of law, in an echo of Novalis's apotheosis of medieval Christianity: "Spirit and law interact only as opposites. Where law commences, spirit disappears; and where spirit has disappeared, law sets up camp."[11]

Sohm's attacks on legal rationality and, by implication, on the liberal theological establishment drew on early nineteenth-century motifs but also opened the path for a modernist turn in the dialectical theology that took shape around the First World War. An important shift in theological discourse had begun around 1900, and Sohm's neoromanticism gave expression to it through the critique of key tenets of Wilhelmine Protestantism. The attack on legality, however, was only one aspect of the discursive shift. Its corollary was the centrality of charisma as the appropriate mode of Christian sociability, for charisma denoted a specifically antilegal organizational form. In addition, Sohm's emphasis on the antinomic issues of legality and charisma, which Weber appropriated, displaced the Ritschlianers' concern with philological authenticity and textual contamination.

Though this changing scholarly interest indicated the gradual transformation of theology from nineteenth-century science to the existentialism of the 1920s, it also signified a more immediate shift in political loyalties and ideological strategies. Harnack's concentration on textual contamination was organized around categories generated by the conflict between German nationalism and the Roman Catholic Church. In Sohm's work, the question of pre-Christian traditions played only a peripheral role, although Sohm was even more passionately anti-Catholic than Harnack. The politics of Protestant anti-Catholicism had undergone a profound metamorphosis, in which the hidden issue was no longer national identity but rather criticism of the bureaucracy, and Sohm projected this antibureaucratic concern in turn-of-the-century culture onto antiquity as the determining feature of the origin of Catholicism.

Between the lines, Sohm's historical narrative implied a parallel between ancient Rome and Wilhelmine Germany. Both empires had reached the zenith of military and political power, but both had lost their internal cultural substance and were reduced to facades, superficially imposing but lacking an authentic spiritual identity. Sohm described the entrance of Christianity into the ancient cultural crisis, its rapid spread and equally rapid secularization. He did not deny Harnack's claim that the influence of the pre-Christian context, with its masses of new converts, contributed to the deformation of the early Christian project. Yet his prime concern was not the syncretic contamination but rather the gradual erosion of the community of faith and its replacement by a secular order. For Sohm, the apostolic church was a charismatic community, a social group without bureaucratic administration or legislative restrictions and characterized by a collective participation in a shared meaning, the new faith. Yet "trust in the free reign of charisma dwindled. As the size of the congregation grew, so did the desire for a solid, external order." This desire for order in turn induced a division of religious labor, a separation of clergy and laity, and therefore the production of a class of religious specialists endowed with a privileged position within the previously undifferentiated ecclesia. For Sohm, the turning point was the establishment of the episcopacy. He was concerned less with the purportedly pre-Christian elements in the Catholic order, as Harnack had argued, than with the establishment of a worldy order per se as the antithesis of the true community of faith. Christ's body, the invisible church, could have no legal form, since legality was necessarily secular and visible.[12] Catholicism appeared thus as the result of bureaucratization opposed to the essence of authentic Christianity, and bureaucracy was perceived as a form of social organization inferior to the model of the charismatic community. The hidden motor of ecclesiastical historiography was no longer the *Kulturkampf* but rather criticism of the bureaucratization of Wilhelmine society.

Sohm's insistence on the fundamental incompatibility of religious spirit and legal rationality influenced his account of the early Christian communities. Even though he admitted that the various members of the congregation might carry out different functions, he insisted that this division of labor represented no more than the Christians' fulfilling their respective callings and not an externally codified, canonic structure. Similarly, he saw each early Christian assembly as the full and immediate manifestation of the body of Christ, not as the local chapter of a centralized organization. The centralization of the second century and the subsequent subordination of the group to the Bishop of Rome was only a later development within the process of Catholic legalization. Law, even divine law—and for Sohm the notion of divine law was necessarily a contradiction of terms—had no place in the charismatic community where spirit, not legal conceptuality, served as the organizing principle. Sohm's ideal emphatically excluded formal structures, for

Christianity was "the popular assembly (the people) of God (of Christ), God's chosen people, the herd that God nourishes and shepherds with His word, the community united by love, by the brotherly love born of love of God. It builds a unity, a body, the body of Christ. But the body of Christ is no corporation, let alone some 'Christian corporation.' "[13] With this broadside against any secular organizational form of the church, Sohm distanced himself radically from the liberal Protestantism of the Ritschlianers and Harnack, who were devoted to the reconciliation of church and state in the spirit of Wilhelmine liberalism. In Sohm's eyes, the church was merely another administrative agency in the maze of bureaucratic institutions, while the essence of Christianity lay precisely in its separation from secular administration and its rejection of the law. Therefore Sohm's articulation of an alternative form of sociability, charismatic community, represented not just an idiosyncratic position on the early history of the church or even a political position on Wilhelmine Protestantism, but rather an alternative to the Wilhelmine cultural crisis altogether, the vision of a society that could escape the inherited vacuity and rediscover authentic meaning.

It was because of these cultural critical overtones that the notion of charisma appealed to Weber as a solution to his categorical antinomies. Weber nowhere favors charismatic organization as such. Often he considers it inappropriate, as in the universities. Yet when he contrasts the ideally charismatic political executive with the dangerously bureaucratic parliamentary parties, he implicitly draws on paradigms central to Sohm's account of early Christianity. Sohm described two alternative forms of religious assembly: "pneumatic anarchy," in which the spirit of the word prevailed and no codified order operated, and the eucharistic meeting, in which by the end of the first century the division of ritual labor in the communion had led to the establishment of a canonized hierarchy. In Sohm's narrative, the church did not adopt the external laws of the non-Christian environment but instead declined into Catholicism because of the legalization and ossification of its own endogenous forms. This transition, which Weber later describes as the routinization of the charisma, implied for the romantic Sohm the extirpation of the spirit. He underscored the opposition between the authentic assembly of the church of Christ and corporate structures and bureaucracy, just as he contrasted the equality of the apostolic church to the subsequent hierarchy of the episcopacy. Sohm's antinomy between Christianity and Catholicism constituted a religious coding of the Wilhelmine crisis, a critique of empty legality, and a search for spiritual renewal. Not surprisingly, both Sohm and Harnack translated their opposing accounts of religion into conflicting notions of culture. For Harnack, the defender of established society, cultural progress was a matter of organized research and scholarly institutions, such as the Kaiser Wilhelm Society and the Prussian library system. For Sohm, culture instead implied personal activity and engagement in the social question, the mission of the spirit.[14] For Harnack, state subsidies carried culture; for Sohm, the medium of culture was charisma, the grace-giving spirit of community.

The problem of charismatic organization that emerged from the Harnack-Sohm controversy shed light not only on the key third term of Weber's sociology but also on the cultural constellation under which modern writing emerged. The young generation of authors was not particularly religious, even though their aesthetic pronouncements were occasionally couched in a religious terminology. Nevertheless, even in specifically secular works, modern writing of the early twentieth century set off on a charismatic crusade: an effort to overcome the rigid legality of a bureaucratic culture that Sohm had projected onto Catholicism. Hence the goal of modern writing was the establishment of a qualitatively new social relationship or new community within literature, between authors and readers, that would at the same time extend beyond literature and generate a new social community.

When in *Economy and Society* (1921) Weber describes the three modes of legitimate authority, he does not present them in a single narrative sequence. He universalizes their relevance and projects them throughout human history. Nevertheless, behind his tripartite system of traditional, legal, and charismatic rule is Weber's response to the experience of Wilhelmine modernization: the backward agrarian society plunged into the categories of a liberal capitalism which inexorably generated its own bureaucratic procrustean bed, restricting ever more the individuality on which it must, by definition, pin its hopes for progress. No linear progress leads out of this iron cage. Salvation can mean only a fundamental break with established logic, a leap sui generis, an act of grace, or charisma.

In *Economy and Society* Weber delimits sociology by setting it apart from the concerns of natural science. Whereas the natural sciences address facts and describe instrumental action, sociology is concerned solely with relationships and acts that are subjectively meaningful, for only meaning can be understood. This distinction between the natural sciences and the humanities was not uncommon in the period, yet when it generated literary scholarship, it tended to produce objective histories of ideas. The objectivity on which such scholarship was based, the unquestioned acceptance of the cultural canon of great works, is no longer plausible. Alternatively, the Weberian insistence on the subjectivity of meaning can shed light on the problem of social relationships in the institutions of literature. Rather than examining the subjective intentionality of the individual author, literary sociology inquires into the structures of communication facilitated by the text. By intervening in its sociocultural environment, the text undertakes a project of social transformation, and thus a political project, which reciprocally determines the formal features of the text itself. Literary sociology therefore examines the social relations in literature, especially those produced by the text and generating communicative structures between author and reader in terms of traditional, legal, or charismatic models.

Though Weber tends to reserve these categories for specifically economic or political matters, on occasion he mentions literary figures as examples of charismatic types, specifically Stefan George and Kurt Eisner.[15] More generally, the Weberian tripartite schema proves useful in examining literary relationships as social relationships having cultural meaning, particularly for the period in which Weber articulated it. Aesthetic legality, the foundation of literary life on principles of rationality and not on arbitrary authority, had represented a central cultural theme of the German bourgeoisie since the eighteenth century. That aesthetic legality, based on the possibility of equal exchange and potential communication among readers, loses its vitality in literature of Weber's day and undergoes a process of bureaucratization: everything continues to make sense in the texts of declining realism, but sense and meaning grow increasingly absent. As culture is transformed into a commodity, it becomes an object of mere display, robbed of its traditional substance.

53

This impasse is the impasse of Wilhelmine culture in general, and charismatic alternatives promise various escapes into another literature and another society. This is the key feature of German modernism: the inseparability of the problems of literary and social innovation. Modern writing, in all its competing forms, promises more than aesthetic originality; the charisma of the literary speaker envisions a new social community. Consider Kurt Hiller's paradigmatic 1917 redefinition of the German intellectual: "We will not be muse-like, we will be moral; not contemplate, but act; we will be speakers, teachers, enlighteners, agitators, activists, law-givers, priests, founders of religions; we will be prophets, we will be writers. Deedless profundity lost value; it lost more; spirit is the goal. Let us no longer be attacked as 'intellectuals'; willfully we want to struggle."[16] Hiller's activist program includes voluntarism, intellectual leadership, and the concept of spirit. More important, however, it is symptomatic of the emergence of modernist German literature. Hiller's rejection of established, merely contemplative literary relationships and his evocation of a new sort of community hold for much of early twentieth-century German writing, especially for that crucial part of it which participates in modernist innovation. Yet the competing programs for a charismatic renewal of literary life cannot be understood without the past; no sociology of modernism can do without an account of the reification of nineteenth-century literature, in particular of realism, against which modernism constantly defines itself.

3

Realism and ·
Commodities

The premodernist institution of literary life during the eighteenth and nineteenth centuries presumes a liberal communicative pattern of equal exchange: in the text the author's reasonable and fundamentally comprehensible message takes on the decipherable forms of expression afforded by a transparent language, while the reader responds with an active direction of attention toward the meaning at hand. The meaning that the author intends to put forward comes into its own only because of the countergesture, the critical attention returned, in which signification is appropriated and produced. This hypothesis of a single overriding structure of literary exchange during the period does not deny the real differences among the competing aesthetic programs and literary movements in early bourgeois culture, such as those between early and high enlightenment, Sturm und Drang and classicism, romanticism, and realism. The specific character of the messages, expressive forms, and reception possibilities in these shifting sociohistorical contexts necessarily change. Literary history has traditionally regarded as its primary task the delineation and separation of these various phases, schools, and styles, but this absolute priority of an even finer periodization is open to question. The shared assumptions that support the panoply of early capitalist literary modes—the possibility of rational communication, the priority of reasonable rules, the exchange of meaning between equals, and the transparency of language—must be recognized as the epistemic structure underlying significantly different, even radically opposite literary tendencies within a single epoch.[1]

The contention of a unified bourgeois literary culture from the middle of the eighteenth century to the middle of the nineteenth is more amenable to a literary sociological approach than to a stylistic approach that insists on the incommensurable character of single movements or texts, for no matter how great the formal differences displayed by the textual evidence, the period is characterized by a relatively stable social composition of the literary public. Despite the spread of literacy and the increase in book production, a relatively homogeneous and predominantly bourgeois readership is a constant.[2] Between the middle of the eighteenth century, when an older, primarily scholarly public oriented toward Latin texts began to be displaced by an educated middle-class of urban merchants, professionals, and civil servants, and the 1860s, when the economic upswing brought about the explosive expansion of the book market and the concomitant emergence of a mass public outside of the older bourgeois stratum—that is, in the century between enlightenment and realism—a set of basic assumptions structures the possibilities of literary production and reception. Despite all the marked ideological differences between the classicist vision of an aesthetic education and the romantic program of a universal poetry, both are grounded in a shared belief in the possibility of progress and the desirability of change, which is always a privileged stance in a society based on the exchange principle of the market. Both, furthermore, organize change and progress in terms of a dialectical tension between universal and particular categories; the individual participates in society in terms of the ideology of a free-market competition guided by an invisible hand. Contemporary literary communication, in its various manifestations, derives its categories from the same basic tropes of bourgeois life: individuality, legal regularity, change and exchange.

The specificity of literary communication in the early period of capitalist development in Germany, during which a fundamental ideology of liberal individuality prevailed, contrasts with the predominant dialogic pattern that preceded it. In the baroque literature of the prebourgeois absolutist period, reception patterns are motivated by religious didacticism and social representation. Instead of the liberal period's discursive exchange between author and reader as potential equals united in an intersubjective, communicative process mediated by the text, the baroque literary message is pronounced with an absolutism that permits no individual subjectivity on the the part of either the recipient or the writer. The social structure of literary participation therefore mirrors the political and economic structures of a predemocratic culture: its unquestionable assertion of a divine and universal system rather than the construction of a social totality through individual inquiry into its rational constitution. The rules of baroque literature are based on the opaque enunciations of religion and inherited authority, while the rules of liberal bourgeois literature purport to be objects of rational scrutiny and therefore take on the character of laws generated by a self-determining literary public.[3] The transcendental guarantors of pre-bourgeois literature are grace and eschatology; the hidden telos of bourgeois literature is social emancipation. The stratified, hierarchical collectivity of presecularized culture, stretched between monarch and beggar, heaven and hell, is replaced by the bourgeois cultural optimism of a collectivity of equal individuals, a literary republic.

As Georg Lukács emphasizes, the development of bourgeois literature culminates naturally in a realist mode. The literature of the mid-nineteenth century sheds much of the premodern sacral character preserved in the aesthetics of the classic-romantic period. This change explains the hostility of critics as diverse as the radical Heinrich Heine and the realist Julian Schmidt to the explicitly idealist aestheticism of the earlier Weimar classicism.[4] Still, their critiques imply no fundamental epistemic break, since even realism relies on idealist assumptions and an understanding of the work of art as an autonomous text mediating between individual authors and recipients without immediately penetrating everyday practices. In the second half of the nineteenth century, realism undergoes a process of external and internal erosion: external because industrialization aggressively transforms the structure of the literary public; internal because the immanent categories of the realist texts diverge increasingly from the character of monopoly capitalistic society. Individuality and exchange, progress and emancipation lose their substantive relevance and thereby the vigor necessary to generate a viable literary program. This process of literary collapse, the reification of realism, mirrors the social crisis of laissez-faire liberalism and the corollary rise of postliberal social forms.

When realism loses its cultural viability, a space opens up in which, after 1900, new ways of writing, the competing versions of modern literature, begin to flourish. The social delegitimation of the individual undermines discursive communication, which in liberal culture is a dramatic exchange of meaning between individuals, so that the omniscient narrator, still credible in realism, gives way to alternative solutions, such as the epic collectivity of Alfred Döblin or the tentative individuality, perpetually rescinding itself in irony and narrative unreliability, of Thomas Mann. Similarly the hermeneutics of the reception process no longer assume individual readers and instead appeal to purported collectives. In the postliberal society of the twentieth century, literature operates with alternative rhetorics of address. Because the source of this modernist writing is not merely stylistic innovation, the term *antirealist*, with its solely formal implications, is too limited; the designation *postliberal* for this literature is preferable because of its intended sociological reverberations.

This distinction suggests the significance of the Weberian tripartite model for a social history of literature. At stake is less the mimetic substance of particular literary contents as statements about their respective social contexts than the character of the social relations within literary life, mediated through the architecture of the texts. Weber's three types—traditional, legal-rational, and charismatic authority—which correspond to his experience of the cultural crisis of Wilhelmine Germany undergoing violent modernization, designate the historical forms of literary institutionalization in postmedieval Germany as well; the authoritative traditionalism of baroque poetics, the rational exchange among the enlightened individuals of bourgeois liberalism, and the charismatic renewal promised by the bohemians, avant-gardists, and modernists once established realism has run its course and become increasingly integrated into the exigencies of a commercialized culture industry. The reification of realism, the loss of its communicative substance, consequently represents the literary-historical counterpart to the Weberian problem of bureaucratization. Just as bureaucracy extrapolates from the initial forms of legal rationality, while at the same time sequestering the subjectivity of rational individuality in the prison of the iron cage, a trivialized realism, which appears late on the scene but was always immanent in the realist paradigm, casts off earlier critical and emancipatory potential, offering instead the affirmation of a frozen status quo: destiny and necessity are its fare, be it in the form of sentimentalized pseudotragedy or ineluctable happy endings. The journey from the implicit rationality of mid-nineteenth-century high realism, even in the case of the ideologically reprehensible chauvinist Gustav Freytag, to the explicit adoration of victimization in the twentieth-century culture industry, even in the case of the ideologically sympathetic liberal Georg Hermann, is the history of the death of realism in the spirit of capitalism. Between these two endpoints are two transitional protomodernist stages: the search for a descriptive realism rendered hopeless by the dynamic of commodity exchange, as seen in Adalbert Stifter's *Der Nachsommer* (Indian Summer, 1857), and the self-criticism of liberal individuality, as seen in Theodor Fontane's *Irrungen, Wirrungen* (*Trials and Tribulations*, 1888).

The elaboration of an aesthetics of realism in the early 1850s was supported by concurrent shifts in society and culture in the wake of the defeat of the 1848 revolution. Of most importance was the emergence of an antitheoretical discourse which favored experience over concepts and passive observation over enthusiastic activism. From the vantage point of the realist theoreticians, the decades preceding the revolution appeared as an era of excessive other-worldliness, populated by religious romantics, utopian radicals, and idealist classicists, for all of whom conceptual thought occluded the concreteness of the material world.

Fontane underscores this cultural shift away from theoretical categories and toward a realist perception in an essay of 1853:

> What characterizes all aspects of our age is its *realism*. Doctors reject all deductions and combinations, for they want experience; politicians (of all parties) pay attention to real needs and lock up their rhetoric of perfection in their desks; military experts shrug their shoulders at the state of our Prussian defense and demand "old grenadiers" instead of "young recruits"; above all practical questions, in addition to those thousands of attempts to solve the social riddle, have come decisively to the fore. No doubt can remain: the world has grown tired of speculation and demands that "fresh, green pasture" which was always so near and yet so far away.[5]

In place of deductions, the age demands observation; in place of rhetoric, real needs; in place of youthful excitement, the experience of age. For Fontane, realism does not imply an eclipse of the social question that began to emerge during the 1840s and exploded during the revolution, but the question for him is no longer a revolutionary matter. Practical concerns now prevail, and the categories of idealism have lost their appropriateness for cultural activity. This comment that "the world has grown tired of speculation" refers to philosophical speculation, since the *belle époque* of capitalist speculation has yet to commence. The comment alludes to a verse from Goethe's "Wanderer's Night Song" (1776) which Fontane transforms in a manner characteristic of the realist shift. "I am weary with contending," proclaims the young Goethe's lyric voice in a dissatisfied rejection of the forms of early bourgeois society, an other-worldly melancholy culminating in a desire for the ultimate peace of death.[6] Fontane inverts the philosophical position; worldly "contending" is no longer denounced, but rather empty speculation, abstract thought, and conceptuality. Furthermore, Fontane transforms the subject from the first-person singular of Goethe's poem to the objectivity of "world." For realism, it is the world that can change; significant activity takes place in the material exteriority of society, not in the soulful interior of idealistic yearning. Real things, not imaginary objects, take priority; hence the literature of realism loses much of the subjective reflexivity and philosophical excursiveness of the pre-1848 writing and adopts a primarily descriptive stance.

This concern with real things explains the descriptive character of realism and the importance of the genesis and structure of the described detail. Realism does not directly reproduce the things of the world, as if the world were some naturally given object. Rather, it turns its attention to the surfeit of strange objects, the new wealth of commodities, which it tries to organize and reproduce within the framework of literary communication: an equal exchange of the images of commodities. This organization, however, rests on another aspect of post-1848 culture, the discourse of unity. Like the criticism of conceptual thought, the insistence on unity has roots in the philosophical idealism of the early decades of the nineteenth century. After the revolution, however, totality becomes a normative ideal, counterposed to particularity or division with which it was formerly engaged in a dialectical process. Totality is also regarded less as the culmination of a philosophical or social teleology than as an immanent feature of the world, evident to anyone prepared to direct a realistic look beneath disjointed empirical details. Realism insists on the primacy of a unified harmony, where accidents and exceptions are absent, and appearance and essence converge (good people look good and the evil are recognizably evil); and realism intends to teach the reader to perceive these laws and to read the world correctly.[7]

This discourse of unity takes on particular importance because it is intimately tied to the one aspect of the 1848 revolutionary program that subsequently dominates political culture. The prerevolutionary alliance of national unification and emancipatory politics falls apart, and only the former remains vital. Especially for the early advocates of realism, the unified territory of the state represents the primary political desideratum. Freytag's *Soll und Haben* (*Debit and Credit*, 1855) ties the Bildungsroman narrative of bourgeois socialization—the education of the hero as a merchant—to the experience of the German colonization of the Polish east and its integration into the Prussian state. Typically the bourgeois figure Anton Wohlfahrt is the one who must defend patriotism and the principle of national unity to his aristocratic interlocutor von Fink, enmeshed in a prebourgeois international nexus. Wohlfahrt addresses his blue-blooded friend: "As charmless as this landscape may be and as unpleasant as most of its inhabitants, I still see it with eyes different from yours. You are much more a citizen of the world than I. You have no great interest in the life of the state, of which these plains and your friend are parts, no matter how small."[8] The middle-class hero does not care if the environment is "charmless" or the population "unpleasant." He is interested in neither the beauty of nature nor the pleasures of companionship. On the contrary, his bourgeois asceticism and antisocial misanthropy, alien to the class character of the sensual and convivial aristocrat, converge in an ideology of patriotism. Fink's cosmopolitanism, with its suspicious lack of loyalty to any particular state, contrasts sharply with Wohlfahrt's anxious desire to subordinate himself as a "small part" to the authoritarian demands of his own state, right or wrong.

At stake in the debate is whether Wohlfahrt will contine to devote himself to the project of colonization and national expansionism or abscond with his friend to seek their fortunes together in an adventure elsewhere. In the bourgeois eyes of Wohlfahrt and Freytag, the aristocrat's sensuality, always suspect, turns out to be an egoism lacking in national solidarity, and the middle-class youth is paradoxically left to defend the historic labor of the German aristocracy, Fink's ancestors, as the authentic founders of the nation.

Wohlfahrt tries to invoke patriotic images by asking, "And who conquered the great region in which I was born?" The oversexed cavalier Fink misses the point and responds characteristically with a gender-linked designation, "One who was a man." Wohlfahrt, who is integrated into nationalism, the Protestant ethic, and the bourgeois economy of production, must correct the representative of an anachronistic and decadent class. Whereas the aristocrat projects an emphatic masculinity tied to a cult of pleasure, the bourgeois regards the world in terms of a principle of accumulation. The natural environment is transformed into property and integrated into a totality organized by the state. Wohlfahrt therefore answers his own question:

> It was an ornery farmer. . . he and others of his clan. With the sword and with cunning, by treaty and attack, in every possible way they conquered territory at a time when, in the rest of Germany, almost everything was dead and pitiful. As the daring men and the good landlords that they were, they ruled their realm. They dug canals through the swamps and planted people in the empty countryside, and they raised a race, tough, industrious and ambitious, like themselves. They founded a state out of decadent or defeated tribes. With great sense they made their house the center for millions, and out of the slime of countless insignificant sovereignties, they created a living power.[9]

Antisensuous asceticism, the repression needed to establish a state, here slides into the ideology of unification. The organizational principle of the state appears superior to the reprehensible particularity of mere tribes, described as decadent or defeated, since the realist insistence on the harmonious convergence of appearance and essence in a sensible world treats defeat as indicative of decay. A productive society replaces the former world of underdevelopment, denigrated by a civilizational bias as "empty countryside." The chaos of division is overcome by a centralizing power which imposes itself onto political confusion "with great sense" as a meaningful order, as if sense were possible only where national order and a unified economy have been instituted. Indeed, for the realist, this sort of unified sense is the sole guarantor of life: where death was, a vital nation shall be. The libidinal "slime of countless insignificant sovereignties," confused, chaotic, and unimportant, gives way to the egocentricity of a unified structure of life in which details for the first time take on decipherable meaning.

This discourse of unity, in which the politics of national unification and sexual repression intersect, supports a central aspect of realist aesthetics. The pre-1848 literature, be it classicism, romanticism, or radicalism, is regularly denounced by realism as disjointed and disorganized, and its fragmentary forms and ironic refractions are treated as signs of underdevelopment. Similarly the antitheoretical commitment of realism denounces the plurality of narrative levels in Biedermeier prose in the name of a privileged central and unifying perspective. The program of national unification as the suppression of political and social particularity finds its aesthetic corollary in the realist preference for the totalizing forms of grand epics. This may explain the relative decline of dramatic production, which, according to contemporary aesthetics, would have demanded the perception of a fundamentally conflictual character in social being, while the harmonizing prose of realism, casting the world in a transfigurative light of reconciliation, flourishes in the ideological denial of substantive contradictions.[10] German bourgeois realism is a literature of conflict denial, and the cultural discrediting of that denial provides the social setting for the emergence of modernist writing in the postliberal period. For Freytag, the Prussian conquest of Poland as the suppression of particularity underlies poetic realism. When realism collapses a half-century later, it is no accident of cultural history that the demise of the paradigmatic Wilhelmine author, Gustav von Aschenbach in Thomas Mann's *Death in Venice* (1913), is thematically linked to the revolt of an oriental heritage that the Prussian conquest of Silesia had only superficially suppressed.

Realism forbids authorial interjections as expressions of personal subjectivity and prefers the omniscient but solely descriptive narrator. The hostility to theory and conceptuality evokes a prose of mimetic reproduction of concrete objects and sensuous, but not sexually sensual, detail, organized in a sensible totality. Realist objects have little in common with the prerational effervescence of baroque collections. Instead, the surfeit of concrete detail, which is the primary characteristic of this prose and its ultimate message, presumes a particular organization of things. Just as realist politics tries to organize the nation in a purportedly sensible manner, realist description collects and orders objects with a specific intent. The ideological makeup of this order can be seen in *Die Grenzboten,* the main journal of literary realism, edited by Freytag and Schmidt, especially in pieces in a series entitled "The Luxury and Beauty of Modern Life." These short essays, which one nonradical antagonist denounced as pure "capitalist lyricism," describe a wide variety of consumer goods and their appropriate usage: Hungarian wine, French cuisine, tea, flowers, winter gardens, and jewelry.[11] In these passages the propagators of realism try to impose their ideals and aesthetic values onto the everyday life of their bourgeois readers— the only readers they are capable of imagining. The strategy has a double motivation: the realist desire to organize details vis-à-vis a public distrusted as suspiciously close to romantic disorder, and the capitalist need to protect a correct mode of consumption from the twin dangers of nonconsumptive lack of interest and economically irrational excess.

The essay "Gold and Silver Articles, Jewelry" (1852) commences with a history of the use of jewelry and concludes with prescriptive recommendations for contemporary taste. The pedantic tone suggests Freytag's probable authorship of the anonymous piece, as does the fundamental intent to instruct the public in the correct organization of objects. The history of jewelry is locked into a universal history of progress from the primitive peoples of the Americas and Africa, outside of the civilizational process, through the Orient of Egypt, Persia, and China, and thence via classical antiquity to the German Middle Ages. This history is one of progress from an initial phase of excess and inability to distinguish noble from ignoble materials—primitive communism—to the triumph of taste and simplicity, order and elegance, in bourgeois culture:

> Work on precious metals was always tied to decoration and splendor, but jewelry was not everywhere made of those materials to which we today ascribe nobility. The tendency to ornament oneself is present in all peoples. We find it as active at the lowest levels of culture, when the Indians of the Americas drill through their lower lip, the Botocudos through the lip and ears, or the Australian through the nasal cartilage, in order to attach wooden sticks or rings to the opening, as it is at the towering peaks of advanced culture, which still permit the piercing of the fine female earlobe. For girls, this piercing takes place in early youth, a custom that stretches over the whole globe and through all epochs of world history,

from its Asian beginnings through classical antiquity and the Middle Ages into the present. The manner, however, in which the ornamental instinct is satisfied, reflects the different levels of culture.[12]

In this passage the elevation of the present over the backwardness of the past is in fact less important than the insistence on the fundamental universality of a code of corporal ornamentation. The realist author recognizes variations in the external use of decorative objects, but he cannot conceive of the possibility of different intents, such as that jewelry might fulfill alternative symbolic functions in terms of religious, sexual, or social orders. Instead, the article of jewelry and the act of self-ornamentation are treated as indicators of a universal human desire to display, to become the object of a scopophilic vision.[13]

The *Grenzboten* author thus transforms jewelry into a universal currency of exchange; one body becomes the object-text for the other as subject-voyeur. This stance explains the privileged relationship of women to jewelry in nineteenth-century culture:

Progressing culture introduces a greater diversity into the form of ornamentation, and if at first the decoration of the body is equally distributed between men and women, it becomes, at the highest levels of culture, generally the prerogative of women alone. The present is starting to appropriate these characteristics of a higher culture of taste. One no longer likes an overloading with jewelry, which should be made of precious metals and stones in beautiful forms. If we do not count tie pins and watch chains as ornaments, then the cultured man leaves jewelry, except perhaps for a ring, to women, who, as the blossoms of social intercourse, have the right to enhance the graciousness of their appearance with brilliance and color. (382)

The hypothetical account of the special relationship of women to jewelry is telling in view of the plausible alternatives. The author proposes neither a sexual-political analysis of the objectification of the female body nor a contention of the privileged female access to aesthetic activity. Instead, the nineteenth-century realist, ignoring and suppressing materialist issues of sexuality, explains the organization of details in terms of dramatic social exchange. Women are regarded as the centripetal force in bourgeois sociality, a counterbalance to male activity and capitalist egocentricity, and the realist explains female ornament as an effort to strengthen social communication. The appearance of details is locked into the web of communicative exchange that organizes bourgeois society. Realism becomes the intentional effort to stabilize the order of society through the display of objects. The author's insistence on the universality of display suggests the need to avoid an underconsumption and disappearance of detail—the threat posed by an excessive Protestant asceticism—and the attack on primitive excess is designed to ensure that the system of objects does not lose its sensible character in ostentatious superabundance.

The essay emphasizes the problem of excess ascribed to primitive cultures, whose tasteless nondifferentiation among materials and lack of proportion in ornamentation are linked to a barbaric absence of freedom and, hence, an exclusion from the Eurocentric vision of world-history, which defines the limits of rational communication. Not until Greek antiquity does simplicity commence the process of rarefaction that leads to modern elegance. Even "our ancestors, the old Germanics"—here the nationalist element creeps in—preferred "massive" ornamental objects, which disappeared only during the triumph of modern bourgeois culture in the sixteenth and seventeenth centuries (386).

The author admits that the historical narrative was introduced in order to demonstrate the universality of the use of ornamental display: "Why I have prefaced my consideration of modern forms with this historical overview hardly needs commentary. Whoever is familiar with the material will know that most of the major forms of jewelry in antiquity and the Middle Ages still continue to exist, i.e., that in this branch of human activity and pleasure, too, historical continuity stretches influentially into the present" (388). Not only jewelry and ornament but, on a fundamental level, the detail recognized by realism as the token of social exchange in the society of display are declared perpetual and unquestionable. Although the specific forms may vary or improve in the history of progress, social being as a network of communication and exchange is an absolute. The author can therefore describe a variety of contemporary usages.

Although the historical passages demand a relativizing hermeneutics in order to explain forms no longer immediately comprehensible, the essay introduces a decidedly normative tone, whereby the author declares to his public what is appropriate and what is not:

Strong hairpins, which hold the knob of hair in the neck and with decorated heads to act as ornaments, are very popular. The following form of head is beautiful: attached to the golden pin is a somewhat stronger golden ring, like an enlarged wedding band. On each of its sides is a nicely formed fantasy leaf of blue enamel which closes the opening of the ring in such a manner as to permit one to see, through the open spots, the golden backside of the leaf itself. The form thereby combines a good deal of freedom with massive solidity. (388)

At first this passage interests because of its banality: the apodictic declaration of good taste invokes no explicit values, for there is no hidden meaning behind the shapes of the pin. Rather, the display of the pin, as a signifying detail, sets up the communicative structure. Ideology does not lurk behind the ornamental object—it is not, for example, the emblem of a political party—but inheres in the form itself, where the balance of freedom and solidity, as well as the coquettish allusion to fantasy, declare the wearer to be an actor within the bourgeois exchange of meaning, the constant chatter of display. Meaning is less the articulation of substantive positions than the readiness to participate in the social exchange of sense. This display of details as units of meaning transports the structure of the bourgeois market into the habits of everyday life.

In 1852, on the eve of the expansion of German capitalism, this author addresses a public rapidly accumulating a new wealth which he intends to organize. Hence his constant admonition to simplicity and against ostentation. "Necklaces have become simpler than ever," he insists, and "Simplicity is the ruling law of modern elegance and the criterion of culture" (389-391). The consumers with their new wealth will want to show it, but they need the critic's advice on its presentation: realism attempts the aesthetic organization of the world, because the bourgeois public lacks the representational traditions of the aristocracy that regulated earlier forms of display. No bourgeois item of jewelry can have the objective significance of a royal crown, but by claiming for the new public a privileged access to culture and elegance, the author locates it at the Olympian apex of civilization. The mid-century bourgeois displays the possession of meaning without revealing its content. The public assertion of a private life runs up against the discretion of a reserved middle-class increasingly trapped within its secluded individualism.[14] The bourgeoisie flaunts the presence of emotions with a proud possessiveness which crushes their vitality and reduces them to tokens of a semiotic exchange of signs without referents. The article continues: "Fashion has fully banned the collet. But one does wear chains of thick pearls with a diamond clasp from a solitaire around the neck, or a fine Venetian gold chain on which an enamel ivy leaf may hang or a small book wrapped in ivy. In the leaf or the book there is a small capsule to hold a memento" (389). The older aristocratic forms, heavy, overladen, and therefore strangely tied to the precivilized world of the primitives, have been banished by fashion, the ultimate arbiter of the new culture, and this same fashion apparently decrees that, as real experience grows increasingly inaccessible, memories are to be displayed as signs. The capsule holding the memento displaces genuine experience, and significance undergoes the dialectical polarization of the commodity: antisensuous asceticism diminishes concrete usefulness, while the principle of exchange upholds the emptied form as an object of display. The exhibition of the capsule advertises an encapsulated subjectivity. In the prose fiction of realism the surfeit of details corresponds to an accumulation of commodity structures ultimately caught in the same bifurcation.

The link between the dialectic of capitalist possession and realist aesthetics emerges in another essay in the same series, "Planning a Home Library," in which the author, addressing the "wealthy private gentleman," expounds on the appropriate location of literature in the domestic interiors of the affluent bourgeoisie.[15] Here realism does not try to represent the world in a mimetic fiction but rather to structure the place of fiction in the world. As in the other essay, the catalyst is the proliferation of goods, which threaten to erode the erstwhile and appropriate status of literature in everyday life. Although in other areas of consumption a tasteful sense of elegance prevails, the author complains that the middle-class does not treat books with similar respect:

> Yes, a taste for comfort and pleasure has generally spread. If a host invites his friends, the point is no longer just to show heavy silverware and six different kinds of glasses; rather he understands that the forms of his culinary and household utensils must be graceful and attractive in order to please; and when a German housewife gets dressed for society, then she is no longer concerned primarily with the heaviness and high price of the materials in which she formerly had her body

draped, but with the sensible combination of colors and forms according to the laws of beauty. It is very nice that our rich people know how to eat well and to differentiate good wines from bad, and that our ladies are already making demands about the form of a ball bouquet or the color of a sofa cover; but when the same fine people, who cover the muscular hands of their table servants with white gloves whenever others are present, are not ashamed, when alone, to take the dirtied volumes from a lending library into their own soft hands—that is not at all genteel. (103)

This critique involves an economic asymmetry: the generous and sophisticated consumption of silverware, clothing, and wine versus the miserly refusal to invest in literary works. The author blames this underconsumption for many difficulties of contemporary German authors. Nevertheless, even these partially convincing economistic analyses are themselves structured by a more profound contrast between public and private consumption. The host with his tableware or the wife with her dress are placed in networks of social display and reception; the presentation of the possessed commodity is the basic unit of communication. The concrete labor of the servant's muscular hands is hidden—correctly, according to the author—by white gloves as the cover demanded by social convention. Although other realms of activity are organized as orderly public displays, literature unfortunately is not. What impoverishes literary life is not therefore merely the reluctance to spend money on books but the fact that this reluctance is derived from the prevailing character of private and unsocial literary reception.

The author of the essay is no cultural pessimist; he does not envision a perpetual and inevitable decline in the status of literature in everyday life, but he describes two very real threats to the integration of literature into social life. Each represents a faulty mode of commodity possession: underconsumption and overconsumption, insufficient accumulation and excessive acquisitiveness, dangerous lack of interest in material goods and equally dangerous venality, precapitalism and exaggerated capitalism. The first of each pair is the aristocratic position:

In many of the castles of our great landowners, there are indeed old book collections, often from the time of their grandfathers, who preserved a French veneer along with a respect for the French writers of the seventeenth and eighteenth centuries. But these book collections are regularly booty for spiders and bookworms; in the best of cases they are poorly and gracelessly arranged; and the funds used for new acquisitions are so small and the lack of judgment in the selection of new books is so great that they often make an uncanny impression on the stranger who stumbles upon them. (105)

In a period of capitalist expansion and rapid commodity accumulation, tradition and genealogy provide inadequate matrices of order. The real organization of aristocratic culture is incomprehensible for the bourgeois critic, who therefore regards it as an "uncanny" realm of decay. The perceived disorder of aristocratic libraries is thereby linked to the same motif of death with which Wohlfahrt denounces the ancient Germanic tribes, who entered life only when they were integrated into the unifying economy of the national state, which suppressed nature in order to guarantee cultural meaning. Because these textual mausoleums slumber outside the vitality of social exchange, it is only a "stranger, who stumbles upon them." This dystopic literary world is entered not because of hospitality, order, or law but by desultory accident.

For the bourgeois realist organizers of commodity possessions, the aristocracy threatens the social status of literature through underconsumption, backward traditionalism, and insufficient sociability. The antinomy of ostentatious consumption and forced sociability endangers the social bonds with unfettered acquisitiveness and an inflationary display of wealth:

The ladies of the house would do very well to show their guests and girl friends pleasingly ordered and firmly bound books rather than old Franconian porcelain cups, pretentiously arranged in glass cases with other painted bric-a-brac. In this matter, too, the greatest lack of culture is found in that class of businessman which can be here gathered into the collective name of merchant Hirsch or Levi. Because you have much money, you gentlemen demand that the elite of the state, science, and art mingle with you, but in many of your homes one would find, besides an old, dirty Talmud of your father and perhaps a commercial register, very little that might prove that you understand the best and finest interests of your neighbors. The author of these lines knows very well that several homes in Vienna, Berlin, etc., are brilliant excep-

tions to this sorry rule; but they are, after all, only exceptions.
(106)

As ciphers of excessive capitalist accumulation, Jews, to whom the
names "Hirsch" and "Levi" are supposed to refer in general, weaken
the stability of social bonds by overloading the lines of communicative exchange with the display of amassed wealth. Even more than
underconsumption, ostentatious overconsumption threatens to con-
fuse and destroy the language of possession, the semiotic order of
goods. This polar relationship between subcapitalist aristocrats and
supercapitalist Jews returns with a vengeance in the fundamental
structure of *Soll und Haben*, where the correct bourgeois socialization of Wohlfahrt is framed by the contrasting narratives of the decadent aristocratic Rothsattels and the Jew Veitel Itzig, a criminal
only because he takes capitalism too seriously.

The simultaneous attacks on aristocrats and Jews—both seen
as extranationalist elements by the patriots of realism—reflect the
ideological self-understanding of bourgeois realism. The sympathy
and attraction for aristocrats and the antipathy to Jews correspond
to the German bourgeoisie's class alliance with aristocratic forces
as well as to its constant reliance on a scapegoat mechanism to
deflect anticapitalist sentiment toward a purported opponent, cast
from the start in the role of perpetual victim. Nevertheless in
"Planning a Home Library," the realist author denounces both aristocrats and Jews as social types incapable of generating a socially
viable organization of possessions and, in particular, of instituting
literature as a form of sociability in everyday life. Neither group
participates correctly in the bourgeois exhibition of property. Just
as the display of wealth in corporal ornamentation ought to bind
together the potentially misanthropic egos of the laissez-faire war
of all against all, so too, according to the realists, should the literary
life serve to support a harmonious social life in which real social
differences are overcome in the transfigurative light of aesthetic
illusion.

According to the essay, between the worm-eaten libraries of aristocratic desolation and the soulless bric-a-brac of parvenu opulence,
realism locates a space for literature in the domestic library as the
place for a normal sociability. This literary life has little to do, at
least initially, with an authentic assimilation of the aesthetic material and is rather a semiotic display of a culture possessed by those

who can afford it. The survival of literature apparently depends on the noblesse oblige of a new bourgeoisie seeking external legitimacy, not on its own readerly acumen: "And if his strenuous activity rarely allows the man of the house to improve himself with [literature], he should nevertheless consider that he can give his family no better and lasting pleasure than this library. The condition of the library in a family is under all conditions the primary measure of the spiritual culture and inner life of its members, and an outside guest, who enters, need only examine the books available in order to judge the culture of the house" (106). The author justifies book ownership primarily in the nuclear family and implicitly on gender-linked terms. This appeal contrasts with the earlier image of aristocratic genealogy in which libraries are the inheritance of ancestors long deceased. These alternative versions of family structure contrast with the complete absence of family life in the third element in the equation, the Jewish milieu, for there realism assumes that participation in literary life constitutes merely one tactic in a venal strategy of ethnic assimilation. What ultimately promises to succeed is not the family that reads together but the bourgeois family that owns books together—and displays them actively: literature is first of all a mechanism of socialization. In addition, the possession and display of volumes ensure the integration of the family unit into the sociability of the class. Instead of the "stranger" who accidently "stumbles" into the aristocratic library, one encounters now the "guest," the invited stranger, the figure at the juncture of private and public spheres, who consciously and legitimately enters. Aristocratic libraries are places of lugubrious confusion, whereas the outside observer in the domestic bourgeois scene is capable of discerning culture, if only the paterfamilias will overcome his asocial avarice and activate the mechanism of literature as social exchange.

Despite the poverty of literary life in the German bourgeoisie, the essay treats this class as the likely agent of a social exchange that neither aristocrats nor Jews can perform. It is the middle class, with the means to invest and own, which can establish private libraries and engage in a regular exchange of meaning. Guidelines for the bourgeois accumulation of volumes can be obtained from "friends of the family," since literary culture is naturally at home in this class, and if personal acquaintances cannot provide the necessary advice, then the collector can rely on reference works and periodicals which the author of the essay recommends, including his own *Die Grenzboten.* Literary life may be suffering from underinvestment, but in principle it ought to be able to function well. The library can become "the privileged room of the house," since literature is, for the realist critic, the privileged mode of social exchange, and exchange is the privileged mode of sociability in the market economy (106-108). Similarly, the exigencies of a market economy explain why the author does not shrink from an appeal to national competition with his allusion to England where "it is necessary for every gentleman to maintain a library." Challenged by literary Albion, the Germans cannot afford to remain sleepy bumpkins.

Finally, the essay presents the bourgeois library as a realist utopia. Here is order, here is taste, here is domestic tranquillity. Neither chaos nor ostentation penetrates into the sanctuary of literary accumulation and display:

> Whoever begins a library should take care to have simple and tasteful binding for his volumes. Only in the past few years have tasteful bindings become popular in Germany, but it is still necessary to keep after the binder; no unnecessary overloading with golden ornamentation, but a precise display of the title on the back in clear letters. Books in smaller libraries should preferably be uniformly bound, in larger sizes perhaps, with different coverings in the various cases and shelves. Always maintain a precise list of the books present. In larger collections number the single volumes continuously with an indication of the location of the case. In smaller libraries let a member of the family be the librarian; a lady of the house will gladly take on this duty and take maternal care of the order and cleanliness of the books. (107)

Women are charged with the maintenance only of smaller collections, since larger ones would exceed their capacities. In any case, they are to care for these signs of bourgeois wealth and culture with motherly talents, for if books are truly the signs of meaning in the culture, then they are certainly as significant as male offspring.

Once these volumes have been mobilized in the project of socialization, it follows dialectically that the fundamental principles of bourgeois education—external order and mathematical regularity—should be directed at the library collection itself. This display of ordered details solves the realist problem. Books as objects are organized and thereby saved from the dangerous chaos that perpetually

73

threatens an acquisitive class. The realist library is the blueprint of the realist world, where meaning is evident, language is transparent, and the rules of being are accessible to whoever is willing to see: "A bright room, if possible with a view into nature, with bookcases along the walls, a special case with drawers for charts and prints which can be stored in folders; in the middle an elegant work table with comfortable chairs and in the corners small alcoves with statues and vases, if not of marble then of pewter or a modest terracotta, and historical portraits on the empty wall space" (108-109). Literary life is here a bourgeois idyll, characterized by commodity display and the exchange of meaning, as well as by family life and contact with strangers. The conversation among equals can generate liberal ideals under the perpetual gaze of collected objects. But it is no place of charisma. Social contradictions are banished. God's in his heaven, all's right with the world—or soon will be, once the realist order of the patriarchal household asserts itself as the universal principle of organization. That extension of the realist order takes literary shape in the novels of the period, those modestly bound volumes, numbered, catalogued, and perched carefully on an oaken shelf under the watchful eye and tireless dustcloth of the maternal librarian.

The realist ordering of the domestic library transforms it into a microcosm of the world perceived in bourgeois terms, displaying order, regularity, and reconciliation. Tragic conflicts are absent; harmony is fundamentally possible; and where harmony has not yet been achieved, a realistic political and social policy can easily overcome any vestigial difficulties as long as it succeeds in asserting itself against atavistic romanticism and idealism. For realism, the world itself has a textual character which demands a hermeneutic reading supported by the class vision of common sense. Hence the repeated calls for realism, or a realistic reading of the world, in politics, science, commerce. Realist literary texts do not interlock with this cultural strategy in the explicit propagation of middle-class programs alone. More important than their thematic calls for national unity, bourgeois hegemony, or monoethnicity is the function of these texts as primers in the realist vision. The reception of the texts trains the reader to interpret the world in a similar dialectic of appearance and essence robbed of any theoretical self-reflexivity. The social function of realist literary production is thus the production of the reader as realist, as a specifically formed agent of perception and judgment, integrated not only into literary life but also into the particular vision of mid-nineteenth-century bourgeois society.

The confrontation with the images of a mimetic reproduction of the world can cultivate the facility to understand that world because meaning is thought to be lodged in such images and their concrete details, and not in theoretical reflections upon them. Once the Protestant ethic located significance in this-worldly signs of grace, capitalism began to carry out a radicalized process of secularization in order to transform concrete labor and material possession into objects of regular and rationalized desire. The antitheoretical commitment of mid-century realism represents a decisive step forward in the progressive elimination of an autonomous realm of the spirit, which Schmidt indicates as early as 1848: "From their inapproachable heights, accessible only to the initiated, ideas have entered into the depths of life. The spirit no longer stands opposed to reality. It embraces reality now and struggles to master it. Freedom is no longer a poetic dream, a merely philosophical postulate. Instead its idea spiritually pervades the social order and individuals as well, eager no longer to flee the state or to destroy it but instead to realize itself within the state."[16] The assertion of the immanence of meaning renders the examination of concrete details the locus of significant exchange and consequently disqualifies the exclusively theoretical stance. Theory, as a late stage of an extraworldly religious posture, cannot provide access to the meaningfulness projected onto the object, which is consequently transformed into the object of interest and desire. This redirection of the reading process away from the anemic fare of irony and criticism of the prerevolutionary period and toward the growing collection of possessions teaches the reader to love the world more than thought, or commodities more than reason. Every realist text, regardless of its explicit ideological message, therefore functions as an adverstisement for the accumulation of property and the extraction of surplus value. This desire for possession leads Schmidt directly to a desire for the state as the guardian of the laws of ownership. The nationalist politics of the bourgeois realists derive as much from the need to protect the objects of display as from the insistence on the priority of unity—that is, a unified Germany—as the source of cultural meaning.

Not only does theoretical examination of reality necessarily misperceive the world's specifically real character, but so does its opposite, a materialistic fact-orientation which fixates on the surface of the world and therefore confuses the merely given with the authentically true. This antinomy of other-worldly conceptuality and terrestrial facticity repeats the dual alternatives to the realist posture: precapitalist underconsumption and supercapitalist over-consumption, aristocracy and Jewry. The reading of the world in which the German realists endeavor to instruct their public is predicated on an assumption that the immediate appearance of the environment can suggest but not be directly identified with the genuine significance implied by the details. A hermeneutic process must unfold which, because it is nonconceptual, aims at material objects, but which also, because it is antiempirical, never fully identifies reality with them. A "real reality," an "authentic reality," allegedly transcends the directly presented things. The specific character of German poetic realism cannot be grasped if this distinction is ignored; that is, this kind of realism never intends to offer an unmediated "photographic" representation of empirical facticity.[17]

The simultaneity of antitheoretical with antiempirical postures corresponds to the exigencies of capitalist stabilization: the acquis-itive egoism, nourished by its focus on the objects of the capitalist world, commodities, would degenerate into the antisocial behavior of illegal conflict if not limited by the self-corrective projection of law, harmony, and values as regulatory mechanisms. Freytag's Jews are precisely the figures who lack insight into this nonegoistic sphere of values. In historico-philosophical terms, this mechanism repre-sents the secularized version of the post-Reformation duality of pri-vate faith and brotherly love, the latter necessitated by the collapse of the universal system of the Roman Catholic Church and the medi-eval order and the concomitant emancipation of individual subjec-tivity in the market economy. In terms of literary aesthetics, this rejection of empiricism and its regulation by the retarding mechan-ism of a hypothetically privileged reality imply the rejection of a simple mirroring as the principle of written description. Schmidt insists that the duty of art is "to capture not the accidental appear-ance of reality but rather its lasting content." Literary realism dis-plays a multiplicity of facts as the insignia of reality imagined by the acquisitive mind, but it never simply accumulates details. Rather, realists demand the representation of a transfigured world in which all of the components function as sensible units through "appropriate consideration of the normatively viewed nexus of reality, the 'real reality,' and comprehension of the relationship of a factual reality-particle to 'accidentality' and the 'law of reality.' "[18]

The disqualification of the empirical and accidental from the standpoint of a "real reality" signifies a literary historical rejection of romantic fantasy, which by definition is distant from authentic experience. In an 1851 review, Freytag bemoans the legacy of the early nineteenth-century romantic authors E. T. A. Hoffmann and Ludwig Tieck, complaining of "fantastic, often grotesque figures and uncanny situations, mixed with long discussions about art and literature, and yet no characters nor any artistic necessity, everywhere only caprice, whim and arbitrary turns—this was the curse of that period of the novel." Yet the romantic-unreal is not all that realism excludes. A dual-leveled mechanism of normative exclusion also operates in the literary text as the structuring motor. All details point to their encoded meaning; that is, instead of describing people with abstract epithets, the realist author sketches their concrete appearance, suggesting a correspondence between physiognomy and inner nature. Consequently, mixed figures, grotesque or paradoxical natures, are banned on principle from realist narratives. The point of the realist narrative is, after all, to demonstrate successful readings of the world; therefore figurative constructs that resist hermeneutic penetration because of an absolute opacity would undermine the project. As Schmidt observes, "Puzzling, abnormal individualities, for whom neither reason nor feeling make sense, belong neither to reality nor to poetry; they end in insanity, for insanity is nothing but the psyche isolated from the law of reality."[19]

Yet negative figures are present who do not conform to the realist vision and do not cooperate with a gradual socialization into bourgeois practice. Both Baron Rothsattel and Veitel Itzig in Freytag's novel represent abnormal positions which deviate significantly from the values of the Wohlfahrt narrative. They are not excluded from poesy as such, but they are excluded from the poesy of commodities: neither displays the appropriate comprehension of possessions. Consequently, each is subject to a process of exclusion and extermination within the novel. The realist text is therefore defined less by an absence of abnormality than by a perpetual reenactment of the punishment of deviant behavior in order to reassert the unquestionability of the normative law.

In an essay on the poetry of the 1848 revolution that is an important statement of realist aesthetics, Schmidt points out the intimate connection between law and literature:

> The Revolution brought law, administration and even private life out of the closed offices and into the marketplace again; law, constitution and morality are no longer exhausted by general formulas which are put together in idle hours according to the laws of common sense for justice and goodness. Rather the law manifests itself in certain concrete notions and grows into immediately present life. One feels vividly what was otherwise only constructed on the basis of an immature reasoning. The spread and penetration of the ethical idea into the detail of real life is the necessary and sole foundation for a genuine and great literature.[20]

The disprivileging of reason in the name of vivid feeling undoubtedly carries within itself an anti-intellectual component, for Schmidt concludes the essay with a denunciation of "the interminable speeches and resolutions of a few dozen patriotic clubs" as inferior to authentic political passion. This constellation anticipates Bismarck's attack on liberal parliamentary speech in the name of the concrete materiality of blood and iron, a prototypically realistic stance of the German mid-nineteenth century. Still, reality has become more meaningful and therefore susceptible to more realistic interpretation and appropriation. The law is in the world; the physical environment has been restructured according to a bourgeois logic which treats the particular appearance as the expression of the general essence. The realist text, like the realist world, assumes and reproduces a reader able to understand this relationship and to enter into a specifically structured communicative exchange in which, as Schmidt exclaims, one "can with nearly frightening conscientiousness lose oneself in the detail without losing sight of the grand principle."[21]

These dialectical processes between reader and text and between detail and law are the prerequisites of bourgeois realism. The detail must be significant and the reader must be able to recognize the described object as simultaneously both unique and representative of a general class and of an extensive meaning. As long as bourgeois culture could support this economy of meaning, realism could flourish, but its own internal contradictions eventually generated texts that betrayed the tensions within the realist paradigm and the laissez-faire world to which it belonged.

4

The Dialectics
of Liberalism:
Gustav Freytag

Since the end of the Second World War, literary criticism has constructed a canon of post-1848 literature which, confirming the conservative predilections of the New Criticism and its German counterpart, "work immanent criticism," excludes explicitly political authors like Freytag. Yet no study of German culture in the ninety years between the publication of *Soll und Haben* in 1855 and the collapse of national unification in 1945 can be taken seriously which does not include this novel, the epitome of bourgeois thought in its transformation from liberalism to imperialism. Even the conservative Fontane of the mid-1850s drew attention to the problematic political character of Freytag's novel when he complained about its pejorative treatment of both aristocrats and Jews, and this criticism was hardly the harshest. Freytag's contemporary defenders were also emphatically political. At the behest of the national historian, Heinrich von Treitschke, the philosophical faculty of Berlin's Friedrich Wilhelm University praised the prototypically realist author, who "in times of tendentiousness and partisan strife dared once again to hew figures of flesh and blood out of the fullness of German life." Freytag's characteristic nexus of exuberant capitalism, vicious anti-Semitism, and flag-waving chauvinism has received occasional attention, even if an untendentious novel like Gottfried Keller's *Green Henry* (1854), and not *Soll und Haben*, is still regarded as the paradigmatic text of the German realist vision.[1]

Freytag's ideology cannot be dismissed as a simple embarrassment or a historical anachronism after the expulsion of the German population from eastern Europe in the wake of 1945, and neither can it be treated as a merely thematic message external to the aesthetic form. In a literary text, the function of ideology depends less on explicit content than on the structure of the communicative relationship that helps determine the social character of the readership. While Freytag passes on the fundamental realist message concerning the organization and comprehension of the practical details of life, he simultaneously establishes a tentative communicative pattern with his public: the mid-nineteenth-century bourgeois public, which is in the process of abandoning the romantic revolutionism defeated in 1848, settling down to the business of business, and bringing about the economic miracle of German industrialization. Unlike the modernists of the early twentieth century, Freytag can still assume the presence of a hermeneutically mature public with homogeneous values and shared educational backgrounds, and therefore capable of understanding the literary text he presents. Yet the realist Freytag distrusts the public's ability to manage details both in literature and in life because the accumulation of new commodities is growing increasingly rapid. *Soll und Haben* demonstrates this dual concern: thematically it prescribes a specific mode of capitalist activity, and formally it trains the reader to view the world with a realistic eye.

The economic, or liberal capitalist, and aesthetic, or poetic realist, concerns converge in a condemnation of accident and the insistence on a fundamental law and order. Capitalism demands the possibility of rational calculation in the material world as well as the presence of individuals able to perform such calculations and therefore to perceive the general law encoded in the particular detail which only the untrained might misperceive as accidental. In this manner the social strategy generates the aesthetics of realism, as Freytag explains in the foreword to the novel, addressed to "His Highness Ernst II, Duke of Saxony-Coburg-Gotha," to whom the book is also dedicated.

The foreword begins with the recollection of an idyllic setting in the ducal gardens, a harmony of nature and civilization guaranteed by aristocratic power: "It was a smiling May evening on the Kalenberg. Up around the castle, spring blossomed and filled the air with its scents, and the leaves of the red acacia cast their jagged shadows onto the damp lawn. Down in the darkness of the shadow, tame deer sprang from the brush and looked longingly for the appearance of their mistress, who grants the sweet blessing of hospitality to anyone who nears the castle, be it a matter of men or of birds or beasts" (9). This harmony, however, is only a utopian enclave, for Germany and the European world have been shaken by violent political tremors. Such a strife-torn setting is not conducive to aesthetic production of the best sort, at least according to a realist who is typically fixated on models of order and balance. Fretag complains that the contemporary author cannot devote himself solely to visions of harmony, since his pen will inevitably succumb to the rampant political bitterness: "Whoever forms poetry in such an age—pure love will not flow out alone, hate too will pour from the pen; the place of the poetic idea will be easily usurped by practical tendency, and instead of pure feeling the reader may find an ugly mixture of coarse reality and affected sentiment" (10). In the abstract terms of an aesthetic program, this statement anticipates the triadic structure of the novel. The harmonious desideratum of beauty, love, art, and even freedom is flanked by the two antinomic dangers of clumsy reality, the empirical materialism of documentary journalism and the artificial sentimentality of romantic pretense. Once again the Jewish and aristocratic models endanger the bourgeois solution, just as, in the course of the novel, Anton Wohlfahrt will have to steer his way between the venal Itzig and the noble Rothsattels.

Despite their differences, these dangers can be reduced to a common denominator, according to the foreword. Both diverge from the fundamental order of being, in which bourgeois ideology projects its self-understanding as the fundamental ontology of all things, and are thereby associated with the negative term of accidentality: "Happy will I be if this novel leaves Your Highness with the impression that it truly conforms to the laws of life and poetry and that it never merely copies the accidental events of reality"(10). This credo is much more than a trivial disclaimer that all Freytag's figures are truly fictional. He reveals even before the beginning of his voluminous novel that it is about a realistic order, or the organization of details and their realist perception. Its villains are evil not because they have basic moral failings but because they are carriers of disorder and disorderly modes of vision. For all the wealth of the realist novel, indeed for all the diversity within the whole genre, the ultimate antagonist is always the accident.

Despite this basic ideological and aesthetic orientation, Freytag adopts the curious conceit of setting an apparent accident at the start of Wohlfahrt's developmental path. The realists' antipathy for the romantic and Biedermeier preference for diversity, now denounced as chaos, is a part of the discourse of totality. Realist politics envisioned Germany moving from the plurality of particularism to the monocentrality of a unified state. Wohlfahrt is to undergo a similar process of growth, and therefore Freytag must place the child in an initially confusing situation from which the mature merchant will eventually emerge. It is the confusion of a career choice, allegedly resolved only by an accident: "And because the drawing instructor claimed that Anton had to become a painter, and the head of the class advised Anton's father to let his son study philology, the lad might have, owing to his many talents, encountered the usual danger of gifted children: never to find the appropriate commitment to a single vocation, had not an accident determined his vocation" (12). Yet this apparent accident, on which Wohlfahrt's further career and the whole architecture of the novel rest, turns out to be no accident at all but rather the opposite: the revision of a superficial accidentality by the reassertion of a fundamental law. Wohlfahrt's father, a minor bureaucrat, had once upon a time discovered a misplaced document and submitted it to the courts, where it influenced the outcome of a civil suit:

> Many years ago, in a dusty packet of documents that the courts and men had already given up, the accountant had found a paper in which a large landowner in Posen declared his indebtedness of several thousand talers to a well-known business in the capital. Apparently the admission of debt had been placed in the wrong folder, because of the wartime confusion and disorder. He registered the discovery with the appropriate office, and the business was thereby able to win an otherwise desperate legal battle with the heirs of the debtor. (13)

The grateful merchant, T. O. Schröter, inevitably expressed his thanks with annual Christmas packages to the Wohlfahrts, and this linkage between the two households eventually permits young Wohlfahrt to enter the world of commerce as an apprentice in the

Schröter firm. Thus, the initial event, which Freytag ironically presents as an accident, is in fact a paradigm of the realists' insistence on the presence of basic laws beneath the surface of confusion and chaos.

This introductory anecdote presents three thematic ideological concerns that underly Freytag's realist aim. First, the arrival of the Christmas packages of sugar and coffee provides the first experience with things-as-commodities. Not only does the father subsequently pay close attention to market prices, but the very presence of these goods in the household is repeatedly associated with an aesthetics of desire and possession. Second, the circumstances of the discovery anticipate a central structuring feature of the plot, the search for lost documents, which in turn signifies both the realist insistence on order and the competing strategies of textualization in capitalist culture: the transformation of lived experience into a passive object of hermeneutic labor. Third, the event launches Wohlfahrt's developmental course: his movement from the nuclear family into the patriarchal firm anticipates the grand design of the novel, in which the hero, not as an actor but as an object of exchange, slides back and forth between aristocratic and bourgeois spheres. The realist desire for the poetry of acquisition, the bourgeois reduction of nature to text, and the treatment of biography as a narrative of commodity exchange in which individual subjectivity plays no role set the stage for a cultural development that will lead from the ethic of accumulation in *Soll und Haben* to the frozen imprisonment of Weber's iron cage. The anecdote concludes, therefore, with a movement from sensuous phantasy to bondage, an abstract journey from atomistic freedom to its absolute denial:

> Then the father jokingly asked his son if he would like to become a businessman. And in the soul of the little one, a beautiful picture suddenly took shape like the rays of colorful glass beads in a kaleidoscope, made up of sugar cubes, raisins, almonds and golden oranges, with the friendly smile of his parents and all the mysterious delight he always felt at the arrival of the Christmas package; until he finally cried out: "Yes, father, that's what I want to be!" Let no one say that our life lacks poetic moods. The magician poesy still rules the ways of mortals. But let everyone take care of what dreams he nurtures in the most secret parts of his soul, for when they mature, they easily becomes our masters, our strict masters! (14)

Young Wohlfahrt's dreams of a career as a merchant are realized in the course of the novel, which describes the necessary elements of a successful bourgeois socialization. Entering his benefactor's company as an apprentice, he learns about the nature of commodities and works his way up until he becomes a full partner, an ideal businessman, and the husband of Schröter's sister. His arduous path intertwines with that of Itzig, a Jewish youth, who develops into Wohlfahrt's opposite: the capitalist as dishonest schemer. The alter egos, Wohlfahrt and Itzig, compete in an extended struggle to gain control of the aristocratic estate of the Rothsattels. Although Itzig resorts to criminal methods to acquire the mortgage papers and the deeds to the property, in the end the middle-class hero Wohlfahrt is able to rescue the beleaguered nobles. To do so, he must enter the world of legal ploys and financial dealings. The knowledge that he acquires contributes to the development of his bourgeois personality and increases his distance from the aristocratic milieu to which he was initially attracted; although he follows the Rothsattels from Germany to an impoverished estate in the Polish east, he eventually returns to Germany and the Schröter firm. The novel closes with the inscription of his name as co-owner in the documents of the company.

While describing the integration of the hero into the world of commerce, the bourgeois Bildungsroman *Soll und Haben* conceals most processes of material production. Freytag prefaces his novel with a motto from his collaborator at *Die Grenzboten,* Schmidt: "The novel should search for the German people where they will be found showing their industriousness, that is, at their work." Perhaps Freytag set off in search of the laboring masses, but he never finds them, and he shares this disregard for labor in the decades of industrialization with the realist authors included in the scholarly canon. As Michael Kienzle has pointed out, the novel never describes productive labor.[2] With the exception of some peripheral agricultural figures, it concentrates solely on the sphere of commodity circulation: merchants, their scribes, and, closest to the working class, laborers employed in the trading firm. Nowhere is there a productive proletariat; the barely described construction workers employed to erect a sugar refinery on the aristocratic estate are objects of authorial disdain. Freytag has none of the interest in physical labor suggested by the opening motto. *Soll und Haben* is not about production and work; it is about the accumulation of goods in the form of commodities and the socialization of the hero into the world of commodity exchange.

As in the essays in *Die Grenzboten*, the novel is organized into a three-part equation in which the correct form of bourgeois accumulation, the world of the Schröter firm, is contrasted with two countermodels: the unproductive and hence insufficiently capitalist aristocracy and the excessively acquisitive Jews. Freytag does not suggest that aristocrats cannot accumulate wealth, but an aristocratic figure, like Baron Rothsattel, cannot overcome the legacy of a squandered fortune as long as he continues to act as a member of the aristocratic class: "Like all those whose banners have been inscribed by destiny with family memories of long ago, our baron too tended to think much of the past and the future of his family. His grandfather had had the bitter experience that a single, disorderly thought can be enough to disperse all the grains of gold and honor that industrious ancestors had gathered for their heirs" (29). The aristocrat carries the burden of the familial past; caught in a nexus of tradition and obligations, he cannot act as freely as do the bourgeois capitalist individualists. His economic behavior lacks the same dynamic potential, and when he engages in entrepreneurship, the result is likely to be catastrophic, since his inherited code of aristocratic honor has nothing to do with the world of business. The baron's social standing denies him the flexibility of the bourgeois economic man. Not all of Freytag's aristocrats are impoverished, but all live off resources they are incapable of replenishing.

In their difficult financial circumstances, the Rothsattels, despite their blue-blooded genealogy, remain modest and honorable, whereas Freytag's Jews, even when modest, are ostentatious and untrustworthy: "Herr Ehrenthal was a well-fed man in his best years with a face that was too round, too yellow and too clever to be handsome; on his feet he wore spats and on his shirt a diamond pin, and he walked down the shaded path toward the baron with numerous bows and deep waves of his hat" (32). As if providing an illustration of the anti-Semitism in the essay on domestic libraries in *Die Grenzboten*, Freytag introduces Ehrenthal wearing diamond jewelry, in contrast to the humility of the truly noble Rothsattels. This show of wealth is out of place in the immediate context, since Ehrenthal has come to inspect the baron's stalls. More generally, Freytag denounces this wealth as illegitimate, since it is not based on material production, despite his own reluctance to represent the labor process. Unlike Freytag's aristocrats, his Jews are integrated into the dynamic of capitalism. In fact, the novel presents no Jew who is not linked directly or by family connection to capitalist exchange, and the world of eastern European poverty is fully absent, even though much of the novel takes place in underdeveloped Poland. This capitalist integration, however, is restricted to financial speculation, which, Freytag suggests, leads only to ill-gotten gain. Because neither aristocrats, with their traditionalist burden, nor Jews, with their excessive involvement in speculation, participate in the normative mode of commercial activity, neither is able to achieve the appropriate insight into the fundamental organization of the world guaranteed by bourgeois activity alone. Yet such realist insight is precisely what the novel attempts to impart to its readership.

In the course of *Soll und Haben*, Freytag tries to demonstrate the inferiority of aristocratic and Jewish economics as compared to the model bourgeois capitalism of Schröter. The prima facie narratives of impoverishment and bankruptcy, however, are designed to support a more important sort of paradigm: the novel explains how the negative figures are incapable of a realistic comprehension of the world. When Wohlfahrt begs Schröter to come to the aid of the baron, the merchant replies that the aristocrat fell into the hands of the scheming usurers "because he lacks that which alone imbues life with value: a considered judgment and a constant labor power" (479). The lack of a work ethic necessarily leads to the lack of judgment, and thus of the realist vision. This analysis in turn implies a condemnation of the aristocratic economic mode: "Whoever claims from life the right to pleasure and a privileged position because of his ancestry is often incapable of maintaining the strength necessary to earn such a position. Very many of our old, respected families are condemned to decline, and it will be no misfortune for the state when they disappear" (479-480). In contrast to Wohlfahrt, who at this point is hopelessly enamored of the Rothsattel daughter, Schröter presents a laissez-faire position. His opposition to the aristocracy has less to do with democratic principle than with the concern for the sound management of property and the constant circulation of wealth. Aristocratic traditionalism, incapable of participating in a quickening economic life, ought not be preserved artificially, since such aid only perpetuates the inherited incompetence.

Blinded by tradition and their pretense to privilege, aristocrats lack the acumen necessary to manage their affairs, and they therefore weaken the health of the nation. Because they do not take part in productive labor and instead rely on inherited wealth, they cannot share the realist perception of the world.

Freytag's Jews have no inherited wealth, but, like his aristocrats, they are excluded from the bourgeoisie and therefore from the realist perception. When Veitel Itzig, Wohlfahrt's counterpart, inspects his new quarters at Löbel Pinkus's inn, Freytag provides a suggestive paradigm of Jewish misperception: "Itzig threw his bundle into a closet and stepped out onto the balcony. Finding no other guest there, he started to admire the view with the same degree of interest that a Dutch painter might have had, although not quite with the same intention" (53). Because the view looks out on a dirty canal and urban poverty, Freytag's choice of the term "admire" would be inappropriate if he did not intend to suggest the dubious character of Itzig's designs. The newly arrived guest feels at home in this slumlike underworld because it provides him with the appropriate setting to carry out his criminal plans. He inspects his surroundings carefully—much more so than could an aristocrat—but not with the scrupulous honesty of a merchant devoted to his goods. Itzig is concerned with illegal machinations, and he takes note of hidden pathways that may be of aid in the future:

> Then he noticed that a long, covered stairway led from the end of the balcony down to the water; he saw that next to this stairway a similar one ran down from the house next door, and he figured out that it must be possible to run down one set of stairs—and then to climb up the other and barely get one's shoes wet. He also saw that because of the low water level in the summer, it was possible to move along the houses beside the water, and he wondered whether there might not be people who made use of such a walkway. Encounters with nightwatchmen and police officers need not be feared. (53-54)

The Jewish figure is derided for having an excessive concern with detail, which, as a corollary to the accusation of material acquisitiveness, contrasts with the aristocratic failing of insufficient interest in the present. Both traits are, for the realist Freytag, false modes of perception, unable to penetrate beneath the accidents of surface impression into the dynamic of fundamental laws.

Schröter's complaint that aristocrats cannot understand the world or manage their wealth because they refuse to work and therefore lack judgment recurs implicitly in Itzig's inspection of the scene below the balcony, the poor section of Breslau. Itzig feels at home in this poverty, but Freytag defines the scene negatively by contrasting its present state with its more legitimately admirable past, when it had been the center of honorable activity: "In olden days the respected guild of tanners had occupied this street. The woodwork then was smooth and new, and bright skins of lambs and goats hung from the bannisters until they became soft and pliable enough for gloves for the patricians and leather bags for their wives. Now the tanners had moved away to distant parts of the city, and instead of animal skins, the dirty clothes of poor people hung from the balconies above the splintered woodwork and the worm-eaten beams." Commodity production has moved away, and poverty and crime can enter. Itzig's sharp perception, which can never recognize the superiority of bourgeois legality, is defined by his nonparticipation in honest labor. He cannot see the world through realistic eyes because he does not share the social experience that generates realism. Consequently, he prefers precisely those surroundings of asocial disorder and romantic abnormality which realism tends to disdain: "It was an uncanny abode for any creature, except for painters, cats or poor devils" (53).

Only honest bourgeois entrepreneurship provides the experience that can support a realistic understanding of the world: realism defines the perspective of the merchant class as universal. Capitalism becomes a transparent glass through which to view the surroundings, whereby things-as-commodities allegedly display their essential nature. Participation in mercantile activity can engender the insight and judgment to which aristocrats and Jews have no access. Thus, Wohlfahrt's passage through the Schröter firm is less an economic paradigm than a developmental psychological phase: "the old and well-known trading business had a proud, indeed princely appearance, and, more important, it was made just right to inspire in its partners a sense of secure self-assuredness" (56). Wilhelm Meister's identity formation depended on aesthetic experience; a half-century later, Freytag founds his Bildungsroman on commercial activity, which endows the hero with the proper understanding of the world of details. This bourgeois understanding includes three components: a recognition of basic laws beneath the surface of empirical events, an aesthetic libidinal desire for commodities as a legitimating motor for acquisitiveness, and a tendentially ascetic suppression of this desire in order to restrict sensuous consumption.

Freytag describes Wohlfahrt's initial impression of the firm as a confusing hustle and bustle of customers and salesmen, buying and selling all sorts of goods. Just as Wohlfahrt's own background was characterized by a superficial chaos, so are his first experiences in the business world: "So the business of the day provided the new apprentice with many of the most diverse impressions, people and conditions of all sorts" (56). Anton can hardly make sense of this confusion, and Freytag underscores his perplexity by describing a series of encounters:

> There came material dealers from the province, old, fatherly men of every sort with caps and all degrees of culture and reliability. They bought, shook hands and demanded to be treated as special friends of the business. Further, there came landowners of all levels from the countryside, offering the cash crops, dyer's weeds, spices, etc. Then there were the Polish Jews, black-locked fellows in long, silken caftans, who occasionally made purchases but usually tried to sell the products of their regions—wool, hemp, potash, and tallow. (57)

The list goes on and on. Freytag pursues both the descriptive goal of providing an image of the firm's activity and the psychological goal of suggesting the diversity of details with which the apprentice was confronted. Wohlfahrt does not yet have the insight and maturity to recognize the unifying principle behind this amalgam of mere things; details have yet to be organized in their realist order.

Freytag heightens Wohlfahrt's sense of confusion by shifting into the present tense and by providing a montage of simultaneous discussions in the office. The author breaks the rules of realist narration for a moment in order to indicate the central figure's inability to perceive sense and meaning in his surroundings. Freytag successfully demonstrates the experience of meaninglessness inherent in nonrealist perception. This paradigmatic chaos, however, leads into a model learning experience when Wohlfahrt watches Fink negotiate with the wool salesman Schmeie Tinkeles. Both bargain toughly, and the apprentice, at first bewildered by the apparent irreconcilability of the bargainers' two positions, gains insight into the dynamics of business life. This is his first step toward the realist vision based on capitalist experience, the perception of the overriding goal beneath the superficial detail. Each commodity and each price is good not for its own sake but only for its contribution to the total profit-making enterprise of exchange.

The realist vision, however, does not solely involve the recognition of the hidden totality; it also entails the desire for the materiality of the details, the plurality of the commodities in which Anton discovers a "peculiar poesy" (64). Even young Wohlfahrt's indirect ties to the world of commerce via the Christmas packets are nourished by subliminal yearning; the image of the Schröter firm and, even more so, the strange delicacies that reappear every December illuminate the otherwise musty paternal world with a strange aesthetic glow. Commodities are the objects of desire, but not because of their sensuousness. Wohlfahrt experiences neither the sweetness of the sugar nor the rich, mellow taste of the coffee. Rather, these goods are signs of exchange, which carry with them the aura of exotic differences and foreign places and thereby arouse an erotic interest in the perpetual other:

> Nearly all the countries of the earth and all the races of humanity had labored and gathered in order to pile up useful and valuable objects before the eyes of our hero...A Hindu woman had woven these bast mats, and that box had been painted by an industrious Chinese with red and black hieroglyphs. A Negro from the Congo in the service of a Virginia planter had fastened that reed twist to the bales, this trunk of colored wood had rolled across the sand by the waves of the Gulf of Mexico, that square block of zebra and jakaranda wood had stood in the swampy jungle of Brazil, and monkeys and colored parrots had hopped across its leaves. (65)

Whereas Wohlfahrt's initial experience of confusion in the world of commerce challenges him to penetrate beneath the surface in order to recognize the fundamental order, the infinite mosaic of possession bedazzles him in a manner that ensures the continuity of his acquisitive instinct. The world stands before him as a collection of potential possessions, through which he can appropriate the labor of third-world workers which he himself is never compelled to perform. The contrast with Wilhelm Meister is again apt: capitalism emancipates the aesthetic encounter from the work of art and transfers it to the commodity as the new guarantor of the social order.

The first component of Freytag's bourgeois vision, the recognition of the unifying laws behind empirical details, provides the blueprint for an aggressive economic modernization, but it must be compounded by the second component, desire, in order to fix attention on the objects of exchange. In turn, desire must be checked by the third element, asceticism, lest accumulation collapse into immediate consumption. Before the commencement of the narrative, Wohlfahrt has already undergone an adequate bourgeois socialization with its internalization of the exigencies of suppression; he never enters into temptation, and this explains in part the tedious character of the novel. In contrast, his Jewish counterpart, Itzig, is marked by an unrepressed sensuality, and the figure of a laborer, Karl Stumm, demonstrates the process of self-denial. As the commodities spread throughout the whole of Schröter's house, all social relationships undergo commodification. Individuals are referred to less by their names than by their function. The scribe Pix is called "the black pen," and the warehouse porters are "leather aprons" (83-84).

The first step in initiating Karl, the son of a veteran worker, into the firm is the internalization of the principle of denial. His father leads him into the storeroom, has him taste the almonds and raisins, and then leaves him in front of the open barrels of sweets with the admonition: "Now you have to test how long you can stand in front of these barrels without reaching in. The longer you can take it, the better for you. When you can't stand it any longer, come to me and say you've had enough. This is no command—it's for you and the sake of honor" (85). Goods are the object of accumulation but not enjoyment, just as the jewelry in the essay in *Die Grenzboten* is less for pleasure than display. Possession is subject to the primacy of exchange, not consumption, and this realist order applies as much to the aesthetic form as to the economic credo. The realist novel concerns itself ultimately with the basic order behind the details, but these details are present in a growing plenitude in order to maintain the reader's attention with their sensuousness. This aesthetic materiality never unfolds into unmotivated pleasure, since the details are also tokens of exchange in a communicative strategy, the message of which is the hidden order and harmony. In other words, the realist details attract libidinal interest in their concrete use value, but that value is always subordinated to the exchange value of their primary function as signs of meaning in the discursive interchange between author and reader.

Nineteenth-century German realism, as it emerges in the paradigmatic novel *Soll und Haben*, presents the world of initially disorganized things as an order of commodities. Its aesthetic-programmatic intent and its real function culminate in the instruction of the reader in the correct reading of the semiotic display: the world has a legal structure, its diversity is attractive, and communication is grounded in ascetic self-denial. The converse of this Protestant ethic in reading is the textualization of the world. The goal of teaching the reader presupposes the presence of circumambient nature not as an autonomous being but as a potential object of capitalist possession and hermeneutic penetration: it is there to be had and to be understood. This assumption explains a series of apparently peripheral thematic elements in *Soll und Haben*, for the central narrative of the novel of mercantile development is interwoven with accounts of the losing and finding of texts on which, in curious ways, the fates of the central figures depend. This motif of the search is anticipated in the initial anecdote, when Wohlfahrt's father discovers the misplaced document. The event would amount to little more than a trivial episode if it did not foreshadow a recurrent narrative structure. Not only does capitalism deny to nature its ecological independence and transform it into an object of possession, but capitalist realism treats the world as an object of interpretive appropriation which is exhausted in the act of reading. This textualization of the world consequently ascribes to written texts a special importance as keys to understand an objectified world. *Soll und Haben* includes three different stories about the search for such master-texts, and the three competing textual strategies correspond to the triadic structuring of the novel.

The distance of aristocratic being from the authentic humanity of the bourgeoisie explains the immanent association of the aristocratic group with the category of caricature. Where realism, as the aesthetics of capitalist commodities, swells its pages with sensuous detail, caricature restricts itself to gross outlines and thereby distorts and suppresses the substance of matter. It is an aristocratic mode, the novel suggests, because it corresponds to the lack of substantive activity characteristic of an unproductive class. The travesty and ridiculous misrepresentation innate in caricaturistic description are the accessible modes of expression for a group whose livelihood depends solely on the formation of genealogy and privilege. When exhorted to practice drawing, Lenore, the baron's daughter, protests: "I only draw caricatures. . . they are the easiest, you just make a long nose or short legs, and the fellow just looks ridiculous" (37). Her incapacity to render mimetic reproduction foreshadows the shallowness of her emotional response to Wohlfahrt; between them, the class struggle of aristocratic cabal and bourgeois love is played out once again. The response of Lenore's mother—"You really shouldn't draw caricatures. . . They ruin your taste and make you contemptuous"—in no way disproves the affinity between class and genre, since the novel demonstrates how natural it is for the aristocracy to fall into contemptuous behavior: witness Fink's disdain for bourgeois friendships or the baron's mistreatment of Wohlfahrt. Caricature as the rhetorical mode of the aristocracy even leads the realist Freytag to resort to caricature in his own descriptions of the nobility.

Aristocratic caricature as a strategy of textualization dominates the novel when Fink introduces Wohlfahrt into the aristocratic society at the von Baldereck dance school, where the bourgeois hero first encounters sophisticated intrigue. He enters as "a sacrificial lamb of dark powers, who were about to destroy his inner peace" (155). The youthful participants have divided into two antagonistic parties: "Soon two large alliances arose, between which a few figures swung back and forth, but which generally remained stable and nourished strong, secret antipathies for the other side. It went so far that on one evening all the ladies of one party carried a white camelia in the middle of their ball bouquet, attached to a highly visible brown ribbon hanging down. As a result, on the next evening the opposing party came with red camelias and green ribbons" (173). In contrast to this external display of antagonistic partisanship, Theone Lara, one of Lenore's friends and, along with her, part of the central group of the brown party, keeps an intimate diary, shared only with her confidantes, which therefore becomes a "holy relic" of the clique. Lenore contributes to the elaboration of this sacred text with her caricatures, precisely because of her inability to express authentic emotions, and these caricatures in turn nearly lead to catastrophe when the book is lost one evening, and the girls fear that one of their opponents will find it and make public the ludicrous distortions, with unthinkable consequences: "The holy relic of the alliance was lost. It had fallen into the hands of strangers, perhaps, a horrible thought, into the hands of the greens. On each of the last passages were mischievous remarks about all the gentlemen, with coded names of course—Fink was called Zeisig, Tönnchen was Nussknacker—but who could guarantee that these ciphers might not be understood? And what would happen then? Catastrophe! The ruin of the dance lessons, family feuds, the dissolution of all human bonds" (175).

In this episode aristocratic misperception of the world generates a strategy of textualization which not only fails to produce the authentic effect that mimetic realism alone can provide but also threatens the stability of social order and harmony. It reinforces trivial divisions and leads to strife and dissension. As a mode of writing, the worldly textualization of which the aristocracy is capable belongs to an anachronistic past, and its continuity in the age of realism is regressive. Typically, the bourgeois Wohlfahrt is the one who recovers the text from Fink and thereby averts the impending disaster, but he ultimately only postpones the necessary demise of the aristocratic order. The sort of text to which Lenore reduces the world, abstract caricature without binding substance, repeats the instability of her class background.

Because of the aristocrats' proclivity for an inadequate, merely caricaturistic perception of reality, they are easily entangled in a second textualization strategy, which is equally formalistic but much more powerful. Freytag, who ascribes this second mode of writing to the Jews, develops from it the central plot of *Soll und Haben*, in which the machinations of Jewish speculators lead to the financial ruin of the German aristocracy. This motif nourished central elements in the political anti-Semitism of the late nineteenth and early twentieth centuries. While Wohlfahrt learns the importance of love in the form of national solidarity and bourgeois loyalty, Itzig operates through manipulations of the legal code, which he distorts to his own end of gaining control of the Rothsattel fortune. His fixation on the significance of law is apparent in his first encounter with Anton. The two parallel figures meet on their journey to the city where each, after his own fashion, will try to make his fortune. Itzig proclaims: "It is to be done, that you buy from each man what he has. There is a recipe, and with it you can force everyone you want something from, if he doesn't want to give." In addition to his mercantile orientation and his hunger for power, Itzig is marked above all by the need for a code, which is always a matter of legal knowledge and documents, namely contracts, deeds, and mortgage papers: "When I go to the city, I go to find knowledge; it is written on papers. Whoever can find the papers becomes a mighty man. These papers I want to look for until I find them" (25-26).

While Wohlfahrt busies himself with commodity exchange, Itzig masters the law and gains possession of the powerful papers, documents of mortgage and indebtedness, which grant him control of the Rothsattel estate. The aristocratic baron is caught in the romantic illusions that plague his class and lacks a realistic sense of business. Unable to manage his affairs well, he has borrowed funds and damaged his financial stability. The promissory notes which he has signed disappear, and the search for these texts establishes the nexus of the relationship within which Wohlfahrt and Itzig repeatedly confront each other. Long after their initial discussion, at the end of the book, they face each other again in the battle to gain control of the missing texts:

> Years ago, when the two, who now stood opposed as enemies, had traveled together to the city, it was the Jewboy who searched for papers on which in his childish naiveté he believed his happiness to depend. Then he was ready to buy the baron's estate for Anton. And now the other had set out in search of mysterious documents and demanded the baron's estate from Itzig, who had found his knowledge. He had found his mysterious recipes, and he held the baron's estate in his hands, as his destiny neared its climax. At the same moment both men thought back to their shared journey. (776-777)

In Freytag's apotheosis of the bourgeoisie, Wohlfahrt of course wins out. He acquires the mortgage papers and returns them to the baroness, who can destroy them and thereby rescue what remains of the Rothsattel fortune. The German middle class poses as the benefactor of the aristocracy, and Itzig's criminal escapades cannot rescue his projects from their deserved failure. The grand narrative of the novel, which commences with a desire for the texts and proceeds through their production and disappearance, concludes with their recovery and liquidation. If there is an ideological continuity between Freytag's nationalism and twentieth-century National Socialism, then the victory over these Jewish texts of finance capital anticipates, in its specific form, the book burnings of May 1933: "The baroness held the blind man's hand on the bundle of mortgages as she ripped each one through. She rang for a servant and had the papers carried piece by piece to the oven. The flame shot up brightly and threw red light through the room. It roared and crackled until the fire died away. The evening twilight filled the room, and the baron sat by the bed of the sick woman, burying his head in the covers, while she folded her hands over him and her lips moved in a silent prayer" (829-830). The victory of the church over the synagogue, which eradicates the threat of the Jewish textualization strategy, allows the text of the German bourgeoisie, the realist novel, to draw to an end, for it has achieved its purpose, the demonstration of the superiority of bourgeois commercialism and its aesthetic counterpart over the worldly but excessively capitalistic competition.

Aristocratic caricature ignores living substance and forces matter into distorted forms, whereas capitalist textualization insists on the priority of external form and consequently desiccates living matter. Freytag repeatedly associates the financial documents with antivitalist imagery and death. As Rothsattel sinks into ever more dangerous dealings, his bonds undergo a process of decay to which he reacts with disgust: "The baron drew out his richly ornamented safe, and, in the place of the attractive, white parchments, he set the thick, yellow bundle of documents, soiled by many hands, which from now on represented his estate. He no longer looked inside with the joyous attention he had given the bonds; he closed the top of the box quickly and pushed it into his desk" (225). The documents that sap the life of the agricultural estate themselves appear to wither. The antithetical relationship between the false texts and the healthy life is later made explicit in one of the few instances of the narrator's direct address, just after the death of the baron's son: "Listen, you poor father, holding your breath: it has grown quiet in the castle and in the tops of the trees, but still you cannot hear the one tone of which you constantly thought when you were busy with your pipe dreams and your parchments, the heartbeat of your only son, the first Rothsattel of an entailed estate" (723). The documents share with the "pipe dreams" a fundamental unreality: they are mere representations of life, which are, moreover, false. They are counterposed to their radical alternative, the heartbeat of the son, which stands for the full, authentic being that is denied by the antirealist strategies of textualization. While Lenore's caricatures threaten to explode society in the partisan strife of aristocratic particularism, the capitalist documents erode being through the imposition of a mechanical formality that leads necessarily to a rigor mortis.

Freytag's critique of a Jewish textualization strategy is ultimately congruent with the ideological contents of the essays in *Die Grenzboten* and with the anti-Semitic discourse in fascist literature of the twentieth century.[3] *Soll und Haben,* aside from its generic indebtedness to the Bildungsroman modified in the class interests of the mid-nineteenth-century bourgeoisie, is concerned largely with competing modes of writing. Realism endeavors to teach its recipients to read the world as a text—and because Freytag and his contemporaries can still assume the presence of a culturally homogeneous and mature readership, such instruction is fundamentally unproblematic, but conversely, it presumes that the worldly text is a written document available to the reader's inquiry. Nature is instrumentalized as concept, as it becomes solely an object of human desire. Yet the precise identity of the human subject determines the mode of conceptualization. The repeated quest for the text and the intertextual competitions, in which both the diary and the mortgage documents participate, correspond to a class struggle over the questions of authorship and ownership: who really writes the world, who defines society? The riddle is solved as the novel ends with Wohlfahrt's rite of initiation into the bourgeoisie.

The bourgeois world-view is complete from the start of the novel, carried by the merchant Schröter whom Freytag never subjects to significant criticism. Within the framework of the novel of development, however, Wohlfahrt must undergo a learning process through which he recognizes the superiority of middle-class culture over its competitors. His break with the aristocracy occurs in the Polish episode. Living at close quarters with the Rothsattels, the hero has the opportunity to discover the limitations of their knowledge and understanding: "Most of what Anton read was foreign to the family. When they read the newspaper, he was surprised by their lack of understanding of foreign political conditions. The depths of history were not enjoyed by the baron, and when he denounced the English political system, he could call his own opinion legitimately unprejudiced, since he had absolutely no knowledge of the matter." The aristocrats' nonparticipation in productive activity engenders a distance from the concrete facts of life; even their geographical information is faulty, and Freytag makes clear that these failings are characteristics, not accidental attributes of the Rothsattels. This disinterest in "real reality" is linked to a specific literary strategy by means of one of the few literary critical passages in the novel: "The baroness, who was interested in entertaining reading and valued reading aloud, adored Chateaubriand and read, in addition to fashionable novellas, the novels of sophisticated ladies. Anton considered *Atala* tasteless and the novels boring. He soon recognized that his housemates considered everything that they encountered in the world from a perspective he did not share" (539). Romanticism is explicitly denounced as aristocratic literature, which is therefore incapable of authentic perception. It ignores the world and disdains the bourgeois concerns that Freytag sets as universal and absolute. The Rothsattels' superciliousness toward factual existence finds its ultimate metaphor in the image of the blind baron who cannot recognize the undeniable forces that the realists insist upon as fundamental laws. His is no Homeric blindness which, ignoring surface appearance, gains access to a more profound vision; it is simply the myopic provincialism of an increasingly irrelevant social class.

Unlike the aristocrats whom Freytag presents as constitutionally incapable of sight, or bourgeois realist perception, the Jews in *Soll und Haben* are excessively observant. Their fixation on surface facts, regularly linked to the mechanisms of shady business deals on the border of crime, corresponds to the overdevelopment of materialist acquisitiveness. This constellation of visual modes easily translates back into aesthetic sources: if aristocratic otherworldliness allies with romantic literature, then the opposite stance, Jewish hypersensitivity to facts, pairs with a literary strategy of empirical mimesis, which the poetic realists, insisting on an order beneath the surface, consistently denounce. The distance from the empiricist perspective to the correct bourgeois perception is underscored at an early stage in the parallel socialization processes:

The next morning each of the two boys began his tasks. Anton sat at his desk in the office and copied letters; and Veitel stood...like a detective in front of the biggest hotel of the city in order to observe a stranger from the country who was angry with Herr Ehrenthal and was suspected of meeting with other partners in his room. By copying the letters, Anton acquired some insight into the style and language of his business, and while lying in wait outside the inn, Veitel had the good fortune of learning the address of a passing student who felt it was time to sell his silver watch. (55)

Freytag not only contrasts Schröter's mercantile rectitude with Ehrenthal's plotting but also links each factor to alternative processes of personality development and perception. Wohlfahrt's copying letters leads neither to bureaucratic pedantry nor to obsequious parroting but rather, via mimesis, to integration into bourgeois maturity and the universal vision of commerce. Itzig's more worldly activities lead paradoxically to a much more limited perspective, hopelessly obscured by the chaos of immediate details and the promise of short-term gains. The bourgeoisie constitutes the world as a text to be understood; hence it condemns aristocratic romanticism. Yet the realists also insist on the overarching order of this text in which each detail fits into a universal pattern established by a basic law. Only Wohlfahrt, not Itzig, grows privy to this knowledge, and once his recognition of the bourgeois character of the world has been adequately confirmed, he too can be incorporated into the mercantile order. This rite of passage depends on a third and final sort of text.

Wohlfahrt enters the Schröter family, after breaking off his liaison with the aristocratic Lenore, and simultaneously enters the Schröter firm. The transition is marked by the entry of his name as co-owner in the "secret book of the firm," the founding documents of the Schröter company. Freytag treats these papers as a holy text (834). Therein lies the identity of the enterprise, hidden to all outsiders and preceding all experience, since this book of business determines and defines social organization. From the start, Wohlfahrt has been destined for this initiation, but not until the end is this secret text revealed as both the goal and ultimate law of his biography.

By the end of *Soll und Haben*, the aristocratic and Jewish competitors have been rejected, as have their alternative strategies of textualization: caricatures and mortgages. Bourgeois textualization, the insistence on the order of commodities as the framework for human existence, establishes itself as Wohlfahrt's integration is completed. After the dismissal of the false texts, the ultimate book is discovered, the secret order of capitalist things. Thus, the novel concludes with a telling variation on the life-as-book metaphor: "The old book of his life has come to a close, and in your secret book, you good spirits of the firm, will now be inscribed 'with the help of God': his new debit and credit" (836). The realist Freytag, who condemns the aristocratic reduction of life to caricature and the Jewish manipulation of life as finance, praises the bourgeois textualization of existence as a business ledger. The poetry of poetic realism is the alliterative rhyming of character and commodity, universalized as the structure of biography and the substance of nature. Wohlfahrt's life is to be read by the implied reader of the realist text as an account of the vicissitudes of an initial investment leading to the profits reaped in the offices of the firm and in the arms of Sabine Schröter. Freytag organizes his hero's developmental path as a marketing process in which the personality, which fifty years earlier was the crown of idealist philosophy, is reified as a token of exchange.

Despite the novel's critique of the excessive capitalism of Ehrenthal and Itzig, *Soll und Haben* is first and foremost an apotheosis of commercial exchange. Mercantile capitalism alone produces wealth, builds character, and holds the nation-state together. Neither the unproductivity of aristocratic traditionalism nor the corrosive dynamic of financial speculation is an adequate substitute. This thematic concern of the fable corresponds to the microstructure of the realist text, in which concrete detail takes on the structure of commodity. Poetic realism may present itself as a transparent or a transfigurative representation; in fact, the categories of the representational process are borrowed from the organizing principle of bourgeois society. This principle of exchange also defines the relationship of the text to the reader. Just as Wohlfahrt is compelled to discern the connection between the particular good and the general laws of business, so too the realist text assumes a hermeneutically mature reader able to comprehend the status of the individual detail within the larger order. Despite the politically reprehensible aspects of Freytag's ideology, with its nationalism, anti-Semitism, and philistine mercantilism, this novel also suggests the possibility of liberal communicative exchange and the desirability of progress. The novel truncates these emancipatory elements, diluted remnants of the Enlightenment, by tying them explicitly to bourgeois class interests, the development of which in the unfolding of capitalism would only further blockade the same desirable communication and progress. Later realist authors are much less sanguine than Freytag. Their novels are marked either by a melancholy trivialization, in which hermeneutic complexity gives way to a cult of one-dimensional destiny, or by a frantic search for a wordly meaning that recedes perpetually beyond the grasp of the epistemological subject.

The genre of the Bildungsroman depends on an initial ego weakness of the central figure, the overcoming of which stakes out a space where the plot can unfold. While the development of the bourgeois personality is undeniably the ostensible concern of *Soll und Haben*, a different dynamic is simultaneously operative. The strengthening of Wohlfahrt's identity is asserted more convincingly than it is demonstrated. In many ways, he remains passive and weak, pushed back and forth between the Schröters and the Rothsattels. Both families use and exploit him, and he is always eager to participate in this instrumentalization of his own person. Freytag uses him as well, for in this purported novel of development, surprisingly little attention is devoted to the hero's inner growth. Rather, Wohlfahrt serves as a mechanical device to link the separate German bourgeois and Polish aristocratic accounts; that is, beneath the Bildungsroman artifice, Freytag hides the disjointed structure of a political novel.

Functionalized in this manner, Wohlfahrt ceases to represent a personality undergoing autonomous development and becomes instead himself an object of exchange. Freytag inserts him into the marketplace by wresting him violently out of his family setting. By the end of the first chapter the author has killed off both father and mother and sent Wohlfahrt on his merry way. The absence of mourning is reminiscent of the eagerness with which Bunyan's Christian severs his family ties, which Weber notes in discussing *Pilgrim's Progress*.[4] Cast into the world, Wohlfahrt finds a home in the Schröter household's commercial patriarchalism. By way of contrast, Itzig, who will not be integrated into a bourgeoisie where business acumen and family love are identical, does not experience a similar patriarchal guardianship. Whereas Wohlfahrt lives in his employer's house and dines at his table, Itzig is put into dingy lodgings at the inn in the slums.

The new residence in the realm of the ersatz father is the starting point for Wohlfahrt's substantive development. The newcomer quickly develops a diffuse sense of alienation and a general dissatisfaction with his apprentice status. This discomfort will eventually speed him on his path to maturity. Yet the initial description of Wohlfahrt's malaise displays crucial features of Freytag's capitalist ideology. The unequal distribution of property is accepted as natural, and the divison of labor, like all treatments of authentic labor, is suppressed. In addition, the realist author Freytag attributes Wohlfahrt's feelings of dissatisfaction to nefarious literary influences:

> For his sister the merchant kept a coach and horses, which he never used himself. For her sake he attended soirees and hosted some himself, to which Anton and his colleagues were not invited. The carriages rolled up to the door, uniformed servants flew up and down the stairs, and colorful shadows swayed before the bright windows of the front house, while Anton sat in his attic room and watched with longing the glamorous life to which he did not belong—with ardent longing, for our hero was barely nineteen years old and knew about the bejeweled sociability of elegant circles only from the deceptive descriptions in the books he had read. His reason certainly still told him that he did not belong in the front house—what would come of it if he and his dozen colleagues, whose backgrounds were so different, began to spread out at these parties? Yet what old man Reason says is not always respectfully accepted by young lady Desire, and sometimes Anton crept away from the window with a soft sigh and returned to his lamp and his books. He tried to forget the inviting music of the quadrille by listening to the roar of the lions or the croaking of the bullfrogs in some tropical land.(67)

Wohlfahrt understands that the difference in social status and wealth cannot be called into question by reason, but his rational faculty must compete with an emotional desire that has been nourished by a literature described in pejorative terms. The inability to comprehend reality because of reading experiences, which is reminiscent of *Madame Bovary*, is compounded by sexual (man/woman) and generational (old/young) codings. In Freytag's account, alienation emerges neither from the property differential nor from labor process but solely from the perceptual incompetence associated simultaneously with youth, femininity, emotion, and a romantic-adventurous literature. This constellation conforms to the overall ideological commitments of the realist program. At the same time, these inadequacies set the biographical narrative in motion by introducing an element of dissatisfaction into Wohlfahrt's life. They set the stage for his decision to abandon the bourgeoisie and enter the service of the aristocratic world, and for his subsequent return to the middle-class fold. In this cycle each transition is motivated more by the interests of the respective social grouping than by the logic of Wohlfahrt's own development. The commencement of his employment by the Rothsattels, for example, depends on their family requirements, not on the needs of his inner life or even of his career. His travels from Germany to Poland and back are motivated less by his own self-interest than by his dependence on shifting authority figures: Rothsattel, who needs him to manage the estate, and Schröter, who needs him in the firm. Despite his bourgeois self-understanding, Wohlfahrt always labors for others and has little control over his own fate. The political transition from liberalism to imperialism in *Soll und Haben* includes the psychological transition from autonomy to masochism.

Wohlfahrt does not undergo an autonomous personality development, as the Bildungsroman pattern would demand, but instead is instrumentalized as the object of exchange between two actors. The structure of this exchange process sheds light on the political significance of realism. At first, the cycle seems simple, moving from the patriarchal home—of the substitute father even more than of the natural father—to the dislocation of his travels in the East, and then to return. The cycle has both geographical and social implications, moving from Germany to Poland and back to Germany, and from the bourgeoisie to the aristocracy and back to the bourgeoisie. In terms of the character of the actual work, this movement is from commercial activity, which Freytag misunderstands as solely productive, to an adventurous independence in the service of the unproductive nobility, and then back to the safe world of business. This version of the cycle carries the novel's explicit message: the vindication of the concrete stability of commodity exchange over the fluid lability of the aristocratic milieu. The importance of Wohlfahrt's final return to the sphere of commodities gives away the fundamental homology between his own ostensible path and the cycle of simple exchange, in which a commodity is initially exchanged for money, which in turn is used to acquire a new commodity of equal value. In both the biographic and the economic processes, the middle phase implies the tension of instability and abstraction, which is only resolved in the reconciliation of return.[5]

Yet the equation does not work out that simply. The crucial second phase is the only one in which Wohlfahrt in fact performs physical labor. Furthermore, in the first and third phases Wohlfahrt is regularly and necessarily concerned with money, no matter how much Freytag would prefer to ascribe financial interests solely to Jews. Finally, the completion of the cycle does not return Wohlfahrt to the status quo ante. He is not only richer in experience but also richer monetarily once he becomes a partner in the Schröter firm. In other words, the initial removal from the bourgeois sphere is followed by an investment in concrete activity, from which Wohlfahrt emerges as the carrier of an increased value. After Schröter transfers control of Anton's labor power to the Rothsattels, the labor produces a surplus value, which in the course of the second exchange, leading to the third phase, is extracted as an incrementation of property. Wohlfahrt's biography thus passes through a process of commodification, decommodification, and the production of wealth. The bourgeois cycle of exchange is not an eternal return of the same but a never-ending search for profit, and the ponderous close of the novel, Wohlfahrt's entry into the firm, becomes less credible when one considers the practical consequences of his life as a merchant in a company with global imperialist interests.

This narrative of exchange, Wohlfahrt's oscillation between his different masters, explains the substantive character of his reified existence as well as the capitalist ideology of Freytag's text. More important, it illuminates the dynamic mechanism of the authentic realist novel, whereby meaning is exchanged between author and reader through the text. The point of this exchange in *Soll und Haben* is not the message of the content, the moral of the story. The point is rather the establishment of the exchange relationship itself as the hegemonic trope in capitalist society. On occasion Freytag expresses admiration for certain aristocratic qualities, and he criticizes capitalism, at least its excessive version associated with the Jewish figures. Yet underneath the historically specific class compromises explicitly thematized in *Soll und Haben*, the novel— prototypical of poetic realism—functions as a capitalist text because it establishes plausible relationships of liberal exchange. Author and reader confront each other on an equal footing as individual laissez-faire entrepreneurs. Meaning is passed back and forth between them through the sensuous textual details, the hallmark of realism, which constitute the commodified currency of the literary economy. The immanent crisis of that economy and of the surrounding society soon led to a radical transformation of literary detail, a profound doubt about the function of the text, and a desperate pessimism regarding change, exchange, and progress.

5

The Authority of Address: Adalbert Stifter

T he realist novel as exemplified by Freytag's *Soll und Haben* is the literary corollary to mid-nineteenth-century capitalism. This hypothetical linkage between communicative form and economic structure includes several aspects: the structural homology between realist detail and capitalist commodity and the dependence of the literary carrier of meaning on the dialectic of use value and exchange value; the presumption in realist literature of a legible reality, the world as text, which presents itself passively to the hermeneutic subject anxious to appropriate and instrumentalize nature; and the echo of the ideology of exchange as a structuring device for plot and for literary communication in the new hegemonic relations in exchange society. Poetic realism—not as the content of each and every one of its texts but as a specific mechanism of literary institutionalization—celebrates and reinforces the laws of laissez-faire economy, and Adalbert Stifter's *Der Nachsommer* (1857) presents the guilty conscience of that ideology.[1]

Although Stifter sets his novel in the Biedermeier world of the 1820s, he does not reminisce nostalgically of Metternich's ancien régime. He is not a reactionary, for despite his denunciation of the revolution of 1848, he does not give up his own prerevolutionary liberalism. Instead he transforms it into the utopia of *Der Nachsommer*, where his own never particularly radical version of the Austrian Enlightenment tradition, the Josephinist belief in progress and reason, could be played out far from the democratic zealots of Vienna. Shielded from the real social pressures of the 1850s, these elements of the bourgeois world-view could be pushed to an extreme, which allows Stifter to examine their consequences in vitro. *Soll und Haben* is concerned with the desideratum of mid-century capitalism; *Der Nachsommer* considers its potentialities, the probable results of bourgeois culture. As Uwe-Karsten Ketelsen remarks: *"Der Nachsommer* is not at all a dreamy pre-1848 idyll; it actually presumes the victory of the bourgeois revolution."[2] Stifter's utopia is simultaneously inspired by the moderate ideology of that revolution and by the desire to respond to its consequences. Unlike the sanguine Freytag, Stifter constructs a utopia on the basis of a pessimistic world-view. Both the immanent chaos of natural history and the destructive trajectory of modern society unleash a process that threatens the possibility of meaning and the functioning of exchange. The postliberal novel he constructs and the utopia it describes are intended as alternatives, bastions of order against an impending social and semiotic entropy.

The construction of order in *Der Nachsommer* is mediated through the experience of the first-person narrator, Heinrich Drendorf, the son of a Viennese merchant. Financially independent at the age of eighteen, he spends extended summers hiking in the mountains of Upper Austria. During one such journey, he seeks shelter from an impending storm in the rose-covered house at the Asperhof, the estate of Freiherr von Risach, whose name, like Heinrich's, is not disclosed until much later. The Asperhof is a model farm, and Risach a cultured gentleman who engages his young guest in lengthy discussions of art, nature, education, and society, which all testify to Stifter's urgent search for security.

Risach eventually recounts how he had once fallen in love with the daughter of a wealthy family, Mathilde Makloden. Their relationship had come to a premature end because of misunderstandings and untempered passion. After a successful career in government service, Risach settled at the Asperhof. Later, the widowed Mathilde acquired the Sternenhof estate nearby, where she resides with her children, Gustav and Nathalie. At the conclusion of the novel, Nathalie and Heinrich marry. The young couple's love complements the Indian summer of their elders.

Stifter constructed this image of idyllic harmony in opposition to the historic experience of extreme social unrest. Appalled by the progressive radicalization of the Viennese revolution, he echoed conservative interpretations of the French Revolution a half-century earlier by describing the uprising as a revolt of passion and unreason against sensible order. In a letter of September 4, 1859, he wrote to his publisher, Gustav Heckanst: "When unreason, hollow enthusiasm, then the meanness of emptiness and finally even crime spread and took possession of the world: my heart nearly literally broke."[3] The frantic affirmation of order in *Der Nachsommer* is ultimately a response to the disorders of the revolution. The novel, full of so many reformist plans, is not hostile to change in general but only to revolutionary change, associated solely with the ominously passionate figure of Roland, an artist patronized by Risach. Yet the same Roland whose revolutionism is rejected has the potential to become a great painter because of precisely that fiery temperament which otherwise leads him to idiosyncratic political positions. In any case, Roland, the only figure linked to radical politics, does not play a major role in the novel, and his political disqualification is not a crucial issue. Although *Der Nachsommer* insists on order and denounces revolution, the emphasis on order structures the bulk of the text, while the opposition to revolution is no more than a peripheral concern. This peripheralization is itself a political practice, but the novel cannot be explained away by the hypothesis of a simple causality between Stifter's antiradicalism and the aesthetic form of the work.

The concern with order in *Der Nachsommer* is in fact less a response to the upheaval of the revolution than an integral element of Stifter's own liberalism: the necessary corrective to his vision of human progress. For Stifter, civilization, never a stable structure, is perpetually involved in change. Risach turns down Heinrich's promise never to change anything at the Asperhof since, as he insists to his young guest, change is inevitable. What holds for the individual applies all the more to the species, for which change is also the rule. At stake, however, is the precise character of change. Stifter's liberal hopes are mixed with a profound despair concerning the character of social development. He watches a process of progress unfold that threatens the substance of culture and the possibility of meaning, and he constructs his rigorous schemes of order as a strategic effort to counteract the erosion caused by this historical decline initiated by bourgeois society.

This historical process is thematized most generally as cultural decline; castles have crumbled and churches fallen into disrepair because the authentic values of an earlier medieval age have dis-appeared. Art works of the distant past, deemed superior, are con-trasted with those of the present in order to trace a trajectory of decay. Thus Heinrich's father, the elder Drendorf, comments on his own preference for the painting of the sixteenth century: "It was a strong and powerful race that acted then. Then came a weakly and degenerate time. It was considered an improvement to make the forms richer and paler, to accentuate the color and deemphasize the shadow. The new age gradually came to disdain the old, which is why it let the latter decay. Indeed the coarseness accompanying this ignorance destroyed much, especially during wild and confusing periods" (394). The decay and even destruction of the art works of the former high civilization are indicative of a loss of a sense of quality that is integral to cultural production. The path of histori-cal progress since the Renaissance is marked by a loss of cultural meaning, which might, Drendorf explains, be overcome in the future in the context of profound changes. At this point Drendorf's utopian prediction is still less important than his fundamental denunciation of the present as a period in which cultural quality, unattainable by most, is preserved only in enclaves like Risach's Asperhof.

The various digressions on historical decline reiterate this pat-tern, but they remain abstract. Elsewhere Stifter suggests the specific causes of this process, foremost among which is the commodifica-tion of the object in capitalism, in regard to both its production and possession. While describing the history of his efforts to establish a shop to restore old furniture and works of art, Risach intimates how his own artisanal plans were instituted only against the class resistance of the workers:

Building this house was not at all the most difficult task; it was much more difficult to find the workers. I had several cabinet-makers and had to fire them. Gradually I learned myself, and then the obstinacy of willfulness and station blocked my way. In the end, I took people who were not car-penters in order to train them here first. Yet these too, like the earlier group, had a sin often found in the working classes and probably others as well, the sin of complacency or care-lessness which always says, "This way will do," and considers any further precautions unnecessary. (87)

Risach's complaint that good help is hard to find corresponds to the overall cultural criticism: in an age of declining values and aesthetic barbarism, the erosion of the work ethic contributes, at least from the standpoint of the entrepreneur, to the lowering of production standards. Only the force of the rational carrier of culture who, overriding all artisanal self-understanding of the craftsman, fully determines the labor process can reestablish standards of quality. The Josephinist Enlightenment does not supplant the entropy of decay, which proceeds always on its own accord, but merely holds it off temporarily: progress is an opportunity, but decline is fate. Thus, for all Risach's efforts to obscure the antagonism of class difference—his clothing is egalitarian, and he rejects the artificial codes of hierarchy that prevail elsewhere in Austrian society—these differences reappear with ineluctable necessity in the forced harmony of the Rosenhaus. The gardener's bucolic imbecility and Roland's smoldering passion both reflect their social inferiority vis-à-vis the *grand seigneur*. Risach is modest enough to dine with his more skilled laborers, a patronizing gesture symptomatic of Stifter's liberalism. Unfortunately, however, the economic plans to which he devotes so much attention make this sort of culinary camaraderie difficult. Because the workers rise so much earlier in the morning, they prefer to eat at hours different from those of their employer. Therefore Eustach, Risach's draftsman, "himself requested that he choose the time and nature of his meals" (593). The everyday ramifications of class structure, specifying who must work when and who need not, are thereby attributed to the free choice of the workers. Stifter proclaims the desideratum of a natural fraternity in which the artificiality of hierarchical etiquette has disappeared, but his own utopian schemes reproduce the signs of status in terms of the exigencies of the division of labor. No matter how nicely he treats his employees, Risach still occupies a privileged position from which he can observe the labor process as an aesthetic spectacle.

The class struggle behind the rose-covered facade is one aspect of the novel's seismographic registering of the process of capitalist expansion, which the book nevertheless excludes from explicit thematization. The mechanism of commodity production, with all its related labor conflicts, leads, furthermore, to a certain type of product: poorly made, poorly conceived, and lacking any essential tie to its purported purpose. This critique of modern commodities, which are contrasted with the superior artisanal products of medieval craftsmen, recurs throughout *Der Nachsommer* and represents an additional aspect of Stifter's indirect analysis of the consequences of the developing bourgeois society.

With this motif and, in particular, his prescription for a return to premodern productive modes, Stifter anticipates late nineteenth-century cultural critics like William Morris. In terms of mid-century realism, however, his critique of capitalism overlaps to a certain extent with Freytag's positions. Just as Freytag attacks excessive acquisitiveness in the ostentatiousness of Ehrenthal, Stifter contrasts the modesty and natural behavior of his central figures with the stilted artificiality of the surrounding society, often characterized by a showy elegance in dress. The difference between them lies in their estimation of the fundamental character of contemporary society. In the final analysis, Freytag's Ehrenthal and Itzig are deviant figures whose delinquent behavior separates them from the role of the paradigmatic bourgeois, Schröter. For Stifter, on the contrary, the privileged manner of behavior associated with Risach appears not at the center of real society but in a utopian exile defined precisely by Risach's rejection of the surrounding hegemonic culture. Freytag attacks unfettered acquisitiveness as a corrective to his otherwise unbroken defense of capitalism, while Stifter implicitly attacks capitalism as a senseless accumulation of wealth in the name of cultural stability and order.

Ehrenthal sports gaudy diamonds, while Risach devotes his resources to art collections: both figures extract a surplus from the money economy and devote it to nonproductive consumption linked to mechanisms of display. This theme of consumption indicates again the mid-century realist novel's intimate connection of capitalist expansion with the new surfeit of goods. In *Soll und Haben* this connection is made explicit, since Wohlfahrt must learn to overcome the superficial chaos of new wealth by recognizing the immanent laws of commodity exchange. In *Der Nachsommer* the historical experience of commodity accumulation—the new affluence and its threat to traditional cultural forms—is sublimated and transformed into the imagery of the plenitude of nature. Risach flaunts his roses just as, according to *Die Grenzboten*, the nouveau riche flaunts his bric-a-brac. Nature is not the source of his wealth; it is a metaphor for the historical form of amassed property. Standing in front of the myriad rosebuds on the verge of blossoming, Risach boasts to his young friend: "we are like the rich man who cannot count his treasures. In the spring one personally knows every blade of grass that is among the first to risk its way out from under the earth and one carefully follows its progress until there are so many that one no longer watches them and no longer recalls how strenuously they emerged and one makes hay out of them, forgetting that they had appeared so recently, acting instead as if they had always been there" (203). Unlike Freytag, whose capitalist optimism convinced him that the new wealth could be controlled by the laws of business, Stifter gives expression to a profound underlying pessimism. Accumulation, presented as a natural force, erodes the initial, intimate connection with the object. As commodities are amassed, they are less accessible to full subjective appropriation, and the burgeoning quantity consequently undermines the quality of possession, robbing the surrounding world of meaning. The wealth that cannot be counted cannot be comprehended either and confronts the individual as an absurd mass, a perpetually threatening disorder. This entropy of accumulation derives from the same suppressed capitalist dynamic which engendered the elements of class struggle and declining production quality. It is against this experience of chaos inherent in bourgeois society that Stifter invokes his strategems of order.

Two further social sources of the nascent semiotic crisis of capitalism are located in *Der Nachsommer*. Nineteenth-century capitalism still depended strongly on an ideology of individualism in order to emancipate society from the restrictive legacies of premodern institutions. While the realist theoreticians in *Die Grenzboten* took issue with subjectivity as a form of romantic escapism in the name of a worldly realism, Stifter denounces excessive subjectivity as the cause of chaotic desires which threaten social permanence. Thus, not only capitalism but the corollary form of an individuality removed from a universal order is perceived as a danger. Risach instructs Heinrich:

> Because men are always desiring and praising something, because they leap into one-sidedness in order to satisfy themselves, they make themselves unhappy. If we only maintained order in ourselves, then we would have much more pleasure with the things of this earth. However if there are excessive wishes and desires in us, then we constantly heed them and are no longer able to grasp the innocence of things outside

ourselves. Unfortunately we call them important when they are objects of our passion, and unimportant, when they have no relationship to us, although the reverse may often be the case. (189)

This explicit denunciation of anthropocentrism and the related cult of interiority, Stifter's version of the end of man, parallels the two major narrative lines of the novel: the interpolated account of Risach's failed passion for Mathilde and the lengthy chronicle of the successful love between Heinrich and Natalie. The former relationship presents a negative, the latter a positive formulation of the overt message: the necessity of reconciling individuality with an overarching order. For the neo-humanist Stifter, this sort of reconciliation is possible only if the individual does not engage in an excessive specialization but rather mirrors the external order in his own universal education. That cultural strategy presupposes, however, a society without the division of labor that Stifter is unable to exclude from his own utopia. For Stifter, specialization is not like the Lutheran acceptance of worldly station as an expression of brotherly love; it is only the concretization of a putative self-interest and is linked therefore to individuality, interiority, emotionalism, and all the potential disorder of romanticism. The cipher of this threat is Roland with his sullen anger and his subjectivist painting.

The antinomic complement of romantic individualism, the logic of bureaucratization, also contributes to the crisis of meaning to which Stifter responds with his constructions of order. Paradoxically, the bureaucracy can claim to be the ultimate guarantor of order both in the fictional time-frame of the Metternich era and in the post-1848 context in which *Der Nachsommer* was written. Nevertheless Risach's account of his own experiences in the civil service constitutes a cogent essayistic interlude in which Stifter analyzes the assumptions and cultural consequences of an expanding state administration, which is as much a part of the Josephinist heritage as the more specifically bourgeois aspects of capitalism and individualism.

Near the conclusion of the novel, Risach finally reveals his identity and his past. He had pursued a career in government during the Napoleonic wars and had been more than modestly successful. Yet despite the predictions of a grand career, his insistence on personal independence was incompatible with the exigencies of an administrative bureaucracy. He retired prematurely in order to devote himself to his various horticultural and antiquarian interests in the countryside. He explains his basic incongruity in the civil service in terms of the nature of his own personality:

> You see, I lack two things necessary to be a servant of the state: the skill to obey, which is a basic condition of any organization of persons and things, and the skill of productive integration in a whole in active pursuit of goals beyond the immediately visible, which is also a basic condition of any organization. I always wanted to change the principles and improve the foundations instead of doing my best under the circumstances; I wanted to set the goals myself and to do each task in the manner most appropriate to it without regard for the whole and without considering whether my action might cause a gap somewhere else with consequences perhaps worse than my immediate success. (610)

Stifter is here speaking as the pedagogic reformer and neohumanist liberal who came into conflict with conservative powers in the immobile governmental bureaucracy.[4] Yet it is also Risach who claims for himself the individual autonomy antithetical to the same sort of obedience that he demands of his own workers. The point is not Risach's escape from the bureaucratic Leviathan—he is after all Stifter's fictional cipher of a utopian exception—but rather the central role of bureaucratization itself in the crisis of modernity. Although bureaucracy demands obedience in the name of order, its substantive approach to any problem entails a radical dissection: the whole perpetually disappears from sight as it is divided up into an infinite number of disjointed parts, misperceived, like the atomistic individuals, as fundamentally separate units. Bureaucratic logic, therefore, erodes an initial totality and replaces it with a mosaic of fragments in which only the elite few are capable of recognizing patterns.

The crisis of meaning that ensues from this process of fragmentation is compounded by another of its features, the inability to recognize specific qualities. The state bureaucracy must function like a machine, and it therefore trains its agents in a manner which guarantees a smooth operation; neither individual growth nor individual characteristics can be taken into account. Here Stifter anticipates elements of the grand Weberian theme:

> The substance of this service must have a form that ensures that activities necessary to the state's goals continue without interruption or significant weakening when greater or lesser individual talents variously occupy the individual offices in

which they operate. I could use an example and say that the most excellent clock would be one which was so built that it would run correctly even if all its parts were changed, replacing the good ones with bad ones, and the bad ones with good. Yet such a clock is hardly possible. State service, however, must form itself in this manner or renounce the development in which it finds itself today. It is understandable that the order of state service must be strict and that it is not permissible for individuals to attempt to give the regulations a significance different from the prescribed one: indeed it is understandable that for the sake of the preservation of the whole, an individual task must be performed less well than it might when considered in isolation. (608)

Specificity and particularity disappear in the name of the untroubled functioning of the machine. Furthermore, this disappearance of individual qualities in the homogeneous temporality of the operation corresponds to a disappearance of quality as such. Because bureaucratization ignores quality, it necessarily privileges mediocrity, and those tasks that independent individuals would carry out well are carried out with only mechanical perfunctoriness by the bureaucrat. The order that this bureaucracy institutes is the emptiness of an entropy in which differences and complicated structures are simultaneously ignored and destroyed.

Stifter's analysis of bureaucracy continues implicitly in Risach's account of himself as the epitome of the nonbureaucratic personality. Just as Risach insists on bringing his own individual qualities into play in any activity, he shows particular interest in the individual attributes of every object before him. He directs his attention to concrete features, not generalizing formulas: "Since my childhood I have had a drive to produce things which are perceived with the senses. Mere connections and relationships as well as the deduction of concepts had little value for me, I could not place them in the assembly of matters in my mind." In contrast to Risach, with his sensuous perception and his "pleasure in everything produced that can be perceived," the bureaucracy is abstract and theoretical (611-612). Whereas Risach provides names and labels, the bureaucracy offers empty concepts. At this point, Stifter's antitheoretical stance converges with key positions of the contemporary realists. Their differences, however, are more interesting. Dissatisfied with the idealist predilections of Weimar classicism and the pre-1848 radicalism of the young German authors, the realists transpose the generalizing function of the Hegelian spirit into the matter of the real world. This secularization permits them to claim that meaning is immanent in their world, and their project is the celebration of that meaning and its worldliness. In contrast, the metaphysical presupposition of *Der Nachsommer* is the disappearance of meaning. Modernity in the guise of capitalism, subjectivism, and bureaucracy has initiated a crisis: order is threatened, quality disappears, and the objects of the world, which Stifter so copiously describes, constantly escape the grasp of the subject and fall into the senselessness of disorganized mass. Precisely this recognition of the crisis is the key to the pedantic descriptions: the literary strategems of order constitute a resistance to the imminent entropy—not a reproduction of the capitalist world but, extrapolating its consequences, an effort to deny it. Thus Stifter maintains, "In the work I have wanted to sketch a life deeper and richer than usually appears."[5]

The realist secularization of meaning generates a literary strategy in which detail can plausibly function as the carrier of sense in a perpetual and unregulated exchange between text and recipient. The world is filled with discrete units and specific traits, referring simultaneously to a fictional individuality and a general social type: Itzig's physiognomy, Ehrenthal's jewelry, the Rothsattel furniture, or Schröter's carriage. The realist novel presupposes and, by structuring the communicative relationship, produces the readership able to undertake the hermeneutic penetration of the aesthetic object, with only minimal help from the narrator. Because meaning is supposed to be stable and the readership capable of recognizing it, the process of reception needs no interventionist regulation, no direct commentary or disruptive interjection.

Stifter does not participate in this realist optimism regarding the accessibility of meaning or the fluidity of a laissez-faire exchange between text and reader unregulated by narrational effort. On the contrary, modernity plunges culture, the social structure of meaning, into a profound crisis. For Stifter, the act of writing as an act of address constitutes an effort to resist this crisis by imposing order where it is otherwise eroding. This problematic emerges most clearly as content in a series of key thematic concerns: the preservation of art works against decay, the conservation of the past in terms of local history, and the protection of domesticated nature against destruction. In an era of decline, order is not a replenishable natural resource, an attribute of being, but rather the achievement of those few who can resist the collapse: "They impede the pace of the calamity when the service of art begins to decay, and when the darkness should again become bright, they carry the torch forward" (616). The dictum indicates the strategic intent of Stifter's narrational politics.

In all three major domestic scenes in *Der Nachsommer*—the Asperhof, the Sternenhof, and the Drendorf home—an unbreachable order of things prevails. Nothing is ever out of place, and no object or room is ever used for a purpose other than its authentic one. Works of art and nature are catalogued, measured, and stored. Order must be preserved with such frantic rigor because disorder is always so close, as in the case of the thunderstorm that leads to the initial encounter between Heinrich and Risach.[6] The same principle of order determines Stifter's style, his treatment of details as well as the structure of his sentences. The novel includes lengthy descriptions of the rooms in the various houses and all their furnishings. An object once introduced into the course of the narrative is never forgotten, no matter how inconsequential it seems. Stifter makes a point of describing how the basket Risach holds while feeding the birds is given to a servant in order to return it to its place: "When we had arrived there, he gave that which I had initially thought to be the cover of a basket but which was a specially woven, very flat and long feeding basket to a maid to put in its place, and we went into the dining room" (74). The concern with the basket serves no other purpose than to demonstrate the rule of order, but Stifter is not yet done with it. After a tour of the house and its collections, Heinrich and Risach pass through the kitchen and the servants' quarters, where cleanliness, organization, and industry prevail. Pages later, the basket reappears in this idyll of diligence and order: "The long, fine basket, out of which my host had fed the birds, leaned in its own niche in the wall beside the door, which appeared to be its designated place" (100-101).

In addition to this precise description of minutiae, Stifter uses other devices to impose order on a linguistic world that he considers constantly threatened by fragmentation. These devices are all the more necessary since, unlike Freytag, Stifter does not presume a communicative exchange with a hermeneutically capable recipient. His voice is that of a didact, leaving nothing open to question and no places of indeterminacy in the text. Precision is underscored by his excessive predilection for demonstrative forms, such as "oneself." After the novel's first sentence introduces the father, and the second sentence his house, the third one cannot simply assume the location but must pinpoint it as "in the same house" (7). The desire for order also determines Stifter's use of punctuation, especially his omission of commas in serial listings: "Together with the father she took care of the fruit the flowers and the vegetables" (13). "There were drawings of altars choral balustrades chairs individual figures painted windows and other objects that are found in churches" (92). The separation that the commas would introduce among these discrete units is avoided, and the world takes on the appearance of a seamless totality. The same principle—establishment of unity through a punctuational device—explains the many series of sentences linked only by commas with no periodic breaks. Temporal and locational adverbs, such as "then" and "there," are used to link statements that might otherwise suggest separation (266). The length of a sentence is determined ultimately by the purported internal cohesiveness of an experience, no matter how many individual clauses must be strung together, as in the extended account of Heinrich's panoramic view from the mountaintop.

Stifter's exclusion of disruptive moments from the course of the text and his pedantic attention to the order of things and activities represent his literary response to the crisis of meaning inherent in *Der Nachsommer*. Not only is meaning as a resource in danger of exhaustion, but meaningful exchange with the reader can take place only with the aid of this absolutely closed speech. The epic breadth of Stifter's world is ultimately very narrow, since the horizons are always close. The report of Heinrich's journey after his engagement to Natalie is merely a list of the cities he visited, for to treat them concretely would have exploded the framework of the novel, and explosion is precisely what Stifter wants to avoid. He flees it, escaping into the safety of his periodic structures, just as Heinrich first enters Risach's home in order to avoid a summer storm that never happens.

Of the various sanctuaries of order in *Der Nachsommer*, the libraries are not the least important. As collections of books, they parallel the many other collections of gems, stones, paintings, prints, and roses. Yet in a novel in which the literary act is appropriated as a mechanism to establish order, these architectural centers of literature display a character that is particularly revealing in comparison to the model proposed in "Planning a Home Library" in *Die*

Grenzboten in 1852, five years before the publication of *Der Nachsommer*. There, literature represented a place of sociability and exchange, not only in the reception process between author and reader but also among the readers themselves. Literature was a crystallizing center of a public sphere. Stifter's libraries are very different: the display of books, which the realist critic expressly advocated, is now proscribed. Heinrich's father has placed green silk behind the window panes of his bookshelves: "because he could not stand it if the titles of the books, usually printed in golden letters on their backs, could be read through the glass by everyone, as if he wanted to show off the books he owned" (8). This explanation is not fully credible, since only a few lines later the reader is informed that Drendorf insisted that each room serve only one purpose; thus the library is only for private reading and not for public socializing, so the possibility of even being suspected of showing off his books could not arise.

A more likely interpretation of the curtains is suggested by the image itself and the piety with which the room is treated. The curtains before the texts lend them an aura of holiness and autonomous self-enclosure. Social concerns, indeed the human presence, are out of place in this literary world: "One was not allowed to disturb him there, and no one was permitted to walk through the library . . . He always replaced the book, in which he had read, in its exact spot in the shelf from which he had taken it, and if one went into the library just after he left it, one could see nothing at all which might indicate that someone had just been reading" (8). The library not only has nothing to do with public sociability but also has very little to do with reading at all; the traces of the reading subject are constantly obliterated. No longer a communicative process, literature transforms itself into the contemplative adulation of the cultural object: the cult of art.

The separation of reading and contemplation finds its architectural concretization in the more spacious premises of the Asperhof. Risach's library is ultimately only an extrapolation of the elder Drendorf's on the grander dimensions afforded by greater wealth, just as Risach functions as an ersatz father for Heinrich with more possessions, in a substitutional process indicative of the repressed project of capitalist accumulation. In both libraries the rule holds that every book must be returned immediately to its place. In addition to this external similarity, each room serves only a single purpose. Yet while Drendorf combines the storage of books and their reading, Risach provides two separate spaces: the library itself, where the books are enshrined, and a separate reading room. This expansion clarifies the sacred character of Stifter's concept of literature: "Because nothing happened in the library except that only the books were there, it became sanctified in a certain sense, the books took on an importance and dignity, the room is their temple, and no one works in a temple. This order is also an homage to the spirit which is preserved in so many ways in these printed and written papers and parchments" (193). The library is a sanctuary in which to keep the holy texts whose importance rests on their own autonomy and not on any interaction with their recipient. This denigration of the reception process is thematized repeatedly in the aesthetic excursions in *Der Nachsommer*, where the value of a work of art is treated as separate from and often antagonistic to the nature of its empirical reception.

The recognition that literature is presented not as a subjective experience but as the contemplative acceptance and adulation of hermetic works helps explain the peculiar path of Heinrich's own literary development. Initially he is simply unconcerned with literary matters. His first response to the collection of books at Asperhof is a disappointed, "It was almost only all poets," for whom he has little interest (49). In the course of his maturation process, however, he is gradually introduced to literature and learns to treasure the great authors of Stifter's neohumanist canon: Cervantes, Shakespeare, and above all Homer. Yet unlike Wilhelm Meister, the paradigmatic Bildungsroman hero with whom he begs to be compared, Heinrich merely meets this literature and loves it immediately. There are no interpretive difficulties, no fruitful misreadings, and no important literary critical passages associated with these textual encounters. The *King Lear* episode in *Der Nachsommer* has none of the weighty significance of the Hamlet problem for Goethe's novel. The canon is merely established as such, cultural material arbitrarily declared worthy of preservation. Therefore the literary gifts, a Goethe edition and the *Nibelungenlied*, are presented only as statements with no consequences for the subsequent development of the recipients or for the unfolding of the novel.

By separating the act of reading from social communication and transforming it into the adulation of a cult object beyond rational comprehension, Stifter sets up a social relation that can easily be transferred out of the world of letters and into a realm beyond social meaning: physical nature. Indeed the literary experiences in *Der Nachsommer* are rather scanty when compared with the abundant descriptions of nature, and this nature, which Stifter imbues with a sacred character, is presented as an object of scrutiny, a macrotext, deserving the same reverence accorded to the volumes in both the Drendorf and Risach libraries. Thus Heinrich reports:

> If any history is worthy of thought and research, it is the history of the earth, the most presentimental and appealing one that there is, a narrative in which humans are only a small insertion, and who knows how small, since they may be replaced by the histories of perhaps greater beings. The sources for the history of the earth are preserved deep inside it, as if in a document vault, sources set down perhaps in millions of documents, and it is only a matter of our learning how to read them without letting our eagerness and obstinacy falsify them. Who will ever have this history clear before his eyes? Will such a time come, or will only he know them fully who has known them from eternity? (291)

At first, Stifter here sets up a general category of history, large enough to encompass both natural history, especially the history of the earth—a particular interest of the dilettante geologist Heinrich—and human history. Yet human history quickly loses any particularity: not only is it merely a chapter of natural history, but it is an insignificant one. Stifter transforms the Enlightenment belief in progress into speculation on greater future beings, and the vision of that magnificent future induces a denigration of the present, the domain of social humanity. This implicit antihumanism of the neo-humanist converges with the antisubjectivism arising from both the contemporary critique of romanticism and Stifter's own distrust of capitalist individualism. The antisubjectivism in turn undergoes a misanthropic turn as an antianthropocentrism. Like the world of the realist Freytag, Stifter's world is constructed around a hidden text, but with a radically different intent. In Freytag's case, the textualized world becomes legible for the reader with the appropriate bourgeois vision, and the realist novel serves as the corollary primer. In Stifter's case, the text is as hidden as the books in Drendorf's library. The young geologist can collect minerals and measure lakes, just as Stifter does not expressly deny access to the "millions of documents" preserved in the inner sanctum of the earth. Yet the liberal

Stifter, while not prepared to embrace unquestioned agnosticism, is not hopeful. The likelihood of human penetration of the mysteries of the world is small, and that holy knowledge is in the end reserved for a divine and eternal intelligence.

The reader in Stifter's libraries approaches a book in the same manner as the geologist approaches the earth. Both textual encounters take place in an atmosphere of cult. In both cases the preserved texts are vessels of knowledge, the authenticity of which depends in no way on the recipient's ratiocinative appropriation. Knowledge has nothing to do with social intersubjectivity, but rather with the subordination of the passive subject—whose passivity already implies a loss of authentic subjectivity—to the petrified canon. The matter at hand, be it the book or the mountain, the universalized structures of order, has a distant past and a distant future, but the present is dehistoricized and thereby moved beyond the realm of rational comprehension. Given his fear of social instability, Stifter can defend order only as absolute and impervious to the sublunary tamperings by human agency.

This dehumanization of the world transformed into a cult object provoked a sharp attack from the critic Walter Benjamin in 1918. Conceding Stifter's success in his "wonderful descriptions of nature," Benjamin nevertheless complains that they are intimately linked to "false metaphysical basic convictions . . . about that which man needs in his relationship to nature." Stifter's refusal to differentiate between greatness and smallness, thematized in the foreword to his *Bunte Steine* (Stones of Many Colors, 1853), leads to a privileging of the small, not only of the apparently irrelevant detail in descriptive treatments of nature but also of those aspects of human life closest to nature. The exclusion of greatness, however, leads to a truncation and distortion of human life, robbed of its adult maturity whereby it endeavors to overcome the mere givenness of the natural order by establishing a human one: "He indeed lacks the sense for the elementary relations of man to the world in their purified justification; in other words, the sense for justice in the highest sense of the word." For Benjamin, Stifter's cult of nature leads to a denigration of the proper activity of society, the search for justice, which in this context is both eschatological and political. Justice demands human subjectivity and historical change, both of which Stifter denies. Instead of a reordering of social affairs as specifically human, "in Stifter there was a convulsive impulse to link the ethical world and destiny with nature in another way, which seemed simpler but was in truth subhumanly demonic and ghostly. In truth it is a clandestine bastardization."[7] The utopia in *Der Nachsommer* pretends to be based on nature-as-harmony but in fact depends on nature-as-order, as the immovable and demonic idol of veneration. This act of veneration, in which social obligations are forgotten and the individual bows without resistance to the sheer force of structured power, is universalized as acceptance without will and directed toward nature, culture, and order. The wordly text is fully comprehensible, but no longer in the realistic sense. Gone is the notion that there are fundamental laws which individuals might appropriate in order to act; gone is the assumption that a reciprocal exchange of meaning is possible in communication. In Stifter's frozen world, the sole meaning of the various semiotic systems—clothes and weather in addition to mountains and books—is the exigency of subordination and the command to submit.

In *Der Nachsommer*, the reception structures of nature and literature are homologous. In both types of reception a passivity vis-à-vis the auratic object displaces the hermeneutic maturity of the implied reader in earlier bourgeois literature. Despite this parallel, the novel turns its attention overwhelmingly, in terms of sheer length of description, toward nature rather than literature. With regard to his relative devaluation of cultural objects and the heightened significance of material objects specifically located outside the dimension of intellectual comprehension and social communication, *Der Nachsommer* occupies a crucial position in the historical trivialization of the German Bildungsroman. In the course of the nineteenth century the framing narrative of social integration, which remains the defining feature of the genre, grows increasingly external to the immanent process of the hero's development. For Wilhelm Meister, integration into human society depends on the maturity of the human personality, mediated by the experiential integration of largely aesthetic products of culture. A century later the hero of Gustav Frenssen's *Jörn Uhl* (1901) establishes himself solely on the basis of a technical education: the mastery of nature qualifies the individual to enter a society in which technical logic prevails over human concerns. *Der Nachsommer* stands halfway between the two, still committed to the project of culture but prepared to reduce that culture to the facticity of nature. The cipher of this naturalization of human culture is Risach's mechanism for predicting weather, the extension of his own powers of observation through the nerve systems of animals. This extreme sensitivity to the environment is no ecological utopia but a capitulation to the power of nature in the province of Circe. An autonomous realm of culture falls apart in two directions: the subjectivity of the individual is denounced, while cultural objects, beyond rational appropriation, are integrated into the same cultic contemplation directed at nature.

The priority of nature over literature indicates a similar priority of observation over communication. The aesthetic corollary is the novel's descriptive rather than teleological narrative structure; the perceptual corollary is the preference for visual over verbal elements. Repeatedly Stifter underscores the privileged character of optical perception. Risach himself invokes his preference for concrete designations rather than abstract concepts as an explanation for his inability to carry on in the bureaucracy. Early in the novel the still unnamed narrator underscores his own descriptive nature: "Father used to say that I had to become a describer of things, or an artist who makes objects out of materials...or at least a scholar who investigates the traits and composition of things" (25). This gift of description is transformed into Heinrich's extended efforts in drawing and painting. Not only does he insist that the picture reproduces the object with greater success than does verbal discourse, but he treats the pictorial image as in fact superior to the unmediated observation of the observed object itself:

> I read somewhere once that one comes to understand and to love objects more quickly and clearly if one sees drawings and paintings of them than if one sees them directly, because the limits of the drawing make everything smaller and more particular than in reality, where it may be large and mixed with other matters. In my case, this claim turned out to be valid. When I saw the architectural drawings in the rose-covered house, I understood the constructions more easily, judged them more easily, and I could not understand how I could have been less attentive in the past.(181)

A social order that maintains itself as spectacle rather than substance necessarily grants the image priority over the experience.[8]

The preference for the pictorial representation of an object refers not only, as in this case, to treatments of buildings and art objects but to those of nature as well. When Heinrich begins to paint, he recognizes the limits of his earlier verbal and cerebral appropriation of geological phenomena:

> The mountains stood before me in their beauty and fullness, as I had never seen them before. My research had always treated them as parts. Previously they had been merely objects; now they were images. One could sink oneself into the images because they had depth, and the objects were always spread out for contemplation. Just as in the past I had drawn objects of nature for scientific purposes... now I tried to draw and paint with oils on paper and canvas the full view, in which a series of figures, one behind another, floated in the scented air, in front of the heavens. (292-293)

Stifter has Heinrich present two alternative modes of perception. Painting is associated with an image that renders beauty or charm and totality, in contrast with drawing which is appropriate only for objects of scientific research and teleological instrumentalization. Painting guarantees depth and fullness; drawing is rigid and flat. The antinomies of picture and object and, implicitly, of art and scientific rationality reproduce the same problematic of nature and culture. Stifter denigrates conceptual, rational, and communicative modes in which individuals can function as autonomous beings in the social activity of culture. He privileges structures in which individuals sink away in contemplation, surrender their rational facilities, and subordinate themselves to the object of cultic perception in its brute naturalness. Whereas Freytag's realism culminates in imperialism, Stifter's descriptivism leads to an authoritarian positivism in which power structures are accepted because they are recognized and the subject, ashamed of his powerlessness, assists in his own eradication.

Stifter's cult of the visual is the apotheosis of the given. He does not suggest the presence of laws beneath the confusion of an empirical surface, since the surface, scrutinized by the seeing eye, is itself the law. The empirical is not subject to investigation or rational questioning, and there is no room for communication, for words, or for concepts. The only difference of opinion in the course of Heinrich's discourse, omitting Risach's autobiographical narrative of his past, is the initial debate over the weather. Otherwise every dialogue is marked by reciprocal agreement. Opinions are perhaps reinforced in this reciprocity, but neither of the interlocutors ever shows the need for reinforcement, and it is not negotiated through the subtle mechanisms of exchange that operated in

Schröter's office. No new word is ever spoken, and the exclusion of the catalyst of communicative language from the static world represents a corollary to the visual priority, as Benjamin recognizes: "He can work only on the basis of the visual...this basic characteristic is linked to his total lack of a sense of revelation, which must be *heard*, i.e. it lies in a metaphysical acoustic dimension. Futhermore, the basic feature of his writings can be explained along these lines: quiet. Quiet is namely the absence of any acoustic sensation."[9]

Stifter's nearly exclusive attention to the visually perceivable world doubtless emerges from the same historical experience implicit in the realists' credo, the rejection of theory and speculation in the wake of the defeat of the 1848 revolution. However, this intellectual historical parallel ignores the functioning mechanism of Stifter's text. The descriptivism fuels his frantic effort to hold onto the concrete details that he felt were rapidly escaping his grasp because of the entropy unleashed by capitalism. In addition, the priority of the image over the word guarantees the passive contemplation of an epic cosmos in which subjectivity withers because it is never called upon to speak. The close link between epic structure and submissive silence is at the center of the aesthetics of *Der Nachsommer*, and it anticipates similar problems of vision and spectacle inherent in the trivial realism of the commercial literature which the culture industry provided for the new mass reading public of the twentieth century.

In the explicit aesthetic discussions, Stifter advocates the classicist preferences of his own neo-humanism. Greek art, he argues, displays the moderation absent in modern pomp. Whereas Greek art presents order, wholeness, and truth, modern products are fragmented and false. Each type of art evokes a corresponding pattern of reception: "This is the high value of the artistic monuments of the ancient, serene Greek world...that they fill the spirit in their simplicity and purity...In contrast, in the modern world there is often a restless search for effect which cannot hold the soul but which is rejected by it as something untrue" (335-336). Classical art, whole in itself, engenders order and calm; the contradictions of modern art generate commotion and conflict. The ancients' privileged access to simplicity and purity further indicates a greater proximity to nature: "It seemed to me as if they were more natural true simple and great than the men of the modern world, as if the seriousness of their being and their respect for themselves disallowed the excesses that later ages considered attractive" (292). Not distorted by the subjective independence of modernity, a source of chaos and social entropy, Stifter's Greeks avoid conflict and uphold order because they are natural, which is to say, silent. Their universe is devoid of communication, since the linguistic autonomy of discursive subjects has not broken the social totality. The disparagement of communication and the cultic veneration of the given is appropriated by Risach himself, who collects books in languages he cannot read simply because of their greatness. Private reception is irrelevant, the symptom of an age of excessive individualism and unfettered subjectivity.

Stifter undertakes a strategic effort to counter that subjectivity by recasting the nineteenth century in the image of the epic totality of Homeric Greece. Conflict is excluded from the narrative by the avoidance of dissonant tones, with the exception of the deer-slaying and Roland's painting, and their significance is as peripheral to the central utopia as their peripheralization is characteristic. Conflict is further avoided by syntactic and punctuational devices: the omission of commas suggests an unbroken cosmos, and the order of the periodic structures echoes the regularity of the daily schedule at the Asperhof. Finally, Stifter explicitly imposes Greek forms onto contemporary experience during Heinrich's winter visit to Risach. The hero, immersed in the *Odyssey*, loses himself in contemplative reverie, "until Nausica finally stood at the pillars of the gate, simple and with profound emotion: then the smiling beautiful image of Natalie appeared to me; she was the Nausica of today, so true so simple not flaunting her emotions nor falsifying them. The two figures melted into each other" (600). Stifter had prepared the reader for this double exposure by earlier describing Natalie's physiognomy as similar to the image on one of Drendorf's Greek stones. She is the allegoric cipher for the renewal of epic totality implicit in the propagation of classical aesthetics. This aesthetic position, however, reveals Stifter's specific political project: it is not Attic democracy that he attempts to revive, but the total order and non-conflictuality characterizing his understanding of the Greeks. Silence prevails, and activity recedes in both the art work and the envisioned society. Stifter endeavors to impede the ubiquity of real conflict and change in society with his literary strategy and his message of silent submission. His writing is a mechanism to impose epic terms onto fragmented life by denying contradictions and by aestheticizing politics through the imitation of Homeric models.

This insistence on order and stability potentially conflicts with the dynamism of the capitalist market, the structures of which leave their imprint on the literature of the 1850s. The principle of exchange, for example, organizes the realism of *Soll und Haben* on several levels. The story itself celebrates commodity exchange as an economic mode objectively superior to its two rivals, aristocratic traditionalism and speculative finance capital. The subjective perspective of the novel of development follows the exchange of the hero between competing classes. Furthermore, the narrative address presupposes the possibility of a communicative exchange between text and reader. Reflecting the emerging class compromise between Germany's liberal bourgeoisie and the Prussian Junkers, the novel nevertheless restricts this principle of exchange, at least on the thematic level, by allowing for the possibility of a healthy aristocracy as the the carrier of agricultural development. As long as such a class relies on achievement rather than on inherited privilege, argues the merchant Schröter, it can legitimately sequester its estates from the dynamic of the market. An additional limitation on the exchange principle is implied in the denunciation of consistently capitalist behavior; when one of the colleagues in the Schröter firm praises the fully rational pursuit of individual profit in America, Wohlfahrt responds with praise for personal allegiances and local bonds, the laudable German irrationality of "caprice and fondness."[10] Freytag relativizes his otherwise unqualified enthusiasm for capitalism by insisting on the priority of personal loyalty and national interest, both transfigured as sentimental attachment.

Even more than Freytag, Stifter is worried by the process of destabilization unleashed by a market economy. Yet while the realist Freytag limits exchange by holding onto the heterogeneous correctives of nationalism and the aristocracy, Stifter transforms the character of exchange itself. In his hands exchange loses the excited dynamic that brought the world together in a "poesy of commodities" in the Schröter firm, and the individual actors in the exchange lose their atomistic mobility. Instead, exchange becomes a highly formalized ritual, pervaded by a rigorous conventionality and designed to ensure the stability of a society threatened by catastrophic disorder.

Compared with Freytag, Stifter is considerably more consistent in his liberalism. Nowhere does he display the obsequiousness toward aristocratic privilege that Freytag demonstrates both in his foreword to the novel and in his ultimate sympathy with the Rothsattel clan. The power Risach exercises over his laborers is derived not from a feudal title but from the capitalist division of labor. All of Stifter's central figures—Risach, Heinrich and his family, Mathilde and her children—are of bourgeois origin, and the sole authentic aristocrat, the baroness, who is in any case a minor character, functions less as an aristocrat than as the center of a bourgeois salon. This universalization of bourgeois class relations in the novel suggests the possibility of a universalization of bourgeois economic relations in the future: after the current period of transition, an age may well come, owing to the progress of science, which will even surpass antiquity because of its perpetual exchange of information and commodities: "What will it be like when we can send messages across the whole earth with the speed of lightning, when we ourselves will be able to reach the most diverse places on earth with alacrity in the shortest of times, and when, with the same speed, we will be able to transport great shipments? Will not the goods of the earth then become common property through the possibility of easy exchange, so that all will be available to all?" (459). Stifter's extrapolation of the market dynamic ends at a point where communism and consumerism converge: the total availability of goods is equated with their accessibility to the totality of society.

This process demands its own unrestricted unfolding, for all heterogeneous limits and correctives to the exchange principle must be eradicated. The world becomes fully an object of marketing only when a world market is established: "Today a small country city and its hinterland can close itself off with what it has, what it is and what it knows: soon it will no longer be so, it will be torn into the universal intercourse." Freytag's praise of the marketplace in muddy Polish villages shrinks into insignificance next to the exuberance of Stifter's capitalist cosmopolitanism. In Risach's utopia, horticulture and craftsmanship are not aspects of a pathetically privatistic Biedermeier retreat from the concerns of the world but are blueprints for a social organization designed to sweep across continents, intolerant of any resistance: "Owing to the demands of universal contact, it will then be necessary for even the least member of society to know more and to have greater abilities than today. Those states which, through the development of reason and culture, first acquire this knowledge will be foremost in wealth power and splendor and will even place the existence of the other states in question" (459).

Here the neohumanist facade is dropped and knowledge is overtly instrumentalized in international power struggles. Education does not complete the personality; it contributes to the strength of the nation destined to impose its will on weak, imbecilic rivals. Stifter, like the fascist modernist author Ernst Jünger after him, does not plead the case of any particular nation. Freytag comes to an explicitly imperialist position through a defense of the German national interest, whereas Stifter—again more consistent in drawing the consequences of the bourgeois organization of society—describes the emergence of imperialism from commodity exchange.

Despite this central theoretical defense of exchange as a force of progress, Stifter excludes explicit commodity exchange from the novel. Although the reader learns how committed Heinrich's father is to his business dealings, the substance of these dealings is never revealed. Whether he sells candles, carrots, or cocaine is not discussed, as if that detail, even for the descriptivist Stifter, were simply irrelevant. Similarly, although the exceptional agricultural productivity of the model estate keeps many dreary conversations going, the commercial transition from wheat-in-the-field to flour-at-the-market is nowhere described.

This apparent antipathy toward overt treatments of exchange is carried over into the narrative itself. For example, Risach explains that, although he once engaged in exchange in order to establish his collection of paintings, he no longer does so; that is, he has imposed an artificial barrier between the market and his own possession. Exchange may be able to modernize the world, and it can certainly lead to a bounteous accumulation. Nevertheless, Risach's complaint is evidence of Stifter's fundamental suspicion that exchange can also break bonds, erode order, and isolate the individual. The fear of losing familiar objects represents a subjective reflection of the crisis of meaning, in which the world ceases to surround the subject as a home, becoming instead alien territory, impenetrable to reason and hostile to sentiment. Stifter attempts to counteract this tendency with his detailed descriptivism and his Homeric aesthetics. He does so as well, however, by transforming the mechanism of exchange itself.

The original sin in *Der Nachsommer* is the premature exchange of declarations of love between Risach and Mathilde. This transgression caused each to lead an unhappy life and is ultimately atoned for only in the union of Heinrich and Natalie. This second exchange of vows is, in a sense, inevitable after Heinrich first enters Risach's home, since there is no subsequent break in the chain of visits that eventually leads to his marriage. Nevertheless the approach to Natalie is tediously slow and time-consuming, and this contrast with the excessive speed of the older couple provides the key to Stifter's treatment of the exchange problematic. Exchange must take place, even within the epic stability of his world, but its destructive potential is defused by the impeding mechanism of convention. Certain speech is disallowed for years in order to avoid the harm caused by a too rapidly achieved intimacy. This lesson of the errors of Risach and Mathilde is carried into the novel in another way: the names of the central figures are not disclosed, either to the reader or to each other, until very late in the course of the narrative. Because Risach does not introduce himself by name to Heinrich, Heinrich, out of politeness, refuses to inquire, just as he refuses to pose many questions that might be deemed out of place.

The postponement of the intimacy of an act of exchange guards against the isolation that might follow from a too egregious failure. After the turmoil of romanticism and revolution, Stifter endeavors to introduce conventional regulation into the social sphere. This regulation takes on the character of a ritual. Nowhere are the rules expressed, let alone scrutinized. They are nevertheless always implicit in the constantly recurring patterns of order. The ritual is most evident in the exchange of gifts: the specific character of the gift is often ignored, since the point is rather the establishment of a social bond through the act. Neither the object that changes hands nor the dynamic process of change is significant, but only the establishment of order through the ritualized intercourse. When Heinrich visits distant relatives with his father, he discovers that the latter has brought gifts for everyone, although he did not even know whom he would encounter. Regardless of the specificity of the recipients, the objects are distributed as signs of gratitude for hospitality. This distribution, Stifter emphasizes, does not take place prematurely: "He had not wanted to bring the gifts at his initial arrival, for, although the people were only the normal valley inhabitants of this region, he considered it impolite to arrive loaded with presents, as if he wanted to say to them: 'I think that this is what you consider important.' Now, however, he had become indebted to them and could demonstrate his gratitude for the hospitable reception" (560).

Like his son and Natalie but unlike Risach and Mathilde, Drendorf knows how to wait and how to respect the silently codified tropes of exchange. Excessive emotionality can only weaken the cohesiveness of social bonds, just as excessive individuality leads to isolation. The postponed exchange of names signals Stifter's radical denunciation of romantic subjectivism but also his answer to the social crisis. Convention, caution, and ritualized interaction may not guarantee eternal stability for the social order, but they can retard the processes which plunged the older generation into catastrophe. Heinrich shows how well he has learned the novel's lesson with his exclamation at his wedding: "Caution itself has led me to my fortune" (718).

All exchange processes depend on rules, but ritualized exchanges grant greater importance to those rules than to the substance of the specific process. In *Der Nachsommer* ritualization is evident in the lack of concern with the exchanged material, in contrast to the underscored importance of the hidden goal of the process itself. The prolonged omission of names in a novel in which so little takes place indirectly and inadvertently creates a minimal suspense. The resolution occurs, however, not with the revelation of the names, which is a rather parenthetical event, but with the recognition that respect for the rules of communicative exchange—Heinrich's not asking the question—was the point all along. Thus Risach assures Natalie of Heinrich's goodness with the explanation: "He was always very modest, never pushed or inquired in a forward manner, and will certainly become a gentle husband" (717).

This dynamic of ritualization determines not only the exchange of names and gifts but verbal exchange in general. Speech is robbed of its communicative substance, becoming instead a mechanism to establish formal social bonds. Heinrich first meets Risach when, believing a storm is imminent, he asks for shelter. Risach responds with the correct prediction that it will not rain but, more important, explicitly splits Heinrich's concern with the weather from the request for hospitality: "Those are actually two questions" (44). By discounting Heinrich's concrete fear but nevertheless inviting him in, Risach establishes a social bond which culminates, hundreds of pages later, with the marriage. In the interim, the nameless figures are designated repeatedly by reference to this initial social institution as guest and host. Verbal exchange therefore does not function at all as a medium to exchange particular information; the use value of communication is eclipsed by the exchange process itself, designed to hold society together. Language is not externally referential; it is not about anything. It is rather the droning ritual chant with which the community cements its internal cohesion. Risach admits at the end of the bonding process that he first enmeshed Heinrich in linguistic exchange not out of selfless altruism (for there was, after all, no threat from the weather) but out of selfish interest in Heinrich as a potential suitor for Natalie. Risach even boasts to her that it was he who found her a groom. Therefore Risach's extended discourse with Heinrich does not constitute instruction addressed to a Bildungsroman hero; it is rather a seduction, carried on by the ersatz father, acting for the unmarried daughter.

No difficulties trouble the speech in *Der Nachsommer*. No disputes or differences arise between speakers, and no speaker ever stumbles over his own words. No voice is ever raised; no whisper overheard. The long discussions, never interrupted, about flowers or art or history are devices to establish and display social stability. Benjamin identifies the perfunctory character of this talk: "Language, as spoken by Stifter's figures, is ostentatious. It is a display of feelings and thoughts in a deaf space. He absolutely lacks the capability of presenting any emotion the expression of which is what man primarily searches for in language."[11] This speech is neither communicative nor authentically expressive, and both failures indicate the absence of full personalities. Stifter's figures interact solely in terms of the instrumentality of social stability. The accounts of Heinrich's speech are concerned neither with his personal interiority nor with the communicative accumulation of information necessary for growth, but solely with the establishment of his position in the silent world of epic order. Instrumental bonds are cemented through the perpetual speech acts, and the character of these bonds allows no room for deviation or motion.

Not only does the ritualization of speech among Stifter's characters ensure the immobility of the utopian order, but the speech directed at the reader represents an attempt to impose that order on the real world. Freytag tries to establish an exchange between equals, between the omniscient narrator and the hermeneutically mature readership that he presumes. Stifter presents a first-person narration characterized by an authoritarian mode of address. The narrator establishes the bourgeois context in the first sentence of the novel—"My father was a businessman"—but he does not introduce himself nor give the reader any hint of his own particular perspective. There is no anticipation of later events, and no interpretive openings are made via commentary. Rather, the reader is expected to submit to the course of the narration with no hint as to its probable direction. The objectivity of the account suggests a speaker without subjectivity and induces a similarly structured interlocutor: the implied reader of *Der Nachsommer* is expected to ask as few questions as did Heinrich in his sojourn at Risach's estate.

This suppression of the recipient's curiosity and the denial of individual subjectivity in general constitute the political act of the novel. Stifter responds to the perceived social crisis with a linguistic machine designed to produce order by denying individuality. Since Heinrich is satisfied not to know the name of his host, the reader ought not to expect to learn about the narrator. The fact that meaning is denied, and critical inquiry blocked, explains the conservative reception of the novel in the twentieth century. The limitation of exchange by convention and its counterpart, the ritualization of speech, determine the inner workings of the novel and the structure of its reading as well. The silence imposed on the reader testifies to the immanent ossification of realist prose. Despite Risach's diatribe against bureaucratization, the disappearance of individuality and the restrictions on freedom of which he complains reappear in the reader invoked by Stifter's discourse. *Der Nachsommer* is remarkable because it indicates this immanent tendency toward the trivialization of capitalist culture as early as the 1850s. A half-century later, when this reified form of communication had become all but universal, the rebellion of modernist writing would attempt to establish a radically new literary community emancipated from the strictures of established discursive practices.

6

The Dissolution
of Meaning:
Theodor Fontane

*D*espite the general disapproval that met *Der Nachsommer* at its publication and during subsequent decades, Stifter's novel indicates a traumatic cultural experience, the importance of which became evident in literary works during the second half of the nineteenth century. The bourgeois organization of society which Freytag glorified in *Soll und Haben* unleashed a process that eroded the credibility of the realists' thesis of a fundamentally meaningful world. Capitalist expansion and the concomitant accumulation of commodities transformed the middle class's perception of possessions and therefore the status of the literary detail. The reduction of nature to an instrumentalized object of exploitation simultaneously eroded the stability of traditional social structures, leading to the emergence of class conflicts, which were soon thematized as the "social question." The developmental process of capitalism itself quickly climaxed in crises, like the crash of 1873, which made the tenuous character of exchange evident to all. Historically, literary realism represented the corollary to a viable ideology of laissez-faire liberalism as much as it represented the response to the defeat of 1848. The course of realism after the 1850s parallels the vicissitudes of liberalism; realism's internal aesthetic malaise mirrors the demise of liberalism and of its faith in meaning, language, and discursive exchange.

Stifter responded to the crisis of meaning with both thematic and formal strategems of order. He banished the impending chaos from his utopia where it lurked only on the fringes, in the slaughtered deer, Roland's painting, and Risach's reminiscence of his youthful passion. In *Der Nachsommer* the guilty conscience of realism's optimism, with a keen sense for the threat inherent in capitalist modernization, desperately searched for an alternative, but it faced the chaotic consequences only obliquely. Not until the relatively late novellistic oeuvre of Theodor Fontane does realist literature make explicit the confrontation of the desire for order and social disorganization, particularly in *Irrungen, Wirrungen*, the work with which the author established himself as an important writer of prose fiction and which long remained one of his most popular. The title itself proclaims the message which established contemporary society most feared: the proximity of confusion and the crisis of meaning. At stake in the novel is much more than the overt theme of the impossibility of a marriage between an aristocratic officer and a poor woman of the petty bourgeoisie. Instead, like Stifter but with different means, Fontane grapples with the limits of rational understanding in an increasingly confusing cultural world, the noncommunicative functions of speech, and the implausibility of the liberal pursuit of individual happiness, the disruptive subjectivity that Stifter so detested.

Fontane broke with the established literary language of reason and conceptual order as a result of his experiences in an increasingly industrialized press. The modernization of cultural life engendered the collapse of older stylistic and argumentative forms, as he notes in an 1859 study of English journalism: "The leading article in the 'Times' represents the complete victory of the feuilletonist style over the last remains of the style of the chancellery and other deformed sons and daughters of Latin classicism. Long periods are disdained; the sentences follow one another quickly like shots from a revolver." A new writing is freed from the obligation to present knowledge and further the rational comprehension of the world, as it shifts its attention to matters of external form: "Knowledge and details must not take up too much space. The well-written 'Times' article is an arabesque, wrapped gracefully around the question, an ornament, a witty illustration; it is coquettish and wants to please, captivate and conquer, but it does not at all intend to convince, once and for all."[1] The newspaper's renunciation of the comprehensive overview based on a conceptual appropriation of the social totality corresponds to the declining status of the writer as journalist and, more generally, to the crisis of meaning: to the advocates of bourgeois culture, the world, seeming to grow more and more absurd, refuses to submit to the rational ordering that structured the perspective of earlier generations of intellectuals.

Stifter reacted to this immanent disorder with the strategem of descriptivism; Fontane, as a theater critic, develops instead an ethos of observation: "I never go to the theater with prejudiced opinions. I simply wait for the effect."[2] The clear rejection of a normative stance should not be mistaken for a positivist credo. Where the positivists insisted on a disinterested and studious observation, Fontane claims for himself a certain priority as observer; that is, his writing is based on a decidedly subjectivist mode of perception. In the context of the apparent confusion of modern society, an objective order can no longer be maintained, but an observational realism carried out by a privileged subject can at least elaborate a fictional order vis-à-vis the chaos. Order becomes the product of a literary act which is not yet as proudly self-referential as later modern forms but nevertheless refers above all to the self of the writer as an asylum from the threatening social transformation.

The order which Freytag saw inscribed in the worldly text and which Stifter projected onto Risach's utopia becomes for Fontane the voluntaristic act of the literary subject. A crucial episode in his own development made clear that this new sort of ordering represented a response to an aspect of the social crisis which played an exponentially greater role for him than it did for earlier writers: the cultural consequences of the emergence of politicized masses during the Franco-Prussian war and in the Paris commune. The inherited order of bourgeois culture was now confronted with an unmistakable threat, and the ensuing shock could be traced through the subsequent shapes of textual production.

Fontane terminated his long association with the *Kreuzzeitung*, the journal of aristocratic conservatism, in April 1870, and two months later he reached an agreement with the liberal *Vossische Zeitung*, becoming its regular critic of performances at the Royal Theater. News of the outbreak of the war in July reached him in Warnemünde, where he was vacationing with his family, and although he shared the antipathy of the German public toward Napoleon III, he remained critical of the spreading chauvinistic mood. Nevertheless his initial contribution to the *Vossische Zeitung*, a review of *Wilhelm Tell* on August 17, notes the nationalist atmosphere with approval. Similarly the subsequent review of Paul Heyse's *Kolberg* (1868) links literature with the contemporary political context: "The piece was chosen with regard to the great hour that we are experiencing. And rightly so," because it gave expression to the "loyalty, appeal to the people and hatred for the neo-Frankish Caesarism" which the historical moment demanded.[3] Yet several months later, in a review of Karl Gutzkow's *The Prisoner of Metz* (1870) on January 10, 1871, Fontane put forward a very different position, criticizing the drama not simply in aesthetic terms but in political terms for the same nationalism he himself had previously praised.

In the interim, Fontane had traveled to the front and been captured by the French, who suspected him of espionage. The autobiographical account of the episode, *Kriegsgefangen* (Prisoner of War, 1871), sheds light on the development of Fontane's attitude toward the war, literary criticism, and the changing social status of literature in general. In addition to its informational function as reportage, the autobiography repeats the fundamental realist paradigm of initially romantic literary illusions giving way to a sober observation of real experience. This emphasis on factual authenticity generates the subtitle, *Erlebtes 1870* (Experiences 1870). More important, Fontane's first-person narrative underscores how a poetic dreamer is rudely awakened by the brute facts of war and politics. Thus, the initial arrest takes place precisely at the moment when Fontane claims to have lost himself in aesthetic contemplation of the birthplace of Joan of Arc, between the French and Prussian fronts: "I made my notes, then stepped back into the garden and sank once more into viewing this place, celebrated equally in history and poetry. Convolvulus wrapped around the trunks of some cypresses; beds of mignonette filled the air with scent, the nun spoke quiet, friendly words—all was poesy."[4] Suddenly reality intervenes with his arrest and eventually brings him to the military prison at Oléron on the Atlantic coast; Fontane learns the hard way that the world does not readily conform to aesthetic laws. In *Kriegsgefangen* Fontane records how the dimensions of art, illusion, and romanticism are supplanted by reality, politics, and observation in the context of both war and—a key theme throughout the memoir—incipient social revolution. Witnessing the entry of the masses into the social arena, in the form of both the army of the new German nation and the radical crowds of democratic France, Fontane constructs a narrative which describes how an initially aesthetic culture, the culture of the older elite, yields in the course of social modernization to a culture of political realism.

This supersession of traditional aesthetic categories by an observational realism structures Fontane's response to Gutzkow. *The Prisoner of Metz*, labeled "a patriotic comedy," takes place in a sixteenth-century world of military prowess and aristocratic adventure. The French Duke of Aumale, captured and held for ransom by the German Margrave Albrecht von Kulmbach, repeatedly attempts dishonorable escapes with the help of cunning priests and amorous intrigue. Gutzkow uses this constellation in order to present anti-French and anti-Catholic imagery to the patriotic public. Despite its intentional contemporary relevance, the play was not successful. Karl Frenzel, the theater critic of the *Nationalzeitung*, pointed to its formal failings: "Although one must recognize the felicitous idea, the inspiration of the poet to form into art a material that has so many natural ties to the present, the worrisome fullness of the matter appears as a serious weakness."[5] A representative of established literary criticism, Frenzel barely touches on the political significance of the work, directing attention instead to its structure. His complaint that the plot is overly complicated rests on a whole corpus of poetological expectations derived from idealist aesthetics and associating particular characteristics with the various genres: dramatic plots were expected to be simple.

Frenzel's response contrasts with Fontane's critique, in which the traditional aesthetic discourse becomes supplanted by an explicit thematization of the relevant political issues. Fontane does not bemoan the complexity of the material but rather its polemical intent: "merely a hardly amusing pasquinade of courtly life and princes, aristocrats and Catholic clergy."[6] Whatever conservative allegiances may have motivated the reaction against caricatured representations of aristocrats and priests, Fontane defends his stance by rejecting all representations that deviate significantly from empirical reality. Gutzkow's play is presented as an idealistic, aesthetic distortion, implicitly counterposed to a concrete, factual dimension of experience. Thus within the context of the war, to which the play clearly refers, Fontane takes issue with Gutzkow's nationalism not by adopting an alternative, Francophile partisanship but by rejecting parochial, nationalist imagery in general as a mode of knowledge fundamentally unrealistic and therefore inadequate to the situation at hand.

In privileging realist observation over aesthetic or ideological categories, Fontane engenders the feuilletonistic literary critical practice in which subjective experience typically outweighs any conceptual investigations of the literary work. In addition, this relationship between the two dimensions corresponds to the central issue of *Kriegsgefangen* in which Fontane describes an autobiographical passage from art to politics. This development is accelerated by the emergence of the masses, which calls into question the legitimacy of the abstract categories of elite culture. The same argumentative dynamic underlies Fontane's review of Gutzkow. He concludes by locating the art-politics polarity within the qualitatively new quantitative order of sociopolitical events: "The winter campaign of 1870-71 is not going very well for our stage. Nor will this *Prisoner of Metz* be able to change that. Lucky for us that we have one hundred thirty thousand others of the same title." The capitulation of the French forces at Metz in the previous October was indeed one of the important events of the war; the performance of Gutzkow's play was not. Its illegitimacy in the face of real events is underscored, again in numerical terms, in a later autobiographical statement: "Its anti-French character was perhaps all right, but it also turned out to be an anti-Catholic piece, and that above all. And a bigoted anti-Catholicism is something I have always found especially horrible. And at a time when a half-Catholic German army was in enemy territory, at such a time an anti-Catholic play or even just a major figure who presents Catholicism as obnoxious!"[7] Fontane returns to quantitative considerations again and again in order to criticize aspects of established culture that are not adequate responses to the contemporary reality. Be it the masses of French prisoners, the masses of German soldiers, or—as in *Kriegsgefangen*—the revolutionary masses in the year of the Paris commune, Fontane recognizes a new social presence, and although he profoundly fears it, he knows that the anachronistic categories of culture need to give way to realistic observation and empirical experience. In terms of literary criticism this meant a break with the inherited conceptualism and the introduction of new material and new perspectives into the institutionalized discourse.

This implicit shift in the character of the literary critical discourse did not go unnoticed. Though Gutzkow might have accepted a purely aesthetic critique of his play, he bitterly resented Fontane's approach, which broke all the established rules of discursive practice. Gutzkow complains to the editor of the *Vossische Zeitung:* "Let Herr Fontane find some small literary scandal sheet for this method of criticism! The *Vossische Zeitung* deserves a reviewer with objectivity, in control of his desires for personal revenge and subjective humor, who is capable of a measured and calm estimation of what is presented on the stage solely according to the rules of art."[8] Gutzkow's vision of a criticism based on impersonal objectivity and devoted solely to the categories of aesthetic philosophy draws on a central element of traditional bourgeois literary life: cultural communication as a rational legality. In contrast, Fontane's position is based on a partial internalization of the experience of social modernization which in 1870-71 crystallized around the war. Where others applaud the founding of the empire, Fontane, albeit obliquely, recognizes a new popular social force that induces profound changes in the structure of the public sphere. The bourgeois elite could no longer pose as a universal class, and its universalist categories increasingly lost their legitimacy.

While this episode explains how Fontane's rejection of an idealist elite culture and his turn to subjectivist criticism and realist literary strategies were mediated by the historical experience of the war and the commune, the transformation does not imply a partisan identification with the new popular concerns. In fact, Fontane feels uncomfortable with the mass nationalism in Germany, and *Kriegsgefangen* shows him to be even more terrified of the democratic crowds in France. During his imprisonment he insists on the class privilege of treatment "like a superior officer" and devotes considerable energy to maintaining a hierarchical superiority over his servant. The adjustments that he considers necessary in literary culture respond to the results of social modernization but express no solidarity with them. His subjectivism is counterposed to the apparent disorder of an objectivity rent by class struggle. Similarly Stifter, hostile to the revolution, recognized the changed character of society in the post-Metternich era and committed himself to the elaboration of necessarily new mechanisms of order. Fontane's characteristic treatment of the social crisis in *Irrungen, Wirrungen,* after his experiences both in revolutionary France and in the Germany of the late 1880s with its militant working-class movement, places considerably more emphasis on the "social question" than did *Der Nachsommer* and in a much more explicit manner.

As the novel opens, the aristocratic officer, Botho von Rienäcker, and the poor seamstress, Lene Nimptsch, are enjoying a love affair which, because of their class differences, comes quickly to an end. Botho appreciates the simple hospitality offered by Lene and her peers, but when his uncle demands that he marry a wealthy heiress in order to save the family name, he slowly realizes that he will have to accept duty and responsibility. Lene has long understood the impossibility of a permanent union, and her magnanimity and stoicism contrast with Botho's confusion. Each of them fully internalizes the immobile hierarchy of Wilhelmine society.

Yet more important than the novel's overt thematic concerns is its approach to the crisis with the late realist mechanisms of order. In its effort to maintain the detail as a carrier of meaning, its redefinition of the status of linguistic texts, and its response to the failure of exchange, *Irrungen, Wirrungen* still endeavors to uphold social order by the revivification of the bourgeois literary community. The shape of these strained efforts, however, testifies to the intensification of the real crisis underlying the demise of nineteenth-century literary communication.

The text of the novel structures a communicative interchange between author and recipient, mediated by the specific relationship between narrator and implied reader, and the basic currency of exchange is the detail. The changing character of the detail reveals the transformation of literary discourse, which in turn depends on contextual, extraliterary social forces. In the paradigmatic realism of Freytag, the treatment of the detail presupposed both the immanence of meaning in the world and the presence of a readership capable of a hermeneutic appropriation of the narration. The unproblematic optimism regarding literary communication contrasted sharply with Stifter's discourse, which reflected a profound sense of the fragility of meaning. The predicted unfolding of bourgeois society induced a commodification of the environment in which the perpetual exchange of possessions robbed them of their familiarity. With his tediously precise descriptivism, Stifter attempted to counteract this process of alienation, while his authoritarian mode of address to the reader, who was led step by step through the utopian lessons and denied the flexibility of interpretive subjectivity, corresponded to the author's doubts about the maturity of the contemporary public.

The treatment of details in *Irrungen, Wirrungen* diverges significantly from that in *Der Nachsommer*, reflecting the two authors' different characters, their alternative cultural traditions, and the thirty years that separated the publication of the two novels. Yet Fontane's address to the reader is structured by the same crisis of meaning, leading to homologous literary strategies. Realism continues to demand that the detail serve as a carrier of meaning, but the congruence of signifier and signified is no longer the easily accessible natural resource on which the literary communication of the 1850s was based. Because the late realist author must exert himself to ensure the presence of meaning in his descriptive accounts, Fontane is forced to devise new mechanisms, foremost among which is an excessive precision. For the same reason that Stifter relied on particular grammatical forms, such as the eternal return of the demonstrative pronoun, Fontane employs local color.

Biographical factors account in part for Fontane's attention to Berlin and the Prussian landscape and for his successful treatment of the material. Nevertheless his popularity outside of a geographically circumscribed region suggests that the appropriation of local color and other types of extraliterary referentiality responds to immanent problems in the novel and literary communication in general. He addresses this matter in an 1881 defense of the use of precise, nonliterary details in his theater criticism:

> Inspired by the desire to say something beyond the usual critical phrases in order to give the reader a concrete insight, I find myself forced again and again to recur to typical appearances of everyday life which can serve as objects for comparison. Only so, I claim, is the reader able to construct a minimally vivid picture concerning the performance of yesterday's Maid of Orleans or yesterday's Bolingbroke. "The Bolingbroke of Herr X. lacked a courtly demeanor," says absolutely nothing; if, however, after a lively and full experience, I write with conviction: "His Bolingbroke displayed the traits of a county councilor from New Pommerania" or "of a cavalry captain from the cuirassier regiment Emperor Nicholas of Russia;" then I present something concrete and with one stroke let the reader know how well or how poorly yesterday's guest presented Bolingbroke.[9]

The appropriation of nonliterary material, Fontane argues, ensures the viability of a literary communication that would otherwise collapse. Similarly, the use of local color in the novels guarantees their meaning; or, conversely, the meaningful character of the narration would dwindle if the readership were confronted with solely self-referential material without explicitly extra-aesthetic foundations.

The radicality of Fontane's regionalistic precision becomes evident when it is contrasted to the practice of Freytag and Stifter, neither of whom specified the name of the city in which their respective novels took place. Not the texts themselves but only external evidence indicated that Anton Wohlfahrt spent his time in Breslau and that Heinrich Drendorf grew up in Vienna. Both authors assumed that their accounts stood on their own without the need for additional cartographic support. Not so for Fontane, who is compelled to assume a readership familiar with a secondary text, the map of the capital city, or at least desirous of achieving that familiarity through reading the novel. Whereas Freytag could hold his readers' attention by describing questions of national, albeit class-specific, interest, Fontane offers the reader in Hamburg, Munich, and Stuttgart a voyeuristic view of life in the imperial center.

This local color increases the attractiveness of the text and binds the reader in an otherwise difficult exchange of meaning. It is no mere once-upon-a-time-in-Berlin tone that Fontane employs in *Irrungen, Wirrungen*, but a rigorous geographical precision.[10] This is announced in the opening phrase, "At the intersection of Kürfurstendamm and Kürfurstenstrasse, diagonally across from the 'Zoo' " (95). The title, which suggests the fundamental experience of confusion, contrasts markedly with this spatial specificity, but the contrast itself is based on a causal relationship: because of the confusion engendered by modernization, realism retreats into ever more precise details in order to hold onto an evanescent meaning. The author tries to maintain literary communication in the context of social destabilization by insisting at least on the stability of place: the novel is woven around a matrix of real locations—Stralau, Treptow, Rixdorf, Bellevuestrasse, Landgrafenstrasse—and even well-known stores and restaurants.

A related device—the bolstering of the structure of meaning via a surplus of parochial coloration—is evident in the use of dialect speech. In the untroubled communication of Stifter's epic world, language was never interrupted by the difficulties of verbal incompetency; all conversations proceeded through the crystalline transparency of mutual comprehensibility and unanimity. Freytag had his Jewish characters speak with an accent and with Yiddish syntactical structures in order to exclude them from the normative national language shared by all other groups: aristocrats, bourgeois, and laborers. Fontane reserves that normative speech for the aristocracy, for whom oral and written language are identical. The Viennese Jewess Salinger is condemned to speak with Fontane's intentionally humorous version of an Austrian accent, while the lower middle-class figures around Lene communicate with the regional linguistic forms of Berlin. The substance of their speech is thus no more important than its shape. By underscoring the class specificity of language, Fontane upholds the social order, the maintenance of which constitutes the novel's central thematic concern. Like the foregrounded local color, the precise marking of linguistic utterances serves to ensure the coherence of meaning in the novel via extraliterary references comprehensible to the contemporary readers.

The meaningful character of details finds additional support in a secondary overlay of symbolic referentiality. In the German tradition of poetic realism, the symbolic detail was designed to play an important role, especially at key points in the genre par excellence, the novella. In Fontane's novels, the surplus significance guaranteed to the detail by a symbolic dimension is spread so extensively throughout the work, often bordering on the heavy-handed, that it generates an additional, separate level of meaning. In the extreme, each place name points outside the novel to the map of Berlin and each detail, reverberating with symbolic fullness, points to a hidden allegory. The precise detail is not a simple carrier of an autonomous meaning but the locus of an intersection of various referential levels, including local color, symbol, and the overt narrative sequence.

These competing levels not only contribute to the interpretive richness of Fontane's texts but also indicate the crisis of literary communication. The detail is no longer adequate in itself but must rely on external supports, while at the same time signification is disintegrating into only contingently related dimensions. At the beginning of the novel, Fontane introduces the central scene both by placing it with excessive precision in the city, nearly with a street address, and by transforming it into an easily legible symbol:

> Diagonally across from the "Zoo," in the middle of the seventies, there was still a large nursery stretching across the field

with a small three-windowed house set back about a hundred feet in a garden. Despite its size and seclusion, it could be easily seen from the passing street. What otherwise belonged to the full picture of the nursery, indeed its main aspect, was hidden precisely by this little domicile, as if by a theatrical backdrop; only a little wooden tower painted red and green with a half-broken clockface beneath the steeple (not to mention a clock itself) could lead one to suspect that something else might be hidden behind this screen, and this suspicion was confirmed by swarms of pigeons that covered the tower now and then and more so by the occasional barking of a dog. (95)

Partially hidden from view, the building's tower lends it a fantastic quality, and the vestiges of a clock indicate that time has come to a stop. This fairy-tale code, which is modified by the temporal adverb "still," means that once upon a time, "in the middle of the seventies," stories like the following still took place, but in the modern metropolis they have come to an end. The unhappy conclusion of the realistically impossible liaison between Lene and Botho is thoroughly anticipated by the introductory detail.

In another example, after breaking with Botho, Lene develops a white streak in her hair, and Fontane makes sure that the reader does not miss its symbolic significance by having the gardener's wife, Frau Dörr, comment: "My God, Lene. And on the left. But sure...that's where it is...it has to be on the left" (187). Finally, during the lovers' excursion to the countryside, Lene winds a wreath of wild flowers for Botho. Again Fontane ostentatiously underscores the significance of the detail; the flowers are named not simply in order to provide the concrete detail preferred by realism or the regional coloration inherent in the local flora, but in order to link the incident to a symbolic dimension. Lene translates the botanical nomenclature into the aspects of the lovers' relationship and the allegorical subtext of the novel: love (or the impending separation of the two lovers), honor (particularly for the aristocrat Botho), damnation (for the Don Juan), and death (the inevitable termination of earthly happiness).

In all these examples—the timeless tower, the white streak of sorrow, and the encoded flowers—Fontane buttresses the meaning of each detail by embedding it in a symbolic context which accompanies the central narrative in a constant counterpoint reinforcing the primary level of signification. The realist text coheres as a unified narrative only by relying on auxiliary codes of order: the code of place names, the floral code, or even the code of alcohol. The poor drink a coarse cider or schnaps, while the wealthy imbibe elite vintages organized into ever finer gradations. In the course of a luncheon, for instance, the rising spirits of Botho's uncle are mirrored in the increasingly elegant wines: Chablis, then Cliquot, and finally, "Heidsieck. Best Class" (129).

The emergence of this secondary symbolic framework testifies to the continuing impact of the historical trauma. In the context of increasingly radical social conflicts, the hierarchical organization of society loses its appearance as a natural order. From the standpoint of established interests, social reality becomes a locus of confusion, and its details lose their immanent significance. Meaning can be guaranteed only by an external imposition of symbolic order, organizational forms grafted arbitrarily onto the perceived confusion. Such external codes of meaning do not merely embellish the central narrative but grant it a stability which, left on its own, it could not attain. Reality is no longer the carrier of an immanent meaning, and order becomes meaningful and orderly only because of the imposition of heterogeneous matrices.

Whereas the realism of the 1850s counterposed a "real reality" to the idealism and fantasy of romanticism and the *Vormärz*, the late realist Fontane sees an orderly reality to be possible only if held together by voluntarist subjectivity and imagination. Botho's friend Serge insists: "All pleasures are really imagination, and whoever has the best fantasy has the most pleasure. Only the unreal has value and is really the only reality" (131). The class character of the statement, which becomes evident when it is contrasted with Frau Dörr's denunciation of "imagining," illuminates the structure of Fontane's descriptive details. Bourgeois culture faces a social crisis that it understands to be unsolvable on its own legal-rational terms. Abandoning the principle of communicative exchange, the advocate of that culture, who can no longer maintain the objectivity of worldly meaning, retreats to a subjectively constituted reality of arbitrary codes, projected by fiat onto experience. Consequently details in Fontane's text cannot themselves be meaningful but, in addition to relying on both local color and symbolic embeddings, survive as meaningful in the consciousness of the various figures. The connotative implications of "cider" are less important than the meaning that Botho ascribes to it (109). The run-down state of the Dörr's real estate is less important than the figure's designation of it as a "castle" (96). The "real reality" of Schmidt and Freytag is no longer accessible to the participants in a later stage of bourgeois culture who, frightened by the consequences of modernization, hold their private realities together by their loyalty to perfunctory codes which preserve otherwise illegible details. Whereas *Soll und Haben* intended to teach the reader how to interpret the world as the locus of orderly meaning, *Irrungen, Wirrungen* demonstrates the contingency of meaning and the necessary arbitrariness of order.

Given the transformed character of the detail, linguistic communication becomes increasingly problematic. The opening paragraph of the novel concludes with an implied promise which sets up the discursive relationship between narrator and reader. The initial, precise location of the scene of action is followed by a repeated insistence on the imperceptibility of the place. Fontane draws attention to a spot which cannot be seen, just as if, in the center of a photograph of an interesting site, the back of a head were to block the intended view. The narrator simultaneously heightens and frustrates curiosity in the hidden material. The house "could be easily seen," but everything else "was hidden." In fact, the text provokes the reader "to suspect that something else might be hidden" and gratuitously provides additional evidence, the pigeons and the barking dog, that could confirm "this suspicion."

The narrator repeatedly emphasizes suspicion and thereby ascribes to the implied reader a particular interest, leading to a heightened suspense. An as yet inaccessible meaning is posited, and the reader's attention is captured in the hope that this deficit will be overcome. The process is doubled in the next sentence, where the narrator coquettishly grants the voyeuristic reader a peep but really shows nothing: "Where this dog really hid escaped perception, although the door on the left corner, which stood open from morning to night, offered a view of a small piece of the courtyard" (95). The withholding of meaning tantalizes the reader. The open door invites him to enter, but Fontane still places his interlocutor outside, lacking any insight. Although Fontane suggests that a hidden meaning is present, it is not yet apparent.

With the following and final sentence of this introductory paragraph, set off clearly from the rest of the text, the communicative structure of the novel and the raison d'être of the narrational speech are established: "Nothing at all seemed to be hidden on purpose, and yet anyone who walked along this way at the beginning of our story would have to be satisfied simply with the view of the three-windowed house and a few fruit trees in the front yard" (95). Despite the coy suggestion, the initial address to the reader has made such a lack of interest impossible. By implication, the narrator promises the reader that the narration itself will introduce him to the place behind the scenes and make the hidden meaning evident. Narrative speech presents itself as a process of information in which the reader will be granted the insight and knowledge initially denied him. It guarantees entry into a world that is otherwise meaningless or banal and in any case impenetrable.

Irrungen, Wirrungen may seem to keep this opening promise. The narrator leads the reader into the buildings, introduces him to the figures, and lets him follow their paths. But the narrative speech that promises a hidden meaning is concerned here with a place which no longer exists, as the novel's first sentence indicates. The central figures have moved away, and their social ties are broken. The narrator recounts events that have transpired in the past, the conclusion of which was always inevitable, and which have left no mark on the present. The sole documents of those events, Lene's letters, are destroyed in the course of the narration. The narrator has seduced the reader into paying attention to a sequence of events whose irrelevance to the presence is perpetually underscored. Realistic literary speech is about the search for meaning, but here, at least, meaning is ultimately absent. The initial contract between narrator and reader assumes a communicative rationality which, as the text demonstrates, has become anachronistic and lost its plausibility. Demonstrating this distortion of linguistic exchange is the ultimate substance of the novel. Keeping the narrational promise therefore means breaking it, just as the love story of the novel describes the impossibility of love, not just the difficulty of an unequal match.

In *Soll und Haben*, verbal communication, as in the business negotiations between Fink and Tinkeles in Schröter's office, demonstrated the possibility of exchange in the ideal speech situation of liberal capitalism. In *Der Nachsommer*, all discussions were monuments to unanimity and the absolute absence of discord. Fontane's conversations display the futility of speech. Although individual characters may make remarks that refer to the allegorical dimension, the immediate substance of their statements repeatedly underscores their own insignificance. In the first lengthy discourse, Frau Dörr comments extensively on Lene's affair with Botho, claiming expertise because of her own similar affair in the past. Yet she ends by disqualifying her remarks as soon as she sees the aristocratic suitor: "And there he goes. And there. . . really, I think he's turning around. No, no, he's only waving again, and she throws him a kiss. . .Yes, I believe it, I like it. . . No, mine wasn't like that" (97-98). In addition to the retraction of the parallel between the two upper-class lovers, which Frau Dörr had used to legitimate her speech, the internal contradictions and, especially, the alternation of affirmative and negative interjections ("Yes"/"No") render her lengthy exclamation absurd. The meaning she has put forward with characteristic vigor turns out to be nonexistent; the more her verbosity runs on, the more it dismantles itself.

The meaninglessness of speech, the implicit corollary to the confusion of the social order, constitutes the novel's basic concern. Neither authentic love nor authentic communication can take place between individuals. The irrelevance of speech is made painfully clear in the scene in the aristocratic club where, in an atmosphere of intense boredom, the members sit quietly, desperate for gossip but interested only in their card games. Their call for "news" permits the exposition of Botho's situation, but the communicative status quo is fundamentally trivial (130). Elsewhere Botho himself explains to his lower-class friends how conversation is ultimately about nothing and serves only to obscure the meaninglessness of perfunctory social encounters: "Actually it makes no difference what one talks about. If it's not morels then it's mushrooms, and if it's not the red Polish castle, then it's the little castle at Tegel or Saatwinkel or Valentinswerder. Or Italy or Paris or the streetcars or if the canal should be filled. It is all the same. You can say something about anything at all, if you like it or not. And 'yes' is just the same as 'no' " (112). Any topic is possible because no topic is significant, and the only reality counterposed to the self-referentiality of this speech is the club life of male camaraderie and gambling, thus no alternative at all: "And at the club it is really charming. No phrases, reality begins there. Just yesterday I won Pitt's Graditzer mares" (112).

Botho's suggestion that gambling is the alternative to empty speech is a sarcastic remark. In fact, his attraction to Lene, as he repeatedly explains, is owing to her nonparticipation in such point-

149

less word games, her lack of "phrases." She represents for him a natural world undistorted by social artifice where a serious and authentic communication might unfold. It is in such terms that he praises her to her later husband. More important, behind Botho's rejection of one linguistic sphere and his preference for another, a conflict between alternative modes of speech constitutes a key thematic concern of the novel. The conflict appears most clearly in the characterization of Käthe, whom Botho, because of financial concerns and class loyalty, was compelled to marry. She is "a bit silly," which alienates the more pensive Botho, to the chagrin of his comrades (194). Her speech can entertain, but it never compels her husband: "She was entertaining and could even occasionally have a bright idea, but even the best of what she said was superficial and playful, as if she lacked the ability to differentiate between important and unimportant things" (183). This inability constantly forces Botho to recall Lene and her "simplicity, truth and lack of phrases." Nevertheless Käthe is a social success, "because she practices the art of a pleasant saying-nothing with true mastery" (190). Her "enormous talent for talk" and her "loquacity" are universally applauded (192). Thus Fontane contrasts the two women as alternative modes of speech and communication: the promise of authentic but inaccessible interchange with Lene and the reality of mere entertainment with Käthe's verbose irrelevance.

The issue comes to a head, and Botho is forced to choose Käthe over Lene when Käthe, describing the entertaining Englishman, Mr. Armstrong, whom she had met at a spa, complains of Botho's boring seriousness: "Our men, including your friends, are always so terribly thorough. And you're the most thorough of all, and that makes me sad sometimes and sometimes impatient. And you have to promise me to be like Mr. Armstrong, a little more simple and try to chat harmlessly and a little more quickly and not always the same themes" (227). The antinomy of "small talk" and serious speech is now moved into an illuminating context. The fictional linkage of light conversation to an English realm and its alternative, the association of serious conversation with a specifically German language (Käthe speaks of "our men"), refers back to Fontane's own development as a writer, for it was precisely in the English press that he discovered the feuilleton style with its priority of entertainment, and he himself experienced the hostility that this new critical language met when he introduced it to Germany. "Small talk," a term that

Fontane appropriated to describe his own journalistic essays, was deemed insufficiently serious for the weighty matters of theater criticism. Despite the novel's apparent sympathy for Lene and its denigration of Käthe, Käthe is the one who in the end defends the communicative mode associated particularly with Fontane, and it is her speech that Botho is forced to adopt.

Irrungen, Wirrungen in no way suggests the substantial superiority of meaningless noncommunication devoid of genuine content and referential objectivity. "Small talk" is not laudable, but it is the sole sort of speech—or narration—with which bourgeois culture can hope to master the semiotic chaos engendered by capitalist modernization. It is only through such speech that meaning or the illusion of meaning in an otherwise meaningless world is possible. The novel is a text which engages the reader but leads nowhere; speech is an act of social bonding which has no point of reference outside itself. The crisis of meaning, which Stifter attempted to overcome with his precise descriptivism and the other strategems of order, leads Fontane, the late realist, to dissolve the world into conversation, and increasingly so in the novels after *Irrungen, Wirrungen*. On the one hand, this device recognizes the priority of subjective perceptions of meaning over all claims to an objective "real reality." On the other hand, it expresses the understanding that order and class privileges can only be upheld as a linguistic fabrication of arbitrary meanings. Despite this sense of resignation, which determines the entire structure of Fontane's narrative address and not merely its thematic concerns, something else begins to emerge in his late realist work: speech as the mechanism to institute a new community, which anticipates the fundamental practice of modernist texts.

Discussions of literature within literary texts, be it a matter of interpolated critical essays or episodes integrated into the plot, illuminate the intended status of the text at hand and therefore provide a guide to the reader. Similarly, treatments of exchange implicitly structure the character of the communicative encounter between author and recipient. The paean to the market principle in *Soll und Haben* corresponded to the realist's faith in the operation of a transparent literary communication. The ritualization of exchange in Stifter's work emerged from the loss of that faith, in the wake of which both an authoritarian narrator and a passive reader were instituted in a cult of the auratic object. Like Stifter three decades earlier, Fontane recognizes the highly dubious nature of exchange, both literary and economic. Yet instead of attempting to preserve exchange through the regulatory mechanism of conventions and external limitations, Fontane appropriates its impossibility as material for the novel. Thus the bourgeois realist novel, which took shape as the expression of a class ideology of change and exchange, history and progress, survives in its late phase as a demonstration of the failure of the traditional desiderata and the victory of an immutable order and ineluctable fate, the regular fare of the twentieth-century culture industry.

Reflecting a cultural disillusionment with the market principle and, by extension, with liberalism in general, *Irrungen, Wirrungen,* like *Der Nachsommer,* excludes explicit treatments of economic exchanges. Even Jews, who since *Soll und Haben* had been marked as the carriers of business life, are relegated to a peripheral status, as in the case of the merchant Goldstein, for whom Lene works on occasion, and Frau Salinger. Käthe's descriptions of Frau Salinger's wealth echo Freytag's attacks on nouveau-riche ostentation, but only weakly, since in the end precisely this wealth appears attractive to the aristocracy. Although the novel presents no examples of authentic market exchanges, there are several references to false exchange: commerce is not, as for Freytag, a force of civilization and progress, linking distant places together and conquering nature, but rather an incessant deception. The gardener Dörr sells transplanted geraniums, claiming that they were grown in their pots, and derives both additional profit and pleasure from the ruse: "They were all of the sort that had not been grown in their pot but had been transplanted, and with a particular satisfaction and joy he had them carried before him, laughing in advance over the 'Madams' who would come tomorrow, bargain off the usual five pennies, and nevertheless be cheated. He counted this among his greatest pleasures; indeed this was his main intellectual pastime. 'Oh that little scolding. . . If I could only hear it just once' " (100). Another discussion of the deception inherent in commercial exchanges refers to Dörr's habit of bundling the bad asparagus with the good. Instead of contributing to the internal cohesion of society, commercial interests undermine order by introducing distrust and manipulation into social relations. Amorous liaisons, as a mistress of one of Botho's friends tells Lene, should exclude the heart and be designed solely to guarantee the economic well-being of the mistress. Similarly Botho recognizes that his own doubts about the quality of a painting he possesses must not be articulated, lest he depreciate the value of his own property. Because market exchange, at the center of contemporary society, engenders deception, all social exchange takes on a deceptive or at least doubtful character: be it the exchange of love, the exchange of aesthetic judgment, or the exchange of speech, including the literary exchange between narrator and reader.

In *Irrungen, Wirrungen,* there is a further exchange that fails, the exchange between classes. Freytag traced Wohlfahrt's path as a token of exchange back and forth between the bourgeoisie and the aristocracy, and Stifter presented a universalized bourgeois identity, to which there was essentially no outside. Fontane, in contrast, not only excludes an authentic middle class but also, unlike his predecessors, insists on the unchallengeable perpetuity of class differences. The affective and sexual intimacy between Botho and Lene cannot weaken, let alone overcome, the basic separation dictated by the social order. The love they exchange is transitory, their desire to change class positions hopeless. Botho's obligations compel him to marry within the aristocracy from which Lene, the "little democrat," is absolutely excluded (117).

The separation of the lovers necessitated by the social hierarchy constitutes the key narrative concern of the novel, but it is accompanied by two other issues which magnify the problem of exchange. The first is the political discussion that elaborates the failed affair, most obviously through the explicit thematization of class differences. Fontane expands the political significance by means of the historical setting. Written during the conservative 1880s, the novel looks back on the liberal 1870s, specifically the period 1875-1878, the last years before the alliance between Bismarck and the liberals collapsed and, in the context of a protectionist economic policy and repressive socialist laws, the conservative Puttkamer era commenced.[11] Fontane's treatment of the 1870s in *Irrungen, Wirrungen* thus represents a reminiscence and examination of the liberalism that failed. Käthe's confessional tolerance toward Frau Salinger takes place before the anti-Semitic wave of the early 1880s, and thus in 1888 Fontane treats that aspect of liberalism with a touch of irony. The young officers are all supporters of Bismarck, and they all regard the conservative opposition of Botho's uncle, the traditionalist Junker, as a humorous curiosity.

It is the liberal faith in humanity and personal happiness, however, that Fontane scrutinizes most critically. The conservative uncle is denounced for his insistence on hierarchy and his lack of humanitarian ideals. Thus Botho says to his friend Wedell: "I am supposed to have breakfast with an old uncle of mine, new-march blood, comes from the region around Bentsch, Rentsch and Stentsch—all rhymes of Mensch, but of course without any significance or obligation" (123). The antihumanitarian uncle, advocate of the conservative opposition to the liberal Bismarck in the 1870s, is also the agent for crushing Botho's liberal, indeed "democratic," hope for personal happiness with Lene. Political ideology thereby converges with the contour of the plot: the necessity of Botho's break with Lene represents the fictional corollary to the demise of liberalism viewed from the conservative juncture of the 1880s.

The parallel trajectory between liberalism and liaison in *Irrungen, Wirrungen* means that Botho's renunciation of Lene and his marriage with Käthe have political reverberations beyond the overt class loyalty. Thus the shift from lower-class Lene to upperclass Käthe is accompanied by an indication of the weakening of Botho's liberal positions. Botho's location on the political spectrum is determined very early when, in his sole mention of figures at the imperial court, he indicates his proximity to the liberal Crown Prince and his wife. In response to Lene's query regarding the nicknames of his friends, Botho remarks: "Oh, those are just names we use and that we call each other when we get together. The Crown Prince, too, says Vicky when he talks about Victoria" (112). Apparently Botho has also on occasion been "together" with Crown Prince Friedrich. More important, his liberalism comes to the fore when he challenges, albeit timidly, his uncle's anti-Bismarckian tirade.

Three years later, however, in the midst of the political turn to conservatism, a small remark by Armstrong suggests a profound reordering of Botho's political commitments. Käthe recounts Armstrong's equation of stealing horses with stealing land in reference to his family's role in the border wars between England and Scotland. Though conquest of territory by military force appealed to the aristocratic code, horse theft did not, and Botho regards the remark as an effort to denounce territorial annexation by relegating it to the status of an unrespectable crime. Furthermore, he transfers Armstrong's remark from its British context into German politics, with some justification, since Armstrong's cousin served in the Badenian dragoons and the ruling English dynasty had historical ties with the throne of Hannover. Interrupting Käthe's anecdote, Botho labels Armstrong a "disguised Guelph," by which he suggests that the implied denunciation of territorial expansion referred to the Prussian annexation of Hannover in 1866 and therefore amounted to an attack on Bismarck's policy of national unification. The significance of the passage is heightened by a reference to the same political dispute in one of Käthe's earlier letters. Although Botho is here still putting forth a possibly liberal and decidedly Prussian standpoint, he continues modifying his initial rejection of Armstrong with the admission that the "disguised Guelph," the clandestine Hannoverian loyalist, may in fact be right: "But there is something to it" (227). Even this weak recognition of the legitimacy of the Hannoverian claims represents a radical revision of the erstwhile enthusiasm for Bismarck and is tantamount to a rapprochement, if not a total capitulation, to the traditionalist conservatism of his uncle. Thus, just as the overt narrative makes clear that the choice for Käthe over Lene represents the choice for order over happiness, the explicitly political narrative links this thematic message to the contemporary debates between the promoters of individual happiness and the defenders of the established order.[12]

In addition to treating the transformation of Botho's political identity as a reflection of his choice of an aristocratic marriage, the novel analyzes the immanent dialectic of liberalism as a renunciation of its own ideals in order to embrace authoritarian solutions. When Botho and his friend Wedell join the conservative uncle from the "region around Bentsch, Rentsch and Stentsch," they quickly become embroiled in a political dispute. The liberal officers do their best to avoid confronting the crusty Junker, but he does not permit them to escape easily. By insisting on an open exchange of opinions, the uncle, paradoxically, becomes the defender of debate and an advocate of free speech: "But the gentlemen are silent. I beg you, speak. Believe me, I can listen and tolerate other opinions; I am not like [Bismarck]; speak up, Herr von Wedell, speak up" (126). This exhortation to speech and mutual respect contrasts with the positions advocated by the younger generation. The liberal, pro-Bismarckian, and anti-conservative Wedell responds with a defense of naked power and a denigration of legality; his dictum that "power precedes right" echoes the antiparliamentary sentiment of Bismarck's own blood-and-iron realpolitik. Furthermore the liberal Wedell condones and implicitly supports Bismarck's persecution of Harry von Arnim, just as he and Botho, within the political matrix of the novel, must initially support the repressive campaign against the Hannoverian loyalists.

While Wedell transforms liberalism into an apology for intolerance and persecution, Botho denigrates free speech and discursive exchange, in contrast to his uncle's visceral attraction to vigorous debate. The Junker recognizes that his nephew's pallid response amounts to effete equivocation, where bona fide interlocution would be appropriate: "I don't understand you, Botho; what does this 'one can say' mean, if not 'one can also not say' " (125). It is thus the conservative who resents the liberal blurring of the difference between affirmative and negative statements. The traditionalist conservative looks for honest debate and authentic communication, while the liberal Botho again, as in the critique of speech he offers to Lene, mistrusts the very process of verbal exchange. On this point, too, *Irrungen, Wirrungen* echoes the experiences of German political culture: the liberal ideology of exchange and debate collapses in on itself and renounces these ideals just as it renounces the possibility of happiness.

The subordination to Bismarck profoundly changed the character of German liberalism. As early as the mid-1860s, in the wake of Bismarck's crucial victory over the Prussian parliament during the constitutional conflict, the historian Hermann Baumgarten— Weber's mentor—complained of liberalism's immanent weakness. At the end of the Bismarckian era, the liberal leader Ludwig Bamberger analyzed the authoritarian consequences of the Iron Chancellor's regime: "Now that all independent wishes and thoughts have been abolished, we are left with the dogma of subordination— not only to one particular figure but to any figure who becomes the leader; the state thereby acquires unlimited power over all areas of life down to its very roots."[13]

This description of an indiscriminate acceptance of authority as a crucial feature of contemporary political culture underscores the significance of Botho and Wedell as representatives of a liberalism quickly becoming authoritarian. Bamberger suggests, moreover, that the political obsequiousness bequeathed by Bismarck is particularly nefarious because it can be redirected toward any new leader; that is, the political leadership figures can be constantly changed, but the authoritarian structure will remain. This problem appears in

Irrungen, Wirrungen in the exchangeability of names; identity is never permanent, and integrity is consequently eroded.

In a society of epidemic ego weakness, despite the liberal ideology of individualism, personal nomenclature loses its substance. While the old-guard uncle insists on the importance of family names, the young generation toys with a multiplicity of self-designations. The officers have their club names; their courtesans similarly have their false labels, as deceptive as Dörr's claims for his flowers. Even place names, with which Fontane endeavors to ensure the stability of his descriptions, undergo the erosion induced by the crisis of meaning. Käthe tells her husband that Armstrong "was an officer in a Scottish regiment that was in Madras or Bombay or maybe Delhi. In the end it's all the same" (226). This same devaluation of specific nomenclature is repeated in Käthe's remark: "He says he goes fishing sometimes for fourteen days in Loch Ness or Loch Lochy, just think, there are such funny names in Scotland" (227). Similarly the novel concludes with a discussion of names treated as if they, and not the persons who carry them, were the vessels of authentic identity. Precisely this sort of confusion indicates the collapse of liberal individuality and with it the demise of the model of laissez-faire exchange, always a discursive encounter between stable actors with clearly delineated identities. Botho's inability to establish a permanent union, a perpetual exchange of love, with Lene reflects not only the immutability of the social order but, as a corollary, the weakness of liberal individuality in the process of dissolution.

The second issue that bolsters the separation of the two lovers is a sort of allegorical mirroring of the political material. Early references in the text to a "fairy-tale" atmosphere indicate the presence of an unrealistic, otherworldly, mythic framework (95,105). Just as the political analysis recounts the failure of liberal individuality, the allegory describes the futility of individual efforts to escape the spellbound order of an unchanging world. The conflict with the uncle is located at the center of the political analysis, while a contrast with Dörr provides access to the allegory. When Botho, addressing Dörr, indicates that he has brought a gift for Lene, the gardener's wife interrupts with her typical attack on her husband which nevertheless sets up an illuminating antinomic structure: "God, him. He'd never bring a gift. Dörr is only for hoarding and saving. Just like a gardener" (109). This sets up a significant duality between Botho, on the one hand, still caught in the liberal illusion of an individual pursuit of happiness, engaging in the liberal act of exchange, and Dörr, on the other hand, cast as the cipher of perpetual accumulation and non-discursive avarice, unconcerned with the other. Botho is ultimately linked to a privileged world of culture and literature, life and happiness, while Dörr, the gardener, digs in the earth which Botho later learns to associate with death. It is the unchanging world of nature and order that Botho attempts to escape, seen not only in the family obligations of the aristocracy but also in the death fixation of Lene's mother and the antisocial misanthropy of Dörr.

The choice between the two alternatives of individual happiness and collective death is concretized in the two major excursions Botho undertakes. His last hours of utopian happiness with Lene during their excursion to the countryside are linked explicitly to the motif of paradise. The allegorical connection continues when Botho refers to the potential arrival of other tourists as a "banishment from paradise" and then glosses his own remark as an instance of "speaking of the devil." Indeed, moments later the other guests do arrive and put an end to the short-lived happiness, for which Lene, in any case, had never fostered any illusions. The evening before, she preferred to row the boat called "Trout" because she considered the alternative, dubbed "Hope," inappropriate (145).

The banishment from paradise, the garden of joy, takes place in the center of the novel. Transitory happiness comes to an end. Later Botho sets out on a second excursion to the place of eternity, the Jakobi Cemetery, in order to lay a wreath on the grave of Lene's mother. Fontane overlays this journey to the kingdom of death with allegorical allusions: the heat is hellish, the coachman knows Botho's name, the salesgirl at the florist's is described as one of the Parcae, and Botho is caught behind a carriage full of broken glass: "And he looked at it unwillingly and his fingertips felt as if the splinters were cutting him" (211). The end of happiness, signified by the broken glass, and the perpetuity of death are further indicated by the specific character of the wreath which the deceased had wanted and which is discussed throughout the novel: the flowers are immortelles, which point to eternity. These flowers are also wound into the other wreath in the novel at the competing allegorical focal point, the wreath that Lene makes for Botho on their short trip to paradise.

Between paradise and hell, *Irrungen, Wirrungen* describes the fleeting character of human happiness and the ineluctable eternity of nature and death. Happiness is not, as the liberal Botho believes at first, the natural state of mankind, but only a chance moment that the individual can perhaps experience but never preserve. Hence the plenitude of references to games and gambling in the course of the narrative, culminating in the grotesque mixture of an amusement park with games of chance and funeral monuments for sale outside the cemetery: happiness is fortune and luck, but death is inevitable.

The allegorical corollary to the demise of liberalism, the insistence on the transitory character of life, leads finally to the curious aversion to sexuality. Frau Dörr's remarks always point toward Eros, and Lene always resists them. This is no prudishness on her part, for Botho is attracted precisely to her straightforward manner, unhampered by conventional coyness; it is rather an instinctive recognition of the tragic character of Eros. Sexuality in *Irrungen, Wirrungen* is always unproductive. Consider Frau Dörr's remark: "This is all swamp, even though it pretends to be a pasture. Just look at that pond where the stork is standing, looking over at us. Well, it's not me he's looking at. Wouldn't do him a bit of good. And that's just fine with me" (135). An idyllic field turns out to be a swamp, in an obvious reference to the deceptive character of the couple's joy. Furthermore, Lene is here being warned about a possible pregnancy. More important, Frau Dörr rejects the possibility that she herself might bear another child. It is not solely a matter of her age but also her clear antipathy toward reproduction. Fontane's allegory stretches sterility over all his figures with unrelenting rigor. Lene is adopted, the Dörr's son is imbecilic, and Botho and Käthe have no child. The continuity of the species is ensured only by nameless others, aristocratic lineages, and anonymous workers, but none of the novel's central nuclear families has progeny, and no individuals with individual names are born.

The absence of children in *Irrungen, Wirrungen* corresponds, in the allegorical dimension, to the political analysis of the disappearance of the individual and the end of the liberal society of exchange. The message of inevitability and renunciation, the objective meaninglessness of details, the impossibility of linguistic communication, and the failure of exchange constitute the self-destruction of the realist novel where the perpetuity of death and the immutability of monopoly capitalism converge. The genre that set out to institute a literary community of interpretation, comprehension, and discourse is transformed into a documentary demonstration of ineluctable order. The implied reader is no longer called upon to understand the world or the text, only to accept it; its laws, no longer products of intersubjective negotiation, are the untouchable dictates of an impenetrable universe. This metamorphosis sets the stage for a dual development. The explosion of modernist literary strategies around the turn of the century attempts to break the strictures of an increasingly coercive culture which is no longer willing to fulfill its earlier emancipatory programs. Modernist writing attacks the late forms of bourgeois culture in order to rescue its authentic content. Yet while modernist works try to break through this ossification of established literary discourse, hopelessly entangled in its own lust for confusion and helplessness, realism itself collapses into the trivial novels of inevitability and submission that characterize the culture industry of the twentieth century.

7

Culture Industry
and Reification:
Georg Hermann

*B*ourgeois literature, which begins with the pursuit of happiness, ends in a submissive acceptance of melancholy. It promises meaning to individuals but culminates in the absurd collectives from which no one escapes. The laws with which realism commenced organized the possibility of rational participation in social life, but within half a century this law underwent a process of reification, transformed from a mechanism of individual cognition into an incomprehensible destiny, leading to either tragic demise or insipid happy endings, but in either case to a state of perpetual immobility. This rigor mortis which besets the novel defines the process of trivialization: the genre no longer engages the reader in a dramatic exchange of meaning and presents instead a spectacle designed to render the reader passive and unquestioning in a literary iron cage. No matter how many elements of authentic culture the culture industry borrows, including realism and modernism which it imitates in its novels, it does not preserve or evoke the ratiocinative recipient capable of hermeneutic penetration of the text. That recipient is now replaced by the cultural consumer who, subordinated to the text, is taught subordination to the social order.[1]

The culture industry is the expression of postliberal capitalism in which the principles of meaning, communication, and exchange lose their vibrancy. A transformation of the realist categories of detail, text, and communication leads to a trivialized epigonic form of the novel. The term *trivial* is not used here in order to denounce the quality of the text itself, held up against some high cultural standard, but to indicate the changed character of the literary situation. In place of a discursive interchange between author and recipient, a one-dimensional spectacle imposes on the reader an unquestioning passivity, echoed thematically in the fixation on the force of destiny.

These features are evident not only in the widespread colportage literature of the late nineteenth century but even in the highly successful middle-brow entertainment literature of authors like Georg Hermann. Hermann's best-selling novel *Jettchen Gebert* (1906) and its sequel, *Henriette Jacoby* (1908), referred to together as *Jettchen Geberts Geschichte* (Jettchen Gebert's Story), were remarkably popular until 1933.[2] The economic status of the author is treated within the novel itself, where Fritz Kössling, a writer, grows painfully aware of the financial insecurity of the professional author when his own poverty prevents him from marrying the heroine, Jettchen, the niece of a wealthy merchant. The narrative of unsuccessful eroticism is therefore embedded in a milieu of unsuccessful culture, where writing is perpetually reified into constellations of sterility.

The novel is set in Berlin in 1839-1840 and portrays the everyday life of a middle-class Jewish family. Jettchen lives with her uncle Salomon, a businessman, and his wife, Riekchen. Salomon's brother, the aesthete Jason, introduces the gentile author Kössling into the Gebert household. Although Kössling and Jettchen fall in love, she is forced to marry her cousin Julius because the family objects both to Kössling's religion and to the economic limitations of his literary life. Only Jason, the black sheep of the Geberts, shows sympathy for Jettchen, and the two maintain a close intimacy. Yet Kössling's affection for Jettchen continues to grow, culminating in a circumscribed erotic encounter. The tension between financial exigencies and the world of culture, represented by Jason and Kössling, cannot be resolved. Jettchen's unhappy marriage and her emotional turmoil lead her finally to take her life.

Jettchen Geberts Geschichte not only thematizes the relationship between economics and cultural production but is itself a paradigm of the culture industry. After its publishing success, it became a hit on the stage, both as a drama and as an operetta.[3] The musical adaptation, *Wenn der weisse Flieder wieder blüht* (When the White Lilac Blooms Again), draws on the central floral imagery of the novel; that is, the exploitation of the text by the culture industry derives from its own immanent characteristics, above all in terms of its detail. No longer does the author presume an exchange of meaning with a competent readership, able to recognize the relationship between the particular object and its general significance. Instead the novel presents an unbroken spectacle of description. Entities are outlined or places are named not in order to address the recipient's interpretive facilities but solely to be objects of the silent voyeurship ascribed to the reader. Thus the many cultural references in the novel have little to do with the substance of the narrative itself. Instead they are present only to be recognized as references by the reader, whom the narrator manipulates with constant name-dropping: historical events, such as the anti-Napoleonic wars of liberation; literary names, such as Jean Paul, Heine, Novalis, and Eichendorff; or the many place names related to Berlin do not set the stage, as similar elements did in Fontane's reliance on an extraliterary code. They merely embellish the central story, producing further possibilities for nostalgic identification while remaining only ornamental, signifying nothing. They create the illusion of meaning in its absence, heightening the appearance of signification without adding to its substance. The plethora of details bedazzles the reader while never permitting extended interpretive activity.

The details in Hermann's texts neither direct attention to social problems—ugly matters are essentially excluded—nor provide precise observations of specific objects. Instead the world is dissolved into an impressionistic glow which concerns itself solely with objects of beauty. Hence the privileging of three pretty and pleasant domains: fashion, furnishings, and flowers. The heroine herself is introduced as a model, paraded before the reader as enchanted voyeur, to whom the narrator leaves no room for an alternative vision:

> Was that a lovely girl! How she dallied and walked in her little shoes with the wide buckles, all in silver gray, like a spring evening. The rows of flounce on her wide skirt slid, rustled and shook. The broad laces of her shoes really fluttered...broad silver gray silken laces with rosebuds on them; and the long fringes of the Indian scarf she wore around her full shoulders—pulled between the broad gigot sleeves—danced with every step. She wore pale blue gloves, held a fishnet in her hand, a parasol and a little bag decorated with a black lyre embroidered in black pearls, a sort of pompadour.(7)

The initial exclamation in the passage functions as a command directed at the reader to assume the appropriate voyeuristic stance, typical of the culture industry, and to share the same admiration the text dictates by fiat. The fragility of the verbs dally, flutter, and dance, as well as the delicacy of the colors and the lightness of the fabrics, combine to produce an image of charming prettiness which can attract the reader's gaze but disallows any interpretation: the spectacle of the text of the culture industry transforms the reader into spectator.[4]

In the essay "Gold and Silver Articles" in *Die Grenzboten*, jewelry was organized into a system of display in order to support social cohesion and communication. Similarly the detail in the realist text constituted the basic unit of currency in a communicative exchange between reader and text. Anticipating the collapse of such an exchange system, Stifter imposed secondary systems of order onto the details in his utopia, thereby transforming them into objects of antiquarian interest. When Risach led Drendorf from room to room at the utopian estate, Stifter thematized fetishism, which he presented as a stabilizing palliative vis-à-vis the immanent crisis of bourgeois society. Hermann no longer articulates this message, since commodity fetishism has become a thoroughly internalized mode of perception. Whereas Stifter once showed the reader the exemplary educational process of Heinrich's tour of the house, Hermann leads the reader directly, with no intermediate figure of distanciation, past the tasteful decors of the Gebert home. Hermann belabors these descriptions not in order to display meaning but rather, compensating for the social lack of meaning, to appease the reader with a spectacle of wealth and a furtive glimpse of the hegemonic taste of a former age:

> The room was big and bright and painted blue. Along the molding ran a broad, silver cornice. Dark oaken chairs with high-swung backs paraded by the wall in a long line. On the buffet, a smooth, brown sideboard, stood red crystal glasses that glistened and sent little rays of light to the ceiling. They reflected merrily in the polished reading lamp, the sort that is adjustable, and they surrounded the two porcelain candleticks, tall Doric pillars, with thick yellow candles, beside each of which was a set of silver ornamental shears.(30)

In passages such as this one, Hermann's interest in art history and his extended study of Biedermeier culture leave their mark. He describes furnishings and objects as if they were listed in an auction catalogue, coloring precision with subtle indications of high quality and taste. He imputes to the reader an attraction for the object under consideration which, no longer a carrier of meaning to be decoded by the recipient, becomes an object of desire, because of its grace, because of its association with wealth, and because of the age in which the objects are placed, toward which the reader is expected to adopt a nostalgic stance of reactionary yearning. The novel was originally planned with the title "Interiors of the Biedermeier Time," indicative of Hermann's descriptivism.[5] More important, however, than the historical account of pre-1848 Berlin is the character of the reader engendered by this sort of description, which privileges the values of taste, power, and the past to the disadvantage of the realist virtues of inquiry, comprehension, and communication.

The inanimate details of fashion and furnishing which capture the implied reader's attention and trap the fictional figures in a frozen world of immutable beauty depend on a fundamental principle that reaches its fullest expression in the descriptions of nature. The novel's beginning is set in the spring of 1839, and the events described take place in the course of the following year. Because Hermann follows his figures not only through Berlin, which allows him to employ local color as a device to maintain the reader's attention, but also to summer homes in the surrounding countryside of Charlottenburg and Potsdam, he can rely on extended descriptions of flowers to indicate the passing of seasons. His floral imagery has neither the utopian rationalism of Stifter's roses nor the allegorical significance of Fontane's wreaths. Instead the force of nature blossoms forth, overpowering the reader with its brilliance and, once again, fixing his gaze on the object of sheer beauty:

> And it came as it had to come: and the same wonders as in all the years before transpired in the same order. The lilac buds opened up and unfolded green leaves which were still all bright and loose like children tired out by their own growth; and down at the banks of the Königsgraben underneath some bushes in an off-the-way corner was a plot of violets, and the green of their leaves was filled through with blossoms. And whoever crossed the bridge would sniff and say very thoughtfully: there must be violets over there in the garden. The poplars threw down their catkins which grabbed onto the bushes or plopped into the water and were carried away, or they snaked along the pathways in front of your feet like brown, hairy caterpillars. Out of the brown elm blossoms came little balls of green fruit that covered the web of twigs so they looked

like pale green coral branches; and somewhere on a trellis pink peach blossoms fluttered open, while over a high, yellow wall a lonely white blossom branch stretched out its shimmering arm. (117)

Such accounts of the colors and odors of trees and blossoms recur throughout the novel and follow the natural changes in the course of the year. Their function is twofold. First, floral descriptions like those of Jettchen's clothing or the Geberts' living room provide the novel with additional sensuous beauty for the mesmerized reader to admire. Whereas Stifter's Risach used speech to seduce Heinrich, Hermann's narrator uses this imagery to ensnare the captivated recipient. The details themselves are meaningless, but they fill space with the illusory appearances of the same niceties that characterize all kitsch. The transformation of the descriptive detail into an element of empty spectacle was always an immanent possibility of realism, but it could only become the determining mechanism of culture-industry production once the discursive-communicative character of literature had lost its credibility.

The opening lines of the passage indicate the second function of the nature images, to provide a sense of necessity and destiny. Just as the changing of the seasons is inevitable, so is Jettchen's fate and, by extension, the reader's. Hermann intoxicates the reader with the sensuality of nature in order to leave him with the misery of decline and helplessness, the ultimate message of the novel. The metamorphosis of natural objects into social concerns parallels the subordination of human biography to purportedly natural laws, which is the reification of social life that Lukács addressed with his concept of a "second nature."[6] The lesson of unfreedom that the relationship between text and reader imparts is made explicit in the invocation of the inexorable course of nature as the paradigm of experience:

And it came as it had to come. Everything as it had to come. The lilac, the beautiful, young lilac with its blue blossoms, became brown and dry; instead of its golden banners the laburnum soon waved only brown pods in the wind, the pink hawthorne flowers sank away into the leaves, and instead little pieces of red coral that could be seen from afar gleamed forth from the cherry trees. . . And after the beautiful days of spring, when each seemed to surpass the other, there came days with wild winds that stripped the trees and splashing rain that tore the leaves from the branches and, as if it were a naughty little boy, smashed them on the ground. (351)

The imagery of nature transforms the cult of beauty and, more generally, the commodity fetishism that pervades the novel into a cult of doom and decline. Despite Hermann's own liberal sympathies, evident in the sparse references to pre-1848 politics, *Jettchen Geberts Geschichte* immanently reproduces the pessimism of the early twentieth-century right-wing ideology in Germany, expressing the inevitability of decay, the powerlessness of culture, and the ineluctability of an impending catastrophe which, despite its finality, glows with beauty and the desire for death. The principle that structures the floral accounts as much as the treatments of clothing and interiors establishes a fundamental interlocking between the intentionally beautiful detail and the consequently helpless reader, violated by the seductive address.

The realism of the mid-century places the individual as a sovereign in the material world, no longer retarded by the metaphysical idealism of romanticism and radicalism. In Freytag's *Soll und Haben* or, even more explicitly, in Gottfried Keller's *Grüner Heinrich*, with its Feuerbachian inspiration, realism set out to conquer nature with reason and human activity.[7] A half-century of capitalist modernization reversed the relationship, for Hermann's figures are trapped by putatively natural laws from which they cannot escape. It is not a rigid social convention which drives Jettchen to suicide but the force of destiny. The seduction that initiates the final sequence of events is hidden by a circumlocution familiar from the floral descriptions: "And it all came to pass, as it had to come to pass."[8] This phrase is not only the leitmotif of the novel, the advertising slogan of immutability, but also, in its culminating insertion, a pun on the sexual encounter—"to come," which the reader, transfixed as voyeur, is denied, in the final frustration, the ultimate broken promise. In a world populated by objects, described with loving care in order to excite the reader's desire, individuals become the passive objects of irresistible forces, and the reader becomes the manipulated victim of the text, which tantalizes only in order to overpower. This constellation of beauty and power, desire and denial, created by the culture industry, completes a politics of subordination, announced in the tendential masochism of Freytag's Wohlfahrt and the authoritarian address of Stifter's narrator, and finally producing the reader as the victim of a speech which disables by fascination.

The reification of the literary detail, its loss of communicative substance, corresponds to a broader reorganization of cultural material. Instead of a discursive exchange of meaning within the context of bourgeois sociability, culture becomes a pretense, the ideological concealment of the absence of meaning. Both the representations of culture within the novel and the novel itself as a cultural object designate reception processes as a passive consumption that precludes any active, rational appropriation of the aesthetic material.

After the long family dinner which takes up much of the first third of *Jettchen Gebert*, the guests gather in the living room and Uncle Jason entertains them with some popular and humorous songs. The outsider Kössling, however, whom Jason had invited, pays less attention to the music than to lovely Jettchen, who is playing the piano: "But Kössling had barely listened, while always and only watching Jettchen, who sat tall and proud in her chair, the head tilted slightly to the side, half dreaming, and her white hands quietly and effortlessly holding chords that somehow fit the music. She could not play well, he felt; but she had a sense of tone and rhythm because everything about her was music" (85). The conclusion of Kössling's reverie is indicative of the status of culture in Hermann's novel in general. Though he ascribes to her a profound, instinctual understanding of music, she in fact cannot play well at all. Kössling's perception of Jettchen, which the reader is commanded to accept, is designed to augment the impression of beauty: despite her meager talent, "everything about her was music." In addition to all her other attractive attributes—delicacy, grace, charm, beauty ad nauseam—she is also musical, or so the text promises the reader, although her musical ability is in fact minor. Hermann has no need for a practical demonstration of musical talent by Jettchen, but he feels compelled to label her musical in order to add to her yet one more positive quality and to integrate her into the nexus of cultural signs that runs through the novel. In this case culture is promised in the form of Jettchen's musicality, but simultaneously withheld. The novel presents an image of substantial culture to the reader, but the image quickly turns out to be an illusion. The novel of the culture industry, immanently aware of its own trivial character, attempts to drape itself with the emblemata of a high culture which, on closer examination, turns out to be only a facade.

The novel derives much of its suspense and identificational possibilities from a defense of culture located in a conflict between two families. The Geberts are a wealthy family of German-Jewish merchants, the carriers of taste, elegance, and culture. Two of the Gebert brothers—Salomon, Jettchen's uncle and guardian, and Ferdinand—

are married to sisters from the Jacoby clan, less wealthy but upwardly mobile eastern European Jews. Hermann locates their family home in Bentsch, pejoratively placing it, as in *Irrungen, Wirrungen*, in a primitive region deemed, from the standpoint of Berlin, nowhere. The Jacobys are tasteless and greedy; they lack elementary social grace; and, at least in the case of Julius, whom Jettchen is pressed to marry, they lack basic business integrity. To the extent that the Jacobys maintain traditional religious practices—their Uncle Naphtali observes the canonic dietary laws, in contrast to the Geberts who are fully secularized—Hermann subjects them to a bitter parody. In general, Hermann's reproduction of German Jewish hostility toward eastern European Jewry reflects the fundamental categories of German anti-Semitism. Like Freytag's Itzig, Hermann's Jacobys are crude, dishonest, and greedy, ciphers of an excessive capitalism of the nouveau riche, held in scorn by the refined representatives of old money.

The clash of the two families represents a battle between culture and mammon spread out over a geographic code. Salomon apologizes to Kössling for the low level of cultural discussion at the dinner, implying that in the past, before German culture was contaminated by oriental barbarism, the Gebert household had been a haven for the arts. Similarly when Jettchen brings her Jacoby Aunt Riekchen a volume from the library, the aunt complains in terms that are meant to deride her attraction for merely popular, entertainment literature: "Ivanhoe?!—I don't understand why Fernbach has such boring books nowadays. Can't you get anything by Siede or Rambach? I always like those books. Or maybe something by Sue! But always this Scott and Dickens and Dickens and Scott and Sternberg and Schopenhauer" (27). The Gebert heroine chooses Walter Scott, but her aunt, née Jacoby, prefers Eugene Sue or worse. Although Hermann uses this list of authors to add historical color to his narrative, he also once again makes his point regarding the different cultural levels. After the long dinner, Jason sings popular entertainment songs, despite Kössling's request for Schubert lieder, because, Hermann intimates, Jason knows that his Jacoby audience lacks the cultural competence to appreciate serious music. The designation of culture as an exclusively German province and the denigration of eastern Europeans as boorish indicate Hermann's proximity to the ideologies of twentieth-century German imperialism and especially the anti-Semitic component in the fascist redefinition of culture.

This politics converges with the expansionist implications of the cult of destiny.

Yet this dichotomous world, split between the cultured German bourgeoisie and the uncouth barbarians from the East, is itself part of the deception: for all of its melancholy bemoaning the decline of culture, the positive examples of culture are themselves empty, as illusory as Jettchen's musical talents. Jason and Jettchen, and Kössling as well, constantly drop literary names—Jean Paul, Heine, Eichendorff, Thackeray, Balzac—but nowhere does a substantial discussion of literary matters take place, just as, when opportunity presented itself, no expansion on the material of the *King Lear* performance took place in *Der Nachsommer*. In *Jettchen Geberts Geschichte* no critical discourse investigates texts of literary concerns, no debate follows a theater performance, no subjective reflection gives expression to an authentic personal experience of an aesthetic object. Culture is present only as possessions—material possessions or names that are bantered back and forth as material for conspicuous consumption. The war Hermann wages against the Jacobys in the name of culture is, like so many wars, an expression of an internal crisis and the effort to deflect any serious examination of it: as long as the Jacoby yokels are available as illiterate foils, the superficiality of the Geberts can continue unchallenged.

Hermann provides his reader with the opportunity to hold Riekchen in disdain because of her preference for low-brow entertainment literature: that is, the reader is granted an unearned sense of superiority toward a figure who lends herself well to denigration because of both her ethnic background and her sex. In Hermann's account, the dichotomy between high and low culture is projected not only onto the binary system of family and nation but also onto the difference of gender since, with few exceptions, the cultured Geberts are male, while the coarse Jacobys are primarily female. While Riekchen betrays her lack of literary taste by snubbing Walter Scott, her husband, Salomon, whom Hermann casts as the keeper of the family library, appears as the defender of culture. Yet Riekchen at least reads; the same cannot be said for Salomon, for whom books are primarily family possessions. When he finds Kössling admiring the collection, he remarks: " 'Well, Herr Doktor, I am sure you have more books. Look here, this copy of Mendelssohn belonged to my father.' He took a bright, little leather volume and opened it. 'Look here, how cleanly that is printed and how charming the illustration.

No one does work like that nowadays. And here is the first edition of *Nathan!* " A conversation ensues between Kössling and Gebert: " 'You have here the works of Saul Ascher, Herr Gebert!' 'I haven't read them—and I won't read them, but one has to support the man.' 'You think so!' That had slipped out of Kössling. 'Well, then maybe not,' Salomon replied, 'I promise you, Herr Doktor, I don't read him' " (74-75). This passage illustrates the literary culture to which Riekchen's triviality is counterposed. Yet in this demonstration of Gebert sophistication, no significant discursive exchange in fact takes place. Salomon expresses some opinions, but no authentic discussion with Kössling occurs. Moreover, those opinions are introduced by Hermann primarily in order to characterize Salomon with additional local color: the German-Jewish merchant cherishes his Mendelssohn and his Lessing. He recognizes the value of the cultural tradition, but this recognition remains external to literary matters.

Mendelssohn and Lessing are revered as names, while the substance of their works is ignored. Salomon preserves culture like a marmorated heirloom: he possesses the volumes but does not open them. At best he assumes a philanthropic stance toward literary production, as is made clear in the exchange regarding Ascher. Just as Hermann himself introduces details into the novel as signs of meaning otherwise absent, the Gebert library flaunts a cultural identity which has lost its vitality, perpetuated not as a living activity but, first, as a monument to the past and, second, as an ideological defense of privilege threatened by new social groups. Without his unopened volumes, the cultured bourgeois would be no different from his competitor. Unlike the Jacobys, the Geberts have a right to their wealth because they possess a first edition of Lessing's *Nathan der Weise* (*Nathan the Wise*, 1779): literature does, after all, have a social function.

Jason, the aestheticist black sheep of the Gebert family, also has a library to which Kössling is introduced. As expected, Jason is considerably more sophisticated than his businessman brother, and his literary taste is correspondingly more refined. Although again the book appears primarily as a possession, now this fetishism is not ascribed to one of the fictional figures but instead emerges directly from the narration, as Hermann runs his fingers endearingly over the collected volumes: "Beside the coarse cardboard volumes stood the delicate little leather-bound volumes, and a final glow of the reddish sun ran across the golden letters on the green labels and sparkled

in the little golden flowers that decorated the covers." Whereas
Salomon's books expressed family, ethnic, and perhaps political identity, Jason's collection is symptomatic of the book lover; whereas the
novel is placed in 1839-1840, the relationship to the books described
here corresponds to the bibliophilism of the early twentieth
century—not yet the culture of aestheticism but certainly the aestheticization of culture, an object of beauty instead of communicative discourse. Literature, removed from forms of lived sociability
in which authentic discussion occurs, becomes increasingly a matter
of ownership and possession. The book as property implies the collector as property owner, isolated from social exchange. Thus the
pre-1848 Jason gives expression to a fin-de-siècle resignation which
he sees inextricably tied to the literary experience, as he explains
to his guest: "Here I have learned to be modest, here I have entombed
many a hope, and for many hopes that were smashed in the outside
world, I have here found a substitute. A real book-lover—Herr Doktor,
remember that!—can have neither wife nor child nor family. This
here must be all he has" (327). Presented as the alternative to the
active life, Jason's library provides compensation for the worldly
experience of disappointment which Hermann describes as omnipresent and perpetual. It is the locus of neither discursive exchange
nor cultural education but only asylum and escape; it is the iron
cage in which culture is imprisoned and sequestered from society.

In the culture industry the reification of the text arrives at this
provisional conclusion. The mid-nineteenth-century realists envisioned the library as a potential center of sociability, where exchange
and display could coincide in a domestic public sphere. Stifter radically limited the exchange and transformed the principle of display
into cultic preservation, linked, however, to an educational program
still indebted to traditional liberal notions of growth, progress, and
individuality, no matter how truncated. Fontane made the class character of textual competence explicit: Lene could not spell and, despite
Botho's protestations, she knew that her lack of equal education
would make a marriage impossible. Yet Fontane did not examine the
consequences for culture implied by its integration into a class
system. In Hermann's novel culture becomes property, displayed in
order to announce status, and thereby robbed of its own essential
character. The library is not the setting for literary conversation, as
the realists prescribed, nor is literature organized into a program of
education and individual growth. The literary text, which Jason

defines as the guarantor of consoling illusions compensating for the bitter disillusionment of the practical world, is itself an illusion, since it is present only in name, not in substance. The culture industry holds out the promise of a culture in fact absent because culture has been transformed into property.

Thomas Mann's Leverkühn would later dream of a society that would not possess culture but would truly be culture? Here, however, culture as commodity prevails, and in order to preserve that system of property, the cultural deception is necessary; the reader of the trivial Hermann can look down on Riekchen's trivial taste and identify with the sophisticated Geberts, whose sophistication is perfunctory precisely so as to permit the identification by an unsophisticated public. The reader is granted the optical illusion of entry into the world of literature, the same voyeuristic peek into the private lives of the wealthy that constitutes the novel's main libidinal attraction. Yet it is a glimpse from the outside, against a shuttered window. The authentic culture promised to the recipient is never delivered, though the promise itself continues to fascinate, for the basic motor of the culture industry is the constantly renewed credibility of illusions, despite the real disillusionment of history.

The illusion of culture, the representation of a literary and aesthetic understanding that is demonstrably absent, corresponds to a culture of illusions that derives from the principle of market exchange, the structural corollary to realism. Capitalist mechanisms, which fascinated the realist authors, transform the original paradigm of a display of significant details into a universalized display without significance, a spectacle without meaning. Both the descriptions of bourgeois behavior and the structure of literary reception are thoroughly revised.

Realism traces a world of commodities, and action within it is commodity exchange. Hence the preferential treatment accorded to figures from the mercantile bourgeoisie. *Soll und Haben* described the developmental path of the exemplary individual into the hegemonic world of business, and *Der Nachsommer* announced its own class-orientation in the first sentence, one of its most important: "My father was a businessman." *Jettchen Geberts Geschichte*, a half-century later, still draws on this tradition. The Geberts are German-Jewish merchants, while Jettchen's groom, Julius Jacoby, intends to commence a career of business, in obvious imitation of Freytag's Veitel Itzig. A bourgeois ethic pervades the Gebert clan, stressing the importance of work and accumulation, of civic consciousness, and of the emphatic separation of public and private spheres.

Despite the explicit bourgeois coloration of the narrative, the specifically bourgeois sphere of commodity exchange is excluded. The operation of business is assumed, but it is never described. Nowhere is it accorded the same centrality ascribed to it in *Soll und Haben*. In part this is a consequence of gender: the novel's main concern is a female figure herself excluded from the world of business. In addition, the lack of authentic accounts of commerce in a novel so emphatically tied to a commercial milieu repeats the dynamic found in the novel's treatment of culture: Hermann refers to culture and to commerce as local color but never investigates their substance. The promise of any given material can be made because the promise is always broken. In more specific terms, the exclusion of commodity exchange indicates the fundamental crisis of conscience of a bourgeois culture which no longer believes in the legitimacy of the central category of its own definition. The absence of exchange corresponds to the collapse of a laissez-faire capitalism and the consequent denigration of individual entrepreneurship. Hence the ubiquitous passivity and indecision of Hermann's figures; their weakness vis-à-vis ineluctable destiny reflects the irrelevance of the individual facing monopolistic structures and the authoritarian state.[10] The erosion of exchange mechanisms robs the realist novel of the ultimate source of change and action. Only because he was a merchant could Anton Wohlfahrt act, but in *Jettchen Geberts Geschichte* all figures are paralyzed by an insoluble liquidity crisis. The narrative that seems to develop in the initial scenes, the incipient love between Jettchen and Kössling, is never completed, since neither an exchange of goods nor an exchange of opinions nor even an exchange of love is permitted.

The denunciation or even denial of exchange historically played an important role in premonopolistic capitalist culture, as in George Lillo's *The London Merchant* (1731) or in *Soll und Haben*.[11] An excessive capitalism is denounced in order to legitimate the social function of a normal capitalism. Thus the text could successfully address anticapitalist tendencies in the readership without endangering its own distribution by challenging the fundamental principle of the system. In a liberal context, such anticapitalism may have provided a necessary regulatory mechanism for a society perpetually threatened by divisive egoism. In a monopolistic context, however, the ideology of superficial anticapitalism only serves to stabilize the power structure of the status quo, while misdirecting potential oppositional energies toward scapegoats. Hermann drums up a pogrom mood against the Jacobys, but he never questions the alliance of the Prussian state with established capital represented by the Geberts. The denunciation of exchange, of underdeveloped capitalism that has not had the time to gild its crassness and polish its rough edges, benefits those capital groups no longer dependent on the logic of the market. The novel of the culture industry becomes the novel of monopoly capitalism; it poses as anticapitalistic in order to please the poor, but when it attacks the greedy entrepreneur, the real victim is the individual and the real winner is the privileged class, while the lesson designed for mass distribution is a melancholy acceptance of fate, hence a passive submission to monopolistic interests.

The demise of exchange as a viable trope within both literary rhetoric and social ideology has a corollary in the communicative relationship between author and reader. The detail ceases to function as a vehicle of an exchange of meaning; instead, it serves as a cipher for a meaning not accessible to interpretive activity. No dialectic of the particular and the general evokes a hermeneutically active recipient. The world is frozen into objects which attract attention but permit no ratiocinative scrutiny. The novel sets up a spectacle and condemns the reader to a voyeuristic silence. Indeed, both stylistic and thematic elements in Hermann's work combine to condemn the reader to an absolute passivity.[12] With no room for critical interpretation, the reader is guided as rigorously by the author as Jettchen is by fate, but this is precisely the point. German realism culminates in a literature of passivity in which the recipient becomes the helpless object of the narrative discourse. It is this helplessness that the culture industry, in the context of a postliberal antiindividualism, is designed to institute.

The novel produces helplessness by establishing a communicative structure in which the reader is fully subordinated to a sovereign narrator. The autonomy of the narrative voice does not engage the reader in the reciprocity of exchange; on the contrary, it demands his subordination. Thus in the preface Hermann commences the story with an imperial gesture: "You must let me tell a story here simply because I want to do it. For no other reason. I want to lose myself in it and wrap myself up like a silkworm in its own threads. Call it caprice! Consider it a toy that he is building! God only knows why! But—listen!" (1). The sovereign narrator insists on an unquestioning acceptance of the fiction, not because of some purported aesthetic, moral, or documentary value, but simply because of his claim to privilege. In lieu of a justification or apology, the narrator demands obedience by fiat. The authoritarianism of the mode of address implicit in Stifter is made intentionally explicit in the context of imperialist culture: Hermann's narrator expects the same obsequiousness from his readers that the emperor expects from his nation. In fact, more important than the thematic, directly ideological elements in the novel of the culture industry is the production of the obsequious recipient, which constitutes the significant political act of this literature. The structure of the communicative social relationship around the text always has political ramifications, and here, at a late stage of bourgeois culture, the entertainment novel ensures the stability of the structures of social domination.

Acceptance of the omniscient narrator of high realism was based on the assumption of his ability to uncover meaning immanent in the world. In the course of narration, a process of signification was supposed to unfold which could emancipate the environment from its merely empirical appearance without sacrificing it to an idealistic other-worldliness. The reification of literary communication destroys this framework; the authoritarian narrator who demands attention claims to report facts impervious to scrutiny and therefore outside the dimension of intersubjective rationality. Whereas realist narration referred to the immanence of meaning, the culture industry insists on the limits of reason and the priority of senselessness. At the conclusion of the first novel, Hermann appends a brief afterword in which he provides a telling designation of the literary act. Upholding the fiction of the historical authenticity of his figures, he surveys their graves and comments obliquely on their fates, recounted later at length in the sequel. Then he turns his attention to the weathered lettering on the gravestones:

> But even this last sign of loyalty has already begun to rot and crumble, and wind and weather, rain and snow, have long since washed the last traces of gold leaf from the curved letters which have been worn away and are hardly legible now, just as no one preserves the memory of Jettchen Gebert any longer. But later, in a quiet hour, I want to bring new gold to the curled and curved letters of her life, so that they may shine again, clear, bright and for all to read. But to him, too, who was carried down in the current and to whom no one set a stone

and who rests in no protected cemetery. . . the runes of his life, too, lost and undecipherable, will I then frame with gold. (473)

Narration is imbued with a monumental character. The sense and significations of social life disappear, their own self-designations wiped away by inescapable natural forces. This inexorable decline can only be mastered through the mimetic appropriation of the same authority by the narrator; the act of literary speech does not engender the reciprocity of liberal discourse but rather, the same subordination demanded by fate. The novel constructs a monument to its figures only by transforming its readers into speechless mourners, imitating the silence of death. The incomprehensibility of the world implies the denigration of potential rational activity on the part of the recipients, while it liberates the narrator from the limitations that a rational criticism might impose. The narrator's imperial exaltation presupposes and furthers the suppression of the readership, which, denied any interpretive autonomy, is fully dependent on the narrator and incapable of raising questions.

This absolute dependence on the narrator culminates in the final humiliation of the reader in the novel's last nonevent. Hermann's technique involves the elaboration of possibilities of identification and hostility on the basis of superficial features which, on close examination, prove inadequate. Jettchen's pretty charm is heightened by her absent musicality, just as the Jacobys' lack of literary judgment is ultimately not inferior to the Geberts' commodification of culture. The recipient's cathexis is manipulated by a narrator who provides external signs of beauty, culture, and love without any evidence of their substance. This legerdemain of identification with illusion climaxes at the novel's end when, before committing suicide, Jettchen sends a letter to Kössling. Kössling, however, has disappeared and apparently killed himself. Jason takes the letter from Kössling's apartment in order to prevent it from falling into the wrong hands and setting off a scandal. Yet he reads it as well, and Hermann lets us read over his shoulder. In the letter, Jettchen confesses to Kössling that she loves Jason but cannot consider marrying him because she has slept with Kössling, and she insists that Kössling never reveal her true affections to Jason.

The narrative trick with which Hermann manipulates the reader is symptomatic of the fundamental principle of the culture industry. The purloined letter gives Jason—and thereby the reader, who, like Jason, reads the letter and is consequently violently shifted into identification with him as the two lines of vision converge—an expression of love from the cipher of beauty which both Jason and the reader have always desired since she first appeared in the novel and the narrator instructed: "What a lovely girl!" Yet this gift is simultaneously denied, not so much by the reality of suicide as by the auto-da-fé of the letter, which intends to withhold this knowledge from its only reader. Pleasure and happiness are once again promised and once again withheld. The love that is presented is only an illusion, inscribed into a text that permits no criticism. The message is one of helplessness, inevitability, fatalism, and subordination. The novel leaves Jason standing alone in the dark and the reader without any recourse to the process of manipulation, for the culture industry locks the recipient in a prison in which he must dream of freedom, and precisely these dreams turn into the bars and chains.

High realism, emerging from an emancipatory bourgeois culture, still took freedom seriously. Its heroes learned to maneuver in the world, and its readers were asked to interpret, not arbitrarily, but autonomously as mature subjects participating in an equal exchange of meaning. The development of capitalist society in the second half of the nineteenth century reorganized culture. The older ideals of individuality, reason, and progress survived only as reminiscences, quoted in order to institute their opposites, while culture lost its discursive quality, a training ground for maturity, and became a crucial mechanism for social stability in the age of imperialism. The metamorphosis of realist narration from Freytag to Hermann registers these social changes and demonstrates the transformation of the function of culture. Realism is not always and necessarily domination, but it becomes so in the institutional context of the culture industry. The failure of realism, the most profound cultural consequence of industrial capitalism, is the backdrop against which modernist writing now appears, for while the culture industry constantly cheats the reader and leaves him isolated and powerless, modernism in its various versions attempts to break the bonds and emancipate the reader by structuring a new social relationship in the act of literary communication, and therefore, a new social community.

8

The Charismatic Novel: Robert Musil, Hermann Hesse, and Elias Canetti

*R*obert Musil prefaces his early novel *Young Törless* (1906) with a quotation by Maurice Maeterlinck which elucidates the particular philosophical project of the novel while at the same time articulating the general status of literature in the context of a perpetual social crisis.[1] In place of the older laissez-faire liberal values of reason, progress, and exchange, the symbolist dramatist points to the inadequacy of language and the constant destruction of meaning:

> In some strange way we devalue things as soon as we give utterance to them. We believe we have dived to the uttermost depths of the abyss, and yet when we return to the surface the drop of water on our pallid fingertips no longer resembles the sea from which it came. We think we have discovered a hoard of wonderful treasure trove, yet when we emerge again into the light of day we see that all we have brought back with us is false stones and chips of glass. But for all this, the treasure goes on glimmering in the darkness, unchanged. (v)

The concrete beauty of the sensuous object dissolves once it is appropriated by language and introduced into the dynamic of exchange, for exchange no longer functions as a mechanism by which human culture establishes itself within nature by controlling it but rather as a perpetual devaluator: everything becomes solely exchange value, and the mourning for the loss of use value and concrete experience becomes the ultimate source of authentic aesthetic production.[2] A cosmos of immanent meaning exists now only as a utopian projection, the treasure trove far below the surface, below the threshold of reified society. There things are still embedded in an epic wealth of sense. There the detail has its place within a universal totality: "the world is wide and yet it is like a home, for the fire that burns in the soul is of the same essential nature as the stars," notes Lukács in the opening passages of *The Theory of the Novel* (1920). The utopia of meaning—for Maeterlinck, for Lukács, and for Musil as well—is counterposed to the barren desert of social existence in which mechanical details are merely contingent and individuals are caught in the absurd senselessness of empirical accidents.

Given the obsolescence of individual initiative in postliberal capitalism, culture reflects and reinforces patterns of submission and passivity. The literary corollary to the experiential senselessness of the modern environment is the novel of the culture industry in which acceptance of destiny, without reason, without question, and without escape, is proclaimed as the absolute demand of existence. Be it a happy end or a melancholy demise, the final message is the irrevocable character of events, just as the fundamental nature of the reading experience is subordination to the power of the narrator. The thematics of necessity, the narrative of closure, and the consumerist fixation on spectacular detail combine to reduce the interpretive autonomy of the reader and to ensure a stance of voyeuristic petrification vis-à-vis impenetrable events.

The enervation of the reader as the project of realism in its culture-industry phase recalls the Weberian paradigm. Realism, which initially drew on the bourgeois culture of the eighteenth and nineteenth centuries with its values of meaning, progress, and communication, attempts to establish a permanent and orderly exchange between reader and narrator in the text. Yet precisely this literary exchange enters a crisis, just as do contemporary market mechanisms. The literary system of legal authority that prevailed since the early Enlightenment undergoes a process of ossification: the individual figures are still central to the texts of the culture industry, but they no longer function like brave entrepreneurial spirits. Instead, they submit to their fates, while the reader, too, no longer participating in an active social production of meaning, surrenders to the authority of the text and the authoritarian narrator. The realist reader, who began as the hermeneutically competent consciousness able to recognize the dialectic of the particular and the general in the precision of the novelistic detail, ends as the prisoner of a text which the dynamic of society in a late stage of cultural modernization has transformed into Weber's iron cage.

As the mechanism with which the bourgeoisie explored the world and developed the categories and strategies necessary to carry out its own emancipation from absolutist domination and theological idealism, liberal literature accelerated the constitution of bourgeois subjectivity. Yet when that subjectivity, as a specifically liberal category, collided with the objective development of monopolistic society, established literature lost its critical function and became instead a central element of the ideological apparatus designed to guarantee the stability of the social order. The major characteristic of the culture industry is not the loss of aesthetic quality owing to commercialization but the transformation of the aesthetic experience from a developmental moment in the history of the individual into a repressive device. The death of the heroine in Enlightenment drama denounced the social order and called for revolt; the death of Jettchen denounced happiness and called for resignation and acceptance. The primary difference was not a matter of literary quality but rather of the quality that each ascribed to autonomous subjectivity and social self-determination. The denial of social self-determination in Hermann's work, and not the quality of the prose, rendered it trivial because it trivialized the subject and demanded the recipient.

Modernism rebels against the culture industry, not with better or higher prose but with multifarious strategies of destroying the iron cage. Its central concern is the emancipation of the reader from the system of deception perpetuated by established culture. Modern writing presents itself radically as an alternative writing and therefore concerns itself expressly with reading and writing. Hence the apparent increase in self-referential and intertextual features in early twentieth-century prose. The new literature critiques prevailing literary habits not simply as a competitor but as a liberator from the obsequiousness demanded by the institution of trivialized realism. Whereas high realism and its predecessors in authentic bourgeois culture addressed social problems, modernism addresses literature as itself the social problem: the legerdemain of the culture industry on which the overall system of domination vitally depends. In place of the literary system of imprisonment, modernism envisions a charismatic renewal, the thorough destruction of bureaucratic culture, through aesthetic means; the social rejuvenation it preaches is to be carried out through the specific restructuring of the reception processes.

The reification of culture through the second half of the nineteenth century represented only a phase in a much longer process. In the paradigmatic bourgeois biography of Wilhelm Meister, Goethe's hero underwent an aesthetic encounter as a crucial part of his maturation. In 1796 Wilhelm had literature as experience; in 1857 the figures in Stifter's *Der Nachsommer* had literature as fetish objects, toward which a cult of art was directed and which, another fifty years later, became the mere property in the Geberts' drawing rooms. Culture was displayed as possession not in order to establish a space within which social exchange might take place, but rather in order to demonstrate a real or desired class membership through the semiotic exposure of the signs of culture. Precisely because an authentic experience of culture disappeared, its shell was ostentatiously flaunted, both by the bourgeoisie to justify its pretense as the leader of a nation with a cultural mission and by the proletariat to ensure the credibility of the fiction of upward mobility and integration into the same bourgeoisie. Thus the monumentalism of early twentieth-century bourgeois culture and the peculiar conservatism of classical Social-Democratic cultural politics presuppose the same inauthenticity of culture transformed into outward signs of status.[3]

The experience of this inauthentic culture produced the dissatisfaction with traditional writing which Maeterlinck expresses in the passage quoted by Musil. For early twentieth-century authors, literature appeared to have lost its credibility. This legitimation crisis of institutionalized culture could be overcome only through a rejection of the reified communicative structures inherited from realism and a simultaneous insistence on literary works of a qualitatively new character. The innovative narratives of German modernism are charismatic novels, because they both suggest an escape from alienated social relations, providing literature with a new legitimacy, and reject the liberal individualism of the nineteenth century, endeavoring to produce a community of readers outside the culture industry. The modernists probably overestimated the degree to which literary innovation could relegitimize literature and influence social structures. Nevertheless their novels articulate a profound and compelling critique of cultural reification.

This critique is particularly convincing in *Young Törless*. Placed in an elite boarding-school, the novel describes how the perverse educational system leads to a perversion of the students' intellectual creativity and erotic energy. Törless, an exceptionally sensitive student, joins with others in the persecution and torture of one of his peers, Basini. In the course of the sadistic degradation, Törless comes to question many of the precepts of nineteenth-century culture, just as the novel breaks with the forms of nineteenth-century realism by paying close attention to Törless' psychological interiority.

Musil describes the trivialization of culture in a bourgeois society that reduces living thought and art to petrified monuments, which are as obligatory as they are misunderstood in the bourgeois household. The perfunctory respect directed toward the reified cultural object makes any penetration of the object impossible: "Now, in Törless's hearing the name Kant had never been uttered except in passing and then in the tone in which one refers to some awe-inspiring holy man. And Törless could not think anything but that with Kant the problems of philosophy had been finally solved, so that since then it had become futile for anyone to concern himself with the subject, just as he also believed there was no longer any point in writing poetry since Schiller and Goethe" (115). Reverence renders the work inaccessible and simultaneously obviates any further cultural labor. The slavish adulation of the unreachable cultural figure has, as its ultimate focus, not the oeuvre of the particular figure—since Kant, Schiller, and Goethe, are, in this mode of reception, fully interchangeable—but the act of submission itself. Thus the trivialization of the primary text serves above all to trivialize its recipient and to transform him into a frictionless wheel within the machinery of the authoritarian state.[4] The petrification of the text teaches Törless that history is frozen and permits no intervention on the part of a subject repeatedly taught the redeeming virtue of passivity and humility.

Stifter transformed the library from a place of sociability into a sacred space of cult. Musil goes on to demonstrate the intimate reciprocity between culture as property and culture as shrine. The description of the library in the Törless home recalls Drendorf's library: "At home these men's works [Kant, Schiller, Goethe] were kept in the bookcase with the green glass panes in Papa's study, and Törless knew this bookcase was never opened except to display its contents to a visitor. It was like the shrine of some divinity to which one does not readily draw nigh and which one venerates only because one is glad that thanks to its existence there are certain things one need no longer bother about" (115). Musil's point is not so much to caricature the purportedly cultured middle-class as to indicate the setting in which Törless' personality emerges, and this context is in large part culturally determined. The culture industry, as the mechanism that cements the stability of monopoly capitalism, is present both in the literary fare of the students at the military institute—"volumes of sentimental romances and drearily humorous tales of army life"—and in its corollary, the simultaneous denigration and apotheosis of the classics (10). The culture directs toward the classics a senseless obsequiousness, which magnifies the humiliation by the obligatory reverence of the reception process. The difference between classics and pulp novels disappears, for both versions of established literary life have as their goal the production of social habits of subordination and acquiescence.

Thus Musil insists that the reification of culture functions as the cause of Törless' insecurity and his participation in the brutalization of his classmate Basini; that is, the culture industry is a prime contributor to the production of the authoritarian personality:

> This distorted relationship to philosophy and literature in due course had its unhappy effect on Törless' development, and to it he owed many of these miserable hours. For in this way his ambition was diverted from the subjects to which he was really most inclined; and while, being deprived of his natural goal, he was searching for another, his ambition fell under the coarse and resolute influence of his companions at school. His inclinations reasserted themselves only occasionally, and shamefacedly, each time leaving him with a sense of having done something useless and ridiculous. Nevertheless they were so strong that he did not succeed in getting rid of them entirely; and it was this unceasing conflict that left his personality without firm lines, without straightforward drive. (115)

Not only the ultimate inaccessibility of culture forces the developing subject toward barbarism, but the repeated efforts to reach culture and the humiliating experiences of the concomitant failure provide the motor force with which to impose humiliation on the other. The perpetual embarrassment in a culture of illusion, where, as Kafka's hero Joseph K. puts it, deception has become universal, reverses itself in an inexhaustible potential for violence.[5] The reification of culture and the denial of authentic cultural experience, along with their result, the stunted development of the personality—an ego-weakness that becomes epidemic in postliberal society after the category of the individual has lost its former centrality—set the stage for Törless' "indifference" toward terror and his participation in ritualized domination.

Musil not only analyzes the cultural setting and its effect on personality formation but also suggests alternative modes of literary life. On the simplest level, he offers a neo-humanist defense of the classics and consequently criticizes the school's curriculum, which fails to integrate these key texts, thereby leaving the students without the crucial formative experience of cultural development. Musil primarily proposes not a return to Kant, Schiller and Goethe but rather a recovery of an experiential aesthetic dimension which the reification of culture and the general mechanization of alienated social relations have blocked. This alternative dimension appears initially in the allegory of the prince, placed early in the novel in order to set up the basic philosophical problematic of the work. Törless befriends an outsider, a young prince, who, despite his privileged background, is rejected by most of the schoolboys. In fact, Musil describes a barely sublimated class struggle waged by the sons of the middle class against "a scion of one of the oldest, most influential, and most conservative noble families in the empire." The prince's upper-class mannerisms and, especially, his religious piety provoke the anger and derision of the others, who are imbued with the secular rationalism of the liberal bourgeoisie. Nevertheless, Törless experiences a strong attraction for the dimension of grace that the prince represents, in which beauty and religion merge with a transcendent delicacy: "The silence and tranquillity of an ancient and noble country seat, and of devotional exercises, seemed somehow to cling about him still. When he walked, it was with smooth, little movements and with that faintly diffident attitude of withdrawal, that contraction of the body, which comes from being accustomed to walking very erect through a succession of vast, empty rooms, where any other sort of person seems to bump heavily against invisible corners of the empty space around him" (6). Social privilege and confessional religion are basically irrelevant, secondary details which Musil employs to lend his narrative credibility. At stake is really the elegance and calm of another world which Törless has never known: a space of beauty outside the purview of bourgeois experience.

Once Musil sets up this opposition of two separate states, he can break off the episode in order to pursue the consequences of his binary system in the richer fictional context afforded by the other boys, until Törless can discover the prince within himself in the apperception of his own irrational potentialities. Characteristically the narrator achieves the termination of the friendship and reintegrates Törless into the ideological practice of his class by having him attack aristocratic piety with the acerbic scorn of bourgeois rationality: "For as though independently of himself, Törless's intellect lashed out, inexorably, at the sensitive young prince." The authentic cultural experience is destroyed by the exigencies of class society, and the bourgeois subject is left in self-doubt and weakness precisely when he successfully asserts his own class interest, as if bourgeois society perpetuates itself through a constant humiliation of its own participants:

> Törless was indeed obscurely aware that what he had done was senseless, and a glimmer of intuitive insight told him that his wooden yardstick of rationality had untimely shattered a relationship that was subtle and full of rare fascination. But this was something he simply had not been able to help. It left him, probably forever, with a sort of yearning for what had been; yet he seemed to have been caught up in another current, which was carrying him further and further away in a different direction. (8)

Because Törless has no access to culture, he participates in barbarism. Because he has no mechanism with which to regulate the secular rationalism of his background, he destroys his first object of love. He banishes beauty and belief from a world which entraps its own subject in an alienated logic of paranoid causality. Yet Musil wants to sketch the path of Törless' possible escape from the self-mutilation demanded by bourgeois culture: the prince was the first way-station, followed by a series of encounters with the infinite and nonrational that breaks the bonds of a solely conceptual thought. In opposition to the insipid triviality of institutionalized culture, Musil locates an alternative aesthetic dimension, charged with both religious and erotic elements, toward which he leads his hero, until Törless himself becomes the advocate of this alternate state.

Summoned to testify at a commission of inquiry, Törless is asked to account for his participation in the Basini affair. In this dramatic confrontation, Musil is able to counterpose the young student, who gives expression to a defense of the legitimacy of the irrational and charismatic state, to the representatives of an older, desiccated culture, his teachers. Once again, the cultural misery of the period is set up as the context for the modernist revolt. Although Törless at first seems nervous and tongue-tied, unable to articulate his own position clearly, the self-righteous cretinism and intellectual buffoonery of his interrogators, who misunderstand him with reassuring regularity, rob them of any aura of respect they might still have maintained. Established culture collapses under the weight of its own petrification; its pretentiousness, which renders it increasingly labile, exposes its weakness to the critical eye of the outsider who is poised for attack: "[Törless] was standing very straight, as proudly as if he were judge here; and he looked straight ahead, past the men facing him—he could not bear the sight of this ridiculous assembly" (209). The tables have been turned, for now the student stands in judgment over his teachers—the priests of Kant, Schiller, and Goethe—and he finds their priesthood contemptible. The form master's patronizing authoritarianism, the mathematician's pedantic lack of imagination, and the religion teacher's credulous delusions lose their power over the young mind. Törless sees through them and beyond the culture they represent, and only then, with that act of intellectual emancipation, can he proceed to pronounce his defense of a dual vision, simultaneously rational and irrational, which constitutes Musil's message in the novel.

The point here, however, is not the specific character of Musil's fin-de-siècle irrationalism. The issue is rather the confrontation of two antithetical cultural institutionalizations. In Törless' revolt against his elders, Musil provides one cipher for the social genesis of modernism. Against the "ridiculous assembly" of the elders, caught up in the power matrix of institutions and fastened to the "wooden yardstick of rationality," Törless' speech proposes the modernist search for a no-longer "ridiculous" collective, a new sort of congregation in which a new spirit, grace or charisma, would reign supreme. With remarkable insight, his interlocutors almost recognize the significance of his discourse: the form master denounces him as a "little prophet," and his speech is given the pejorative designations always reserved for an other-worldly language: "subjective" and "hysterical" (213). The priests of high culture rely on the institutional power with which they enhance their own dicta to denounce and banish the prophet in order to prevent the establishment of a new community. This banishment determines the very structure of the narrative. After Törless' speech, there is a scene in which the narrator assumes a third-person omniscience. Elsewhere he follows Törless' eyes, but here he describes the teachers in Törless' absence. Their decision to expel him from the school repeats in the plot what the narrative form has already revealed. *Young Törless* thus provides a seismographic registering of the tension within the cultural world of 1900 between the ossification of the inherited bourgeois culture, which ensures the masochistic passivity of the recipients, and the emerging movement to liberate the individual by means of a radical renewal of the literary community.

The description of this tension fuels Musil's diagnosis of the cultural malaise of modernity, and the aesthetic alternative inscribed in the novel represents the crucial antithesis counterposed to the barbarization of the culture industry. The appropriation of the non-rationality of the aesthetic dimension within Törless' experience permits the otherwise stunted personality development to unfold; the successful character of that development remains ambiguous within the text, but its status as an exemplary treatment of contemporary culture is indisputable. An even more explicit analysis of the constellation of personality formation and cultural structures in the specific context of a burgeoning culture industry is provided in Hermann Hesse's *Steppenwolf* (1927).[6] In the context of the cultural crisis, new forms of social cohesion appear which, as in Musil's novel, necessitate a restructuring of both the psychic interiority of the individual and the cultural institutions in which he participates, and precisely this restructuring, in its various versions, is the practice of early twentieth-century modernism.

In *Steppenwolf,* Hesse presents the fictional notes of his hero, Harry Haller, a highly educated European intellectual troubled by the crisis of modern western culture. His essayistic reflections on the modernization of everyday life, the decline of the arts, and the flawed structure of the bourgeois personality are interspersed with a curious personal history. With the help of mysterious figures, Haller makes his way on a pilgrim's progress through a perfunctory established culture, devoid of meaning, to a new organization of cultural life.

In Hesse's account the reification of established culture encompasses both a monumentalization of the literary legacy and, as both cause and effect of this element, a mechanization of life forms. Cultural material loses its vitality, just as middle-class normalcy grows increasingly rigid. With his characteristic moroseness, Haller complains:

> All our striving, all our culture, all our beliefs, all our joy and pleasure in life—already sick and soon to be buried too. Our whole civilization was a cemetery where Jesus Christ and Socrates, Mozart and Haydn, Dante and Goethe were but the indecipherable names on moldering stones; and the mourners who stood round affecting a pretence of sorrow would give much to believe in these inscriptions that once were holy or at least to utter one heartfelt word of grief and despair about this world that is no more. And nothing was left them but the embarrassed grimaces of a company round a grave. (77)

Cultural possessions exist solely as a petrified forest, hardened relics of a formerly vibrant world for which contemporary recipients cannot even mourn authentically, so desiccated has their affective sensibility become. Social life assumes a perfunctory character; its forms are maintained and respected, but they are devoid of immanent meaning, and the participants are "embarrassed" at their own acquiescence, even though they never call it into question. The mechanical constitution of society which systematically excludes emotional depth and genuine happiness goes hand in hand with the desecration of culture: in place of genuine holiness, Hesse pinpoints a sham cultic reverence.

Hesse concretizes this abstract diagnosis of contemporary society in the episode of Haller's visit to a professor, the representative of established culture. Haller leaves no doubt as to his contempt for the formal character of social life: "it is all compulsory, mechanical and against the grain, and it could all be done or left undone just as well by machines" (77-78). The critique of merely formal existence that lacks inner substance or an authentically experiential dimension is repeated in the description of the host. Haller regards the invitation and the evening as fundamentally empty, and the professor himself becomes the cipher for a senseless activity carried on without reflection and without meaning. He pursues his arcane research with mechanical regularity. Now, however, Hesse augments the critique of formal existence with a specifically political dimension by presenting the professor as right-wing mandarin. He is not only the automaton of an absurd existence, hopelessly lost in books, but also the racist reactionary with a taste for culture:

> There he lives, I thought, and carries on his labor year by year, reads and annotates texts, seeks for analogies between western Asiatic and Indian mythologies, and it satisfies him, because he believes in the value of it all. He believes in the studies whose servant he is; he believes in the value of mere knowledge and its acquisition, because he believes in progress and evolution. He has not been through the war, nor is he acquainted with the shattering of the foundations of thought by Einstein (that, thinks he, only concerns the mathematicians). He sees nothing of the preparations for the next war that are going on all around him. He hates Jews and Communists. He is a good, unthinking, happy child, who takes himself seriously; and, in fact, he is much to be envied. (78)

The text relies on the tension between the representation of bourgeois culture and the standards by which it is measured: not only allegedly superior values but a fuller and therefore superior sense of life. Hesse draws on a vitalist critique of Wilhelmine society, asserting that modern civilization has lost touch with the original, creative forces of life.

By holding up a purportedly empty scholarly rigor to derision, Hesse as Haller denounces the established wing of contemporary cultural life which still insists on an immanent significance to cultural production. Yet "mere knowledge," part of mere life, is not enough, and Hesse links it directly to two other implicitly anachronistic liberal values, progress and evolution. Furthermore, he underscores the conservative character of this knowledge, a remnant of Wilhelmine liberalism in the Weimar Republic, by having the professor ignore the intellectual force driving the modernization of culture, just as, in his ivory-tower manner, he ignores the imminent political catastrophe. Thus the cult of "mere knowledge," with its willingness to separate scholarly activity in particular and cultural activity in general from the allegedly more authentic concerns evident to the vitalist consciousness of the novel, leads first to an otherworldly naiveté and ignorance concerning contemporary developments, and then to an authoritarian personality and concomitant militarist politics. The same linkage that was apparent in a rudimentary form in *Young Törless* is radicalized and made explicit here. Reified culture distorted Törless' growth and made him susceptible to the sadistic gang, while the professor, because of the mechanical culture of which he is a cipher, transforms that sadism into a real political program.

Hesse argues that monumental culture and ideology are interrelated. The culture industry is not a matter primarily of the mass-marketing of popular art but of the transformation of social relations through cultural objects in order to maintain the stability of post-liberal capitalism. Culture loses its autonomous status and is integrated directly into the ideological apparatus, and this integration applies as much to the treasures of high culture as it does to popular forms. Its representations express the system of authority and the signs of power, while the purported cultural material itself sinks into the background. Consider Haller's account of a cultural icon in the professor's home:

> It was an engraving and it represented the poet Goethe as an old man full of character, with a finely chiseled face and a genius's mane. Neither the renowned fire of his eyes nor the lonely and tragic expression beneath the courtly whitewash was lacking. To this the artist had given special care, and he had succeeded in combining the elemental force of the old man with a somewhat professional makeup of self-discipline and righteousness, without prejudice to his profundity; and had made of him, all in all, a really charming old gentleman, fit to adorn any drawing room. No doubt this portrait was no worse than others of its description. It was much the same as all those representations by careful craftsmen of saviors, apostles, heroes, thinkers and statesmen. Perhaps I found it exasperating only because of a certain pretentious virtuosity. In any case, and whatever the cause, this empty and self-satisfied presentation of the aged Goethe shrieked at me at once as a fatal discord, exasperated and oppressed as I was already. It told me that I ought never to have come. Here fine Old Masters and the Nation's Great Ones were at home, not Steppenwolves. (79)

The "Steppenwolves" are those who, like the narrator, have grown disaffected with middle-class society without having found a new home or a stable identity. Haller's hostility toward the professor and the portrait corresponds to Hesse's critique of an inauthentic bourgeois culture. Haller insults his host by articulating his contempt for the engraving, which turns out to be a family heirloom, and the incident quickly puts an end to the visit. In this passage, which moves from an aesthetic account of the representation of Goethe through comments on the genre in general to social and political conclusions, Hesse retraces the argumentative connection between cultural reification and social crisis. None of the features recognized in the image is treated as authentic; all are clichés, the obligatory emblemata of the patron saint of national culture: the "chiseled face," "genius's mane," "renowned fire of his eyes," and "lonely and tragic expression." Thus Hesse identifies this portrait with others of its ilk; Goethe hangs in all the drawing rooms of the bourgeoisie, and this is the way he always looks. This constant appearance has nothing to do with the historical personage or with the character of the literary texts, but solely with the bourgeoisie, which remakes its poets in its own image in order to reassure itself of its own legitimacy. Culture loses its authentic substance. Haller cries out against this insipid comprehension of literature when he rejects the "empty and self-satisfied presentation" of the poet. Yet the emptiness is no vacuum; the constellation of clichés sets up a formula for genius as the concurrence of discipline, fire, and tragedy, categories that slide from cultural representation into belligerent politics. Haller realizes as much in the insightful conclusion of the passage, where the ideological system transforms cultural material into an authoritarian cult of masters in which literary grandeur and political power converge. Literature becomes a cult object, and politics is aestheticized in a seamless mechanism of domination. Precisely here, however, the space for an alternative cultural practice begins to open up: established culture excludes Haller, just as the priestly teachers in *Young Törless* cast out the young prophet, and both can therefore explore counterinstitutional cultural possibilities.

The transition from the critique of established cultural forms to the investigation of a new practice occurs immediately after the departure from the professor's home. Haller's exit amounts to a denunciation of monumentalized culture which has no relation to the ultimate concerns of life, and his compulsive oscillation between contempt for the bourgeoisie and desire for its security seems to be finally broken. The exploration of an alternative organization of aesthetic experience ensues under the dual leadership of Hermine, Haller's female alter ego, who guides him through an artistic demimonde, and the musician Pablo, who introduces him to phantasy and hallucinations.

In place of the traditional values associated with the professor, Hesse attempts to redefine the character of culture in both its high and its low forms. In dreams and hallucinations, Haller confronts the prototypically canonic cultural figures of Goethe and Mozart, whom he discovers to be much less cumbersome and staid than their obsequious admirers would expect. Goethe explicitly exhorts Haller to cease approaching the grand figures with excessive respect and awe and to emancipate himself from the submissive patterns associated with such a reception. In a key passage, the poet first parodies Haller's reverence for an immortal culture and then appropriates the epithet in order to overcome the strictures of bourgeois temporality. In both cases, the monumentalization of culture is denounced and the previously serious recipient is urged to recognize the primacy of humor, which breaks the spell of time-bound existence. Here and in a similar Mozart passage, Hesse presents the prescription for Haller's recovery from the painful bifurcation of bourgeois subjectivity: release from encasement in the mundane concerns of the private ego and emancipation of the soul into the immateriality of atemporal being.

Hesse describes the popular culture corollary to this eternity by having Hermine introduce Haller to the world of dance and jazz. At first he expresses total disdain for this mass culture as a symptom of social conformism, Americanism, and tastelessness, allowing Hesse to parody the same middle-class conservatism inherent in his depiction of the professor. Haller rejects the popular culture of pleasure and entertainment, populated, in his view, by the unproductive, the flirtatious, and worst of all, the carriers of an elegance that is only "second-rate"; he looks at it with a corresponding mixture of contempt and desire (121). Yet just as the novel records the transformation of Haller's attitude toward high culture and his discovery of authentic culture's resistance to its bourgeois marmorealization, so too does his disdain for the jazz-filled dance hall end. Pleasure and entertainment are never accepted just as such, for Hesse is too much of a moralizer to allow for simple fun. Instead, he revises the initially negative judgment of dance as just so much pleasure by transforming it into a religious experience during which a new type of individual and a new sort of social bond come to the fore during the artists' ball:

> An experience fell to my lot this night of the Ball that I had never known in all my fifty years. . . the intoxication of a general festivity, the mysterious merging of the personality in the mass, the mystic union of joy. . . A hundred times in my life I had seen examples of those whom rapture had intoxicated and released from the self, of that smile, that half-crazed absorption, of those whose heads had been turned by a common enthusiasm. I had seen it in drunken recruits and sailors, and also in great artists in the enthusiasm, perhaps, of a musical festival; and not less in young soldiers going to war. . . I myself breathed the sweet intoxication of a common dream and of music and rhythm and wine and women—I, who had in other days so often listened with amusement, or dismal superiority, to its panegyric in the ballroom chatter of some student. I was myself no longer. My personality was dissolved in the intoxication of the festivity like salt in water. (168-169)

Haller goes on to describe the universality of the erotic experience. Dancing with one woman, he dances with all, while even the barriers against homoerotic love collapse. The experience of communion mediated by music and dance breaks down all borders and differences. Individuality loses its private character, as the contours of the personality expand, until the former subject becomes merely part of a new unity, an ecstatic community, no longer atomized by egoism, time, and material concerns. Thus popular music, like the music of Mozart or the poetry of Goethe, ultimately provides access to a qualitatively different experiential dimension, homologous to Musil's aesthetic state, where the practice of culture takes on a radically new character. Haller's assurance at the novel's end that both Mozart and Pablo would wait for him does not necessarily indicate an absolute convergence of high and low culture, for the precise musical forms may remain very different. Yet Hesse is certainly attempting to outline a tentative reinstitutionalization of culture in which the character of each is redefined: high culture loses its monumentality, while low culture ceases to be superficial. Each contributes in its own way to the destruction of the bourgeois personality with its impoverished binary structure, and each engenders instead the new cultural community, ecstatic and emotive, no longer rational or egocentric. More so than in *Young Törless,* the modernist revolt in *Steppenwolf,* which constitutes the substance of the novel's program, thematizes its social consequences as the search for a new type of collectivity, outside the logic of market exchange, carried by a charismatic spirit. In the enthusiasm of the dance, a utopian communism is inscribed, just as the thematic critique of individuality reflects the prevailing postliberal social forms. Against the background of the social crisis projected onto a single personality, the redefinition of cultural institutions as the project of modernism takes shape, and this redefinition has not only an individual-psychological but also a collective-social dimension, as modernism sets out to change the world through literary innovation.

In *Young Törless,* modernist innovation was grounded in a reorganization of the personality that Musil linked to a newly discovered aesthetic dimension. In *Steppenwolf,* this modernist subjectivity is radicalized. Instead of Musil's dual structure, Hesse advocates an infinitely shattered ego, which is linked to a renewed social collective. Modernism emancipates the individual from the desiccation of a mechanized rationality and reinvigorates the charismatic community. Both transitions are mediated by aesthetic experiences: abstractly for Törless in the encounters with the aesthetic state, and concretely for Haller in the musical episodes. Yet modernism often defines this mechanism of transition precisely within itself: it describes itself as the agent of the renewal within its own texts in an inscribed aesthetics. Though self-defining elements are evident in all literary periods, they are particularly salient in modernism where literary self-consciousness and, especially, the recognition of the function of the opponent literature of the culture industry are strongly developed.

Although both Musil and Hesse provide direct accounts of a denigrated mode of culture, its reification and trivialization, the antithesis, an alternative cultural practice, remains implicit. In Elias Canetti's *Auto-da-Fé* (1936), the character of the modernist alternative is made explicit in opposition to a hypertrophic petrification of established culture.[7] The scholar Peter Kien has constructed a library around himself which hermetically seals him off from the world in an unmistakable concretization of the literary iron cage. The renowned sinologist loses himself in the study of ancient Oriental literatures and sequesters himself from all living human contacts in his regular pursuit of knowledge: "Punctually at eight his work began, his service for truth. Knowledge and truth were for him identical terms. You draw closer to truth by shutting yourself off from mankind. Daily life was a superficial clatter of lies. Every passerby was a liar. For that reason he never looked at them" (15). Although Peter's library is a collection of great works, culture is not merely that, as it was in Stifter's library, at the Geberts, or in the Törless home. Rather Canetti makes clear that reified culture is itself the means with which authentic human relations are blocked and prevented. Even the sort of friendship that might emerge via cultural labor, based on mutual scholarly interests, is impossible for Peter who, defining himself repeatedly as a "person of character" (17), retreats into the library as an impervious carapace in order to ensure the impossibility of any outside penetration. Peter's library is therefore his counterpart to the skirt of his housekeeper, Therese: "Her skirt was a part of her, as the mussel shell is part of the mussel. Let no one try to force open the closed shell of a mussel" (54). In both cases, the image serves as a philosophical cipher, permitting Canetti to raise the issue of the individual separated from society by the impermeable character mask which alone guarantees the continuity of the isolated personality in its textual imprisonment.

The principle of noncommunicative order embodied in the library explains the other elements that characterize Peter: acrimonious misanthropy as a result of being closed off from the world, but because of this very isolation, hopeless naiveté and helplessness. Peter's cult of order and discipline, his reluctance to enter into spontaneous exchanges, also implies a certain aesthetics, especially a distaste for the novel as a literary form. When obliged to lend a volume to his housekeeper, he chooses a soiled copy of Willibald Alexis's *Trousers of Herr von Bredow,* not only because its sorry state offends his own bibliophilic taste, but also because his idealization of classic order leaves little room for the empathy and identification central to the generic reception process:

> A novel was the only thing worth considering for her. But no mind ever grew fat on a diet of novels. The pleasure which they occasionally offer is far too heavily paid for: they undermine the finest characters. They teach us to think ourselves into other men's places. Thus we acquire a taste for change. The personality becomes dissolved in pleasing figments of the imagination. The reader learns to understand every point of view. Willingly he yields himself to the pursuit of other

people's goals and loses sight of his own. Novels are so many wedges which the novelist, an actor with his pen, inserts into the closed personality of the reader. The better he calculates the size of the wedge and the strength of the resistance, so much the more completely does he crack open the personality of his victim. Novels should be prohibited by the State. (42)

The imagery of "wedge" and "cracking open" links the aesthetic problem to the personality as a mussel shell. The corrosion of the character mask which the novel allegedly carries out represents the diametric opposite of the labor that Peter performs in order to maintain his own protective encasement: where he closes himself off, the novel opens the individual to a confluence with other interests and desires and, hence, to the erotic intimacy that Peter never experiences. Threats to the order of the reified psyche, novels are also, in Peter's eyes, threats to the social order, since they demonstrate a fundamental relativism among competing points of view. Thus the classicist Peter ponders their prohibition. By proscribing genuine human contacts and their aesthetic representation, the state could guarantee the untroubled reproduction of reified personalities and an immobile social order. A ban on the novel could prevent the emergence of an adversarial readership which, because of its desire for intersubjective communication, could threaten political authority. Peter rejects the novel in a manner reminiscent of Haller's initial arrogance toward popular music and dance: both cultural conservative figures denigrate "low" forms of art by associating them with modes of pleasure, which they designate as inferior in order to maintain their taboo. However, just as Hesse revised Haller's hostility to dance, Canetti retracts Peter's denunciation of the novel, not through a process of growth and change—for Canetti's figures do not grow, showing the modernist distance from the liberal rhetoric of development—but through the introduction of a competing aesthetic position which proves itself superior both within the novel and as a key to the reading of the text itself.

The alternative to Peter is embedded in the figure of his brother, George Kien, a psychiatrist in Paris who remains absent until the middle of the third and final section of the novel. Canetti introduces this figure, who arrives in Vienna to rescue his brother, to set things in order, and—so the reader expects—to bring things to an auspicious conclusion at the novel's close, by way of a contrast which sets him in a positive light. George became director of a psychiatric institute when he married the widow of his predecessor; Canetti presents that former director as an insensitive tyrant, unmoved by the plight of his patients, whom he treated only in order to demonstrate the validity of his theories: "[He] had embraced official psychiatry with the obstinacy of a madman. He took it for his real work in life, to use the vast material at his disposal to support the accepted terminology. . . . Human beings, especially nerve cases and criminals, were nothing to him. He allowed them a certain right to existence. They provided experiences which authorities could use to build up the science. He himself was an authority" (395). This nameless director, who regularly preferred severe judgments to mild ones, instrumentalized his environment in the name of his theories and thereby lost genuine human contact: he forced his first wife to leave him, his second to beome insane, and his third to commit murder. His patients despised him, and they therefore love his successor, George Kien, all the more.

The critique of the authority of the director is a metaphor for the legitimation crisis of nineteenth-century literature. The inversion suggested by the image of a psychiatrist acting "with the obstinacy of a madman" corresponds to the transformation of liberal realism from a communicative discourse into the reified narration of the culture industry. Therefore the construction of an alternative psychiatric practice within the novel should be understood as a program for the charismatic novel.

The contrast between the two psychiatrists does not merely provide material for a secondary fictional narrative. Rather, Canetti develops the alternative in order to raise an issue at the heart of his philosophical concerns in *Auto-da-Fé*, one with particular relevance to its literary status. Whereas the predecessor, a therapeutic nihilist, typically ignored the speech of his patients, George draws on the Freudian model of a "talking cure" and urges them to speak, liberating the narratives of the insane from the incarceration imposed on them by the authoritarian conceptuality of official psychiatry: "In the hard school of his predecessor [George] had developed quickly into his exact opposite. He treated his patients as if they were human beings. Faithfully he would listen to stories he had heard a thousand times before, and would express spontaneous surprise and amazement at the stalest dangers and anxieties. He laughed and cried with the patient he had in front of him" (396).

At stake here is not primarily a turning point in the history of psychiatric therapy but an alternative model of communication that will ultimately illuminate Canetti's literary project. George opens the discursive interchange that generates extensive speech on the part of the patients, and this in turn permits George to penetrate the other's interiority. This "possibility of sliding into the other's soul" refers once again to the problem of encasement and entry; Peter's own self-encapsulation finds its opposite in George's therapeutic practice. Although this sort of communication transforms the status of the speaker, namely the patient, who for the first time is treated not as evidence but as a human being, it also changes the recipient. George's empathy and insight demands a perpetual flexibility from him: "He advised them with crystal cleverness, as though their wishes were his own, cautiously keeping their aims and their beliefs before his eyes, cautiously shifting ground, expressing doubts in his ability, never authoritative in his dealings with men, so diffident that many smilingly encouraged him; was he not after all their chief minister, their prophet or their apostle, occasionally even their chamberlain?" As interlocutor, George renounces the authoritarian privilege he could claim as administrator and scientist; instead, he subordinates himself to the meandering confabulations of his partner and consequently surrenders the continuity of his own identity, slipping from role to role as demanded by the constantly generated text. Yet this extended discourse with the insane and his willing participation in their delusions does not erode George's own personality; on the contrary, it enables him to escape Peter's fate, for he develops no ossified character mask, and the human character of his encounters with others leaves its mark on his face in an absence of rigidity: "In time he developed into a remarkable actor. The muscles of his face, of exceptional mobility, would fit themselves in the course of a day to the most various situations" (397).

Authoritarian communication fosters and reflects the hardening of character masks which interrupt human interaction, whereas empathetic communication, or the willingness to lose oneself in the other in a hermeneutic immersion, breaks the spell of alienation and liberates the self from monadic imprisonment. The alternative modes of psychiatry reproduce the problem of the novel, namely the entrapment in shells, including the library, versus the attraction for the infinity of otherness. The opposition of the two communicative patterns simultaneously provides a comment on the communicative structure of this novel in particular. The extensive ramblings of insane figures which have occasionally led critics to reject the novel in fact represent Canetti's effort to produce a new sort of literary discourse and thereby a new personality and literary community.[8] The interior monologues of Peter, Therese's erotic fantasies, or Fischerle's dreams are not neatly coded allegories which can be solved by a clever matrix of concepts; they thrive instead on the baroque richness of their material which the reader may enter, in all its confusion and polyphonic particularity. *Auto-da-Fé* presents itself to its recipient much as the discourse of the insane encountered George, demanding a renunciation of privilege and authority and producing a reader able to escape the character mask generated by the hegemonic communicative patterns of the culture industry.

Precisely this link between the thematics of personality structure and literary form, derived from the antinomic psychiatric models, is made explicit in the subsequent sequence describing George's own medical background. The problem implicit in the two versions of psychiatry is now reintroduced into two stages in George's biographic development, and each is associated with a literary-linguistic mode. Drawing on familiar clichés, Canetti constructs a former, trivial stage in George's career as a Parisian gynecologist for the fashionable circles. Neither his concern for medicine nor his participation in social life is particularly profound, and this superficiality is associated specifically with the reading of French novels: "Reading was fondling, was another form of love, was for ladies and ladies' doctors, to whose profession a delicate understanding of *lecture intime* properly belonged. No baffling turns of plot, no unusual words, the more often was the same track traversed, the subtler was the pleasure to be derived from the journey. All fiction—a textbook of good manners. Well-read men are obsessed with politeness. Their participation in the lives of others exhausts itself in congratulations and condolences." This reading is both superficial and prurient; it instructs the reader in the mechanisms of alienated social contact by the presentation of paradigmatic models as well as by the mechanical character of the communicative situation established in the text. This pejorative characterization of the novel denounces the genre for the opposite reasons from those that had concerned Peter. For Peter, the novel endangered the protective shield which, surrounding the psyche, prevents the individual from participating in the lives of others. Here, however, literature is itself entangled in the societal mechanisms of isolation, perhaps is even one of the major agents of reification, contributing to the construction of the character mask: "he was indeed cut off, by the books he read, the sentences he spoke, the women who ranged round him in a greedy close-built wall" (398-399).

Peter rejects novels because of their alleged ability to generate empathetic social contact. George suffers from novels which prevent empathy. In both cases, *Auto-da-Fé* thematizes the relationship between the institutionalization of literature and the character of social relations. Processes of aesthetic reception, which depend on specific literary forms, contribute to the character of extraliterary social and political structures. By parodying Peter's misanthropy, Canetti denounces cultural conservatism and a classicist high culture. The account of George's literary situation expresses a critique of trivial culture where literature assumes a negative social function as the source of the carapace of isolation. The social consequences of the reification of culture, which were evident as early as Stifter's libraries, become unmistakable here. Canetti spells out the results of the culture industry, the paranoid personality, denied authentic human contact but at any moment prepared to plunge into the hysteria of the fascist mob.

Canetti, however, also describes a linguistic and existential alternative to the atomistic readership of the novel. This alternative model is anticipated when, in the course of describing George's success as a gynecologist in the empty luxury of Paris, Canetti chooses a religious image: "Surrounded and spoilt by innumerable women, all ready to serve him, he lived like Prince Gautama before he became Buddha" (399). The new language that George learns from his most crucial patient permits this charismatic renewal, the renunciation of all worldly goods, and the attempt to establish a new community, the result of which is the utopian character of his regime in the psychiatric institute. Whereas the old language and literature sequestered the self in an impermeable shell, the new language emancipates objects from a rigid system of nomenclature by linking sound with gesture in an expressive system: "Each syllable which he uttered corresponded to a special gesture. The words for objects seemed to change. He meant the picture a hundred times and called it each time something different; the names seemed to depend on the gesture with which he demonstrated them. Expressed and accompanied

201

by his whole body no sound appeared indifferent" (401). In contrast to Törless' perpetual indifference, owing to the monumentalization of culture and the concomitant warping of his personality, or to Peter Kien's absolutely unperturbed manner, George's empathetic modus vivendi establishes a new cosmos in which things are called to an orphic life. The spell of reification is broken, and an immediate relationship between personality and world is established. Concepts give way to relations, as theories yield to passion in the verbal universe of a magic language.

Because of his encounter with this new language, George, like Buddha giving up his princely patrimony, renounces the luxurious world of elite gynecology and enters on a career as psychiatrist, albeit with a profound respect for the insane as the carriers of an authentic alternative knowledge. He intends to learn from them rather than to cure them, and this permits him grand discoveries regarding the construction of the self and its relationship to the collective. The charismatic rejuvenation of language induces the recognition of the fundamental community of human life. George's careerist assistants, like his authoritarian predecessor, are entrapped in an official psychiatry, which holds the insane, with their access to a preindividuated collective, in contempt in order to construct artificial forms as the encasements for individual personalities: "Of that far deeper and most special motive force of history, the desire of men to rise into a higher type of animal, into the mass, and to lose themselves in it so completely as to forget that *one* man ever existed, they had no idea. For they were educated men, and education is in itself a *cordon sanitaire* for the individual against the mass in his own soul" (410-411).

Beneath the forms of reified individuality, but still within every single person, lies the force of communal experience, "the mass-soul in ourselves." Its suppression defines the project of the normal personality; its periodic upsurge explains the possibility of selfless acts, the expression of a preconceptual solidarity with the others of the species: " 'Mankind' has existed as a mass for long before it was conceived of and watered down into an idea. It foams, a huge, wild, full-blooded, warm animal in all of us, very deep, far deeper than the maternal. In spite of its age, it is the youngest of the beasts, the essential creation of the earth, its goal and its future." Canetti provides a phylogenetic framework for his thematic treatment of character mask and intersubjective communication. Encapsulation is a problem not merely of the pedantic intellectual Peter, unconcerned with the world around him. Peter is only an example of a broader malaise of impermeable individuation. Personality is encased in a shell in order to avoid the collective experience, which will nevertheless eventually reassert itself. Individuality is a historical episode, concluding not simply biographically in death but also collectively in the rediscovery of human solidarity: "for there will be no I, you, he, but only it, the mass" (411). The cracking of the shell, the liquidation of the paranoid personality, is the *telos* of the species. Canetti's envisioned restructuring of literary communication—involving the rejection of traditional novels, which reinforce stereotypical behavior, and the elaboration of a simultaneously empathetic and expressive language—is designed to hasten the emergence of a postindividual community. The open confabulations of Canetti's novel are his contribution to the institutionalization of a modern literature, the charismatic novel. It stands in opposition to the culture industry, which appears in *Auto-da-Fé* as the bibliophilic mausoleum. The modernist rejuvenation of culture, always iconoclastic, destroys a no longer viable literary mode: hence the final immolation, when Peter's library goes up in flames. This auto-da-fé of reified literary culture represents the passage from a paralyzing entrapment to a new freedom.

In *Törless, Steppenwolf,* and *Auto-da-Fé,* modernism is presented thematically as a project to reinstitutionalize culture. Inherited literature has lost any vibrancy, and traditional patterns of reception are incapable of perceiving literature's authentic character. The legacy of the past has degenerated into the object of a reverential lip-service, symbolized in the perfunctory respect paid to the classics in the Törless home, in the kitsch portrait of Goethe, and in the petrification of the Kien library. The reification of the literary experience, which already marked the distance between *Wilhelm Meister* and *Der Nachsommer,* is articulated as an explicit crisis in early twentieth-century modernism. Just as the bourgeois notion of culture comes under attack, so does the whole range of values that had structured that world: individuality, conceptual reason, and market exchange. The rejection of this historical substance generates the material of the modernist text: *Törless* revises the understanding of psychological interiority; *Steppenwolf* outlines a rejuvenated communication for the new individual; and *Auto-da-Fé* links these sub-projects, the individual and collective aspects of modernism, to literary change.

Gone are the resigned acceptance of fate and the lessons of submissiveness that came to dominate late realism and its twin, the novel of the culture industry. In their place, modernism articulates a literary means to a charismatic community, liberated from the rigid strictures of bourgeois law, unencumbered by the borders of pusillanimous personalities, and therefore dependent on new patterns of communication. In the linguistic contours and literary forms of the modernist novels are inscribed the paths to the charismatic transformation of society: modernism is political not primarily in its occasional themes but in its mode of address, and the competing forms of modernism correspond to alternative political projects. With the address to the reader, the modernist author establishes a new social relationship of communication in conscious opposition to established communicative lines, and the character of this intended communication is itself the primary locus of the politics of the new literature, with its textual intervention into the moribund discursive context. In other words, the various modes of modernism invoke different types of implied readers, corresponding to radically different conceptualizations of the social relations in innovative literary institutionalization. All models of modernism share the sociopolitical implication of rejecting the older bourgeois literature, although for different reasons and with varying consistency. Three models in particular, addressing a regenerated fascist folk, an epic collective, and an aesthetic social individuality, mark off the domain of the German modernist novel.

9

Fascist Modernism: Ernst Jünger and Hans Grimm

A sociology of modernism centered on the category of charisma lends itself naturally to an account of the literary strategies allied with fascist politics that stretch across the European landscape: Eliot, Pound, Lewis, Céline, Hamsun, Marinetti, Benn, Jünger, Grimm, Johst. It was none other than Weber who pushed the problem of charisma, which he had found in the contemporary ecclesiastical debates, in the direction of the charismatic leader. Towering above his devoted acolytes, the great leader appears as the credible source of a transfigurative grace that destroys the brittle structures of inherited tradition or rationalized bureaucracy and therefore gathers the inspired masses around himself, the authoritarian revolutionary. Yet this fixation on authority betrays Weber's own indebtedness to the Wilhelmine cultural context and the antiliberal legacy of the Bismarck cult. The notion of charisma, which Sohm elaborates as an alternative to a purportedly bureaucratized Catholicism, has nothing to do with the leadership of Christ or the divine representation of the episcopacy and everything to do with the character of a renewed community within which the spirit dwells without a specialized leadership figure. This desire for community fuels the various modernist projects, and the differences among them concern the programs for societal restructuring in a renewed literary community.

Without doubt, fascist modernism, at least in the German context, regularly invokes images of leadership figures toward which an unmistakably homoerotic desire is directed, either explicitly, as in the case of Hans Grimm's Cornelius Friebott in a bestseller of the Weimar period, *Volk ohne Raum*(Folk Without Room, 1926), or covertly, as in the chief ranger in Ernst Jünger's *Auf den Marmorklippen* (*On Marble Cliffs*, 1939), which is often read as a camouflaged critique of the Nazi regime but nonetheless presents the villainous leader as the carrier of a power and blood lust that fully ensnare the fascinated narrator. These leaders, however, obvious corollaries to the right-wing denunciation of parliamentary democracy, rarely occupy the center of the literary works; they function rather as ideological addenda to a more profound project, the production of the fascist community defined in terms of nation, race, and above all, the supersession of the categories of liberal subjectivity. The collapse of entrepreneurial capitalism corresponds to the disappearance of the individual as the organizing principle of epic narration and the emergence in his stead of a collectivity in which psychological interiority gives way to the surface lines of power and the seamless matrix of order. The reader is invoked no longer as the agent of a hermeneutic penetration but as the locus of a double passivity, determined by the knowledge of the race inherited from the past and by the duty of the present in the preservation of the collective. Because history as the narrative of progress is rejected in the name of hypostatized order, activity becomes the perpetual repetition of preordained roles, and curiously, the legacy of liberalism can be found, grotesquely distorted, solely in the figure of the leader, the only carrier of subjectivity in an otherwise fully organized mobilization. Still the leader merely provides the mirror in which the unceasing iteration of the transfixed community can be reflected as overpowering spectacle.

The idiosyncratically conservative character of German fascism and its ideological appeal to the antiurban sympathies of the urban masses generate images of a premodern community of the folk. Nevertheless, the specifically modernist origin of the postindividual collective emerges clearly in the memoirs and essays of Ernst Jünger, where the worker and, above all, the soldier in the modern mechanized war become interchangeable units of the regenerated social organization. The binding force is no longer a social contract between autonomous monads but rather a charismatic spirit that overcomes a purportedly anachronistic individuation. In *Der Kampf als inneres Erlebnis* (Combat as an Internal Experience, 1922), a description of the fundamental ontology of military encounters, Jünger underscores the importance of a common belief in the necessity of courage: "Courage is the living fire that welds the armies. It surpasses all other things, no matter how beautiful their names may be. A soldier without courage is like a Christian without faith. Therefore in an army courage must be the most sacred object. It has always been deleterious, when its clear source has grown dark." Courage is not mere bravery; it is mood, spirit, enthusiasm, the presence of a binding force that overcomes the separation of inherited atomization and structures the human machinery into a unified agent of power. It transcends the categories of individualism and hierarchy, ego and privilege: "Courage is its own reward, a bond that surrounds all equally."[1] This sentence resonates with the illusory promise of the fascist community as an ideological response to the capitalist crisis. The congregation of courage surpasses the disappointments of wage labor, for the spirit "is its own reward"; asking nothing in exchange, it moves beyond the logic of exchange society. Similarly it holds out the image of equality that liberalism, in its historical flight from democracy, constantly invoked only to deny.

These two components of fascist ideology—the rejection of exchange and of privilege, or the return to the immediacy of use value and the obliteration of particularity—arise as by-products of the fundamental principle, the magic of the collective inspiration: "A final element: ecstasy. This condition of the saint, the great poet and great love is also given to courage. Enthusiasm tears masculinity so beyond itself that blood boils as it beats against the veins and glows, foaming through the heart. It is a drunkenness past all intoxication, a release that breaks all restraints."[2] A community is established by dionysian seduction. The cultivation of subjective interiority in liberal culture led only to failed eroticism, as in Botho and Lene, Jettchen and Jason. Here is where the strategies of fascist literary address emerge, calling individualism to account, pointing to its sexual misery, and generating images of a new collective of perpetual union. T.S. Eliot's *The Waste Land* stands as a paradigm. The power of attraction is clear, but so are its limits, for participation in this union demands the renunciation of individuality, the dissolution of the profile of subjectivity, in order to join the congregation. The social crisis is to be solved by insisting on the absolute priority of the whole over the individual who, robbed of all particularity, becomes the perpetual repetition of the next unit: the worker, the soldier, the member of the race, among whom no exchange can ever take place, since all are the same and since difference, as privilege, is denied.

While the transition from laissez-faire to monopolistic capitalism poses the problem of the individual from a contextual perspective, it can be addressed equally as a transformation of literary material. Before 1800 the category of the bourgeois as aesthetic individual took shape in the classical novels of development of Wieland and Goethe; its transformation into the bourgeois as businessman appeared in the credo of the nineteenth-century middle-class, *Soll und Haben*. The truncation of the figure, the reduction of freedom from the dialectic of subjectivity and objectivity into a matter of entrepreneurial activity, was carried on into *Der Nachsommer* where, despite the resurrection of the aesthetic experience, an authoritarian ethos prevailed which privileged structures of unquestionable order over individual particularity and spontaneity. Nevertheless the restrictions on exchange were intended to maintain a bourgeois world against the chaos it generated as its own contradiction: consumerism and class struggle. After Stifter, the commitment to bourgeois society as specifically bourgeois collapsed, and the novel in general was displaced from the narration of bourgeois maturation. The hiatus that marked the distance between bourgeois and postbourgeois, premodern and modernist literature ran between the self-location of Stifter's narrator in 1867—"My father was a businessman"—and Jünger's dictum of 1932 in his treatise symptomatically entitled *Der Arbeiter* (The Worker): "The German was never a good bourgeois." Between the two statements an "existential revolution" has taken place that radically transformed the literary project.[3]

The liberal novel of development presents, in one form or another, the growth of a particular individuality and its integration into a social system. Precisely this concern with the individual disappears in the *völkisch* literature of reactionary populism out of which fascist modernism develops. This becomes clear in a transitional work, Gustav Frenssen's *Jörn Uhl*, which retained widespread popularity throughout the National Socialist period. It still operates with the characteristic tropes of the genre while at the same time demonstrating their anachronism. Its Bildungsroman features are salient: the genealogy of the hero, the traits inherited from father and mother, the path from childhood to maturity, education, pivotal experiences, and the struggle for orientation in a world that initially confronts the subject as hostile. Nevertheless the traditional genre has undergone major revisions. For one thing, Jörn is a peasant, no bourgeois subject. This matter of content is only the outward sign of a fundamental shift away from an ethos of exchange to its vilification. Exchange is precisely the problem in the form of the loss of the patrimonial estate, the peasant's land. In contrast to Stifter's restriction of exchange mechanisms for the sake of preserving order, Frenssen formulates a nascent right-wing anticapitalism. *Jörn Uhl* also diverges from the novel of development in its central mechanism, for the hero's stuggle with father and society does not fuel an authentic development. The oedipal conflict is not a motor of growth, for ultimately the hero does not experience a process of immanent change. On the contrary, change appears solely as an external force of destiny that has elected Jörn from the start and accompanies him on his path. Maturation is therefore not the medium of the potentially autonomous individual but rather the submission to a heteronomous authority as the sole source of strength and virility.

Frenssen's destiny, which eradicates the possibility of individual freedom, is presented specifically as oblivious to individuality, for Jörn provides the paradigm of a mass experience: "What happened to Jörn Uhl, happened to many." This denigration of particularity is made explicit in a crucial episode, the hero's participation in the Franco-Prussian War. Finally escaping the limits of his native village, he encounters a grandeur before which his individuality shrinks into an insignificance overshadowed by the collective of the folk: "How small Wentorf has become! Wentorf, the middle and navel of the world! There must be ten thousand villages in the world and people like the grains of sand by the sea. At first their battery had been alone, back then when they had crossed the Elbe in two steamships. Then they had become a regiment, then a corps, and then an army. Since yesterday they were a folk."[4] The experience of the same military masses, as well as those of democratic France, forced Fontane into a self-referential causerie that recognized the limits of subjectivism without daring to peer beyond them: the swan song of the bourgeois ego. Frenssen takes a different path, for in addition to the blatantly nationalist political reverberations of the text, the passage indicates the literary transition to postindividualist tropes. The rhetoric of individual development gives way to the perpetual invocation of a collective, an early form of the same fascist charismatic community that Jünger would describe so vividly three decades later.

The historical experience of military mobilization marks the transition from individual to collective narration, and Frenssen underpins the national substance with a diachronic structure that stands in fundamental opposition to any specifically historical account: myth. In significant interludes the constitution of identity is overtly linked to two elements located outside of normal temporal development: a distant, racial past of prehistoric Germanic tribes and a magical presence of supernatural beings, "children of the earth," carriers of a superior knowledge and guardians of privileged mortals.[5] Their perspectives relativize the consciousness of contemporary individuality to such an extent as to make its insignificance unmistakable. The collective which supersedes the bourgeois subject is not simply the national community of the present but the unbroken presence of past generations as well. The end of atomistic individuality, at least in its fascist version, therefore holds out an additional ideological promise: the victory over death. The erotic union in which isolation is overcome produces no new generations; indeed the literature of race and blood is marked by a ubiquitous fear of reproduction, most certainly linked to a profound misogyny. But this literature offers the hope of redeeming the past generations, retrieving them from an other-world of forgetfulness. Hence the monumental character of fascist modernism, holding onto images of ancestors, in contrast to the commitment to progress in the ideology of liberal individuation.

This disappearance of the individualistic center of the novel of development in the national collective is radicalized in the work which may be treated as the epitome of the fascist version of the genre: Grimm's *Volk ohne Raum*.[6] Again the skeleton of the Bildungsroman is present, in the parentage of the hero, his childhood and youth, his education and maturity, but only as a reminiscence of the literary tradition with which the work breaks. Grimm's text is exponentially more extreme than Frenssen's. Where Jörn lost his farm, Grimm describes the loss of Germany's African colonies, and the novel can be read simply as a political novel arguing for a new colonialism. More important, where Fressen framed his hero's story with reference to the emergent collective, Grimm has his hero, Cornelius Friebott, become himself the spokesman for the nationalist collective. Individual development is insignificant, overshadowed by the tendentious message of the priority of the fascist community. In purely formal terms, the political exigency of agitation repeatedly interrupts the traditional literary concern of biography. Thus the novel itself does not commence with the narration of the individual; on the contrary, the story is postponed for pages while the narrator proceeds with an account of the destruction of community, the erosion of the German peasantry forced off its land by overpopulation and capitalist expansion:

> The men who have to go away and move and leave the valley and the country and the woods and the relatives and the neighbors and the ancient connections of the fathers. . .the emigrants will follow the wages, again and again the higher wages and will fight for them until death somewhere; they can never say again, tomorrow my land comes first and my pasture and my cattle and my farm, tomorrow I work unpaid for myself. They will no longer be lords of their own destiny, their land and their arms, because they will have lost their land, and land and work cannot be reunited in the overpopulated fatherland, not with sweat and not with plans. Sure, if these peasant children were British and had the wide plains of Canada and Austrialia and New Zealand and South Africa, they'd have a different choice than only the march to the factory and the big city! (I, 16-19)

The traditionalist community ends, capitalist competition and atomization set in, and Grimm's imperialist solution is the reestablishment of a colonial empire to provide land for an expanded peasantry. The corollary to this imperialism is the abolition of the literature of atomism, the recentering of the narrative around the new national collective instead of around a privileged, private subjectivity. Friebott's story is ultimately merely a device to provide Grimm with a speaker for his political vision. The authentic hero of the novel is not the individual Friebott but rather the folk, which the literary narrator describes and to which the political narrator appeals. In fact, Friebott, forced out of the German countryside and into colonial adventures in Africa, returns to Germany as an agitator for imperialist expansion. He is both an example of and the mouthpiece for Grimm's politics. No distance separates the consciousness of the narrator from the subjectivity of the hero.

The fascist response to the erosion of traditionalist society is the invocation of a new national community, pursued both as overt content and as a strategy of address in the novel. Grimm's programmatic imperialism explains that the community defines itself precisely as an alternative to competitors, who are denounced in pejorative terms, particularly the British. The internal cohesion of the community is guaranteed by a male bonding. Heterosexual love is either unsuccessful or so repressed and postponed that it does not emerge as a relationship between a man and a much younger woman until the conclusion of the lengthy novel. Attraction and intercourse take place overwhelmingly between men, who provide each other with a support and comfort that Grimm claims is not forthcoming from women. The German problem is presented as excessive separation and particularism, divisions among men, including the splits in the working class, and these wounds can be healed only by male interaction: Cornelius's friend Martin woos him to join him in the colonies, and Grimm himself can hardly disguise his libidinal attraction for his hero. Moreover, misogyny and male loyalty determine Cornelius's own account of his family background: "I'm not guilty of my father's sorrows, certainly not the way he means it and not the way mother tries to justify herself. I'm not guilty and won't condemn myself. But if I were home now, I could sit by my father, and if he didn't blame me, I could maybe, maybe do what mother never did—stroke his hand and give him love, so that he might really feel love, my father" (I, 414).

Where the bourgeois Bildungsroman generally commenced with an absence of paternal authority in order to place the nascent subjectivity in a situation of confusion out of which the process of maturity might lead, Grimm sets a fundamental linkage between male generations against the unloving female. The fascist community privileges the male by insisting not only on a male realm of military heroism but above all on a male solidarity against women, for women, as the potential bearers of change, represent a radical threat to the specific order that is to be erected against and in place of traditional subjectivity. The disappearance of individuality, as a central feature of the modernism of fascist literary strategies, therefore means concretely the elaboration of a constellation of male power and the trivialization of the female domain.[7]

Jünger, as usual, provides the fullest and most sophisticated account of this new constellation of power, defined repeatedly in opposition to the foregoing bourgeois age of society and effeminacy. Democracy, liberalism, and civilization have restrained and corroded the warrior instincts of the race, which nevertheless reappear in the crucible of industrialized urbanization and warfare, allying the archaic and the futuristic against the emasculating nineteenth century: "We have grown old and comfortable like the aged...Weaned of real drunkenness, we have found men and power repulsive." The values of the bourgeois age have generated a valuelessness in which quality disappears in the incessant frenzy of exchange and self-congratulation, engendering an insipid collective where heroism is impossible, the mass: "Politics, drama, artists, cafés, patent leather shoes, posters, newspapers, morality, the Europe of tomorrow, the world of the day after: the thundering mass."[8] This is the world that fascist literary modernism rejects in its effort to evoke alternative readers and collectives.

Jünger's novel *Afrikanische Spiele* (*African Games*, 1936) therefore thematizes the bourgeois society as an object of negation, just as it purposefully parodies and destroys the contours of the bourgeois novel of development. Instead of the hero's integration into society, the narrative traces his flight from society into adventure and the antisociety of the foreign legion, not in order to effect a final reconciliation, but rather to lead him to a more consistent, more mature rejection of middle-class security. As a modernist reformulation of the Bildungsroman, the text displays parallels to *Young Törless*. In place of the undefined irrationality of Musil's aesthetic state, however, Jünger's antithesis to liberal philistinism exudes the violently antisocial aggression of a militarized heroism. The hero escapes the boredom of bourgeois existence by enlisting as a mercenary. Stationed in Africa, he encounters a military world replete with values hostile to the liberal middle-class, and although his adventure comes to an end when he returns home, these new values are not revoked. Thus the ironic narrator, looking back at his own youth, approves his adolescent instincts:

> I suspected correctly that one can approach the natural sons of life only by turning one's back on legitimate order. Sure, my models were drawn on the measure of a sixteen-year-old who does not yet recognize the difference between heroes and adventurers and spends his time reading bad books. Yet I possessed health insofar as I suspected the presence of the extraordinary outside the sphere of society and morality which surrounded me. That's why I did not want to become an inventor, a revolutionary, a soldier, or any other benefactor of humanity,

as is common for that age—instead, I was attracted by a zone in which the struggle of natural powers emerged purely, with no purpose beyond itself.⁹

Instead of an integration into society, morality, aesthetics, or business, the fascist novel of development enacts the process of desocialization into aggression and an alienation marked as heroic isolation. This isolation constitutes the basic unit for the fascist collective in which the central features of bourgeois individualism—subjective interiority, personal development, and participation in social exchange—have no place.

Jünger encounters this new collective in the modernized battlefield. In *Der Kampf als inneres Erlebnis,* he reports how it fills him with an "intoxicating sobriety"—not a neoromantic intoxication of emotional subjectivity but a rationalized fascination with the cold lines of technological power, reminiscent of "the centers of our metropoles or the images of power fields in the concepts of modern physics."[10] The nineteenth-century tropes of organic development and individuated autonomy have disappeared. In their place, the terms of a new community are articulated as instrumental strength and mechanical functioning. The prose itself bears their marks, as its enthusiasm is devoid of particular ideals or personal commitment. At stake is solely the success of the organization which institutes itself with no regard for the specific interests of its own participants:

> This is the new man, the storm pioneer, the elite of Central Europe. A brand new race, smart, strong and full of will. What appears here in battle as revelation will be tomorrow's axis around which life will swirl faster and faster. . .The glowing sunset of a dying age is also the dawn in which preparations are made for new and more difficult struggles. Back in the distance, the giant cities, the armies of machines, the realms whose internal ties are being rent asunder by the storm, await the new man, audacious, used to battle and ruthless toward himself and others. This war is not the end, it is the prelude of power. It is the anvil on which the world is beaten into new borders and new communities. New forms want to be filled with blood, and power must be grabbed with a hard fist. The war is a grand school, and the new man will be cut like us.[11]

Jünger excludes any account of the teleology of warfare, for teleology itself is hopelessly enmeshed in the liberal discourse of development and subjectivity. The war has no goal and no purpose outside itself:

not Germany, not nationalism, not the ideals of an imperialist culture. Instead, war without any external values provides the paradigm of organization as the abstract matrix of force.

This matrix tolerates nothing but power, and the individual, whose demise is the threshold of all modernisms, is now replaced with the abstract unit of instrumentality. The single person is present only to the extent that he serves the functioning of the machine, and both battlefield and industry are the privileged loci of the production of that unit. In *Der Arbeiter* Jünger writes: "The individual, who is basically nothing but an employee, becomes a warrior; the mass becomes an army; and the revision of the social contract is replaced by the promulgation of a new order of command. This removes the worker from the sphere of negotiations, pity and literature and raises him to the deed; it transforms his legal ties into military matters—that is, in place of lawyers, he will have leaders, and his being will become the measure instead of requiring interpretation."[12] Here the fascist modernist declaration of the end of man, linked to an expressly anti-working-class politics, provides an ideological justification for the destruction of the unions and the abolition of the legal safeguards, Jünger's "lawyers," that took place soon after the establishment of the National Socialist regime in 1933. The text can be read as an exhortation to these attacks on the working-class movement by the fascist state.

The explicit politics of the passage are further linked to ominous rhetorical structures: the obsolescence of the individual turns into a programmatic rejection of both the forms of individual communication and the reciprocity of linguistic form organized around patterns of exchange. The drama of legal advocacy, the dialogue of adversarial confrontation, presupposing not only conflict but the potential legitimacy of individual interests, gives way to a functional speech that tolerates no response and in which no individual speaker is even envisioned who might mount such a reply to the power field of order. Oppositional resistance is not merely declared illegal; its ontological basis disappears in the cult of an order that declares all particularity illusory. The monodirectional directive of command instead of the polyphony of contractual negotiation corresponds to the extinction of the forms of language that a plurality of individuals could invoke in the institutionalized responses of a courtroom exchange: instead of law as a medium of interchange, it is reified as the impenetrable command of the leader which can only be repeated, not transformed. Hence the central trope of fascist rhetoric is iteration, the constant return of the immutable message. In turn, this message, which can undergo permutations but no development, congeals as a measure, a cipher of frozen order, that repels any inquiry into its meaning, or any interpretation. The obsolescence of the developmental rhetoric of hermeneutic exchange therefore implies the end of an interpretive project in the fascist cultivation of the impervious surface of power. All that remains is the acceptance of the authority, presented as command and image. The recipient, no longer a potential interlocutor, becomes the passive spectator in the infinite iteration of orderly function.

The modernist rhetoric generated by the topography of the bat-tlefield induces in turn a new literary topography. The submersion of the individual in the nexus of power implies the demise of literary forms dependent on the category of individuality, including drama as the discourse of individuated speakers, the novel as the unfolding of the subject, and lyric poetry as the objectification of private sub-jectivity. The new forms that emerge in fascist modernism rely ulti-mately on an antithetical ontology. The fact that Jünger himself writes two novels in the fascist period, *Afrikanische Spiele* of 1936 and *Auf den Marmorklippen* of 1939, does not disprove this tendency, for the high point of fascist literary production in Germany falls in the years before the historical reality of the fascist state, a chrono-logical disjunction which is not difficult to explain. The National Socialist state does not nourish literary activity; even quantitatively, literary production quickly falls below the levels of the Weimar Republic.[13] In addition, the experience of the established fascist regime collides with the ideological illusions of its significant intellectual prophets, and rather quickly Gottfried Benn, Martin Heidegger, and Jünger grow estranged from the Nazi culture bureaucracy, no matter how the objective content of their work may still converge with a fascist project. In any case, Jünger's version of a fascist modernism is purest in his pre-1933 writings, such as the war memoirs *In Stahlgewittern* (*Storm of Steel*, 1920) or the programmatic essay *Der Arbeiter*, which represents the ideal type of a fascist epic, the substitute for the novel of bourgeois subjectivity in a postsubjective cultural context.

The end of liberal individuality renders the literature of subjec-tive interiority obsolete. In the mechanized temporality of the bat-tlefield, Jünger insists, there is no time for "novelistic development."

Conventional eroticism and affairs of the heart are replaced by hasty encounters characterized simultaneously by a presubjective instinctuality and the postsubjective metallic coldness of the machine age: "When red life crashes against the black reefs of death, pronounced colors come together in sharp pictures. These are epochs of unveiling and release, distant from everything subtle, gentle and lyric. Everywhere life springs back into barbaric fullness and force, not least of all in love and art. This is no time to read your 'Werther' with teary eyes."[14] The sentimentalism of bourgeois individuality, the priority granted to the life of emotions since the eighteenth century, is denounced. The weakness of the suffering hero, passive in life but active in his heart, is rejected in the name of the militarized hero, caught up in the active power field of embattled forces and therefore eager to surpass any enervating lachrymosity. The cult of interiority becomes an anachronism as soon as the rhetoric of inside and outside, suggesting unfolding and development, gives way to a fixation on the absolute facticity of the surface. The surface is nowhere relativized by hidden desires, inside or below, once these other places disappear from the hegemonic tropic catalogue.

Instead of a literature of subjective sentiment, Jünger formulates the program for a modernism of "intoxicating sobriety," a quotidian terror where the threat of the unknown is integrated into the everyday. The other, which denies bourgeois order, is not sequestered in a netherworld but stalks the streets of modernity making mockery of their security and superficial civility. It is an irrationality, not as the vessel of individual emotion, but as the barbaric passion that destroys the universe of the rational ego:

> Everyone has sometime had a terrifying dream, and if he considers it he will find: its factuality was nothing against the uncanny power that moved it. E. Th. A. Hoffmann is the poet of these breakthroughs; from his privy councilors and philistines, the ghostly suddenly slides up, just as the sight of a doorknob can conjure a suffocating experience. Dostoevsky knew this too. Otherwise he could not have written Ivan Karamazov's feverish talk with the stranger in everyday dress. Yet how can this be explained to those who are only at home between the four walls of the comprehensible?[15]

Hoffmann and Dostoevsky become ciphers of the antirational forces of terror, of a panic fear that attacks bourgeois order in a manner which Jünger appropriates for fascist terrorism. Indeed, terror becomes the goal of fascist modernism, as literature undergoes a radical reinstitutionalization. Literature is no longer the stage on which the subject can display its significance in conflict, development, and confession. Instead it becomes the machine, the weapon, with which to accost the atavistic remnants of subjectivity so as to conquer them for the new order of function and power.

Because an antiquated concept of individuality lay at the center of bourgeois art, the preservation of traditional culture is condemned as political escapism. Here Jünger's fascism diverges markedly from the familiar forms of conservative nationalism which presented Germany as the carrier of an authentic culture against the trivial civilization of western capitalism. Weber was certainly not free of that nationalism, which found its classic expression in Thomas Mann's *Reflections of a Nonpolitical Man* (1918). Jünger in no way calls for war in the defense of old culture; in his world that project would in fact appear contradictory. Instead, war, the new, mechanized war of modernity, able to generate its own culture of power, needs to emancipate itself from the stuffy legacy of the bourgeois era with its self-indulgent sentimentality and dysfunctional insistence on privacy. Though all modernisms direct an iconoclastic hostility toward the cultural legacy of the nineteenth century, fascist modernism does so in the name of a totalizing political power: "The cultural establishment is nothing more than the last basis of bourgeois security. It supplies the superficially most plausible excuse for escaping political responsibility."[16] Culture distracts from the urgent demands of the day, the establishment of order and power so as to guarantee the continuity of the state.

For Jünger, nothing, not even the cultural heritage with which the Weimar Republic ostentatiously draped itself, can compete with the priority of preserving the state. The portraits of poets on postage stamps and currency, the streets and squares named after composers of the past, all the official gestures that might indicate to the critical observer the demise of a culture which these external efforts vainly endeavor to maintain—this cult of culture enervates and, Jünger complains, draws attention away from the authentic duties of the age:

> It is a kind of opium which hides the danger and produces a deceptive sense of order. And this is an unacceptable luxury in a situation in which it is no longer a matter of invoking

tradition but of creating tradition. We live in a historical period where everything depends on a monstrous mobilization and concentration of available forces. Perhaps our fathers still had the time to bother with the ideals of an objective science and an art that existed for its own sake. We, however, are clearly in a situation where neither the former nor the latter but the totality of life is in question.[17]

A strain of Marxism denounces religion as an opiate that obscures the real character of class society and state power in order to ensure their stability. Jünger uses the same metaphor for an opposite purpose: culture is the narcotic that distracts from the objective disorder. The force of the iconoclasm is a modernist trait, reacting against a bourgeois culture that has lost its vibrancy and moved into reified forms. The substance of this iconoclasm, however, a rebellion in the name of order, constitutes its specifically fascist character: authoritarian revolutionism.

Modernist iconoclasm, a hostility toward the established cultural heritage of the nineteenth century, leads elsewhere to Marcel Duchamp's urinal, Bertolt Brecht's attacks on Aristotelian theater, or the revocation of Beethoven in Mann's *Doctor Faustus*. In the fascist modernism of Jünger, iconoclasm leads straight to an exhortation to the persecution of the representatives of traditional intellectual and artistic labor. It is hardly an accident that this modernism translates its antitraditionalism into political terrorism, since terror and power belong to its central categorical panoply. Nor should the historical ties of German fascism to certain conservative elements obscure the modernist nature of Jünger's hostility to the heritage of the liberal, Wilhelmine world of bourgeois culture. Autonomous thought and aesthetic activity become the objects of a blatant threat:

> This sort of [individualistic] artistry will be found in Germany with deadly regularity in close connection to all those powers whose overtly or covertly treasonous character is written right across their faces. Fortunately one finds in our youth a growing sensitivity for this sort of connection; and one begins to suspect that in this realm the mere use of an abstract spirit has the significance of an act of high treason. A new kind of Dominican zeal has the nerve to complain about the conclusion of the persecution of heretics—have patience, such persecutions are under preparation, and nothing will stand in their path as soon as one recognizes that for us the belief in

the dualism of the world and its systems is sufficient evidence of the crime of heresy.[18]

Belief in dualism—that is, insistence on the autonomy of art and its separation from the system of political power—is declared to be a heresy which Jünger promises to subject to persecution. Again the date of 1932 is crucial, for the notorious book-burnings took place a year later, in May 1933. The attack on the bourgeois institution of autonomous art, the central project of the historical avant-garde, need not necessarily lead to a fascist conclusion, but this fascist conclusion is certainly one possibility of the modernist revolution against the culture of liberalism.

Jünger denounces the anachronistically individualist and politically irresponsible character of inherited culture and, as an alternative, refers to the quotidian irrationality of an anti- individualist terror, associated with Hoffmann and Dostoevsky. Yet he does not thereby provide a substantive program for a fascist literary modernism. He turns to the novel, a classically individualist genre, only after the mid-thirties as he is drawing away from the reality of the fascist state. His more purely fascist modernist prose, above all the war memoirs which break with bourgeois forms of epic prose by renouncing any claims to fictionality, belong to the twenties.

Jünger's specification of a fascist modernism has a substantive aspect as a mechanism to overcome individuation. For example, he devotes special attention to the film as a sign of the disappearance of the individual. In the mass of the audience and on the screen, the unique and separate private persons come to an end. Although the argument anticipates the motif of collectivization in Benjamin's examination of the cinema, the point of Jünger's film is not the evocation of a critical mass but the integration of the viewers into an unbroken totality. Benjamin couples an aesthetics of montage with a politics of contradiction, whereas Jünger privileges a seamless neoclassicism as the corollary to a totalitarian whole. Art must relinquish all claims to autonomy, just as the atomized individuals of the bourgeois age are to combine in the mass mobilization.

Ultimately Jünger's designation of the social function of aesthetic representation echoes the central project of the Wagnerian *Gesamtkunstwerk*, the total work of art, the anticipatory blueprint of German fascist aesthetics in its regenerative ideology and its antiliberal politics linked to a mythic unity of the folk. Jünger's version is more technologically modern, but the organizing rhetoric, with its attack on separation and difference in the name of a totality to be instituted by art, might have been borrowed from Wagner's program for a revolutionary music drama: "For the same power that the art of politics represents in authority is revealed by art in its formative activity. Art must demonstrate how, from a lofty vantage point, life is understood as totality. [Art] is nothing separate, nothing that possesses validity in itself or because of itself. There is, on the contrary, no realm of life that could not be regarded as material for art." Four decades earlier the final sentence might have represented a claim by art of its right to thematize new material traditionally excluded by established aesthetic definitions. The naturalists, for example, such as Hauptmann in *Before Dawn*, appropriated the seamy sides of social life or medical reality, matter largely absent from the literature and art of the earlier nineteenth century. Yet Jünger does not argue for the emancipation of art from the restrictions of conservative taste. On the contrary, he exhorts art not to restrict itself to its traditional and even its traditionally bohemian material but to redefine itself in terms of a project for the aestheticization of the totality of life. Art is to be no longer merely a matter of private reading experiences or Sunday visits to museums. Instead, art seizes control of all aspects of social intercourse in order to imbue them with the form that represents the same power inherent in politics. This is the "aestheticization of politics" that Benjamin recognized as the essence of the fascist project.[19]

Jünger concretizes the argument by referring neither to literature nor to painting but to architecture and city planning, art forms that can no longer be treated easily as the expressions of individual subjectivity and are no longer matters of private connoisseurship, separate from the affairs of the world. The aesthetic organization of urban topography in order to provide a perpetual representation of state power demonstrates the specifically fascist turn of this modernism. Whereas the avant-garde attacks the inherited notion of autonomy in order to break down the barriers between life and art, fascist modernism does so in order to aestheticize life: not by imbuing life with the values of beauty and autonomy previously sequestered in art, but by imposing form and order, with arbitrary authority, onto the contradictions of social relations in a period of profound crisis.

The imposition of aesthetic form onto the contradictions of politics in order to guarantee the stability of power addresses the reader not as an aesthetic individual but as a member of the collective. Grimm invoked a mythical racial solidarity, while Jünger appeals to a modernized, technological sobriety. The texts produce readers who are devoid of individuality, members of a collective of infinite repetition, and this principle is itself repeated in the foremost trope of fascist literature: iteration. The works of fascist modernism are primers in a language of repetition. The privileged locus of this rhetoric is the metaphor of the pseudohero who assiduously avoids development, for he is present as the vessel of an antiliberal knowledge that is complete at the start. In place of a teleological organization of events, the plot collapses into a plethora of interchangeable episodes, each demonstrating the radical incompatibility of the figure with established society. Experience does not accrue, knowledge is not produced, constellations are only repeated again and again. The concentration of iterative structures around the central figure effects the denunciation of the Bildungsroman and all that it represents, which is a central goal of the ideology of fascist modernism.

Iteration has further functions. In fact it is able to borrow from the melancholy cult of fate that emerges in the late realism of the culture industry, transforming it into a glorification of the ineluctability of destiny and destruction. The valuation has been reversed, for bourgeois resignation still recognized helplessness as a negative condition. The fascist insistence on power and the submission of the individual to its structures celebrates helplessness as the insight into necessity that a bad Hegelianism would deem appropriate. Destiny is the eternal repetition of the destruction of subjective projects, and this recurrence becomes the mark of beauty, as in the inferno at the conclusion of *Auf den Marmorklippen*. Jünger's novel describes how the peaceful guardians of culture are overrun by vicious barbarians. The prose becomes most compelling in the accounts of combat and catastrophe, especially the final images of the end of a civilization. The conflagration in Canetti's *Auto-da-Fé* signifies the failure of a reified literary structure; Jünger's flames suggest the perpetual inevitability of destruction:

> While we watched the rue-garden hermitage, its windows grew bright, and out of its gable a flame leaped up to the heights of the marble cliffs. Its color was. . .deep, dark blue, and like the calyx of a gentian blossom, its crown had a sawtooth edge.

We watched the harvest of many years of work fall prey to the elements, and with the house our labor turned to dust. Yet in this world we must not hope for completion, and he must be praised fortunate whose will does not dwell all too painfully in his striving. No house is built, no plan conceived in which destruction is not the cornerstone; what lives in us as indestructible does not find peace in our works. This was clear to us in the flame, but its gleam also carried joy.[20]

Destruction is inescapable, and it is fated to recur repeatedly. The narrative account is not a unique event, toward which a reaction of empathy might be appropriate, but merely a further episode in the perpetual mirroring of decline and catastrophe. Thus it is useless to consider avoiding the holocaust that awaits. On the contrary, only the recognition that a submission to the flames of destruction is imperative provides insight into the character of being, and only an acceptance of this repetitive being ensures happiness.

Iteration not only demonstrates the nullity of individualism and the vanity of subjective aspirations but is intimately tied to a further feature of the critique of bourgeois liberalism. Where the discourse of exchange assumed the presence of qualitative differences, the ideology of repetition suggests an alternative to market relations in the insistence on eternal sameness. The object that avoids commercial bartering by submitting to destiny—that is, the trade-off between liberal capitalism regulated by the market and monopolistic control—can retreat to the illusory security of a myth of use value. Courage, Jünger claims, is its own reward, not dependent on the false exchange of wage labor. In the literature of fascist modernism, the things that in realism were caught up in the dynamic of the commodity retain an aura of noncommodifiable entities. They glow with a magic that prohibits the quantification of value, so essential to the negotions in the offices of Schröter's firm in Freytag's novel. They escape the subordinating objectification by the capitalist subject and become their own masters in a process of remythification. Again, the modernist rejection of the bourgeois age generates an alliance between the archaic and the futuristic.

This magic is particularly evident in Jünger's luminescent description of the snakes in *Auf den Marmorklippen:*

Above all [the child] Erio loved the biggest, most beautiful animal which Brother Otho and I called the griffin and which, as we deduced from the legends of the peasants, had been living in the chasms since ancient times. The body of the lance adder is a metallic red, and scales of bright, bronze glow are often sprinkled in its pattern. In the griffin, however, the pure, immaculate gold was pronounced and toward the head merged into a jewel-like green with an even greater gleam. When angered, she could stretch her neck into a shield that sparkled like a mirror during the attack. It seemed that the others paid her respect, for none came to the little bowl until the golden one had stilled her thirst. Then we saw how Erio played with her, while she, as cats sometimes do, rubbed her pointed head on his jacket. (197)

The mythological deisgnation, the mysterious beauty, and the paradoxical proximity of childlike weakness and magical danger indicate the autonomy of the powerful object. No discourse of exchange can appropriate this material, no textualization of nature can transform it into an object of exploitation: Wohlfahrt will not be able to sell the griffin. The attraction of the account resides precisely in this preservation of its nonexchangeability. Though iteration surrenders the object to destiny, it can also preserve its uniqueness by refusing to substitute it for the arbitrary other of a commodity. The fascist rejection of bourgeois liberalism not only denies subjectivity and calls for order but also promises to retrieve the use value of objects that otherwise threaten to be emptied of meaning in the dynamic of capitalist exchange.

Nineteenth-century interlocution and exchange are replaced by iteration and stability. Hermeneutic interpretation runs up against the permanence of power, and individual autonomy disappears in the mechanized collectivity. From the absolute position that Jünger assumes, to which he cannot, because of the terms of his own ideology, ascribe subjective particularity, these transformations appear to generate a structured totality. From the standpoint of any participant—all of whom, as individuals, Jünger must disregard— the institutionalization of the fascist collective means a loss of power and a subordination to authority. Denied the flexibility of interpretation, the recipient cannot respond but can only repeat the command. The order of power thereby acquires precisely the aesthetic form that Jünger intends to project onto it. Similarly the subject tendentially loses subjectivity when confronted with the aestheticized politics which disallow autonomous participation. The corollary to iterative speech, in which nothing new can be enunciated, is therefore the spectacular image, which transfixes the viewer without the possibility of understanding. This other tropic form of fascist modernism combines the helplessness of the victimized spectator with the untouchable formal beauty of even the most repulsive substance. Yet because substance is excluded from discursive inquiry, this contradiction can never be thematized.

The spectacular quality of fascist literature is nowhere clearer than in the battlefield descriptions in Jünger's war memoirs. Their political character does not lie in any obvious ideology; in fact, they are remarkably free of overt nationalism or xenophobia. Even the military values of masculine heroism and soldierly discipline seem secondary to the imagistic power of the descriptions which ascribe to the experience of war an irresistibly seductive power: "The sections of the front to our left were enveloped in white and black clouds of smoke; one after another heavy explosions spurted high as towers; above them flashed the lightning bolts of hundreds of bursting shrapnel. Only the colored signals, the muted cries of help for artillery, betrayed that there was still life in the positions. For the first time I saw fire that could only be compared to a spectacle of nature."[21] Jünger's descriptions provide vivid accounts of the appearance of the battlefield through their reliance on concrete nouns, sensuous adjectives, and visual metaphors. Warfare has less to do with human confrontations or national-political projects than with the kaleidoscope of sensory data that the writer organizes in his presentations. Moral judgments are excluded altogether or dwindle into occasional references to the stench of cadavers, yet these details, too, fit into the mosaic of physical perceptions which constitutes the writer's overriding concern. This is the aestheticization of politics and war as objects of contemplation; they are to be judged in terms of their surface appearance and beauty, not in terms of an interior content, for the spectacle is characterized precisely by its lack of an inside.

Battle becomes spectacular theater, an artistic performance that can be watched. The opposition of the hostile armies tends to lose its importance next to their ultimate cooperation in the construction of the visual totality of the event. The notion of spectacle, implying vision and fundamental cohesion, stands in contrast to a dramatic concept of war that inquires into the conflict and its conceptual roots, asking why the forces stand in opposition and how their alternative goals find linguistic articulation. Such a political inquiry into battle necessarily assumes the importance of the alternative subjects, their

225

conscious intentions, the balance of their forces, their past history, and their understanding of their future goals. Yet from the standpoint of Jünger's modernism, all these points are implicated in the metaphysics of an antiquated liberalism and its intellectual baggage of subjectivity, partisanship, and development. The fascist alternative is the rhetoric of spectacle, or the accumulation of sensuous data, totalized into an unbroken form, without meaning beyond its own self-production. The spectacle is therefore the point where fascist modernism can best be understood as a response to the crisis of the hermeneutically mature recipient assumed by nineteenth-century realism. The disappearance of a homogeneous public sharing key values and a basic educational background with the author—a process that sets in gradually around 1870 and generates early in the twentieth century self-conscious avant-garde movements characterized by a vicious hostility toward the public—is the fundamental datum for a sociology of literature of the period. Its converse is the increasing generation of texts that no longer operate with the assumption of the interpretative facility of the reader. Spectacle is not the only possible solution; both the leftist modernism of Brecht and the aesthetic modernism of Mann work with strategies of paradox and provocation in order to produce and prod a reconstructed reader. The corollary in the fascist version is the meaningless spectacle which produces its collective reader, either the archaic racial collective or the masses organized into the futuristic technology of power.

While iteration represents a break with the rhetoric of development and spectacle implies a denunciation of the interpretive subject, yet another feature of fascist prose, its pseudo-documentary character, defines a rejection of nineteenth-century notions of fictionality. One possible consequence of Jünger's complaint about the escapist tendencies in traditional culture is the call for a literature that claims a factual connection to contemporary reality. This tendency, which explains why fascist literature fulfills its own program less in a novel than in a memoir, mimics contemporary leftist predilections for an operative, documentary literature, especially reportage.

The point is not that left-wing and right-wing documentary tendencies are identical; their substantive politics, aesthetic forms and poetological defenses are in fact significantly different. Yet the fascist literary model, like other contemporary models, criticizes traditionalist literature as merely aesthetic and psychological and advocates instead a pedagogic-informative writing able to further collective political struggles. The rejection of bourgeois aesthetics is linked to the critique of nineteenth-century liberalism, for which literature was only a superficial "embellishment of life." *Völkisch* or reactionary populist literature considers it crucial to escape this ornamental status and to become more than fiction, or that which is not fiction, by documenting allegedly authentic political and social conditions. This dynamic explains the critic Paul Fechter's comment on *Volk ohne Raum*: "Hans Grimm's novel is namely—this must be underscored again—for all its artistry that the author hammered out of his story in difficult labor, not just a novel. It is much more than a mere piece of art."[22] Fechter insists on Grimm's having surpassed the limits of aestheticism in order to explain how the novel goes beyond elitism to address "the large whole, the folk," and how it fulfills a practical political function, which traditional aesthetics would have prohibited, as "a guide [*"Führer"*] and aid for clarification of the necessary." The novel has the operative ability "not only to speak to the folk and to say something to everyone who is part of the folk but also more importantly: to participate in the work of creating this folk, which still stands before us as a challenge." Translated out of the jargon of fascist literary criticism, this means that the novel is not restricted to aesthetic representation, since it participates directly in the political project of the radical right. Whether the characterization of Grimm's novel is valid or not, Fechter's point echoes the requirement that Jünger placed on contemporary art, to escape traditional notions of autonomy—here meaning the limits of bourgeois fictionality—and to participate in the construction of a totalitarian order.

The preference for a politically effective, instructional literature, which forms the basis of Fechter's review, recurs within *Volk ohne Raum* itself in an interpolated literary critical episode. Having isolated his hero in a barely settled region of German Southwest Africa, Grimm confronts him with two books, and the different responses they evoke offer insight into the fascist literary model of the midtwenties. The novel, *Buddenbrooks*, at first, seems to be privileged "because it contained formed and finished life"; that is, it is illusionist fiction. But the recipient is gradually repelled by the description of decline: "As the fate of the merchant family began to dissolve into weakness, clearly because of its limitations, a resistance emerged in the reader." Gradually the hero's alternative book, the factual prose of political essayism and economic argumentation of Gerhard Hillebrand, who provides a defense of colonialism, takes on importance. Thus Grimm sets up a competition between two antithetical literary modes: "And while the enervated material of the novel carried little into the next day except greater sensitivity and, at best, a rejection and disinterest in real things, the thoughts of the second book continued to ride and work and hunt like manly companions" (II, 278-279). Political writing wins out over bourgeois fiction; informational and argumentative stances displace literary autonomy.

Given this program, the episode is not surprisingly the only aesthetic experience of the hero in the course of the voluminous novel. The work does not concern itself with aesthetics; it is interested solely in politics and therefore integrates lengthy political essays into the main text. The main text even attempts to present itself as no longer fiction. Although the narrative plays on many features of traditional novels of development, the rejection of traditional fiction implied by the literary critical passage induces Grimm to qualify the fictional status of his own text. At two key points the narrator, who otherwise maintains a traditional third-person objectivity, suddenly appears within the text, not as an additional fictional figure but as Grimm himself. As soon as Grimm claims to have encountered the novel's hero, however, the narrative ceases to act as fiction and assumes the character of a memoir, documenting purportedly authentic events.

The insistence on documentary authenticity, which is merely implicit in Grimm's novel, becomes more distinct in the propagandistic novels of Artur Dinter. The issue is not their ideological content—the vicious anti-Semitism, racism, and reified idealism— but the status of the text. The main body of *Die Sünde wider das Blut* (The Sin Against Blood, 1919) extends for some three hundred pages of apparent fiction with occasional essayistic interruptions. It is followed by seventy-five pages of allegedly documentary commentary which refers back to footnoted passages. These comments are presented as scientific explications of the issues raised by the fiction: the biological risks of miscegenation, the correlation of criminality and race, and the exegesis of Jewish religious codifications. Although Dinter addresses these matters in the terms of his own lunatic-fringe version of the fascist message, he shares with Grimm the curious mixture of fictionality and documentary claims. The importance of this second aspect is indicated by the responses of contemporary critical opponents, which question the legitimacy of Dinter's documentary contentions, i.e. a debate ensues around hard facts, not literary forms.[23]

Although the validity of Dinter's references is questionable, his project of augmenting the fictional narrative with texts allegedly referring directly to the extra-aesthetic historical world is not. This insistence on the documentary status of the text demonstrates the relationship of this literature to the overall crisis of the literary institution of the bourgeois nineteenth century. Traditional fiction is denounced as mere entertainment, which Dinter wishes to replace with a literature of information linked to political action: "In contrast to the goal of the vast majority of today's novelists, I am not concerned with combating the boredom of my readers but with providing them with ethical, religious and spiritual values and an elementary knowledge of the questions on the solution of which the *völkisch* rebirth and the renewal of our unhappy folk depend. My books should be readers and primers for the folk."[24] This pedagogical program determines the typical form of informational presentation, which is not an unstructured montage of documents but a series of extended excursions that communicate both the fact and its significance within fascist ideology. These excursions are located either in the footnotes or in the text itself as lectures or speeches.

This aspect of fascist literature, documentary speech, takes on a grotesque character in Dinter's *Die Sünde wider den Geist* (The Sin Against Spirit, 1921), which is concerned with the occult, a phenomenon in which the spiritist Dinter firmly believes. A spirit from beyond appears at various seances, and the messages he delivers correspond to Dinter's political program. In the afterword to the novel, Dinter assures the reader that these messages are themselves literal reproductions of authentic spiritist pronouncements: "The spiritistic phenomena that I have described in this political novel are authentic: I myself experienced some of them and others were experienced by reliable observers, whom I personally know; others are based on indisputably proven events recorded in spiritological literature."[25] Dinter admits that the plot of the novel is a fictional invention, but it serves only as a framework for the presentation of these authentic documents. To disbelieve Dinter and recognize the pseudo-documentary character of the material is hardly a form of intolerance. Nevertheless the issue remains, as with Grimm, the self-presentation of fascist literature as fact and not as fiction.

The affinity of fascist literature for documentary forms is also evident in Jünger's writings. He approaches the readers of the twenties largely through the purported authenticity of battlefield memoirs and not through traditional fictionality. In addition, his comments on anthologies of war recollections shed light on the implicit aesthetic program. Grimm privileged the political essay over bourgeois fiction; Dinter preferred informative instruction to entertainment. Jünger now deems the authentic statement of the front soldier superior to the pronouncements of the professional literati. A new writing associated with practical experience thus displaces the old writing of elitist armchair commentators, the literary representatives of autonomous aesthetics and independent theory. As Jünger comments in the introduction to *Hier spricht der Feind* (This is the Enemy Speaking):

> Therefore it is much more important for us to learn about the attitude of the simple and authentic soldier on the other side who made history, for example, at the fortress of Verdun or on a destroyer at the battle of Skaggerak than to pay attention to that pathos that is so easy to fabricate at any desk in Europe. A collection of documents of this sort therefore not only provides an incomparably sharper insight into the picture of the war; it also probably serves the true spirit of peace better than that whitewashed European politeness which spreads like a thin veil over the dangerous situation that the peace treaties have left behind.[26]

Aside from the ostensible politics of this passage, its critique of the Versailles Treaty and the heroization of the soldier, Jünger participates in the articulation of a fascist literary model. Elitist culture is rejected, and writing is to become factual and effective, documentary and operative. Although the texts Jünger gathers differ from the pseudo-documents in Dinter's novels or the purported memoirs in *Volk ohne Raum*, all three examples share a disparaging judgment of traditional fiction, all lay claim to a nonaesthetic, historical reality, and all intend to participate directly in a contemporary political battle perceived as an impending fascist regeneration.

The rejection of fictionality and the search for documentary forms as the medium of power are thematized even within the fictional text of Jünger's novel *Auf den Marmorklippen*. The locus of culture, which at the novel's conclusion is consumed by the flames of destruction, is a place of scientific investigation, botanical collection, and classification, not of traditional literary life. Its specificity becomes clear if compared to the other libraries. In contrast to the realists' place of sociability, Stifter's cultic adulation of art, and Hermann's reified culture as possession, Jünger's library is the location of the word that controls nature. The shift is anticipated in the conclusion of Frenssen's protofascist Bildungsroman, which bypasses the traditional entry into a world of autonomous art by leading Jörn to study natural science and technology.

Jünger's herbarium combines the antiquated magic of romanticism with the modernist concern for power and structure: "The word is simultaneously king and magician. We started out from the grand example of Linnaeus, who entered the chaotic worlds of animals and plants with the marshal staff of the word. And more miraculous than all the kingdoms won by the sword, his authority over the fields of flowers and legions of worms continues" (204-205). King and magician, power and magic, fascist future and mystical past— bourgeois subjectivity and its cultural modes are outflanked by a literary strategy that invokes the regressive temptations of a preindividuated state in the service of postindividual domination. Writing has nothing more to do with an exchange of a comprehensible meaning between an accessible text and an autonomous reader. Instead, modernism as fascism guarantees the maintenance of an order beyond question or communication. Iteration that denies change, spectacle that denies inquiry, and facticity that presents documents demanding acceptance combine in a literary strategy that constructs a new authorial authority. The implied reader that these texts intend to produce must submit and merge into the new collective. This literary community escapes atomization but replaces it with a frozen order, a collectivized iron cage. Although fascist modernism breaks with the fundamental organizing principles of bourgeois liberalism, it preserves the passivity of the recipient toward which Brecht and Benjamin addressed their critiques. The iterative spectacle does not condemn the audience to private isolation, but the collective it generates still lacks the potential of autonomous activity that was always implicit in liberalism as an unfulfilled promise.

10

Leftist Modernism: Alfred Döblin, Oskar Maria Graf, and Walter Benjamin

*L*iterary texts always engage in a multiplicity of political practices, but this ascription of a universally political character to literature is necessarily abstract, since it sets itself above the specific status of particular aesthetic programs and works. Not all literatures are equally political, nor are all politics the same. One can certainly argue, for example, that a private, subjectivist writing may imply a certain political stance; it would be foolish, however, to deny that it differs from a literary program that consciously defines its goals in public terms. In the case of the emergence of German modernism, the break with the hegemonic aesthetics of the nineteenth century is accompanied by precisely such a distinction, for nineteenth-century literature is largely embedded in an institution of private contemplation and reception in which the category of the individual provides the central organizing principle. The crisis of that individuality, implicated in a full matrix of political ramifications, sets the stage for new literary projects organized around collective, that is to say, public and political categories. The divergent character of these competing political projects generates the multiple rhetorics of modernist writing.

As a collectivist literary project, modernism does not merely reflect the collapse of the empire, the revolution of 1918-1919, and the transition to the Weimar Republic. Nor do the historical events merely provide authors with new material to be integrated into traditional literary forms. Rather, the radical reshaping of political categories in terms of the exhortation to popular participation coincides with the immanent crisis of literary strategies. The ideology of democracy provides literature with the *demos*—the people, the masses, the class—as a new interlocutor around which new literary strategies can crystallize.

The political character of Weimar modernism is by no means an idiosyncratically leftist project. It includes both a right-wing, fascist modernism and a modernism of social individuality proposed by Thomas Mann. Again, not all politics are equal, and there are competing political projects and designations of the collective. Not only does the left have no particularly privileged relationship to political modernism but the emergence of a leftist modernism takes place no earlier and certainly with no fewer difficulties than do other modernist breaks with inherited bourgeois aesthetics. In fact, the Marxist left, with its strong ties to the nineteenth-century cultural prejudices of Marx and Engels, probably had a more difficult passage to a modernist aesthetics than did other participants in the Weimar scene. The representative Marxist literary critic of the Wilhelmine age, Franz Mehring, had regularly polemicized against the modernist innovation of the German naturalists and against politicizing efforts to develop a specifically proletarian cultural program. His influence continued to determine leftist aesthetics in the early years of the Weimar Republic during which both working-class parties endeavored to present themselves as the true heirs to traditional bourgeois culture. The Social Democrats proved fundamentally hostile to efforts to politicize culture, while the Communists—especially the cultural editor of the *Rote Fahne*, Gertrude Alexander—denounced modernism, including the explicitly Communist modernism of Erwin Piscator, the radical innovator on the German stage.[1]

Influenced by the convergence of avant-gardist aesthetics and revolutionary politics in the Soviet Union, German authors close to the Communist party eventually organized themselves in the Association of Proletarian Revolutionary Writers, in order both to further the development of a revolutionary literature and to defend their interests against the denigration of aesthetic matters current in the party. Nevertheless it was in their own journal, *Die Linkskurve*, that leftist antimodernism ultimately triumphed, for it was there that Lukács launched his attacks against Willi Bredel and Ernst Ottwalt, treated as paradigms of modernist innovation. These attacks announced the fundamental swing toward an aesthetics of socialist realism after 1930. Explicit political discourse was denounced as tendentious, a position that could credibly invoke the testimony of Engels, and the realist novel of the nineteenth century was upheld as a model worthy of imitation. Modernism quickly became relegated to the sphere of a bourgeois decadence, no longer able to generate the progressive vision of social totality provided by the paragons Balzac and Tolstoy, and was quickly associated with the reactionary regression of fascism.[2]

Thus, the model of a leftist modernism was perpetually besieged. As leftist, it was regularly subject to legal persecution by the agents of the Weimar state bureaucracy and the extralegal attacks of right-wing organizations. As modernist, it was denounced both by the defenders of traditional aesthetic principles like Alfred Kerr and by leftists devoted to the same conservative aesthetics interpreted as progressive. Despite this beleaguered situation, leftist modernism represents perhaps the most important locus of cultural productivity in the Weimar Republic. It was here that Bertolt Brecht lay the groundwork for modern theater, Alfred Döblin transformed the novel, and Walter Benjamin elaborated his aesthetics. In addition, figures like Oskar Maria Graf, Johannes R. Becher, Marieluise Fleisser, Ernst Toller, and Ödön von Horvath were, in different ways, linked to the central project, which reverberated as well in Bauhaus architecture and the visual arts through Georg Grosz, Otto Dix, and others.[3]

In leftist modernism, the politicization of aesthetics is tied to the goal of a vocalization of the collective. In contrast to bourgeois literature, where the collective is absent and the speech of the isolated individual gradually loses significance, as in Fontane's *Irrungen, Wirrungen*, the leftist work of art is intended as a medium through which the postindividual subject can come to speech. This process of vocalization is linked to a technological optimism inspired by the functionalism of German Bauhaus and Soviet constructivism, while drawing on the motifs of progress in the *Communist Manifesto*. Capitalist modernization produced the mass, while the progress of scientific and industrial innovation provided the mechanisms with which the masses could overcome the conditions of capitalist production. The specifically modernist rejection of nineteenth-century art forms is thus grounded in a materialist dialectic of technological progress: in the age of technical reproduction, the traditional bourgeois aesthetics of artistic originality, the uniqueness of the auratic work, and the isolation of the individual recipient are declared anachronistic and counterposed to social relations organized around characteristically modern structures, such as film and radio.

Benjamin provides the most complete presentation of this position after the Weimar Republic in his 1936 account of the cinema as the place in which the industrially, that is, collectively, produced object (film) is viewed by the collective recipient who, liberated from privatistic contemplation, can in turn approach the object with sovereign critique and articulate rationality. Brecht's speech on "The Function of the Radio" from 1932 is also apt: "Radio is to be transformed from an apparatus of distribution into an apparatus of communication. Radio would be the most important communicative apparatus of public life, a gigantic system of canals, that is to say, it could also be so if it were able not only to broadcast but also to receive; therefore to make the listener not only listen but also speak; not only to isolate him, but also to set him in relation. Radio would have to transcend mere distribution and organize the listener as a distributor." Brecht translates the familiar Marxist distinction between the conditions of production and the productive forces into a question of communication. The available forces of communication include the technological infrastructure of the radio as well as the mass of listeners. Yet the conditions of communications condemn the listener to the silence of passive reception because of the monodirectional operation of the technological apparatus. Brecht's alternative envisions taking advantage of the potential of the apparatus to vocalize the listeners by permitting them as well to broadcast: "The major issue is not only that the public be instructed but that it must also instruct." The object of a repressive communicative structure is to become the subject of an emancipated discourse which replaces the silence of individuality with the collectivized speaker.[4]

Although this optimistic faith in the benefits of technology betrays a futuristic commitment to modernization, the leftist modernism of the Weimar Republic is even more indebted to the archaic material of a popular religion with strong baroque components. It may appear odd to link leftist culture with religious material, yet just as the early twentieth-century neo-Hegelianism permits Lukács to uncover the authentic philosophical substance of Marxism, the renewed interest in religion, particularly in expressionist circles, allows for the rediscovery of important ideational components in the revolutionary project that was obscured by positivist secularism.

At stake are not only the theological coloration of Benjamin's thought and the biblical elements in Döblin's *Berlin Alexanderplatz* (1930) but also the categorical accounts of social life in Brecht's early poetry or Graf's narratives. Individual happiness is shown to be illusory, death ineluctable, and earthly wealth perpetually subject to the vagaries of fortune and the inexorable character of fate. The particular coloration of Weimar leftist modernism depends on precisely this transformation of pessimistic theology into a political stance: anti-subjectivity, a rejection of capitalist wealth, and the secularization of fate as materialist historiography. This religious substructure ultimately grounds the project of collective vocalization, for the content of that voice is not arbitrary; it proclaims the end of egoism and the emergence of a charismatic community of solidarity that recognizes the spirit implicitly by affirming the explicit objectivity of suffering and fate.

Whereas fascist modernism replaces the insistence of bourgeois realism on the privileged status of the individual as the intersection of authentic particularity and universal laws with the totalitarian homogenization of the single unit as an infinitely repeatable item, leftist modernism responds to the crisis of individuality differently. It is less concerned with the failure of individuality than with individuality as the failure of the original collective. The individual who separates himself from the community is burdened with a guilt that inevitably ruins the earthly joys he may have accumulated. The religious denunciation of individual greed as evil slides into the leftist critique of capitalist individuality. Although the two are ultimately inseparable, the theological rejection of mammon clearly provides the foundation for the leftist rejection of capitalism. Thus, in one of Graf's *Kalender-Geschichten* (Calendar Stories, 1929), a narrative of greedy children leads to the conclusion that "the individual is the most deceitful and hypocritical being that wanders across God's earth." His search for accumulation erodes his morality and the bonds to his community. These bonds are always present in Graf's accounts, but they are always broken. The individual has sinned against the social order, and this order responds with a perpetual vigilance of envy, hatred, and misanthropy: "Himmelberg had not been a real village for a long time, but now it became a nest of discord." "They all were delighted with his despair." "Curious, how kind a man can be if he's trying to cause his neighbor's misfortune." "Help no one...he might kill you." Similarly, the hero who gives his name to Graf's novel *Bolwieser* (1931) is sure of his individual happiness in marriage and emphatically sets himself against the collective in his opposition to a strike and in his isolation from village life. Long before his punishment, he is surrounded by the vengeful chorus, spying on him and waiting for the inevitable misfortune. Precisely this constellation of individual illusions and a hostile collective, which Graf plays out in the Bavarian countryside, structures the hopelessness of Franz Biberkopf in Döblin's Berlin, where the individual who hopes to find happiness as an individual is crushed by the city from which he tried to escape. "Alexanderplatz rules his existence," notes Benjamin, and thus the megapolis demands atonement for the hubris of individuation.[5]

Individuation, as a search for earthly wealth at the cost of communitarian solidarity, wounds not only the collective but also the individual, who repeatedly finds that his plans do not come to fulfillment. As little as Biberkopf can become respectable, Graf's characters fail regularly in stories designed to demonstrate the nullity of the best-laid plans. The atomistic alternative to participatory membership in society can lead to isolation but never to comfort. In *Die Chronik von Flechting* (The Chronicle of Flechting, 1925), where Graf's figures continually abuse family and village in order to pursue a course of upward mobility, the narrator finally proclaims: "One could nearly say that you can't build a castle like that without being punished."[6] With the motif of the castle, Graf cites the genre of the fairy-tale, not in order to evoke an other-worldly utopia but rather to show its incongruity in a bourgeois era. The individualist escape into wealth cannot truly succeed, for it brings only pain and sorrow.

This treatment of the individual, not as the potential carrier of success found in realism but as the carrier of a guilt accrued through a crime perpetrated on the community, generates a rhetoric of exemplars. With didactic intent, the narrative account demonstrates the wages of sin. Yet it is not only the individual who is denounced but the content of earthly pleasure as well. This leftism has lost the Saint-Simonist enthusiasm for sensual pleasure that pervaded early nineteenth-century social criticism, as in Heine. Confronted with a capitalism that seems capable of the infinite generation of commodities, no matter how problematic its mechanisms of distribution, leftism develops a profound mistrust of wealth, which combines a subliminal Jacobin asceticism with a baroque hostility to the pleasures of the flesh: "Strange are the paths of man. The winter is cold, the summer is hot, time passes away, and old age and bitterness sit in your bones, before you know it. And in the end— when you think it over, what did it all mean?—Misery, misery, misery! Chance is everything, and nothing."[7] Life is no longer the bounteous collection of sensuous commodities that bedazzled the young Anton Wohlfahrt in the marketplace of liberal capitalism. Gone are the roses of Stifter's utopia; gone, too, is the sensual beauty retained by objects in Fontane's novel, no matter how much they had already begun to dissolve into allegory. The universal eradication of use value hollows out the object and transforms a trust in the senses into a trap: both Bolwieser and Biberkopf locate pleasure in an erotic realm that proves their undoing. It is no accident that Döblin accords so much importance to the motif of the "whore of Babylon."

Döblin describes how the ex-convict Biberkopf succumbs to the forces of the metropolis and returns to a life of crime that leads to his downfall. Graf recounts the fate of the station-master, Xaver Bolwieser, who, betrayed by his wife and entangled in legal disputes, ends in a similar misery. Both Biberkopf and Bolwieser pursue happiness with naive innocence, and both fail to attain it. Biberkopf loves his mistress, Mieze, and his friend, Reinhold, and his consequent blindness leads to his demise. Graf explains Bolwieser's fate even more clearly; from the start, the devotion to pleasure on the part of the individual ensnares him in an inexorable decline. The novel commences in a generalizing manner, for it has to do with the exemplary case of a petty bourgeois sensualist devoured by a retribution he cannot escape: "In a small city, on a radiant summer morning, a nicely furnished bedroom, not yet tidied up, belonging to a couple not married for long—when the bright, white featherbeds and sheets are hung out the window, and the sun gradually sets the whole room aglow—that has something ensnaring to it!"[8] Sensuality and entrapment set the stage for a paradigmatic case: Bolwieser's trust in earthly pleasures does him in. The point is not that leftist modernism is a hotbed of prudishness. Instead, drawing on an iconoclasm that derives from early modern popular movements like the Anabaptists and Puritans (the first volume of Graf's *Kalender-Geschichten* in fact concludes with narratives from seventeenth-century peasant uprisings), leftist anticapitalism is compatible with an ascetic suspicion of wealth and satiated contentment.

The resultant literary rhetoric attributes to the sensuous detail a fundamentally different status from that provided by bourgeois realism or fascist modernism. Bourgeois realism is ultimately concerned with the ordering of the newly accumulated wealth of commodities, and the detail becomes the significant locus of meaning toward which the text endeavors to direct an appropriate desire. Fascist modernism cannot present the detail as meaningful, since, with its abolition of the individual, it has also dissolved the hermeneutic project. The detail appears rather as the intersection of multiple sensuous qualities within the matrix of the capitalist spectacle, designed to ensure the recipient's passivity. In leftist modernism, the detail is no longer ensconced in the order of realist meaning nor does it overpower the reader as in the fascist text. Instead, the central figure, the exemplary individual, succumbs to sensuous details beyond his comprehension, and the tension between individual and objects sets up a dialectical rhetoric with which the reader is confronted and from which—this is the didactic intent—he is to learn.

The rhetoric of exemplars and the dialectic structures are linked to another element in which religious substance and leftist anticapitalism again converge. Fate as the damnation of human existence in fallen nature converges with a materialist insistence on the inescapability of social conditions and the inevitability of historical processes. Fate provides the various accounts of failed individuation with an ultimate objectivity. Fate is not just a series of curious accidents but an expression of the rule of necessity in capitalist society, where freedom is illusory and pleasure always commodified. No matter how one tries, one of Graf's figures complains, "it turns out wrong...it always ends up different."[9] Complaint is precisely the correct term, for in fascist ideology, fate or destiny is the moving force in history that the member of the collective must embrace in order to fulfill a heroic identity, whereas in leftist modernism the category of fate represents the final limit on freedom in an unredeemed world. The society in which fate operates is subject to a heteronomy that negates any individualist hope for reconciliation. Fate is an objective force that cannot be denied in isolation, although it might be overcome through a collective transformation of the social order, which is the political corollary to apocalyptic resurrection.

More significant, however, than this difference between the fascist apotheosis of destiny and the leftist critique of fate is the delineation, implicit in the central works of leftist modernism, of the distance from the precepts of liberal bourgeois ideology. Whereas the Enlightenment presents the individual as emancipated from higher powers, subject only to the rational laws he is prepared to accept, Döblin asserts that this idealist notion of autonomy has no relevance for the figure trapped in the nexus of monopoly capitalism. Biberkopf may think he is free, but the "hammer" of fate strikes him down again and again, and he must eventually capitulate. Döblin often circumscribes this necessity with a telling phrase: "He swore that he would be proper, and you have seen how he was proper for weeks, but that was only a grace period. He'll be drawn into crime, he doesn't want to, he resists, it overpowers him, he must must."[10] The phrase "must must" recurs elsewhere and echoes the idealist version of freedom in G. E. Lessing's eighteenth-century drama *Nathan der Weise*. There freedom is presented as the absence of necessity: no man "must must," no one is compelled to accept compulsion. In the world of free exchange the individual is emancipated from the strictures of feudal communities, according to bourgeois ideology, and this promise in the course of the nineteenth century transforms general civil freedom into the secular freedom of the free market.

Modernism addresses this truncation of freedom by the logic of capitalist development; all modernisms respond to the demise of the credibility of the autonomous individual, but in radically different ways. Fascist modernism embraces unfreedom as the heroic destiny of the folk, while leftist modernism deplores fate as the denial of the freedom promised. In this sense, leftist modernism displays a continuity with premodernist literature, for it too posits freedom as a desideratum, while recognizing its material nonfulfillment. The category of fate therefore forces the exemplary dialectic of leftist modernism toward a concern with the objective character of miserable social relations. It is as distant from the idealism of the bourgeois fiction as from the purely formal homogeneity of the fascist spectacle. Instead, it attempts to assimilate into itself the concrete authenticity of contemporary social life, and its rhetoric consequently assumes an ethnographic character directed toward genuine facts and popular speech, which explains the predominance of dialectic speech from both Graf's Bavaria and Döblin's Berlin. Various leftist demands for a popular literature have their origin in a double intent: the question of fate raises the problem of the material existence of the people, and the elevation of popular speech to a literary language represents a vocalization of the *demos* as a specific strategy of interpellation, that is, an invocation of a collective recipient in order to enable it to address the fateful necessity that denies it freedom.

Against this background of technological optimism and religious melancholy, a leftist modernist theory of narration began to take shape toward the end of the Weimar Republic. In the literary critical essays of Benjamin and in programmatic statements of Döblin, this theory centers on the category of the "epic," borrowed from Brecht's program for an epic theater and, especially, from the antinomy of epic and novel outlined in Lukács's *Theory of the Novel*. Lukács ascribes the epic to "closed societies," such as Homeric Greece, in which the alienation of the individual from collective culture has not yet taken place. Atomization has not separated the individual from society and nature, and the context of individual activity therefore retains an immanent meaning which is always immediately accessible. In contrast to this closed totality, the world of bourgeois individuality is characterized by a lack of meaning, and the characteristic literary account of confusion and disorientation is the novel, determined by a fundamental disjunction between subjective ideals and objective reality and therefore structured in terms of an ultimately fruitless search for values. The neo-Hegelian categories of *The Theory of the Novel* are transformed in the early twenties into Lukács's Hegelian Marxism of *History and Class Consciousness* (1923). More important for the development of aesthetic theory in the Weimar Republic, however, is the distinction between, on the one hand, the epic as a literary form associated with a historical situation in which individual and collective stand in a nonantagonistic relation to each other and, on the other hand, the novel as the prototypical genre of an isolated privacy, severed from collective social experience.

Like Lukács, Brecht operates with an antinomic aesthetic structure, in which the epic form of theater is counterposed to a dramatic form. Moreover, he shares with the young Lukács the fundamental linkage of epic material to nonindividuated experience, while the drama appears as the locus of features associated with bourgeois culture: emotional subjectivity, evolutionary development, and a passive, quietistic reception. Yet a profound chronological reordering distinguishes Lukács's argument in *The Theory of the Novel* from the Brechtian program for an epic theater. For Lukács, the epic as the art form of the Homeric utopia serves as a foil for the novel, which is the necessary aesthetic structure in an age of ubiquitous atomization; that is, the novel has replaced the epic as the paradigmatic form of modernity. For Brecht, the revolutionary innovator, epic theater is about to banish the moribund dramatic theater of bourgeois isolation from the stage. No longer merely archaic, the epic now also encompasses the features of a modern, futuristic project, in which prebourgeois and postbourgeois, preindividual and postindividual forms converge, and the public is transformed into the vocalized collective. Thus the program for an epic theater counters each of the features of bourgeois drama with an alternative, designed to generate a new recipient: instead of private emotions, public reason prevails; instead of a logic of individual development and organic growth, a montage of independent scenes permits the rational observer to observe the breaks and contradictions; and instead of the enervating contemplation of the dramatic work by the emotional recipient condemned to silence, an argumentative presentation challenges the recipient, "awakens his activity," and "demands a decision."[11] Unlike dramatic theater, which induces an emotional stance in the public and therefore empowers individual professionals with critical authority, epic theater sets as its goal the production of a collective recipient as the carrier of critical reason. This vocalized community is as antithetical to privacy as the fascist folk, but it is precisely the opposite of the pacified victims of the fascist spectacle.

In a review of *Berlin Alexanderplatz*, Benjamin mixes the Lukácsian designation of the epic as an archaic form with the Brechtian critique of individualistic aesthetics and an insistence on the need for a contemporary renewal of a collective narrative mode. The theory of leftist modernism is organized in terms of the tension between private silence and public speech:

> For the epic, being is an ocean. There is nothing more epic than the ocean. One can of course treat the ocean in very different ways. For example, lie on the beach, listen to the surf and collect the shells it washes ashore. That is what the epic author does. One can also travel the ocean. With many goals and none at all. One can take an ocean voyage, and then, out there, with no land in sight, only sea and sky, wander aimlessly. That is what the author of the novel does. He is truly lonely and mute. Epic man is only at rest. In the epic, the people rests after the day's labor; it listens, dreams and collects.

The novelist has separated himself from the people and its activity. The birth chamber of the novel is the isolated individual who can no longer discuss his most important concerns in an exemplary manner, who is confused and oblivious to advice. In the presentation of human existence, the novel pushes incommensurability to an extreme. One can feel the difference between the novel and the true epic by thinking of the works of Homer or Dante. Oral tradition, the material of the epic, has a make-up different from the substance of a novel. The novel differs from all other forms of prose—the fairy-tale, the legend, the saying, the funny story—in that it neither derives from nor enters into an oral tradition. It differs most clearly, however, from the narration of epic prose. Nothing contributes more to the dangerous silencing of the human spirit, nothing stifles the soul of narration more thoroughly than the shameless expansion that the reading of novels has undergone in all of our lives.[12]

Benjamin, who elsewhere provides the Brechtian project for an epic theater with its almost important critical elaboration, here transfers the key categories into the discussion of prose. The contrast between epic and novel generates a series of distinctions that describe the significant features of the model of leftist modernism. The novel is embedded in an individualistic world-view, in terms of both its content, the confusion of the individual lost at sea, and its addressee, the isolated reader. The epic, in contrast, constitutes the discourse of the people with itself, the sedimentation of collective traditions perpetually renewed through public narration. In a review of *Bolwieser*, Benjamin presents this opposition in a radicalized formulation: "It is a matter of life or death for the new epic to liquidate this privacy from which the novel derives its legitimacy."[13]

This liquidation of the individual, the aesthetic corollary to the abolition of private property, implies, in Benjamin's account, an end to individualistic confusion. Whereas the novel recounts the vicissitudes of personal disorientation, the epic provides knowledge, above all by treating its material as examples from which the recipient can learn. The initial distinction between the individual and the collective is thus compounded by a second distinction, between oblivion and insight. Here the leftist modernism of Benjamin with its didactic intent reveals its indebtedness to an Enlightenment tradition of instruction. The German idealist separation of aesthetics from science, which distanced the former from conceptual knowledge and pushed it toward a subjective irrationality, gives way to a program for the epic as a medium of learning and objectivity. In the *Bolwieser* review Benjamin sharpens the attack: "While the Bildungsroman constructs a personality, the epic author demolishes it. In the Bildungsroman the hero has his experiences that form his personality. Here, in the epic realm, the subject of the experiment has experiences that reduce him." The novel of development presents the emergence of a unique aesthetic individuality which integrates itself as a full personality into bourgeois society. The epic account reverses the process and inverts the goal, confronting the recipient with an exemplary failure. In the case of *Bolwieser* this means the paradigmatic decomposition of the petty bourgeois sensualist for the cognitive benefit of the readers. The reduction to which Benjamin refers is salient in Graf's narrative, where the station-master is cast out of established society and returns to the Bavarian landscape and the peasantry, although without any of the fascist nostalgia for rural life. Bolwieser leaves the bourgeois modernity of commodified hedonism and railroads and ends in poverty as a ferryman, a mythic image in an epic realm. Yet this myth—Benjamin refers to the metamorphosis as a fairy-tale, another popular form—is not hostile to reason, for the demolished individual becomes a scientist, a meteorologist, from whom the peasants can learn more than the bourgeois reader from a traditional novelist.[14]

The polarity between individual and collective narrative forms as well as the increment of knowledge associated with the epic are tied to a final distinction Benjamin makes between novel and epic, the distinction between written and oral communication. Although the works of Döblin and Graf are written and printed, Benjamin suggests they are written in a manner not antithetical to the principle of oral recapitulation. For example, they rely on an authentically oral language, dialect forms, in contrast to the artificial and elite language of the hegemonic novel, a language that is never spoken. In addition, the privileging of the oral compounds the project of collectivization by integrating a multiplicity of voices in the polyphony of montage, especially in *Berlin Alexanderplatz*. The juxtaposition of heterogeneous texts, which is the literary corollary to dadaist collages, produces a heteroglossic speech. This "universal discourse," in Heiner Muller's phrase, represents the radical alternative to the predominance of the single speaker in realist narration, isolated from any concrete interlocutors and condemned therefore to a de facto silence.[15] This intratextual polyphony, the point at which Döblin moves closest to the liberal modernism in Thomas Mann's *Doctor Faustus,* corresponds to the underlying goal of the oral principle, to vocalize the objective collective. Whereas the novel mutes the recipient, who in any case is isolated and therefore speechless, the renewed epic shatters the silence of bourgeois culture by invoking the people as a potentially articulate agent.

Categories similar to those of Benjamin's are evident in Döblin's programmatic statements. As early as 1915, in the context of expressionist activism, he insists that literature is a "public concern" and criticizes individualistic orientations by calling for a "depersonation" of the author and an end to "authorial hegemony." In an address of 1929 he argues that the true epic is not a mere conceit relying on the suspension of disbelief but rather a valid medium of truth and knowledge because of its concern with exemplary figures and "elementary situations of human existence." Epic writing is not the expression of private concerns but the "collective work of author and public," for the author "carries the people within himself." Similarly, the creative function of "living langauge" is the vocalization of the collective.[16]

The substance of the leftist modernist theory of narration emerges even more clearly as an inscribed aesthetics in Graf's narratives. Two of his *Kalender-Geschichten* address alternative institutionalizations of literature. In "Fame Deceives," Graf describes the interlocking elements of urban literary life: the bohemian underground, established salons, and the publishing industry. They provide fame and fortune, but as the central figure learns, they also defuse the text, which vanishes into insignificance. Even the grossest hostility and misbehavior on the part of the author can be assimilated and transformed into marketing mechanisms: the more the bourgeois novelist speaks, the more he is silenced. Graf presents an alternative in "Joseph Leiberer, May He Rest in Peace." Leiberer is a storyteller operating in a popular, nonprofessional setting, offering oral narration as a collective event in an inn. Graf emphasizes that he is discussing the ontology of an independent genre by distinguishing between Leiberer's "narrating" and "crazy novels." The adjective "crazy" alone indicates that the oral narrative is to be privileged as the locus of an objective knowledge absent in the bourgeois genre. This knowledge, however, is inseparable from the theological substructure of leftist modernism, especially its melancholy recognition of the inevitability of death: "And when he started thinking it all over, he always ended up saying: 'Oh Lord, what are we after all... A pile of dirt, and nothing more!' That was strange about him. He always began, so to say, with life and ended up with death. He always was thinking about this ending. Strange!" The objectivity of Leiberer's narration depends on the collective context as well as on the content, a recognition of the materialist finality of human life. This familarity from the outset with the ashes-to-ashes conclusion functions in the manner of a Brechtian alienation effect: the recipients avoid excessive emotional identification and can watch the experiment unfold. Thus, unlike the "crazy novels" of urban literary life, Leiberer's stories do not promise happy ends, and unlike the bourgeois novellas, they do not linger over unheard-of events or the unique successes of particular individuals. On the contrary, all three examples of Leiberer's stories end with death. Each provides a further sort of knowledge by inverting an implied, moralizing subtext. The first story contradicts trivial idealizations of wartime partings between lovers, and the second story demolishes urban idealizations of the healthy peasantry. In the third story, the narrated death converges with the death of the narrator. Yet this final account balances on the theological border between melancholy and resurrection. Its title, "When Everything Finally Becomes Just," transforms the religious category into a potentially political apocalypse: the objectivity of grace becomes the foundation for the revolutionary community.[17]

Bolwieser similarly examines alternative narrative models. Whereas *Kalender-Geschichten* describe separate sociological institutionalizations of narration, the novel concerns the immanent character of the texts. The novel's review of competing forms of narrative speech occurs close to the end, where the bulk of the plot has already unfolded, and attention can now be paid to the mechanisms of recounting. The interruption itself is characteristic of the epic program: in place of the unbroken, organic teleology of individual development, the epic constantly anticipates and reconsiders in order to provide the recipient with the opportunity for critical reflection.

In Graf's novel, Bolwieser returns home, a broken man, and his story is retold in three different ways. First the author describes the version presented by a neighbor:

> You can imagine that bright and early the next morning, Käserin was running around the neighborhood, telling her

story with exaggerated importance. Like greedy, sucking gullets, the ears of her respective listeners swallowed her words. And what words they were! At times they were quiet and groping, slowly growing louder and louder. Or else they clogged up like a stifled urge, until they poured out in a rush or simply flowed forth smoothly. Every sound seemed planned, and every gesture had its own effect. It was masterful, like the most vivid newspaper account, the way the old woman managed to capture the people's attention. The more curious they became, the more romantic, frightening and expansive did she ornament her tidings. (319)

This is not simply a matter of gossip; it is a model narration, to which Graf ascribes a literary historical category, "romantic," which in German reverberates with the word for novel, *Roman*. This narration is compared with an institutionalized form of written narration, popular journalism. By consciously manipulating the recipients, it appeals to a solely emotional, inherently prurient interest. The account of the unique event provides no authentic knowledge. On the contrary, the extraordinary character of the happening organizes the recipients as passive viewers, not critical observers. Graf points out the effect of this narration: "Behind the windows of the houses all around the train station, excited voyeurs stared out on and on at Bolwieser's apartment" (320). The recipients are isolated; the experience is privatized; and in place of the vocalization of the collective, which epic narration sets as its goal, Käserin's sensationalism engenders voyeuristic individuals, trappped in a silent, scopophilic watching.

In contrast to this romanticism, Bolwieser has his own account of his story. Alone in his apartment, he discovers a chronicle of his marital troubles that he had kept before the catastrophe came to a head. It is a record of everyday facts, without judgment or interpretation. After providing the reader with a sample of these data, the narrator offers a literary critical judgment: "These sorts of notes were repeated in a boring series. Bolwieser shook his head and had to laugh strangely. His marriage had just amounted to this pettiness and snapping, and he had never noticed it? Yet despite all these thousands and thousands of insults, he found it all still somehow blissful" (329). The sober chronicle seems to be the opposite of Käserin's sensationalist elaborations, but it too represents a narrative failure. It records facts but generates no judgments; Bolwieser loses himself again in the sense certainty of empirical perception and, once again, learns nothing. If, however, the epic antihero never understands his situation and always fails to draw correct conclusions—and this is the role ascribed to Bolwieser—the demonstration of this failure is designed to confront the recipient with the narratological problem. Graf presents two antinomic but equally insufficient narrative strategies: a hysterical romanticism which guarantees the recipients' regression, and an ascetic facticity that ensures continued ignorance. Both are grounded in the principle of isolation.

The genuine alternative is provided by the metanarrative itself, the account of Bolwieser's decline, which neither mobilizes emotional identification nor solely reports the facts. Its objectivity depends on an almost scientific stance, the observation of a paradigmatic case. This objectivity takes on a rich sociopolitical content at the end of the novel. In the final chapter, the narrator's voice merges with that of the peasantry. Bolwieser's return to the people corresponds to a changed tone that incorporates elements of popular forms—the fairy-tale, the myth, and the legend—for here the folk becomes the narrator: "The villagers told it like a dark fairy-tale" (355). The emergence of the collective narrator implies a generic shift at the center of the program of leftist modernism, from the optimistic novel of the bourgeois individual to the melancholy account of an inescapable objectivity. History gives way to myth, individuality to community, and the rhetoric of development dissolves into the exemplary dialectics of the people.

Because all modernist models represent reponses to the same crisis of liberal individuality, they share certain formal features. The fascist tropes of iteration, spectacle, and the pseudo-document are homologous with the corresponding gestures of leftist modernism: exemplars, dialectics, and ethnographic authenticity. In each case, the rhetoric attempts to fill the gap left by the ossification of realist narration. Yet the difference between the respective terms is determined by the antithetical character of the two modernist projects. Thus, for example, fascist modernism replaces the logic of bourgeois development with the nondevelopment of extended repetition; nothing changes, and nothing new is conceivable, for the model presumes structures of eternal stability. In contrast, leftist modernism counters realist narratives of successful individuation with a series of paradigmatic failures. Both the iterative and the exemplary tropes share a serial character incompatible with liberal development, but where the iterative proclaims the impossibility of change, the exemplary insists on its urgency by underscoring the deficiency of the repeated material. Consequently the typical unit of fascist iteration is the hero, such as Grimm's Friebott, who never needs to learn or grow, since his knowledge of the reactionary message is already complete, whereas Bolwieser's inability to grow serves to exemplify the merely ideological character of bourgeois individuality that could be overcome solely by the nascent collective. It is in this sense that Benjamin insists on the exemplary character of epic narration: these are case studies designed to provoke the recipient to draw conclusions not explicitly stated and therefore to complete the developmental growth that the subject of the narration resists.

The exemplary narrative presents the mournful tale of the unhappy specimen. With its didactic intent, it verges on the parable form, and even the large novels of leftist modernism, like *Berlin Alexanderplatz*, collapse into a series of parabolic episodes with inherent instructional value. Where the nineteenth-century novella characteristically concluded with a restoration of order, the epic parable presents the contradictions of nonreconciled being, where the principles of individuation and fate perpetually clash. Döblin provides the model for this sort of narration in the story of Zannowich, representing the ultimate failure of the isolated subject, which anticipates Biberkopf's own trajectory. The Zannowich material is narrated as a barely modernized form of an archaic genre, the rabbinic dispute, and the conflict between the two commentators generates the paradigmatic reception situation of leftist modernism, for the conclusion is left up to the recipient, who is called upon to intervene. Biberkopf's exegetic inability, the opposite of the hermeneutic competency presumed in bourgeois realism, opens a space for the actual recipient; that is, the weakness of the exemplar is the prerequisite for the functioning of the narrative mode. Similarly Graf's figures are never able to draw adequate conclusions from their experiences, and the constellation of contradictions calls on the reader to do so actively.

The activation of the reader whom leftist modernism endeavors to invoke is therefore dependent on the passivity of the represented hero. Contrary to expectations, there are few Communist heroes, carriers of a correct consciousness proclaimed directly to the reader. To the extent that such figures do occur in socialist realist literature after the mid-thirties or earlier in the proletarian-revolutionary novels, the texts do not partake of the same modernist innovation associated with Benjamin, Brecht, and Döblin. Their heroes are anti-heroes, as confused and disoriented as the central figure of any bourgeois novel, but this confusion is presented as a problem for the reader to solve in society and not as a task to be overcome within the fiction in a unique course of development. The leftist antihero must consequently be a passive agent in order to preserve the space in which the invocation of the reader can take place. Precisely this passivity describes the stupidity of Biberkopf and the weakness of Bolwieser: "He had never known how to rise up against anything. He was a pliable man with no will of his own" (339-340).

Malleable Bolwieser succumbs to Hanni's machinations just as Biberkopf knuckles under to Reinhold as the agent of fate. These figures "must must" because they lack the strength of character to resist compulsion; and their incompetence permits the narrative to demonstrate the force of objective circumstances that the idealism of bourgeios realism would have relativized as mere context. Freytag's Wohlfahrt had logistical problems but no existential difficulties in colonizing territory; Biberkopf is colonized by Alexanderplatz. Leftist modernism inquires into this mechanism of submission and therefore requires personalities susceptible to domination. The material of oppression is subject to rational scrutiny—this is the role ascribed to the reader—but only if the case study involves a specimen himself incapable of rational conclusions or emancipatory acts.

The substantive weakness of the exemplar is presented as an implicitly parabolic object of study through a variety of framing devices. Ideally they present the failed individuality as a model to scrutinize, not to emulate. These devices take several forms, most notably the direct address to the reader. The narrators in *Berlin Alexanderplatz* and *Bolwieser*, as well as in the *Kalender-Geschichten*, regularly disregard the illusionist prohibition of realist fiction. This iconoclasm corresponds to a denigration of merely aesthetic contemplation in the name of a purportedly superior discourse of knowledge and objective truth. Leftist modernism eagerly drops the guise of fiction in order to thematize authentic conceptual concerns. The narrators formulate the problems at hand, recapitulate plot developments, and point out the central figures' failings. Furthermore, these surplus accounts of the diegetic trajectories are regularly phrased in abstract, generalizing terms in order to underscore the paradigmatic significance of the case. The concern with malleable figures is, after all, not intended to generate an identification on the part of the reader with regressive personalities, though that may well have been the historical case, especially in terms of the actual reception of epic theater. Instead of learning from Mother Courage's mistakes, the audience may feel empathy with her Sisyphean plight. This is the Achilles heel of leftist modernism, for the investigation of oppression necessitates its depiction, and this can potentially engender its reproduction. At stake is the adequacy of the devices of distanciation. Where they fail, or where a historically new public proves impervious, leftist modernism runs the risk of turning into its opposite: the affirmative representation of exemplary helplessness.

The putative logic of leftist modernism must assume that the distanciation will succeed and that the represented material, the exemplar, will not be identified as the locus of a positive message. This assumption points toward the next characteristic tropic form of this narration, a dialectical structuring of opposites that resists sublation and synthetic motion. This negative dialectics of modernism responds to a specific understanding of the contours of monopoly capitalism and therefore indicates a fundamental distance from realist discourse. The hermeneutics of realism drew on the discursive exchange of laissez-faire negotiations, as Wohlfahrt's experiences in the Schröter firm. The initially confusing plethora of sensuous details dissolved quickly into the orderly laws of commodity exchange. Mercantile consciousness perceived the object simultaneously as use value and exchange value, as particular and universal. The dialectical polarity was overcome within the process of liberal capitalist maturation, and once the immanent economic laws were recognized, the superficial diversity submitted to an orderly closure. Similarly the implied reader of bourgeois realism was assumed to be able to maneuver through this triadic structuring and follow the perpetual confluence of sensuous detail and abstract rule.

Modernism takes shape in a situation where this liberal dialectic has ceased to operate successfully. Fascist modernism responds by collapsing the dialectic, for the spectacle represents the abstract rule as immediately sensuous and therefore impervious to hermeneutic appropriation. Fascist modernism is contiguous, however, with the bourgeois dialectic in its insistence on closure, recast as an existentialist order, not as the historical product of exchange. In contrast, leftist modernism severs the dialectic, maintaining opposition and difference without resolution. This denial of sublation corresponds to the assessment of the anachronism of traditional models of liberal exchange, as becomes clear in *Bolwieser* when the father-in-law Neithart, a brewery owner, arrives in town and initiates negotiations to purchase a local inn. Where Freytag's Fink and Tinkeles engage in a relatively delicate linguistic ballet, Graf's capitalist, described as a "mountain of flesh," uses power and his earthy vitalism to intimidate his disadvantaged interlocutors (61). The ideal speech situation of liberal capitalism has turned into a naked display of brutality. More important, however, than this not unexpected pejorative characterization of contemporary capitalism by a leftist author is a generational difference which points toward a decisive historical shift. Neithart persistently boasts how well he can negotiate, while Bolwieser, the passive figure and exemplar of weakness, admits he cannot. With his comfortable postion, his wife, and his bureaucratic security, he has no interest in entering the risky world of business. Behind these alternative personality types lies Graf's evaluation that traditional capitalist exchange has become anachronism and that modern monopoly capitalism generates a timid individuality too committed to a petty bourgeois consumerist sensibility to recognize broader social interests.

The liberal dialectic breaks down because of the bureaucratic personality's inability to perceive larger concerns. Stifter's Risach recognized precisely this tendency in the logic of capitalist development. Ensnared by his senses from the start, Bolwieser becomes the prototype of the privatized consumer who refuses to know the public. In a typically generalizing passage that indicates the exemplary character of the material, Graf's narrator makes the point explicit:

> A comfortable bourgeois wants to give up none of the pleasures of life. In fact he will be continually driven by the desire to have it much, much nicer. He is fully private and therefore considerably more hedonistic than he is generally assumed. The authentic entrepreneur tries to expand his business and his power. The worker fights with his peers for better living conditions. The petty bourgeois, by way of contrast, does not want the former and already has the latter. He desires the derivative splendor that one sometimes sees in old-fashioned movies. He loves a tester-bed, plentiful lace and bric-a-brac. He purchases excessively ornamented furniture and all those actually superfluous things that weigh like a fetish on one's

feelings and senses. That is why he does not understand that there are people who feel and think differently than he does. As soon as he feels the least threat to his interests and passions, he becomes cowardly and malicious. (106-107)

Entrepreneurs, like Neithart, and politicized workers are active figures, engaged in social transformation. The petty bourgeois civil servant Bolwieser, on the contrary, is entrapped by the signs of status with which he has surrounded himself and beyond which he cannot see. He adopts a self-deprecating posture toward the capitalist and approaches the workers with misanthropic contempt. He is truly comfortable only with the accumulated commodities, which are transformed into fetishes that, like everything else, overpower him. Precisely this commodity fetishism blocks the completion of the liberal dialectic, since the enervated ego can never surpass the surface of a sense certainty that turns out to be more treacherous than expected. The amoral pleasures of the flesh, with which the privatized, asocial individual is solely concerned because he can perceive nothing else, attract him, enchant him, and then destroy him. Leftist antihedonism here converges with elements of the theological denunciation of mammon.

The truncation of the dialectical process is presented as well with reference to transformed family structures. When Neithart, the brutal capitalist endowed with animal vitality, arrives, he inquires into Bolwieser and Hanni's plans for children. While the stationmaster stands by sheepishly, his wife replies that they have decided to do without a family in order to enjoy themselves all the better. Her account goes straight to the heart of the theological substance of leftist modernism and the critique of commodified wealth: "No, no, Daddy, we won't take on that cross! We have it so beautiful now. . .Today it's no longer like it was before the war. Today people usually just live for themselves. . .Times have changed, Daddy" (62-63). The opposition of cross and beauty, or of religion and sensuous pleasure, is fit into a historical periodization. The prewar era, associated with the vitality and family commitments of Neithart, supported a culture of living for others; in the postwar period one lives for oneself, the cross is rejected as well as the family, and the desideratum is addressed in aesthetic terms: a beautiful life. Bolwieser and Hanni are exemplary consumers, fully privatized, caught up in their subjective, or novelistic, concerns. This sort of individualism implies a disdain for community and a devotion to commodified wealth, the critique of which is located at the point where theology and anticapitalism intersect. For Bolwieser, this fixation on pleasure again retards the dialectic: the new generation will not be born, and consciousness is trapped in the polarities of the given, since the progess of sublation is blocked.

Like Bolwieser, Döblin's Biberkopf remains childless and the substitute for the family unit fails to generate an immanent course of progess. The polarities of the present are frozen or bypassed but never overcome. The women who pass through Biberkopf's life are not motivated by personal concerns. These relationships do not come to maturity and natural conclusions; on the contrary, they are constantly subject to the arbitrary, external will of Reinhold. The modernist course of Biberkopf's loves therefore stands in marked contrast to the amorous structures in bourgeois realism. Wohlfahrt wavered between middle-class and aristrocratic sexual objects until the entry into the capitalist family was confirmed with incontrovertible closure. Drendorf, too, experienced the slow arousal of desire that culminated in an ultimately achieved satisfaction, mirrored in the image of the blossoming cactus, suggesting infrequent coital completion.[18] In the narratives of Fontane and Hermann, erotic union was never achieved, for liberal exchange had entered into its crisis phase, but the erotic failures were still individual instances. Döblin draws the conclusion by describing Biberkopf's series of love affairs, each of which is terminated by the intervention of an external authority. The dialectic of love loses any claim to autonomy, opposites no longer converge in marital reconciliation, and the individual experiences social forces as hostile and violent agents of heternomous power.

Whereas Graf explained the obsolescence of a sublationist dialectic in terms of the social psychology of the petty bourgeois, Döblin addresses the crisis of liberal capitalism directly. Alexanderplatz is the slumlike center of the monopolistic economy where hawkers and minor criminals, engaging in hopelessly antiquated modes of exchange, encounter an increasingly incomprehensible world. The merely vestigial character of liberal commerce is made explicit at a turning-point in the novel where Biberkopf encounters one of the most significant allegorical figures. Biberkopf's rite of passage into the underworld—in which in all innocence he joins up with the Pums gang, participates in one of their break-ins, and loses his arm—is introduced by a curious encounter with one

Bernhard Kauer, whose livelihood reproduces the structure of the capitalist liquidity crisis. He spends his time following up on classified ads and negotiating deals with private parties forced to sell some of their possessions:

> And again and again I run up the stairs and buy and make deals and am pleased with myself, and the people are pleased too that the business went so smoothly, and I think, what luck I had, there are so many nice things, splendid coin collections, I could tell you stories, just people who suddenly have no money, and then I come up the stairs, look the stuff over, and they tell me right off what the story is and how miserable everyone is, and if they could just get hold of a few pennies, I've bought things in your building too, the people really are poor, a dryer or a little refrigerator, they're glad to get rid of them. And then I go back down and really want to buy it all so much, but then the worries get hold of me: no money, no money. (221)

Although Kauer constantly enters into the ritual of exchange negotiations, he has no intention of carrying through with the deal. He shows Biberkopf the mimeographed postcards he carries with him with the message that "due to difficult circumstances" he is forced to withdraw from the planned purchase. On occasion he does not even bother to mail the postcard but just slips it through the letter slot after he leaves the apartment.

Like the passive heroes who have no progeny, Kauer's negotiations never come to fruition. The episode demonstrates the sterility of discursive exchange and the restructuring of the dialectic which never achieves a successful conclusion. As soon as the traditional carrier of action, the bourgeois subject, is metamorphosed into the victimized exemplar, action can come to no subjectively determined termination. The contradictions remain open, and even in linguistic encounters, an exchange of opinions fails to generate a consensual agreement. On the contrary, the lines of opposition are abstracted from their purported origins, the individual speakers, and are concretized as a geometric problem: "The words, vibrating waves, waves of noise, filled with content, oscillate back and forth through the room" (91). Speech is separated from its particular source, "depersonated," and the contradictions of the spatialized debate are frozen in an open dialectic which is never closed.

This denial of closure, grounded in the specifically open dialectical tropic structure of leftist modernism, explains the functioning of the exemplaric rhetoric. The antihero is not intended to be the carrier of a conclusive meaning but rather the locus of a failed logic. Nonclosure implies a constant difference from and nonidentity with the ostensible text, as evidenced by a series of characteristic figures. Bolwieser and Biberkopf are seen to be regularly drawing fatefully wrong conclusions from their experiences; instead of appropriating these judgments as valid insights, the reader is expected to recognize their necessarily erroneous character. Similarly, in the *Kalender-Geschichten*, moralizing conclusions are drawn that diverge significantly from the sense of the narrated events. For example, the bloody suppression of the peasants' uprising is labeled a "victory of the just," or in another political parable, a widow whose husband was murdered by reactionary troops during the revolution of 1919 draws a misanthropic conclusion that fully contradicts the deceased's activities and the thrust of the account.[19] The importance of the difference between articulated message and reported experiences anticipates the ambivalence of irony in liberal modernism.

Another figure associated with the open dialectic of leftist modernism is the predilection for the emphatic presentation of contradictory constellations. Where the exemplars pronounce their erroneous closures, the narrators underscore the problematic character of the material. The works therefore take on a processual and experimental character, in the course of which the reader is permitted to observe the gradual clarification of the initial question, which in *Bolwieser* is the transformation of sensual pleasure into the enslavement intimated in the opening passage, and in *Berlin Alexanderplatz* is the conflict between Biberkopf's vain hopes and the brutality of his "grave, true and illuminating being" (47). Yet the problem of contradictory configurations is not exhausted by the logical structure of the thematic issues. In terms of aesthetic content, it leads directly to the use of montage devices, for which Döblin's novel is the classic example. Popular songs, newspaper accounts, weather reports, train schedules, and biblical citations are juxtaposed with each other and intertwined with the central plot. Similarly, descriptive passages are made up of a mosaic of fragments, never subsumed to the unified, omniscient perspective that characterized realist narration. Consider Döblin's urban landscapes and their mixture of commodified diversity and polymorphous political speech. They are not merely evocations of the city or simple local color, like Fontane's Berlin references. In *Irrungen, Wirrungen* extra-aesthetic references were integrated into the novel in order to alleviate the crisis of meaning; regionalism provided the closure that exchange could no longer achieve. In *Berlin Alexanderplatz*, experience of the incomprehensible detail is addressed directly. Concrete objects or voices do not submit to integration into an individualistic perspective, and consequently they overwhelm the individual with their multiplicity. Montage does not simply shock; its fundamental purpose is instead to demonstrate the priority of the principle of contradiction without resolution.

The substantive plurality inherent in the contradictions of the open dialectic leads finally to a polyphonic structure. Because the hero has become an antihero incapable of action, it is not legitimate, as it was in the realist novel, to relegate the other characters to the status of minor figures. All the voices are significant, not only that of the protagonist, who has ceased to serve as a carrier of a message. Thus the novel of leftist modernism is structured around the immanent contradiction between its own multilateral constitution and the foolish individualism of its exemplar. In *Berlin Alexanderplatz*, Biberkopf's search for a private solution is played out before the plurality of voices that provide commentary on his efforts: the biblical narrator, the chronicler of the cityscape, the psychological observer, and the various fictional companions. These speakers do not address one another, nor do they reach any sort of consensus. The universal discourse comes to no decisive conclusion. Yet it takes place perpetually behind Biberkopf's back, as a multi-faceted totality which the antihero can never comprehend. With all its contradictions, this collective totality provides the narrative with an objectivity concerned with a pursuit of truth beyond the limits of traditional fiction. This quest relies on the last major trope of leftist modernism: ethnographic authenticity, the vocalization of the genuine collective.

The modernist dissatisfaction with the literary life of the nineteenth century engendered a variety of iconoclastic gestures, particularly attacks on the established notion of the work of art as an object belonging to an aesthetic sphere fundamentally different from everyday life practice. Peter Bürger identifies this rejection of the ontological separation of life and art as a hallmark of the early twentieth-century avant-garde.[20] In terms of prose narration, this break implies above all a dissatisfaction with the inherited notion of fiction and a search for a literary practice that would escape the limitations of traditional fictionality by participating immediately in the concrete concerns of everyday life. The fascist modernist pretensions to a pseudo-documentary literature arise at precisely this point, as in Grimm, Dinter, and Jünger. The various programs for a fascist aesthetics formulated different models of a literature that would escape, to use Paul Fechter's term, the solely "ornamental" status ascribed to the art work in liberal culture and would participate instead in the reactionary revolution.

Just as structural homologies link iteration and exemplars as well as spectacle and dialectics, fascist and leftist modernisms mirror each other in terms of their tropic features of pseudo-documentation and ethnographic authenticity, despite their fundamental differences. They share a rejection of bourgeois fictionality, especially its disregard for material existence. They both claim to imbue their texts with an indisputable veracity. The designation of the fascist version of modernism as "pseudo-documentary" indicates, however, a critical willingness to question the allegedly genuine facts and to distinguish between true and false material. Dinter cites documents in *Die Sünde wider das Blut;* the leftist modernist Ernst Ottwalt likewise claims that the events described in his novel of the Weimar justice system, *Denn Sie Wissen Was Sie Tun* (For They Know What They Do, 1931), are based on facts. A formalist aesthetic response that identifies them both as "documentary" would thereby reveal only its own limitations, for Dinter's "facts" include fabricated blood libel charges, while Ottwalt's accounts are based largely on authentic court cases.[21] Unless facts are to be dissolved in the manner of revisionist historiography or truth is to be denied in the manner of poststructuralism, it remains crucial to distinguish between valid and invalid claims of referential legitimacy.

Fascist modernism tends toward the pseudo-document, as in Dinter's attraction to the protocols of seances. Leftist modernism endeavors to establish an authenticity modeled initially on the principles of reportage, as if the mere presentation of facts would prove the leftist case. Yet the inadequacy of the journalistic posture, like that of the new sobriety, lies in the passivity of the implied reader, who could register the reported scandals and merely bemoan them. Benjamin derides this stance as "left-wing melancholy."[22] Authentic facts are not enough unless the status of their recipients is radically transformed through the establishment of a new literary community, as Ottwalt suggests in the foreword to his novel:

This book is no roman-à-clef. Yet the figure of the judge Friedrich Wilhelm Dickmann is only a product of the imagination insofar as it is based on the model of no particular German judge. However, all legal cases, court hearings, sentences and events discussed here are documented facts from the years 1920–1931. All the accounts of the inner workings of the German legal system are also based on facts. Because of the peculiar history of the German republic, the reader may find some of these facts incredible. Therefore the author requests that the reader contact him via the publishing house if any doubts should arise concerning the documentary character of this or that description in the novel. All such inquiries will be answered with a presentation of the factual material on which the questionable passages are based.[23]

Doubts concerning the authenticity claims of journalism in leftist modernism do not lead to an alteration of the facts but rather to a transformation of the public sphere and its communicative structures. The opposite holds for fascist modernism with its pseudo-facts addressed to the pacified recipient. Ottwalt both claims a nonfictional objectivity for his text and, more important, attempts to set up an innovative relationship with the readers who are condemned otherwise merely to accept the reported data.

This combination of authentic reportage and an exhortation to the public to participate in the determination of facts was characteristic of the left-wing subculture of the Weimar period. Most notably the movements of "worker photographers" and "worker correspondents" were based on the principle that nonprofessionalized photographers and journalists could record genuine events in their communities and factories and publicize these data as a form of partisan propaganda.[24] The principle assumes a collective participation in a literary life that is concerned with the production of information in social life and not with fictional otherness. This program for a collective reportage, or a narrative mode in which the *demos* speaks the facts of its own life, not only distinguishes leftist modernism from the fascist pseudo-documentation that lacks any notion of a collective subjectivity, but also echoes the fundamental assumptions in the theory of epic narration. From the invitation to the public to participate in an examination of the data in Ottwalt's text, it is not far to Brecht's program to supplant the individual theater critic with an authentically critical public or to Döblin's insistence that the "author carries the people within himself" during the creative process. In all cases a privileged, nonfictional character is projected onto the aesthetic object in the context of an explicit or implicit collectivization of the author.

This collectivization of the author, however, is nothing less than the vocalization of the collective, the program for a participatory literature in which the people comes to speak. The work is no longer merely fictional because it is ethnographic; it is not simply a naturalistic description of the "real life" of the people but a text written by the people itself. Brecht's program of technological optimism for an inversion of the communicative structure of the mass media corresponds to Döblin's claim for the centrality of the people in his own imaginative process. This explains the predominance of dialect language in the novels of leftist modernism, works written in the popular language. For Fontane, colloquialisms produced a humorous effect and reenforced the codings of class society; for Graf and Döblin, they represent the medium of authentic speech. The predominance of dialect forms in leftist modernism marks as important a transition as did, for example, the integration of bourgeois material into the tragedies of the eighteenth century. Each reflected political visions of radical social change, and each was accompanied by corresponding innovations in literary content: the bourgeois family in Enlightenment drama, the proletarian city in the modern novel. Leftist modernism is based on a narrative strategy intended to produce the charismatic community of the emancipated people, the dialectical inversion of the represented exemplars of petty bourgeois individualism. The objectivity of its facts depends on the presence of a collective subject able to articulate a narrative which is authentically popular and popular because authentically democratic.

11

Modernism as Social Individuality: Thomas Mann

*T*he Weberian matrix has so far accounted for central transitions in the rise of the modern German novel. The hypothesis of a bureaucratization of literary relations within the framework of late realism explains the origin of the culture industry and its pacification of isolated recipients through strategies of illusion and a thematics of destiny. The modernist alternatives involve the establishment of charismatic literary communities, produced through rhetorical devices designed specifically to invoke the innovative reader as a collective. Competing versions of modernism diverge in their understanding of the character of this subject and employ correspondingly different modes of address. They share, however, the fundamental goal of producing a recipient capable of participating in literary relationships antithetical to the institutionalized readership patterns of late realism.

The literatures of fascist and epic leftist modernism were particularly concerned with the establishment of charismatic communities. In each case, the literature was intentionally linked to political programs of mass movements, and the literati of the respective political associations could well collapse their literary and political projects into single efforts to invoke new collectives. In the context of explicit politicization, literary innovation concerned itself most readily with the production of a public. The interest on the part of Jünger and Grimm or Graf and Döblin in a postindividual collective subject was in itself not surprising, given their political loyalties.

Yet the political modernisms on the right and the left do not exhaust the full terrain of innovative literature. In fact, the concept of modernism is associated more frequently with writers in whose works political matters have appeared to be of secondary importance at best. The canonized modernists of the literary critical establishment—Mann and Kafka, Gide and Proust, Joyce and Beckett—can hardly be divided between the two ideal types of the political extremes. Their works themselves—difficult, hermetic, and indebted to a thematics of individual alienation—seem unlikely to demonstrate a necessary connection between modernism and community. But if the charismatic thesis failed to address the literary projects of this central grouping, then it could hardly be presented as a plausible sociology of modernism.

These apparently unpolitical texts of modernism in fact reveal within themselves the problem of community, which calls into question their purportedly unpolitical character. Consider an extreme example: the same Kafka who has been presented as a prophet of alienation and hopelessness declares that "literature is an affair of the people." His biographic connection to anarchist circles in Prague is known, as is his reliance on the archaic, popular narrative structure of parables. From these details it would be possible to constuct a new Kafka, inimical to the established image, as a radical in search of a collective.[1] The point is not that the historical Kafka possessed a fully developed political consciousness, but that his literary strategy includes an implicit political goal. The specific writerly strategies constitute a political project, the production of community, which is available to a critical decoding.

A similar interpretive problematic applies in the case of the representative German modernist, Thomas Mann. As with Kafka, the political dimension in his oeuvre has been either denied or presented as specifically elitist. That Mann himself directly addresses the intended interrelationship of literature and politics makes this denial all the more egregious. The obsolescence of laissez-faire individuality and the effort to integrate a transformed individualism into a social collective characterizes the trajectory of Mann's writings. Even at his most impenetrable, Mann is involved in an effort to produce a new reader who participates in a rational collective. The hypertrophic erudition of his late work is not intended to reserve the texts for a mandarin elite but, on the contrary, plays an important role in the political project of narrative address: superficial elitism is inverted into democratic politics. Hostile to the Marxism of Döblin and the fascism of Jünger, though in varying degrees, Mann pursues a hermetic modernism oriented toward the possibility of a new social individuality. This interpellation has much in common with the homologous features of the competing modernist strategies. The centrality of the problem of the renewed collective in Mann's works demonstrates its centrality in the modernist project.

Mann's fiction approaches the issue of the collective through a constant inversion of the analysis of the individual. Be it in terms of the family in *Buddenbrooks* (1901), the personality in *The Magic Mountain* (1924), or the hermetic work of art in *Doctor Faustus*, the contradictory structure of the individual is presented implicitly as the corollary to the social totality. This holds not only in the sense of microcosm mirroring macrocosm but, more importantly, in the sense of the immanent crisis of traditional individuality pushing toward collective solutions inherent in various versions of deindividuation. This constellation dominates several of Mann's short stories. "Tristan" (1902), for example, does not simply pose the familiar antinomy of bourgeois and artist, although that certainly constitutes its major concern. Rather, it elaborates an ironic critique of both established bourgeois individuality and its corollary, aesthetic form. The merchant Klöterjahn and the author Spinell are twins as much as they are opposites. Although the narrative focuses on the inadequacies of the neo-romantic writer, it subjects the businessman as well to a scathing attack and then transplants the failures of laissez-faire individuation into the aesthetic sphere. Hence the account of Spinell's morbid attraction for a Wagnerian loss of identity in the central music passage. The point, however, is that Mann proposes no solution. Not only does the irony directed toward the author recall Nietzsche's Wagner polemic, but the portrayal of the alternative to the decadent aesthete, the philistine bourgeois and his excessively healthy offspring, represents an ironic recapitulation of Nietzschean vitalism. The story is a comic representation of the tragic antinomies of turn-of-the-century bourgeois individualism, trapped within vacuous social forms but incapable of formulating an adequate program of self-transcendence.

The separation of bourgeois and artist in "Tristan" disappears in "Death in Venice" (1912), where the complementary categories are collapsed into the single personality of Gustav von Aschenbach. The story describes the internal erosion of a superfically stable cultural constellation in a manner that indicates the tensions in Wilhelmine culture. Aschenbach, the prototypical writer of the late nineteenth century, travels to Venice where instinctual forces erupt and challenge his authoritarian personality structure. Anticipated in a dream of primitive barbarism and dionysian rites, his demise is associated with a ubiquitous moral decline, a comment on European society on the eve of the First World War and, more important, on the labile status of established literary practices. The narrative commences with Aschenbach's crisis of literary production, which is apparently tied to essential structures of his personality: the repression of the aesthetic-romantic legacy in the name of a reified social integration and establishmentarian success that has brought him many honors, in particular the inclusion of excerpts from his works in bureaucratic anthologies for the schools. His literary life has flourished solely by stifling its own dionysian sources, although the rediscovery of these sources necessarily implies the demise of the bourgeois artist. This dialectical inversion is announced long before the feverish dream when the narrator comments on the problem of morality and form. The efforts of the mature artist to synthesize aesthetics and ethics produce a merely formal morality which, unable to reach substantively into life, declares life to be a realm outside of form and therefore outside of ethics. From the standpoint of the moralizing narrator, identified with the social hierarchy, the attraction to the erotic origins of art appears to be an indication of a damnable weakness, and this is precisely how the text itself has been interpreted. Yet the logic of Aschenbach's decline as well as the self-righteous tone of the narrator provide evidence that Mann's goal is less the condemnation of a unique decadent than the analysis of the objective construction of contemporary individuality.[2]

The breakdown of moral order that the narrator alleges to follow Aschenbach's dream must be balanced against the initial order of repression and self-denial, which is a violent, merely external ordering, waiting to collapse. The ultimate decline is a consequence of the character of the Wilhelmine cultural crisis as described within the terms of Aschenbach's psyche: the path out of the ossification of institutionalized culture leads through the dionysian charisma of the dream. In that dream, the former, death-desiring deindividuation of Spinell is replaced by the oneiric vision of a primitive community, a new grounding for both society and art, which anticipates the accounts of democracy beginning in "The German Republic" (1923) as well as the aesthetic strategy of mythological typology in *The Magic Mountain*. The neoclassical Aschenbach appears as the monadic individual, lacking any authentic social ties and engaged solely in an entrepreneurial literary production, until he confronts a subliminal collective force that overturns the categories of established society in order to initiate a reorganization in specifically social, or postindividual, terms. It is senseless to ascribe a particular tendentious designation to the appearance of the dionysian force in "Death in Venice," and it is irresponsible to treat that force as the direct precursor of the dancers in Mann's "Mario and the Magician" (1929) eighteen years later, or even of the fascist collective of Nazi Germany.[3] The story merely registers the crisis of liberal individuality and Wilhelmine art and the emergence of the previously suppressed categories of the charismatic community.

Mann does not, however, describe all communities as desirable. The irrational collective of Cipolla's victims in "Mario and the Magician," for example, is presented in negative terms by others than the narrator, whose judgments are not universally valid. Reporting on a vacation in a coastal resort in Italy, the narrator describes an evening in which the hypnotist Cipolla was able to dominate most of the audience, despite considerable resistance; his power was broken only when he pushed one of his subjects, Mario, too far.

Because the novella examines the character of fascist domination in Mussolini's Italy, it is important to inquire into the sociological composition of the mass. No group is impervious to the hypnotic powers of the dictator, although as Lukács points out, the working class offers the most consistent resistance.[4] Mann devotes attention to the susceptibility of the otherwise civilized middle-class when describing the seduction of Signora Angiolieri. The narrator, too, whose apolitical, educated bourgeois consciousness constitutes the foreground speech of the story, is never able to muster the strength to break the spell of the magical power. This inability is emphasized by the contradictions between his own recognition of the nefarious character of the situation, so inimical to his role as paterfamilias, and his fascination with the phenomena he is ready to condemn on a rational plane. The enervation of the narrator represents Mann's own doubts concerning the likelihood of a bourgeois resistance to the nascent *Volksgemeinschaft,* the fascist organization of the masses as a racial community.

Yet Mann allows his narrator a moment of insight into a dynamic of domination, which illuminates the problem of individual capitulation to the irrational collective. A "gentleman from Rome" proposes to resist Cipolla, whereby the term "gentleman" serves to indicate class membership and the geographical reference reverberates with reminiscences of the classical republic. The best ideals of bourgeois freedom and individuality challenge the collectivist menace: "we were beholding a gallant effort to strike out and save the honour of the human race." If Mann were simply the proponent of an abstract rationalism against Wagnerian irrationalism qua fascism, here at least the outcome should be different from what it is, for classical order turns out be helpless in the face of the powers of the romantic unconscious. Bourgeois freedom fails in its efforts to resist the attraction of submission, and as the narrator recognizes, this failure is no accident but rather a necessary consequence of the class character of that freedom: "If I understand what was going on, it was the negative character of the young man's fighting position which was his undoing. It is likely that not willing is not a practicable state of mind; *not* to want to do something may be in the long run a mental content impossible to subsist on. Between not willing a certain thing and not willing at all—in other words, yielding to another person's will—there may lie too small a space for the idea of freedom to squeeze into."[5] The "gentleman from Rome" incorporates the principle of laissez-faire freedom, a negative freedom involving the absence of restrictions in the abstract space of the unregulated market. It is a freedom incapacitated by its own lack of content and therfore as ripe for collapse as is the repressive order of Aschenbach. In both cases, bourgeois existence is denounced as merely formal, and the narrative traces the inevitable collapse when bourgeois existence encounters the substance of irrational life. Thus the specific political material of the novella, the etiology of fascism, is implicitly linked to the origin of modernism in the crisis of liberal individuality.

One alternative to failed individuality is the fascist collective of Cipolla's victims, and Mann's political writings of the period present the irrational collective as one characteristically modern, postbourgeois possibility. "Mario and the Magician," however, indicates an alternative path and an alternative understanding of freedom, inscribed in the act of "liberation" with which the narrative concludes. Pensive Mario, with the slender fingers and the melancholy air, is the only one able to carry out a successful resistance. Yet these emblemata of an artistic nature do not suffice to explain the tyrannicide, for Signora Angiolieri, too, is linked to the realm of art, and her aestheticism proves her downfall. Yet Mario has another feature on which both Cipolla and the narrator concur: he is "Ganymede," a waiter, with a "redeeming zeal to serve." In terms of the philosophical constellation of the story, Mario is the antithesis of the "gentleman of Rome," because he has no freedom to defend, no property or privacy. He is the embodiment of pure unfreedom, unmitigated servitude, which from the standpoint of the bourgeois, proud of the profundity of his own "Northern soul," can by definition have no interiority. Thus the narrator states a class relationship to the servant: "We knew him humanly without knowing him personally," since the proletariat appears to be human solely in the abstract, with no attributes of intimacy.[6] In fact, Mario's intimate realm has been destroyed by the unhappy love affair which Cipolla uncovers and which accounts for both Mario's melancholy appearance and his possession of the revolver with which he associates the hypnotist.

The credibility of Mario's psychological motivation is not at stake, but only the structure of the philosophical problem as Mann's statement on the crisis of bourgeois individuality. The successful resistance to the bad collective is offered not by the representative of laissez-faire freedom but by Mario as the cipher of pure servitude. The representative of laissez-faire freedom is associated with an abstract negativity that easily succumbs to the positive content of irrationalism, whereas the cipher of servitude, grounded in a social being that denies freedom, carries the potential of a concrete self-negation which, when confronted with the pure domination of the master, is inverted as the negation of oppression, or liberation. Thus the failure of traditional bourgeois individuality does not mean the necessary victory of an authoritarian community. On the contrary, in "Mario and the Magician" Mann begins to articulate the principles of an alternative community in which freedom can be reestablished on new terms. By the late twenties Mann had already begun to elaborate his own idiosyncratic version of socialism as the successful mediation of individual and collective principles. In Mario he fashions the carrier of freedom as a proletariat, not in an empirical sense, for Mario is separate from the rest of the working-class figures in the novella, but as the servant who has nothing to lose but his isolation and servitude.

Mann thematizes the crisis of individuality and the concomitant search for an alternative community. This search for a social dimension is the basis for treating Mann as a further example of charismatic modernism, no matter how much his constitution of the envisioned collective diverges from the corollary constellations in fascist and epic leftist literatures. His oeuvre illustrates the urgency of a politicizing exploration of collective possibilities in the allegedly apolitical texts of classical modernism.

Mann underscores this convergence of literary and political projects in his public addresses after the First World War. Thus, "The German Republic" is not only an important document on the rapprochement of the intelligentsia with Weimar democracy but also a key to the redefinition of aesthetic practice in the light of the postrevolutionary social context. In an effort to convert the largely conservative academic youth of the universities, a hotbed of antirepublic sentiment, into supporters for the new state, Mann recalls the social preconditions of the prewar hostility toward participation in politics on the part of the carriers of literary culture. He claims that the nonpolitical character of the cultured middle-class was based on the monopolization of politics by the aristocracy within the monarchy. The divorce between nation or culture, on the one hand, and the state, on the other, enforced the disenfranchisement of the literary intellectuals in a context in which they lacked political power or influence and in which, both politics and culture were consequently impoverished. The end of the monarchy, however, changed both the political structure and the relationship of culture to politics: "The State, whether we wanted it or not, has fallen into our laps. Into the lap of every single one of us; it has become our job, which we must do well."[7] The republic by definition calls upon writers to participate in politics and therefore initiates a politicization of culture. The transformation of the status of the carriers of culture effects a revised institutionalization of literature. The aesthetic model of Spinell, who two decades earlier stood outside the social life of the nation, belonged to the culture of the empire, in which writers were obliged to concede the political sphere to an aristocratic state. That model of literary behavior becomes an anachronism in the new republican political text.

Culture is not fully replaced by politics, however, nor does Mann advocate an indiscriminate politicization of culture. Designed to convince a conservative nationalist audience of the benefits of democracy, the speech argues for a specifically "German" version of politics capable of synthesizing cultural and political, individual and collective principles. This synthesis appears initially as a distancing from two pejorative state models, in each of which one moment of the German synthesis predominates. Extrapolating from Novalis's comments on the relationship between the individual and the universal, Mann describes an ideal balance between federal and decentralistic principles in a possible future European state order and then returns to the abstract discussion by presenting a "German" solution as the mean between competing but less successful alternatives:

> It is a German, or generally speaking, a Germanic instinct to cherish the idea of a state-shaping individualism, the idea of association which recognizes humanity in each of its single members, the human idea, in short, which I have characterized as inherently a possession of the single human being and of the State, aristocratic and social at once, and as far removed from the political mysticism of Slavicism as from the radical and anarchistic individualism of a certain West: the union of freedom and equality, the "true harmony"—in a word, the Republic.[8]

Mann relies on the same cultural geography that structured Weber's analysis of the East Elbian agrarian question. While Germany successfully mediates between the state and the individual, it is bordered by territories in which only one or the other principle prevails: in the East, the "political mysticism of a slave state," a term reflecting both contemporary conservative anti-Bolshevik sentiments as well as an older, prewar perception of czarist Russia as the locus of an irrational, primitive collective; and in the West, the unfettered egoism of Manchesterism, the antisocial greed of the laissez-faire bourgeois personality. For Weber, these two principles collided within Germany, initiating a process of social destabilization which would have to be retarded by state intervention in order to ensure the continuity of national survival. For Mann, the new German state, as the mechanism with which the competing principles find resolution, provides the ultimate guarantor of national identity.

The cultural identity of the nation is preserved in a state which is characterized by its ability to synthesize the antithetical principles. The dialectic that in "Tristan" was frozen into unreconcilable antinomies achieves sublation in the postwar social context. Mann's characteristic version of modernism delineates the necessity of a collective in which the substance of the individual does not disappear, in contrast to the solutions in the competing fascist and epic leftist versions of modernism. Mann's modernist collective is defined as the elevation and preservation of individualism, no longer tenable in its prepolitical form and reinvigorated by its insertion into the social nexus. In "The German Republic," Mann labels this modernism "humanity": "It is the mean between aesthetic isolation and undignified levelling of the individual to the general; between mysticism and ethics; between inwardness and the State; between a death-bound negation of ethical and civic values and a purely ethical philistine rationalism; it is truly the German mean, the Beautiful and Human, of which our finest spirits have dreamed."[9] This modernism is, moreover, the mean between Spinell's aestheticism and Klöterjahn's mercenary spirit, between Aschenbach's repressive neoclassicism and the temptation of dionysian release. The cultural agenda of modernism demands a recognition of collective exigencies without an annihilation of the individual, a simultaneity of politics and culture.

"The German Republic" focuses on the political transition from monarchy to democracy as the context for a reformulation of the cultural project in terms essentially homologous with the competing versions of modernism, since modernist culture sets as its goal the foundation of a new community. In a 1923 address dedicated to the memory of Walter Rathenau, who was assassinated by right-wing extremists, Mann restates his defense of the new state: "The Republic is . . . the unity of state and culture." Now, however, the emergence of the republic is located within the specific dynamic of German culture in a manner that concretizes the modernist substance. Mann argues that traditional German culture has suffered from an excessive subjectivity, a cult of the private sphere that necessarily denigrated political interests. This legacy explains the hostility to the Weimar Republic, perceived as foreign to national identity by the carriers of the specifically conservative cultural heritage. In "The German Republic" Mann appealed to Novalis to demonstrate the compatibility of the cultural canon with democratic principles; here he invokes Goethe, whose *Wilhelm Meister*—a Bildungsroman, the prototypical genre of subjectivist inwardness—culminates in a transition "from interiority to the objective, political republicanism." Since Mann's Goethe interpretation is motivated by the political tactic of reclaiming a cultural figure for his own democratic cause, Mann emphasizes the illegitimacy of the conservative presentation of the novel as solely a document of private culture. Political matters were in the past excluded from German cultural consciousness, although they in fact have a solid foundation in the masterworks of the canon. The truncated legacy can therefore achieve the completion of its own inherent project only through a politicization of culture and an explicit incorporation of "the thought of freedom."[10] The call for political modernization in "The German Republic" finds its corollary in this programmatic insistence on a cultural modernization. Since the republic is "the unity of state and culture," the culture in the republic necessarily participates in the state, politics, and collective concerns. Mann counterposes an erstwhile privatistic culture of the isolated bourgeois personality to the imperative of a public culture of the many. The category of the charismatic community, the alternative to the desiccated individualism of the bourgeois era, therefore emerges within the program for literary modernism as one of its central constituents.

Mann elaborates on the collective character of modern cultural production in his "Address at the Founding of the Section for Poetry in the Prussian Academy of Arts" (1926). He earlier emphasized the transition from a prerepublican aesthetic isolationism to the collective character of a democratic culture. Here an additional theme comes to the fore, one rooted in the cultural geography that played a role in Mann's conflicts with his brother Heinrich during the war. Heinrich's Francophile sympathies were linked to a commitment to values designated as specifically "western." These values included an activist, democratic literary ethos to which Thomas had earlier counterposed an idealized vision of Germany as the defender of authentic, nonpolitical culture. The same antinomy recurs in the 1926 speech where the integration of art in society is viewed as a western, particularly a French characteristic. Mann refers to the "French author, whose social—I nearly want to say: sociable—instincts are so much more developed than those of the German author. In fact literature over there plays a very different role than with us, a greater one, if you like: a more fortunate one. It is socially acceptable, a career, recognized, familiar, trusted."[11] In general, France is presented as the more successfully integrated society, while Germany is the locus of romantic isolation. In particular, German writers, Mann suggests, tend naturally toward an aristocratic contempt for social matters and therefore distrust any social recognition. This distrust extends to the specific context of the speech itself: the state's recognition of authors through the establishment of a literary academy.

Having addressed the German author's native resistance accepting a social role, Mann insists that this fear of the sociopolitical realm can be overcome through self-reflection and a discovery concerning the nature of the author's putative isolation:

> [The author] discovers, at first with disbelief and then with growing joy and sentiment, that his loneliness and isolation was an *illusion*, a *romantic* illusion, if you like. He discovers that he was an expression, a mouthpiece; that he spoke for many, when he thought he spoke only for himself, only of himself. He discovers that he was at best only more sensitive and expressive than the majority of others, but not different, not strange, not really lonely, and that works of art and the intellect are not only socially *received*—they are socially *conceived* as well: in a deep, adventurous loneliness, which—who would have thought it?—turns out to be a particular form of sociality, a *social loneliness*. In other words, he discovers and experiences with authentic conviction that art, poetic writing, is truly. . . an organ of national life, no matter how incomprehensible, adventurous, audacious, dreamlike and playful the mechanism. The German poet discovers his sociality.[12]

As in "The German Republic," Mann takes pains to indicate that the politicization of culture in no way implies a thorough abandonment of the romantic legacy. On the contrary, democracy is discovered through a radicalization of precisely that romantic isolation. Whereas the French author participates in society directly, the German writer, according to Mann's version, encounters society only by first rejecting it. The social dimension, initially antithetical to the individual, turns out to be the mechanism of its preservation, because the modernist collective rescues the values of nineteenth-century culture by integrating them into society where they can flourish and undergo democratization. Much like Döblin, Mann insists on the congruence of individuality and collectivity in the aesthetic process. Yet where Döblin collapses the individual and the collective in line with the epic theory of modernism, Mann holds onto their difference while insisting on their compatibility. This differentiated simultaneity leads him in the address "Culture and Socialism," (1928) to the formulaic slogan of synthesis of Greece and Moscow, Hölderlin and Marx, culture and politics—that is, the values of the individual and the needs of society.[13]

Mann's insistence on the necessity of escaping romantic isolation and participating in democratic society initially coincides with his own defense of the young Weimar Republic. Yet he also locates this fundamental cultural shift in historicophilosophical terms that transcend the specific political developments of 1918–1919. Again he draws on Goethe in order to indicate an immanent dynamic in bourgeois culture to break through the limits of laissez-faire individuality and therefore to lose its limited bourgeois character. In "Goethe as the Representative of the Bourgeois Age" (1932), Mann insists that Goethe himself anticipated the end of bourgeois individualism and the necessity of a socialist organization of society. The immanent tendency in the earlier reference to the novel of development is now made emphatic:

[Wilhelm Meister] is really about the self-overcoming of individualistic humanity and a prophetically audacious rejection of it in the name of human and pedagogic principles and convictions, which are very contemporary and have only today achieved general recognition. . .The dissatisfaction with the individual, which is predominant today, is there: humanity can only be achieved by all human beings together, the individual becomes a function, and the concept of society, community, comes to the fore; and the Jesuit-military spirit of the pedagogical province, despite its aesthetic levity, leaves little of the individualistic, "liberal," bourgeois ideals.[14]

This passage parallels statements by Jünger and Döblin that the bourgeois era, organized in terms of individuality, privacy, and development, has come to an end and is replaced by a new mode of social organization. Mann's version is marked by the effort to locate an anticipation of postbourgeois culture in the bourgeois legacy itself. The attempt to preserve the nineteenth-century in the twentieth deviates from the radical iconoclasm that generally colors modernism, but it also indicates Mann's particular modernist project, the preservation of the individual within the emergent collective:

> Through technical-rational utopianism, the bourgeois enters the world community and, if one takes the word in a sufficiently general and undogmatic sense, communism. . .The new, social world, the organized, unified and planned world, in which humanity will be freed of subhuman, unnecessary and irrational suffering, this world will come, and it will be the work of that great sobriety, subscribed to today by all who reject a rotten, petty-bourgeois, and stupid soulfulness. It will come, because an external, rational order, corresponding to the achieved level of the human spirit, must be instituted or, in the worst case, established through a violent uprising, so that soulfulness can once again be viable and have a humanly good conscience.[15]

Organization will replace individuality not in order to stabilize the technical machinery of Jünger's military utopia nor because of the ultimately illusory character of individuation, as for Döblin and Graf, but rather in order to achieve a situation in which individuality and subjectivity—here "soulfulness"—can once again flourish. Mann does not reject the bourgeois legacy; he points instead to the anachronism of laissez-faire principles in the context of the world economic crisis, just as, soon after 1933, he would point to the anachronism of isolationist lassitude when facing the threat of the aggressive fascist state.[16]

Mann is pushing toward a redefinition of individuality and culture, anticipated in the heroization of the servant Mario as the carrier of freedom. The nineteenth-century reason of the atomistic individualism proves inadequate in the current crisis which can, in Mann's view, be mastered only through an emphatic synthesis of the social and individual, a socialization of the individual. The bourgeois era does not come to a final conclusion, replaced by a fundamentally foreign principle of social organization. Mann's modernism is instead a sublation of the inherited antinomies preserved within the new historical stage of social individuality which renders both capitalist egoism as well as its aesthetic corollary, romantic isolation, obsolete.

The obsolescence of capitalist egoism indicates a necessary revision of the traditional understanding of freedom in line with the master-slave dialectic in "Mario and the Magician." The cipher of laissez-faire independence from concrete social ties, the "gentleman from Rome," proves incapable of mustering the "militant humanism" that alone could counter the threat of fascist domination. Instead, the servant Mario is the one whose metaphysical designation as unfree allows him to become the agent of liberation. The same dialectic is explicated in *Doctor Faustus* when the composer Leverkühn and his bourgeois friend Zeitblom explore the implications of serial composition. Mann projects a political theory onto the musicological categories, which is easy to decipher because the question of freedom is posed explicitly: the status of the note in the composition represents the implied status of the individual in the social whole. Leverkühn completes his presentation with a generalization: "The decisive factor is that every note, without exception, has significance and function according to its place in the basic series or its derivatives. That would guarantee what I call the indifference to harmony and melody."[17] All notes derive their legitimacy from their participation in the overriding systems within which all carry an equal value.

The ensuing exchange counterposes the contrasting versions of compositional theory and social freedom. When Zeitblom, the voice of liberal bourgeois culture, complains that the dodecaphonic composer would relinquish all freedom, Leverkühn replies that he would be "bound by a self-imposed compulsion to order, hence free." Zeitblom recognizes correctly that serial composition severely truncates the traditional version of the composer's aesthetic creativity. The course of composition apparently allows for no expressive subjectivity, nor is there any immanent development of the musical subject itself. In both cases, categories of bourgeois culture—subjectivity and development—are negated through their submission to the predetermined series. Leverkühn's modernist project appears to his liberal humanist friend to be a cipher for a lack of freedom, and just such an interpretation of the novel, with the corollary equation of Leverkühn and totalitarianism, has flourished. The composer replies, however, that freedom becomes concrete through participation in the freely chosen order; that is, the individual note finds its freedom guaranteed within the series in which it has its fixed place. This is not Wagner, Schopenhauer, or Nietzsche, Mann's more familiar mentors, but a subjectivist version of Hegel, which corresponds to the modernist positions on cultural practice elaborated in Mann's political essays since the late twenties. The bourgeois understanding of freedom associated with Zeitblom, like the negative freedom of the "gentleman from Rome," is defined precisely by its lack of internal substance which leads to a perpetual weakness. In "Mario and the Magician" it ends in capitulation to Cipolla, while in *Doctor Faustus*, where it is translated into aesthetic terms, it is "a freedom that begins to lie like mildew upon talent and to betray traces of sterility."[18] Unfettered egoism, freed of all inherited conventions, becomes unproductive, and its promise of freedom turns out to be empty. Mann advocates through Leverkühn an alternative freedom, beyond the laissez-faire ego, dependent upon integration into a social totality. He makes the transition from romantic isolation to political participation through an evidently Hegelian insight into necessity.

This passage sheds light on the central historicophilosophical discussion in the novel, following the Kretzschmar lecture. In a public discussion of Beethoven's final sonata, the speaker describes how the secularization of art since the Middle Ages emancipates music from the strictures of cult and establishes the institutions of bourgeois culture; yet where the universal system of religion provides cultic music with a social objectivity—mirrored, according to Kretzschmar, in the innately objectivist character of polyphonic form—secularized culture lacks such objectivity, concerning itself instead with the increasing radicalization of subjectivity as an individualistic category. The exaggerated subjectivism finally weighs on art and hinders its flourishing, whereupon the motif of a return to a social totality again emerges:

> What principally impressed him. . .was Kretzschmar's distinction between cult epochs and cultural epochs, and his remark that the secularization of art, its separation from divine service, bore only a superficial and episodic character. . .he speculated in the void and in precocious language on the probably imminent retreat [of art] from its present role to a more modest, happier one in the service of a higher union, which did not need to be, as it once was, the Church. What it would be he could not say. But that the cultural idea was a historically transitory phenomenon, that it could lose itself again in another one, that the future did not inevitably belong to it, this thought he had certainly singled out from Kretzschmar's lecture.
> "But the alternative," I threw in, "to culture is barbarism."
> "Permit me," said he. "After all, barbarism is the opposite of culture only within the order of thought which it gives us. Outside of it the opposite may be something quite different or no opposite at all."[19]

The supersession of culture implies here a regained objectivity via participation in a substitute for the universal system of medieval religion, hence also a renunciation of the bourgeois principle of aesthetic autonomy. For Zeitblom, however, any tampering with the principle of culture denotes a regression to a precultural barbarism. Again the passage proves the identity of the modernist composer Leverkühn with the principle of National Socialist totalitarianism less than the willingness of critics to adopt Zeitblom's judgments at face value. In fact, the historicophilosophical speculation represents Mann's efforts to designate the specificity of the modern era as emphatically postbourgeois in the terms of his own literary-philosophical discourse. Leverkühn's desire for a regained objectivity, which he later achieves through his elaboration of serial composition, corresponds to Mann's essayistic insistence on the obsolescence of subjectivity in the postbourgeois era. In other words, the third era, after cult and culture, is not necessarily either the Third Reich or the barbarism that Zeitblom fears, but rather a modernism in which aesthetic production, like social being, can take on a qualitatively new character.

The corollary to the obsolescence of capitalist egoism in social organization is the demise of romantic isolation in aesthetic terms. The anachronism of an unpolitical cultural productivity is the central theme in Mann's aesthetic thought after the end of the First World War. He links the necessity of revising the stance of the artist to society both to the exigencies of the democratic state and to the conclusion of a laissez-faire bourgeois era. Thus the program for an integration of social concerns into art represents a specifically modernist program, since literature is henceforth involved in the production and regulation of the social community. This implication in society determines the parallelism of art and society in *Doctor Faustus*, which can be viewed as an encyclopedia of Mann's theory of modernism. This crucial tendency is recapitulated and radicalized in a late essay, "The Artist and Society" (1952), which presents the social character of art not as a tendentious addition to an initially purely aesthetic project but as the ontological designation of art, or at least literature. Commencing with the apparent separation of aesthetics and ethics—an antinomy that was concretized both in "Tristan" and in the parallel biographies of the Rodde sisters in *Doctor Faustus*—Mann proceeds dialectically by claiming that art's very lack of concern with social matters, its solely personal significance, is the locus of its transpersonal value. Its emphatic insistence on its bohemian status, its nonintegration into the bourgeois world, inverts into a critique of the bourgeois world: the antiethical refusal reveals itself as a denunciation of prevailing ethical standards. Similarly, art's immanent predilection toward self-criticism, realized in the institutionalization of literary criticism, betrays an affinity to criticism in general, including social criticism. Whereas fascist and epic leftist modernisms define themselves in terms of a radical break with traditional understandings of art, Mann grounds his project for a socially critical literature in an essentialist substance of art. Modernism appears as an advanced stage of an original aesthetic self-consciousness rather than as a fundamentally iconoclastic renunciation of established art.

For Mann, the function of art as criticism and, therefore, as a vehicle for the establishment of a new social community is grounded in the character of language as the carrier of the spirit against the mere materiality of life. The modernist program is a belated restatement of a critique of early twentieth-century vitalism. It opposes "an obstinate and dumbly mean human essence, which has always constituted the fate of the poet-writer." Although Mann goes on to quote Goethe, he has in fact come around to the position of his brother Heinrich, put forth in the essay "Spirit and Deed" (1911). Commitment to social change is not a subjectively tendentious choice on the part of individual writers but the essence of literary activity itself. Heinrich Mann gave this activism the label of *ratio militans*, miltant reason; during the thirties, Thomas Mann adopted the slogan of "militant humanism." In both cases, a modernist stance is elaborated and simultaneously ascribed to literature as its fundamental calling, and in both cases this modernism involves the mobilization of art in a project of social change designed to generate new forms of democratic, social organization. For Thomas Mann, who begins with the nineteenth-century perception of the incompatibility of aesthetics and ethics, aesthetic writing necessarily conjoins with social moralism, and art turns out to be ultimately inseparable from political, social, and moral questions, since all participate in the category of humanity and the production of the postliberal community.[20]

Although the substance of Mann's account of modernist culture diverges significantly from the fascist spectacle and the program of epic leftism, it shares the basic thesis of an epochal break with the categories of nineteenth-century liberalism. This congruence determines the specifically modernist character of his aesthetics and explains the appearance of homologous tropic forms. Whereas the competing versions of modernism translate the obsolescence of individuality into rhetorics of iteration and exemplars respectively, Mann's texts characteristically employ structures of seriality in place of the developmental narratives of liberalism. Many of the major texts after the First World War invoke the genre of the novel of development, yet the traditional developmental dynamic is embedded in nonhistorical forms of repetition and simultaneity. Just as the historicophilosophical commentaries suggest a coincidence of the individual and the social, the texts themselves foreground an omnipresent tension between diachronic developmental narration and elements of synchronic structuration. This tension, which constitutes one of the specific attributes of Mann's modernism, applies in different ways to the coexistence of Bildungsroman material both with mythology in *The Magic Mountain* and with the atemporality of montage in *Doctor Faustus.*

This perpetual inversion of history into seriality and vice versa owes as much to the tensions of Weimar culture as Jünger's prose does to contemporary militarism and Döblin's novel does to left-wing radicalism. The collapse of the monarchy, which presented itself as the culmination of a linear national history, and the establishment of the republic, viewed by many as the imposition of an alien power structure, delimit an intellectual context in which traditional understandings of a universal history of progress, under attack since the vitalism of the turn of the century, are jettisoned and replaced by a fundamental ontology of historicity. In *Being and Time* Heidegger displaces the possibilities of historical change from dimensions of social practice and rational critique into ultimately inaccessible existential structures, universal determinants of being. This particular retreat from teleological history has conservative implications: "Its political sense is. . . an authoritarian one, evident in the abstract form in which individual and history are thought together. . . It is the gesture of founding meaning, which the philosophical leader assumes in the face of the absurdity of human existence." Whereas the nineteenth-century sanguine faith in progress lost its credibility, the Heideggerian account appears both to perpetuate the social crisis by representing it as existential and to allow for a resolution solely in terms beyond the purview of rational criticism. In response to the insistence on the permanence of fundamental structures of being, Adorno sketches an alternative historiography in "The Idea of Natural History" (1932). The term undergoes a dialectical decomposition, whereby nature refers to a mythic eternal sameness and history refers to trajectories of change or progress. Again, a voluntaristic invocation of Hegelian teleology is impossible, but Adorno avoids the Heideggerian solution and its own voluntaristic, existentialist consequences through an argument of reciprocity and inversion. Nature as myth becomes history in the form of fate, while history in alienation declines into mythic nature. The dual theses anticipate the first chapter of *The Dialectic of Enlightenment* (1947), indicating that Adorno's pessimism predates the trauma of Auschwitz.[21] Yet the pessimism coexists with the inevitability of change. Adorno's melancholy presents a radical alternative to the authoritarian conformism of Heidegger's ontology.

Mann's modernism activates tropic structures homologous to Adorno's historiography. Narrative development coexists with mythological permanence. In fact, as suggested in the "Snow" episode in *The Magic Mountain*, a recognition of mythic permanence is itself the precondition of biographical progress. Cultural optimism and subjective individuality rely on their opposites, the pessimism of ritual horror and sacrificial irrationality. Yet it is impossible to establish a privileging of one of the two parameters. The ambivalence of serial permanence and development progress persists through the debates of Naphta and Settembrini in *The Magic Mountain* and in the paradoxical antinomies of Leverkühn and Zeitblom in *Doctor Faustus*. The oscillation itself describes the contours of Mann's modernist strategy.

Both Jünger's fascist modernism and Döblin's epic leftism reject the liberal nineteenth-century faith in unbroken development. Jünger does so in order to declare the permanence of a fundamental ontology; Döblin in order to denounce the permanence of alienated social relations. The modernist Mann also breaks with a simplistic insistence on progress by thematizing the tensions between order and change. His account of the oscillation between synchronic and diachronic aspects of cultural organization itself undergoes considerable change in the course of his life. Permanence prevails and progress is least apparent in the leitmotifs of *Buddenbrooks*. Consciously modeled on the similar devices in Wagnerian composition, they are inserted as elements of characterization in order to express an unchanging, vitalist substructure beneath the vicissitudes of the family chronicle. This relatively simple technique is expanded in *The Magic Mountain*, as well as in the Joseph novels, into a massive mythological endowment of individual figures, and myth becomes the device by means of which the individual problematic is endowed with universal ramifications.

This structure has a dual significance within the sociology of modernism. First, myth radically heightens a tendency already evident in the realism of Fontane, where details were overlaid with surplus allegorical meanings because the original realist dialectic of the individual and universal no longer functioned without such additional intervention. For Mann, the foregrounded narrative constantly turns out to be mere pretext for the expatiations inherent in the mythological emblemata. Yet this does not at all imply that developmental history is subordinated to mythic permanence. Second, Mann's use of mythological material amounts to an effort to retrieve it from conservative irrationalism in order to direct it against the pessimism of fundamental ontology. In Adorno's terms, myth becomes history and recuperates its original role as enlightenment. As the guarantor of universality, mythology emancipates the narrative from romantic isolation and discovers the possibility of social practice, just as in *The Magic Mountain*, Hans Castorp escapes the hermetic escapism of the sanatorium through a process of hermetic elevation.

In addition to the repetition of leitmotifs and the transindividual functioning of mythologization, tropic seriality incorporates the technique of montage, which operates within a dynamic significantly different than that which prevails in epic modernism. Instead of the shock effect caused by the juxtaposition of heterogenous materials, as in the Brechtian distanciation effect, the layer of montage in *Doctor Faustus* constitutes a compositional structure that concretizes the aesthetics of Leverkühn's serial composition. The independent units are organized in an arrangement in explicit counterpoint to the foregrounded biographical narrative. They represent both an alternative voice to the purported history and the substance of the historian's *parole*. Thus the montage structure itself demonstrates the legitimacy of the composer's musicological argument against Zeitblom, for through a repetition of the arbitrary series or montage, narrative autonomy, which later in the novel is referred to as expressiveness, is renewed in a historical context where traditional narration and autonomy have ceased to be possible. The destruction of time in the synchronicity of citation paradoxically guarantees the teleology of the diachronic narrative. This radical insistence on seriality represents the aesthetic corollary to the theological doctrine of predestination that is at the root of Mann's post-liberal treatment of the Faust myth, for Leverkühn has no choice and no subjective freedom. The pact is not a liberal contract, negotiated between equal individuals. All the salient stigmata of his eventual decline are inherited from his genealogy, and the fateful infection is contracted before the encounter of the devil. Damnation precedes choice—in Zeitblom's naive terminology, "a sort of composing before composition"—and only a mournful recognition of this wretchedness permits a promise of hope to appear as the miracle of grace at the end of Leverkühn's composition.[22] Thus theology, composition, and the temporal structure of the work converge in an uncompromising seriality, the thoroughness of which alone allows for the possibility of a dialectical inversion.

The oscillation between developmental history and mythic permanence and the inversion of damnation into hope govern the functioning of seriality in terms of another tropic feature in the modernism of social individuality: ambivalence. The mimetic representation inherited from nineteenth-century realism is omnipresent but permanently dissolved through the familiar structures of Mann's irony and parody. The particular detail no longer opens onto a universal content. Instead, it borders on a slippery other, while the meaning sways indeterminately in the balance. Hence, for example, the frustrating elusiveness of the message in a story like "Tristan," where all figures are subject to an ironic critique. Hence, also, the textual refusal to resolve conclusively the permanent debate between Leverkühn and Zeitblom, as well as the ambiguity of the judgment on Aschenbach.

This ambivalence is largely a function of the reduced narrator who has lost the compelling omniscience of realism and whose observations and opinions are always linked to the caveat of unreliability. On this point, Mann's modernism displays ties to the prose of Hermann Broch as well as to texts by Henry James and Ford Maddox Ford.[23] Ambivalence is also closely related to the dialectics of Döblin and Graf, as well as to the program of epic theater, where the nonclosure of the work destroys the stability of realistic mimesis in order to present the unresolved problematic. This linkage is crucial, since narrative unreliability has a political function that cannot be subsumed into a philosophy of indeterminacy or a poetics of decentered discourse. On the contrary, the ambivalence of narrative speech establishes an interlocutionary encounter with the recipient who is wrested out of passive contemplation and drawn into the contradictions of the textual debate. In polemical terms, the weakness of the narrator does not signify an absolute deconstruction of speech; instead, it opens a space for dramatic dialogue with the recipient, who is urged into a critical stance vis-à-vis the text. Ambivalence is one of the central mechanisms with which modernism endeavors to produce its recipients and to emancipate them from the fascist spectacle and the illusions of the culture industry. In this sense, the encyclopedic character of *Doctor Faustus* is not at all directed at an esoteric cultural elite. Through the vagaries of the narrator, the text tries to involve the reader in the problem of modernist culture, presented as if in a primer, not a novel. This project itself emerges from the historical diagnosis of the text whereby, in the wake of the cultural catastrophe of National Socialism that contributes to the distortion of the foregrounded narration, the ambivalence of the text provides a Socratic education to the anticipated recipients of the future.

The pedagogic strategy, grounded in the dialogic interlocution with the ambivalent narrator, is thematized explicitly in the novel. The work not only evades closure through the unresolved tensions between Zeitblom and Leverkühn but expressly denies itself even tentative completion prior to the process of reception. Zeitblom comments:

> That date [April 1944], of course, is the point where I now stand in my actual writing and not the one up to which my narrative has progressed. . . I do not know why this double time-reckoning arrests my attention or why I am at pains to point out both the personal and the objective, the time in which the narrator moves and that in which the narrative does so. This is a quite extraordinary interweaving of time-units, destined, moreover, to include even a third: namely, the time which one day the courteous reader will take for the reading of what-has been written; at which point he will be dealing with a threefold ordering of time: his own, that of the chronicler, and historic time.[24]

The montage of independent voices produces a polyphonic texture into which the reader is inexorably drawn, for he can participate in it as an equal among the strictly fictional personae. The contradictions generated by ambivalence do not produce a shock intended to distance; they underscore instead the nonidentity of an aesthetic object open to the scrutiny and exploration of the recipient. The pedagogy refuses the explicit, authoritarian presentation of the intended message to which the student could only submit. On the contrary, as Lukács comments, Mann "is an educator in the Platonic sense of anamnesis: the pupil himself should discover the idea within him, and bring it to life."[25]

The universally modernist rejection of the categories of nineteenth-century realism implies a particular hostility toward traditional notions of fictionality. The pseudo-documentary claims of fascist modernism led to Jünger's predilection for putative memoirs and to Dinter's pseudo-scientific footnotes. Leftist modernism displayed a similar tendency in Döblin's "depersonation" of the author, Ottwalt's reportage, and the ethnographic authenticity inherent in the incorporation of dialect speech. In Mann's modernism, a homologous rejection of fiction is inherent in its repeated insistence on the social function of literature. The other-worldly fiction of Spinell is denounced as equally vacuous and ridiculous, and literature is presented as the mouthpiece of collective experience. This theoretical definition of the objectivity of literature has its tropic corollaries. Most notably, the limits of traditional fictionality are broken down in a plethora of essayistic interpolations within the various narratives. The Platonic dialogues in "Death in Venice," the elaborate commentary in *The Magic Mountain,* and the theoretical discourses in *Doctor Faustus* are specifically modernist in the sense that traditional German realism proscribed explicitly conceptual speculation where mimetic representation alone should reign. The contamination of the aesthetic presentation with philosophical language, paralleling the aestheticization of literary critical discourse at the turn of the century, produces a hybrid text that unabashedly transgresses against the earlier separation of art and science.[26] As art integrates a scientific philosophical vocabulary, however, it appears to acquire the objectivity associated with conceptual knowledge.

Like essayism, montage also provides the work with a new objectivity. Rejecting the nineteenth-century bourgeois separation of art and life, the principle of montage integrates extra-aesthetic material directly into the aesthetic work. The formal structure of *Doctor Faustus* is based on the coexistence of a traditional fictional narrative with passages which erode the priority of fictional narration.

Thus Leverkühn's biography is framed by a recapitulation of Arnold Schoenberg's dodecaphonic compositional theory, quotations from Adorno's study of modern music, and reports on the course of the Second World War. In all these cases, nonfictional material is integrated into the literary text, whose fictional status thereby becomes questionable. Montage pushes the novel toward the character of a document, a tendency reminiscent of *Berlin Alexanderplatz*. In this sense, the work is indeed less a novel than an encyclopedia or an anthology of culture. By including theoretical and documentary material, the modernist novel assumes new cognitive functions.

Yet essayism and montage only touch the surface of the tropic objectivity of the modernism of social individuality, for the significant objectivity of these texts is intimately linked to the production of that social individuality which is at the center of Mann's project. Again the inscribed aesthetics of *Doctor Faustus* are a guide to an understanding of postliberal literature. The Kretzschmar lecture describes bourgeois culture as a historical consequence of secularization and the collapse of a universal system of values. The disappearance of the traditional prebourgeois community sets the stage for an emphatic subjectivity which leads in society to the emergence of isolated individuals and, in art, to the elaboration of an aesthetics of autonomy. Art is emancipated from the demands of the church or the absolutist state and henceforth represents either the expressivity of the isolated artist or the immanent logic of aesthetic material.

In this account, bourgeois culture assumes that the constantly radicalized pursuit of individual happiness can maintain a cohesive society. Yet precisely this radicalization undermines the communicative potential of cultural production; the rational exchange of meaning, the model of nineteenth-century realism, turns into the irrationality of the culture industry. The pathos of subjectivity, with which the bourgeoisie emancipated itself from medieval constraints, becomes the iron cage of isolation that precludes any substantive intersubjectivity.

Doctor Faustus does not merely describe the limitations of bourgeois individuality and the insufficiency of realist narration. It also outlines the goal of the modernist project, the achievement of a new objectivity in a revitalized culture, in terms of both the social reintegration of art and the integrated compositional technique proposed by Leverkühn. Mann's modernism can hardly meet the first criterion, the real production of a new collective. It can formulate the project of a redeemed society, the charismatic community of a free order, and it can endeavor to produce this community through the strategies of interlocution. Yet here it participates in the limits of all modernisms, which must eventually discover that literature may have a political power, but that power is always a weak one, insufficient to transform society alone. In this sense, modernism is always incomplete, and *Doctor Faustus* still participates in the subjective culture it has declared anachronistic.

Yet the novel can meet the other criterion, the elaboration of an aesthetics which anticipates community. *Doctor Faustus* not only articulates a postindividual aesthetic theory but is itself a manifestation of the theory, for the strict style of composition is reproduced in the novel itself in the form of the explicitly polyphonic structure. The lines of the narrator, his subject, and his reader interweave in a three-part fugue, maintaining their independence and generating an objectivity as the complicated web of intersubjectivity in a "self-imposed compulsion to order." In this sense, the novel achieves aesthetically the objectivity that it sets as a social goal, toward which the novel urges the reader but which the novel alone cannot reach. The disjunction between society and art, social change and aesthetic innovation, is recapitulated by the philosophical structure of the work as the nonidentity of subject and object: the absence of the envisioned community, the perpetuation of the iron cage of a sterile individuality alienated from a social collective.

The modernist project of redemption in charisma has been unable to melt frozen melancholy, not for lack of ardor, but for the apparent solidity of real conditions that have overpowered the overestimated strength of literature. Modernism has recognized those conditions, however, and has articulated their critique, and therein lies its continued relevance and the prematurity of a postmodernist quietism that bears the marks of the neoconservative era in which it has arisen. There is little point in advocating a reified canonization of the specific literary techniques of early twentieth-century modernism. Modernism, in all its varieties, defined itself in terms of aesthetic innovation, and a rejection of further innovation would itself constitute a profoundly antimodernist or postmodernist gesture. Yet the question of modernism is ultimately not purely formal; it is a question of translating aesthetic innovation into strategies of societal emancipation, and until that project is achieved, modernism and its charismatic promises remain the order of the day.

Notes
Credits
Index

Notes

1. The Geography of Wilhelmine Culture

1. Gilles Deleuze and Felix Guattari, *Kafka: Pour une littérature mineure* (Paris: Editions de Minuit, 1975), pp. 29-50.

2. Friedrich Sengle, *Biedermeierzeit: Deutsche Literatur im Spannungsfeld zwischen Restauration und Revolution 1815-1848* (Stuttgart: J. B. Metzler, 1980), III, 1047-1058.

3. Hans-Ulrich Wehler, *Das deutsche Kaiserreich: 1871-1918*, 2nd ed. (Göttingern: Vandenhoeck und Rupprecht, 1975), pp. 96-100.

4. See Murray Bookchin, *Toward an Ecological Society* (Montreal: Black Rose Press, 1980)

5. Edward Said, *Orientalism* (New York: Pantheon Books, 1978).

6. Johann Wolfgang Goethe, "Mignon," in *Selected Poems*, ed. Christopher Middleton (Boston: Suhrkamp/Insel Publishers, 1983), p. 132.

7. See Kenneth Attwood, *Fontane und das Preussentum* (Berlin: Haude und Spener, 1970); Hans-Heinrich Reuter, *Fontane* (Munich: Nymphenburg, 1968).

8. Theodor Fontane, *Causerien über Theater*, ed. Edgar Gross, in *Sämtliche Werke*, vol. 22 (Munich: Nymphenburger Verlagsbuchhandlung, 1964), pt. 1, pp. 139-141.

9. See Russell A. Berman, *Between Fontane and Tucholsky: Literary Criticism and the Public Sphere in Imperial Germany* (New York: Peter Lang, 1983), pp. 49-53.

10. Friedrich Schiller, "Das Mädchen aus der Fremde," in Schiller, *Werke*, ed. Paul Stapf (Berlin und Darmstadt: Tempel Verlag, 1962), p. 167; Martin Green, *The von Richthofen Sisters: The Triumphant and Tragic Modes of Love* (New York: Basic Books, 1974) p. xi; Arthur Mitzman, *The Iron Cage: An Historical Interpretation of Max Weber* (New York: Knopf, 1970).

11. Fontane, *Causerien über Theater,* pt. 2, pp. 37–38.

12. See Ernst Bloch, *Erbschaft dieser Zeit* (Frankfurt: Suhrkamp, 1973).

13. Eduard Baumgarten, *Max Weber: Werk und Person* (Tübingen: Mohr, 1964), p. 53.

14. Klaus L. Berghahn, "Von Weimar nach Versailles," in *Die Klassik-Legende,* ed. Reinhold Grimm and Jost Hermand (Frankfurt: Athenäum, 1971), pp. 65–71; Eckart Kehr, "The Social System of Reaction in Prussia under the Puttkamer Ministry," in *Economic Interests, Militarism, and Foreign Policy,* trans. Grete Heinz, ed. Gordon A. Craig (Berkeley: University of California Press, 1977), p. 113.

15. Heinrich Hart and Julius Hart, "Das 'Deutsche Theater' des Herrn L'Arronge," in *Kritische Waffengänge* 4 (1882): 3; Berman, *Between Fontane and Tucholsky,* pp. 69–85; Heinrich Hart and Julius Hart, "Paul Lindau als Kritiker," in *Kritische Waffengänge* 2 (1882): 26.

16. Hart and Hart, "Das 'Deutsche Theater' des Herrn L'Arronge," p. 8.

17. Marianne Weber, *Max Weber: Ein Lebensbild* (Tübingen: J. C. B. Mohr, 1926), pp. 133–35 (indicated hereafter by MW in text); Theodor W. Adorno, "Auf die Frage: Was ist deutsch," in *Gesammelte Schriften,* vol. 10, ed. Rolf Tiedemann (Frankfurt: Suhrkamp, 1977), pt. 2, pp. 693–694.

18. Baumgarten, *Max Weber,* pp. 99–100.

19. Ibid., p. 99.

20. Ibid., pp. 90–91.

21. Ibid., pp. 92–93.

2. The Category of Charisma: Max Weber

1. Martin Green, *The von Richthofen Sisters: The Triumphant and Tragic Modes of Love* (New York: Basic Books, 1974), pp. 106–107.

2. Max Weber, *The Protestant Ethic and the Spirit of Capitalism,* trans. Talcott Parsons (New York: Scribner and Sons, 1976), p. 182.

3. Engels to Paul Ernst, June 5, 1908, in *Marx and Engels on Literature and Art,* ed. Lee Baxandall and Stefan Morawski (St. Louis: Telos Press, 1973), pp. 86–89.

4. D. Carl Stange, *Albrecht Ritschl: Die geschichtliche Stellung seiner Theologie* (Leipzig: Dietrich'sche Verlagsbuchhandlung, 1922), p. 7.

5. Albrecht Ritschl, *Die Entstehung der altkatholischen Kirche: Eine kirchen- und dogmengeschichtliche Monographie,* 2nd ed. (Bonn: Adolph Marcus, 1857), pp. 1–3, 436–460; Stange, *Albrecht Ritschl,* pp. 14–15.

6. Wilhelm Maurer, "Die Auseinandersetzung zwischen Harnack und Sohm und die Begründung eines evangelischen Kirchenrechts," *Kergma und Dogma* 6 (1980): 194; Agnes von Zahn-Harnack, *Der Apostolikumstreit des Jahres 1892 und seine Bedeutung für die Gegenwart* (Marburg: N. G. Elwert, 1950).

7. Adolf von Harnack, *Lehrbuch der Dogmengeschichte,* 3rd. ed. (Freiburg im Briesgau and Leipzig: Mohr, 1894, orig. 1885, pp. 133, 134.

8. Ibid., p. 135, 301; Adolf von Harnack, *Entstehung und Entwickelung der Kirchenverfassung und des Kirchenrechts in den ersten zwei Jahrhunderten: Nebst einer Kritik der Abhandlung R. Sohm's: "Wesen und Ursprung des Katholizismus"* (Leipzig: J. C. Hinrich'sche Buchhandlung, 1910), p. 182; Harnack, *Lehrbuch der Dogmengeschichte,* p. 303–304.

9. Ibid., p. 304.

10. Rudolph Sohm, *Kirchenrecht* (Leipzig: Verlag von Duncker und Humblot, 1892), I, 700; Rudolph Sohm, *Kirchengeschichte,* 11th ed. (Leipzig: E. Ungleich, 1898), p. 30.

11. Wilhelm Maurer, "R. Sohms Ringen um den Zusammenhang zwischen Geist und Recht in der Geschichte des kirchlichen Rechts," in *Zeitschrift für evangelisches Kirchenrecht* 8 (1961/62): 30, 33.

12. Sohm, *Kirchengeschichte,* pp. 1–2, 31; Rudolph Sohm, *Wesen und Ursprung des Katholizismus* (Leipzig and Berlin: B. G. Teubner, 1912), pp. 65, 54–55.

13. Ibid., pp. 27–28.

14. Ibid., p. 61; Max Weber, *Wirtschaft und Gesellschaft: Grundriss der verstehenden Soziologie,* 4th ed. (Tübingen: J. C. B. Mohr, 1956), p. 143; Sohm, *Wesen und Ursprung,* pp. xxxi–xxxiii; Adolph von Harnack, *Aus Wissenschaft und Leben* (Giessen: Verlag von Alfred Töpelmann, 1911); Rudolph Sohm, *Die sozialen Pflichten der Gebildeten* (Leipzig: Kommissionsverlag von Reinhold Werther, 1896).

15. Weber, *Wirtschaft und Gesellschaft,* pp. 140, 142.

16. Kurt Hiller, *Geist werde Herr: Kundgebungen eines Aktivisten vor, in und nach dem Krieg* (Berlin: Reiss, 1920), p. 38.

3. Realism and Commodities

1. See Peter Bürger, *Theory of the Avant-Garde,* trans. Michael Shaw (Minneapolis: University of Minnesota Press, 1984); Michel Foucault, *The Order of Things: An Archaeology of the Human Sciences* (New York: Pantheon Books, 1970); Jürgen Habermas, *Strukturwandel der Öffentlichkeit: Untersuchungen zu einer Kategorie der bürgerlichen Gesellschaft,* 6th ed. (Neuwied and Berlin: Hermann Luchterhand Verlag, 1974, orig. 1962).

2. Friedrich Uhlig, *Geschichte des Buches und des Buchhandels* (Stuttgart: C. E. Poeschel Verlag, 1953), pp. 39–49; Ilsedore Rarisch, *Industrialisierung und Literatur: Buchproduktion, Verlagswesen und Buchhandel in Deutschland im 19. Jahrhundert in ihrem statistischen Zusammenhang* (Berlin: Colloquium Verlag, 1976), p. 19; Russell A. Berman, "Writing for the Book Industry: The Writer under Organized Capitalism," *New German Critique,* no. 29 (Spring/Summer 1983): 39–56.

3. Bürger, *Theory of the Avant-Garde,* p. 47; Habermas, *Strukturwandel,* pp. 42–75; Peter Uwe Hohendahl, *The Institution of Criticism* (Ithaca and London: Cornell University Press, 1982), pp. 52–53.

4. Hohendahl, *The Institution of Criticism*, pp. 61–68; Clifford Albrecht Bernd, *German Poetic Realism* (Boston: Twayne Publishers, 1981), pp. 17–28.

5. Theodor Fontane, "Unsere lyrische und epische Poesie seit 1848," in *Literarische Essays und Studien*, ed. Kurt Schreinert, *Sämtliche Werke*, vol. 21 (Munich: Nymphenburger Verlagsbuchhandlung, 1963), pt. 1, pp. 7–8.

6. Johann Wolfgang Goethe, *Selected Poems*, ed. Christopher Middleton (Boston: Suhrkamp/Insel Publishers, 1983), p. 58.

7. See Hermann Kinder, *Poesie als Synthese: Ausbreitung eines deutschen Realismus-Verständnisses in der Mitte des 19. Jahrhunderts* (Frankfurt: Athenäum Verlag, 1973).

8. Gustav Freytag, *Soll und Haben: Roman in sechs Büchern* (Munich and Vienna: Carl Hanser Verlag, 1977), p. 624.

9. Ibid., p. 625

10. Friedrich Sengle, *Biedermeierzeit: Deutsche Literatur im Spannungsfeld zwischen Restauration und Revolution, 1815-1848* (Stuttgart: J. B. Metzler, 1972), pp. 1040–1047; Peter Szondi, *Theorie des modernen Dramas* (Frankfurt: Suhrkamp, 1969).

11. Paul Lindau, cited in Michael Kienzle, *Der Erfolgsroman: Zur Kritik seiner poetischen Ökonomie bei Gustav Freytag und Eugenie Marlitt* (Stuttgart: Metzler, 1975), p. 11.

12. "Gold- und Silberarbeiten, Schmucksachen," *Die Grenzboten* 11.1 (1852): 382.

13. See Laura Mulvey, "Visual Pleasure and Narrative Cinema," *Screen* 16. 3 (Autumn 1975): 8–9.

14. See Richard Sennett, *The Fall of Public Man* (New York: Alfred A. Knopf, 1977), pp. 161–74.

15. "Die Anlage von Hausbibliotheken," *Die Grenzboten* 11.2 (1852): 102.

16. Wolfgang Iser, *Der Implizite Leser: Kommunikationsformen des Romans von Bunyan bis Beckett* (Munich: Wilhelm Fink, 1972), pp. 13–56; Kinder, *Poesie als Synthese*, p. 171.

17. Kienzle, *Der Erfolgsroman*, p. 10

18. Kinder, *Poesie als Synthese*, pp. 176, 169.

19. Gustav Freytag, "Wilibald Alexis," *Die Grenzboten* 10.1 (1851): 402; Kinder, *Poesie als Synthese*, p. 168.

20. Julian Schmidt, "Die Märzpoeten," *Die Grenzboten* 9.1 (1850): 11–12.

21. Ibid., pp. 13, 11.

4. The Dialectics of Liberalism: Gustav Freytag

1. Theodor Fontane, review of *Soll und Haben*, in *Literarische Essays und Studien*, ed. Kurt Schreinert, *Sämtliche Werke*, vol. 21 (Munich: Nymphenburger Verlagsbuchhandlung, 1963), pt. 1, pp. 214–230; Michael Kienzle, *Der Erfolgsroman: Zur Kritik seiner poetischen Okönomie bei Gustav Freytag und Eugenie Marlitt* (Stuttgart: Metzler, 1975), p. 12; Hans Mayer, "Gustav Freytags bürgerliches Heldenleben," in Gustav Freytag, *Soll und Haben: Roman in sechs Bänden* (Munich and Vienna: Carl Hanser Verlag, 1977), pp. 837–844.

2. Kienzle, *Der Erfolgroman*, p. 13.
3. See Uwe-Karsten Ketelsen, *Völkisch-Nationale und Nationalsozialistische Literatur in Deutschland, 1890-1945* (Stuttgart: Metzler, 1976); Russell A. Berman, "Wurzeln und Ausprägungen faschistischer Literatur," in *Propyläen Geschichte der Literatur*, ed. Erika Wischer, vol. 6 (Berlin: Propylaen Verlag, 1982), pp. 72–96.
4. Max Weber, *The Protestant Ethic and the Spirit of Capitalism*, trans. Talcott Parsons (New York: Scribner and Sons, 1976), pp. 107–108.
5. See Karl Marx, *Capital: A Critique of Political Economy*, trans. Ben Fowkes (New York: Vintage Books, 1977), I, 247–257.

5. The Authority of Address: Adalbert Stifter

1. Adalbert Stifter, *Der Nachsommer* (Munich: Winkler, 1978).
2. Peter Uwe Hohendahl, "Die gebildete Gemeinschaft: Stifters *Nachsommer* als Utopie der ästhetischen Erziehung," in *Utopieforschung: Interdisziplinäre Studien zur neuzeitlichen Utopie*, ed. Wilhelm Vosskamp (Stuttgart: Metzler, 1982), p. 335; Uwe-Karsten Ketelsen, "Die Vernichtung der historischen Realität in der Ästhetisierung des bürgerlichen Alltags," in *Romane und Erzählungen des bürgerlichen Realismus*, ed. Horst Denkler (Stuttgart: Reclam, 1980), p. 191.
3. Ibid.
4. Sepp Domandl, *Adalbert Stifters Lesebuch und die geistigen Strömungen zur Jahrhundertmitte* (Linz: Oberösterreichischer Landesverlag, 1976), pp. 78–80.
5. Hohendahl, "Die gebildete Gemeinschaft," p. 334.
6. See Marianne Schuller, "Das Gewitter findet nicht statt oder Die Abdankung der Kunst," *Poetica* 10 (1978): 25–52.
7. Walter Benjamin, "Stifter," in *Gesammelte Schriften*, vol. 2, ed. Rolf Tiedemann and Hermann Schweppenhäuser (Frankfurt: Suhrkamp, 1977), pt. 2, pp. 608–609; Peter Demetz, "Walter Benjamin als Leser Adalbert Stifters," in *Neue Rundschau* 91. 1 (1980): 148–162.
8. See Guy Debord, *Society of the Spectacle* (Detroit: Black and Red, 1977).
9. Benjamin, "Stifter," p. 609.
10. Gustav Freytag, *Soll und Haben: Roman in sechs Bänden* (Munich and Vienna: Carl Hanser Verlag, 1977), p. 271.
11. Benjamin, "Stifter," pp. 609–610.

6. The Dissolution of Meaning: Theodor Fontane

1. Theodor Fontane, "Die Londoner Presse," *Politik und Geschichte*, ed. Charlotee Jolles, in *Sämtliche Werke*, vol. 19 (Munich: Nymphenburger Verlagsbuchhandlung, 1969), p. 242.
2. Theodor Fontane, *Causerien über Theater*, ed. Edgar Gross, in *Sämtliche Werke*, vol. 22 (Munich: Nymphenburger Verlagsbuchhandlung, 1964), pt. 2, p. 316.

3. Fontane, *Causerien über Theater,* pt. 1, pp. 7, 9. See also Hans-Heinrich Reuter, *Fontane* (Munich: Nymphenburger Verlagsbuchhandlung, n.d.), p. 444.

4. Theodor Fontane, *Kriegsgefangen: Erlebtes 1870* ed. Edgar Gross, *Sämtliche Werke,* vol. 16 (Munich: Nymphenburger Verlagsbuchhandlung, 1962), p. 11.

5. Karl Frenzel, *Berliner Dramaturgie* (Hannover: 1877), I, 230.

6. Fontane, *Causerien über Theater,* pt. 1, p. 25.

7. Ibid., p. 25; Theodor Fontane, *Von Zwanzig bis Dreissig: Autobiographisches,* ed. Kurt Schreinert and Jutta Neuendorff-Fürstenau, *Sämtliche Werke,* vol. 15 (Munich: Nymphenburger Verlagsbuchhandlung, 1967), p. 392.

8. Fontane, *Von Zwanzig bis Dreissig,* p. 649.

9. Fontane, *Causerien über Theater,* pt. 2, p. 37.

10. Theodor Fontane, *Irrungen, Wirrungen,* in *Sämtliche Werke,* vol. 3, ed. Edgar Gross (Munich: Nymphenburger Verlagsbuchhandlung, 1959).

11. See Eckart Kehr, "The Social System of Reaction in Prussia under the Puttkamer Ministry," in *Economic Interest, Militarism, and Foreign Policy,* trans. Grete Heinz, ed. Gordon A. Craig (Berkeley: University of California Press, 1977), pp. 109–131.

12. See Otto Brahm, *Kritiken und Essays,* ed. Fritz Martini (Zürich and Stuttgart: Artemis, 1964), pp. 487-488.

13. Hermann Baumgarten, "Der deutsche Liberalismus: Eine Selbstkritik," *Preussische Jahrbücher* 18 (1866): 455–515, 575–628; Ludwig Bamberger, *Die Nachfolge Bismarcks* (Berlin, 1889), p. 28.

7. Culture Industry and Reification: Georg Hermann

1. See Max Horkheimer and Theodor W. Adorno, "The Culture Industry: Enlightenment as Mass Deception," *Dialectic of Enlightenment,* trans. John Cumming (New York: Seabury Press, 1972), pp. 168–208; Jürgen Habermas, *Strukturwandel der Öffentlichkeit: Untersuchungen zu einer Kategorie der bürgerlichen Gesellschaft,* 6th ed. (Neuwied and Berlin: Hermann Luchterhand Verlag, 1974, orig. 1962), pp. 193–210.

2. Georg Hermann, *Jettchen Geberts Geschichte,* in *Gesammelte Werke* (Stuttgart: Deutsche Verlagsanstalt, 1922), vol. 1

3. C. G. van Liere, *Georg Hermann: Materialien zur Kenntnis seines Lebens und seines Werkes* (Amsterdam: Editions Rodopi, 1974), p. 57.

4. See Russell A. Berman, "The Recipient as Spectator: West German Film and Poetry of the Seventies," *German Quarterly* 55 (1982): 499–510.

5. Van Liere, *Georg Hermann,* p. 144.

6. Georg Lukács, *The Theory of the Novel: A Historico-Philosophical Essay on the Forms of Great Epic Literature* (Cambridge: MIT Press, 1971), p. 62.

7. Hermann Kinder, *Poesie als Synthese: Ausbreitung eines deutschen Realismus-Verstandnisses in der Mitte des 19. Jahrhunderts* (Frankfurt: Athenäum Verlag, 1973)

8. Georg Hermann, *Henriette Jacoby* (Berlin: Egon Fleischel, 1911), p. 350.

9. Thomas Mann, *Doctor Faustus: The Life of the German Composer Adrian Leverkühn as Told by a Friend*, trans. H. T. Lowe-Porter (New York: Vintage Books, 1971), p. 322.

10. Van Liere, *Georg Hermann*, p. 162.

11. See Peter Szondi, *Die Theorie des bürgerlichen Trauerspiels im 18. Jahrhundert*, ed. Gert Mattenklott (Frankfurt: Suhrkamp, 1973), pp. 15–96.

12. Van Liere, *Georg Hermann*, p. 155.

8. The Charismatic Novel: Robert Musil, Hermann Hesse, and Elias Canetti

1. Robert Musil, *Young Törless*, trans. Eithne Wilkins and Ernst Kaiser (New York: Pantheon Books, 1982).

2. See Hans-Jürgen Krahl, *Konstitution und Klassenkampf: Zur historischen Dialektik von bürgerlicher Emanzipation und proletarischer Revolution. Schriften, Reden und Entwürfe aus den Jahren 1966-1970* (Frankfurt: Verlag Neue Kritik, 1971), pp. 345–347.

3. Frank Trommler, "Working-Class Culture and Modern Mass Culture before World War I," *New German Critique*, no. 29 (Spring/Summer 1983): 60–64; Christoph Rülcker, "Arbeiterkultur und Kulturpolitik im Blickwinkel des 'Vorwärts' 1918-1928," *Archiv für Sozialgeschichte* 14 (1974): 115–20.

4. See Max Horkheimer, "The Authoritarian State," *Telos*, no. 15 (Spring 1973): 8–9.

5. Franz Kafka, *The Trial*, trans. Willa and Edwin Muir (New York: Schocken Press, 1974), p. 220.

6. Hermann Hesse, *Steppenwolf*, trans. Basil Creighton (New York: Holt, Rinehart and Winston, 1957).

7. Elias Canetti, *Auto-da-Fé*, trans. C. V. Wedgwood (New York: Continuum, 1982).

8. Hans Magnus Enzensberger, "Elias Canetti: Die Blendung," *Der Spiegel* July 8, 1963, p. 48; *Canetti Lesen: Erfahrungen mit seinen Büchern*, ed. Herbert G. Göpfert (Munich: Hanser, 1975).

9. Fascist Modernism: Ernst Jünger and Hans Grimm

1. Ernst Jünger, *Der Kampf als inneres Erlebnis*, in *Werke* (Stuttgart: Ernst Klett Verlag, n.d.), V, 56–57. See also Carl E. Schorske, *Fin-de-Siècle Vienna: Politics and Culture* (New York: Vintage Books, 1981), pp. 116–146.

2. Jünger, *Der Kampf*, p. 57.

3. Jünger, *Der Arbeiter*, in *Werke* (Stuttgart: Ernst Klett Verlag, n.d.), VI, 17, 115.

4. Gustav Frenssen, *Jörn Uhl*, in *Gesammelte Werke* (Berlin: G. Grotesche Verlagsbuchhandlung, 1943), III, 354, 237.

5. Ibid., pp. 213, 224, 269, 400–413.

6. Hans Grimm, *Volk ohne Raum* (Munich: Albert Langen, 1926).

7. See Russell A. Berman, "Wurzeln und Ausprägungen faschistischer Literatur," in *Propyläen Geschichte der Literatur*, ed. Erika Wischer, vol. 6, (Berlin: Propyläen Verlag, 1982), pp. 85–88.

8. Jünger, *Der Kampf*, p. 58.

9. Jünger, *Afrikanische Spiele*, in *Werke* (Stuttgart: Ernst Klett Verlag, n.d.), IX, 16.

10. Jünger, *Der Kampf*, p. 107.

11. Ibid., pp. 76–77.

12. Jünger, *Der Arbeiter*, p. 32.

13. Dietrich Strothmann, *Nationalsozialistische Literaturpolitik* (Bonn: Bouvier, 1960), p. 356.

14. Jünger, *Der Kampf*, pp. 41–42.

15. Ibid., p. 97.

16. Jünger, *Der Arbeiter*, pp. 218–219.

17. Ibid., p. 219.

18. Ibid., p. 250.

19. Jünger, *Der Arbeiter*, p. 232; Walter Benjamin, "The Work of Art in the Age of Mechanical Reproduction," in *Illuminations*, ed. Hannah Arendt, trans. Harry Zohn (New York: Schocken Books, 1969), p. 242.

20. Jünger, *Auf den Marmorklippen*, in *Werke*, IX, 293.

21. Jünger, *In Stahlgewittern*, in *Werke* (Stuttgart: Ernst Klett Verlag, n.d.) I, 87–88.

22. Heinz Kindermann, *Die deutsche Gegenwartsdichtung im Aufbau der Nation* (Berlin: Junge, 1936?), p. 10; Paul Fechter, "Ein deutsches Volksbuch," *Die neue Literatur* 32 (1931): 466–467.

23. See Hermann L. Strack, *Jüdische Geheimgesetze?* (Berlin: C. A. Schwetschke, 1920), pp. 24–30.

24. Artur Dinter, *Die Sünde wider das Blut* (Leipzig: Ludolf Beust, 1929), p. 342.

25. Artur Dinter, *Die Sünde wider den Geist* (Leipzig and Hartenstein: Matthes und Thost, 1921), p. 236.

26. Richard Junior, ed., *Hier spricht der Feind* (Berlin: Neufeld u. Henius, n.d.), pp. 11–12. See also Ernst Jünger, ed., *Das Antlitz des Weltkrieges: Fronterlebnisse deutscher Soldaten* (Berlin: Neufeld und Henius, 1930), pp. 9–11, 238–259.

10. Leftist Modernism: Alfred Döblin, Oskar Maria Graf, and Walter Benjamin

1. Frank Trommler, "Working-Class Culture and Modern Mass Culture Before World War I," *New German Critique*, no. 29 (Spring/Summer 1983): 63; Manfred Brauneck, *Die Rote Fahne: Kritik, Theorie, Feuilleton, 1918-1933* (Munich: Fink Verlag, 1973).

2. Helga Gallas, *Marxistische Literaturtheorie: Kontroversen im Bund proletarisch-revolutionärer Schriftsteller* (Neuwied and Berlin: Hermann

Luchterhand Verlag, 1972); Fredrick Engels to Margaret Harkness (draft), April 1888, in *Marx and Engels on Literature and Art*, ed. Lee Baxandall and Stefan Morawski (St. Louis: Telos Press, 1973), pp. 114–116; Georg Lukács, *Essays on Realism*, ed. Rodney Livingstone, trans. David Fernbach (Cambridge: MIT Press, 1981), pp. 23–75; Eugene Lunn, *Marxism and Modernism: An Historical Study of Lukács, Brecht, Benjamin, and Adorno* (Berkeley: University of California Press, 1982), pp. 78-85.

3. See Richard Wolin, *Walter Benjamin: An Aesthetic of Redemption* (New York: Columbia University Press, 1982); Peter Gay, *Weimar Culture* (New York: Harper and Row, 1968); Walter Laqueur, *Weimar: A Cultural History* (New York: Putnam, 1978); John Willett, *Art and Politics in the Weimar Period: The New Sobriety, 1917-1933* (New York: Pantheon, 1978).

4. Walter Benjamin, "The Work of Art in the Age of Mechanical Reproduction," in *Illuminations*, ed. Hannah Arendt, trans. Harry Zohn (New York: Schocken Books, 1969), p. 234; Bertolt Brecht, "Der Rundfunk als Kommunikationsapparat: Rede über die Funktion des Rundfunks," in *Gesammelte Werke in acht Bänden*, ed. Suhrkamp Verlag and Elisabeth Hauptmann (Frankfurt: Suhrkamp, 1967), VIII, 129, 131; Hans Magnus Enzensberger, "Constituents of a Theory of the Media," in *Consciousness Industry: On Literature, Politics and the Media*, ed. Michael Roloff (New York: Seabury Press, 1974), pp. 95–128.

5. Oskar Maria Graf, *Kalender-Geschichten* (Munich and Berlin: Drei Masken Verlag, 1929), I, 300; 273, 217, 218, 194; Walter Benjamin, "Krisis des Romans: Zu Döblins 'Berlin Alexanderplatz,' " in *Gesammelte Schriften*, vol. 3, ed. Hella Tiedemann-Bartels (Frankfurt: Suhrkamp, 1972), p. 234.

6. Oskar Maria Graf, *Die Chronik von Flechting: Ein Dorfroman* (Munich: Drei Masken Verlag, 1925), pp. 194–195.

7. Graf, *Kalender-Geschichten*, II, 295.

8. Oskar Maria Graf, *Bolwieser: Roman eines Ehemannes* (Munich and Berlin: Drei Masken Verlag, 1931), p. 7.

9. Graf, *Kalender-Geschichten*, I, 121.

10. Alfred Döblin, *Berlin Alexanderplatz: Die Geschichte vom Franz Biberkopf* (Olten and Freiburg im Breisgau: Walter Verlag, 1961), p. 344.

11. Bertolt Brecht, "Anmerkungen zur Oper 'Aufsteg und Fall der Stadt Mahagonny,' " *Gesammelte Werke*, VII, 1009.

12. Benjamin, "Krisis des Romans," p. 230–231.

13. Walter Benjamin, "Oskar Maria Graf als Erzähler," in *Gesammelte Schriften*, III, 310.

14. Ibid., pp. 310–11. Cf. Graf, *Bolwieser*, pp. 358–359.

15. Heiner Müller, "Reflections on Post-Modernism," *New German Critique* 16 (Winter 1979): 55–57. See also Arlene Teraoka, "The Silence of Entropy or Universal Discourse: The Postmodernist Poetics of Heiner Müller," Ph.D. diss., Stanford University, 1983, pp. 43–46.

16. Alfred Döblin, "An Romanautoren und ihre Kritiker," in *Aufsätze zur Literatur* (Olten and Freiburg im Breisgau: Walter Verlag, 1963), pp. 15, 18; Alfred Döblin, "Der Bau des epischen Werkes," in *Aufsätze zur Literatur*, pp. 106, 116, 120, 132.

17. Graf, *Kalender-Geschichten,* II, 65–91; I, 243–258.

18. See Martin Selge, "Stifters Kaktus: Zur naturwissenschaftlichen und (sexual-) symbolischen und ästhetischen Dimension des Cereus Peruvianus im Nachsommer," *Stifter-Symposium 1978: Vorträge und Lesungen* (Linz: Linzer Veranstaltungs-Gesellschaft, 1979), pp. 28–37.

19. Graf, *Kalender-Geschichten,* I, 177–94, 371.

20. Peter Bürger, *Theory of the Avant-garde,* trans. Michael Shaw (Minneapolis: University of Minnesota Press, 1984), pp 49–54.

21. See Russell A. Berman, "Lukács' Critique of Bredel and Ottwalt," *New German Critique,* no. 10 (Winter 1977), 165.

22. Walter Benjamin, "Linke Melancholie," in *Gesammelte Schriften,* III, 279–283.

23. Ernst Ottwalt, *Denn Sie Wissen Was Sie Tun: Ein deutscher Justiz-Roman* (Berlin: Malik-Verlag, 1931), n.p.

24. Willet, *Art and Politics,* p. 141; Jürgen Kleindienst, *Wem gehört die Welt: Kunst und Gesellschaft in der Weimarer Republik* (Berlin: Neue Gesellschaft für Bildende Kunst, 1977), pp. 462–479.

11. Modernism as Social Individuality: Thomas Mann

1. Franz Kafka, diary entry of Dec. 25, 1911, *Tagebücher, 1910-1923,* ed. Max Brod (New York: Schocken Books, 1949), p. 208; Gilles Deleuze and Felix Guattari, *Kafka: Pour une littérature mineure* (Paris: Editions de Minuit, 1975).

2. Thomas Mann, "Death in Venice," in *Death in Venice and Seven Other Stories,* trans. H. T. Lowe-Porter (New York: Vintage Books, 1963), pp. 14, 13; Dorrit Cohn, "The Second Author of 'Der Tod in Venedig,'" in *Probleme der Moderne: Studien zur deutschen Literatur von Nietzsche bis Brecht,* Festschrift für Walter Sokel, ed. Benjamin Bennett, Anton Kaes, and William J. Lillyman (Tubingen: Max Niemeyer Verlag, 1983), pp. 223–245.

3. Helmut Jendreiek, *Thomas Mann: Der demokratische Roman* (Düsseldorf: August Bagel Verlag, 1977), pp. 260–265.

4. Egon Schwarz, "Fascism and Society: Remarks on Thomas Mann's Novella 'Mario and the Magician,'" *Michigan Germanic Studies* 2 (1976): 47–67; Georg Lukács, *Essays on Thomas Mann,* trans. Stanley Mitchell (New York: Grosset and Dunlap, 1965), p. 37.

5. Thomas Mann, "Mario and the Magician," in *Death in Venice,* pp. 173–174. See also Hubert Orlowski, *Prädestination des Dämonischen: Zur Frage des bürgerlichen Humanismus in Thomas Mann's 'Doktor Faustus'* (Posen: University of Posen, 1969).

6. Mann, "Mario and the Magician," pp. 181, 177, 176, 141.

7. Thomas Mann, "The German Republic," in *The Order of the Day: Political Essays and Speeches of Two Decades,* trans. H. T. Lowe-Porter (Freeport: Books for Libraries Press, 1969), pp. 13-14.

8. Ibid., p. 29 (translation modified).

9. Ibid., p. 45.

10. Thomas Mann, [Geist und Wesen der deutschen Republik] [Dem Gedächtnis Walter Rathenaus], in *Politische Schriften und Reden* (Frankfurt: S. Fischer Verlag, 1968), II, 133, 134–135.

11. Ibid., p. 156.

12. Ibid., pp. 157–158.

13. Ibid., p. 173.

14. Thomas Mann, *Schriften und Reden zur Literatur, Kunst und, Philosophie* (Frankfurt: S. Fischer Verlag, 1968), II, 87.

15. Ibid., pp. 88–89.

16. Thomas Mann, "The Coming Victory of Democracy," in *The Order of the Day*, p. 143.

17. Thomas Mann, "Europe Beware," in *The Order of the Day*, p. 82; Thomas Mann, *Doctor Faustus: The Life of the German Composer Adrian Leverkühn as Told by a Friend*, trans. H. T. Lowe-Porter (New York: Vintage Books, 1971), p. 192.

18. Ibid., pp. 192–193, 189.

19. Ibid., p. 59.

20. Thomas Mann, "Der Künstler und die Gesellschaft," in *Schriften und Reden zur Literatur, Kunst, und Philosophie*, II, 344, 346; Heinrich Mann, "Geist und Tat," in *Essays* (Hamburg: Claasen, 1960), pp. 5–14.

21. Alfons Söllner, "Leftist Students of the Conservative Revolution: Neumann, Kirchheimer, and Marcuse at the End of the Weimar Republic," *Telos*, no. 61 (Fall 1984): 55–70; Bob Hullot-Kentor, "Introduction to Adorno's 'Idea of Natural History,' " and Theodor W. Adorno, "The Idea of Natural History," *Telos*, no. 60 (Summer 1984): 97–124; Max Horkheimer and Theodor W. Adorno, *Dialectic of Enlightenment*, trans. John Cumming (New York: Seabury Press, 1972), pp. 3–42.

22. Mann, *Doctor Faustus*, pp. 488, 192.

23. Consider the narrators in Hermann Broch, *Der Versucher* (The Tempter, 1953), Henry James, *The Sacred Fount* (1901), and Ford Maddox Ford, *The Good Soldier* (1915).

24. Mann, *Doctor Faustus*, pp. 251–252.

25. Lukács, *Essays on Thomas Mann*, p. 32.

26. See Henry Sussman, *The Hegelian Aftermath: Readings in Hegel, Kierkegaard, Freud, Proust, and James* (Baltimore: Johns Hopkins University Press, 1982), p. 125; Peter Uwe Hohendahl, *The Institution of Criticism* (Ithaca: Cornell University Press, 1982), p. 19.

Credits

Index

Academic socialists, and *Verein für Sozialpolitik*, 20

Adorno, Theodor W.: on modernism, vi; on German anticapitalism, 20; "The Idea of Natural History," 280

Aestheticization of politics, 221, 225

Agrarian question: and *Verein für Sozialpolitik*, 20; Thomas Mann and Max Weber, 269

Alexander, Gertrude, hostility to modernism, 233

Alienation, Freytag on, 102. *See also* Reification

Alldeutscher Verband, Weber's resignation from, 23

Allegory, in *Irrungen, Wirrungen*, 157, 158, 159

Ambivalence: irony and parody, 282; and deconstruction, 283; and the recipient, 283

America, North: emigration to, 21; pursuit of profit, 127; and mass culture in *Steppenwolf*, 193

Anarchy: and liberalism, 47; pneumatic, 51

Anticapitalism: after 1873, 18; and German imperialism, 20; and German bourgeoisie, 71; as regulatory mechanism, 174–175; right-wing, in Gustav Frenssen, 209; left-wing, 238; and theology, 254

Antiliberalism, and anticapitalism, 18

Aristocracy: cosmopolitanism of, 61; and sensuality, 61–62; literary habits, 69–70, 71, 72, 92–94, 98; and Jews, 71; Freytag on, 85, 86–87; and politics, 268

Asceticism: as regulation of consumption, 91; in leftist modernism, 238

Ascona, 3

Association of Proletarian Revolutionary Writers, 233

Asynchronicity: experience of modernization, 10–11; and German industrialization, 20

Austria, conflict with Prussia, 5. *See also* Josephinism

Avant-garde: Russian, 1; and